THE VOLUNTEER
MANAGEMENT HANDBOOK

NONPROFIT LAW, FINANCE, AND MANAGEMENT SERIES

The Art of Planned Giving: Understanding Donors and the Culture of Giving by Douglas E. White

Beyond Fund Raising: New Strategies for Nonprofit Investment and Innovation by Kay Sprinkel Grace

Budgeting for Not-for-Profit Organizations by David Maddox

Charity, Advocacy, and the Law by Bruce R. Hopkins

The Complete Guide to Fund Raising Management by Stanley Weinstein

The Complete Guide to Nonprofit Management by Smith, Bucklin & Associates

Critical Issues in Fund Raising edited by Dwight Burlingame

Developing Affordable Housing: A Practical Guide for Nonprofit Organizations, Second Edition by Bennett L. Hecht

Faith-Based Management: Leading Organizations that are Based on More than Just Mission, by Peter C. Brinckerhoff

Financial and Accounting Guide for Not-for-Profit Organizations, Fifth Edition by Malvern J. Gross, Jr., Richard F. Larkin, Roger S. Bruttomesso, John J. McNally, PricewaterhouseCoopers LLP

Financial Empowerment: More Money for More Mission by Peter C. Brinckerhoff

Financial Management for Nonprofit Organizations by Jo Ann Hankin, Alan Seidner, and John Zeitlow

Financial Planning for Nonprofit Organizations by Jody Blazek

The Fund Raiser's Guide to the Internet by Michael Johnston

Fund-Raising Cost-Effectiveness: A Self-Assessment Workbook, by James M. Greenfield

Fund-Raising: Evaluating and Managing the Fund Development Process, Second Edition by James M. Greenfield

Fund-Raising Fundamentals: A Guide to Annual Giving for Professionals and Volunteers by James M. Greenfield

Fund-Raising Regulation: A State-by-State Handbook of Registration Forms, Requirements, and Procedures by Seth Perlman and Betsy Hills Bush

Grantseeker's Toolkit: A Comprehensive Guide to Finding Funding by Cheryl S. New and James Quick

High Performance Nonprofit Organizations: Managing Upstream for Greater Impact by Christine Letts, William Ryan, and Allen Grossman

Intermediate Sanctions: Curbing Nonprofit Abuse by Bruce R. Hopkins and D. Benson Tesdahl

International Fund Raising for Nonprofits by Thomas Harris

International Guide to Nonprofit Law by Lester A. Salamon and Stefan Toeplar & Associates

Joint Ventures Involving Tax-Exempt Organizations, Second Edition by Michael I. Sanders

The Law of Fund-Raising, Second Edition by Bruce R. Hopkins

The Law of Tax-Exempt Healthcare Organizations by Thomas K. Hyatt and Bruce R. Hopkins

The Law of Tax-Exempt Organizations, Seventh Edition by Bruce R. Hopkins

The Legal Answer Book for Nonprofit Organizations by Bruce R. Hopkins

A Legal Guide to Starting and Managing a Nonprofit Organization, Second Edition by Bruce R. Hopkins

Managing Affordable Housing: A Practical Guide to Creating Stable Communities by Bennett L. Hecht, Local Initiatives Support Corporation, and James Stockard

Managing Upstream: Creating High-Performance Nonprofit Organizations by Christine W. Letts, William P. Ryan, and Allan Grossman

Mission-Based Management: Leading Your Not-for-Profit Into the 21st Century by Peter C. Brinckerhoff

Mission-Based Marketing: How Your Not-for-Profit Can Succeed in a More Competitive World by Peter C. Brinckerhoff

Nonprofit Boards: Roles, Responsibilities, and Performance by Diane J. Duca

Nonprofit Compensation and Benefits Practices by Applied Research and Development Institute International, Inc.

The Nonprofit Counsel by Bruce R. Hopkins

The Nonprofit Guide to the Internet, Second Edition by Michael Johnston

Nonprofit Investment Policies: A Practical Guide to Creation and Implementation by Robert Fry, Jr.

The Nonprofit Law Dictionary by Bruce R. Hopkins

Nonprofit Compensation, Benefits, and Employment Law by David G. Samuels and Howard Pianko

Nonprofit Litigation: A Practical Guide with Forms and Checklists by Steve Bachmann

The Nonprofit Handbook, Second Edition: Volume I—Management by Tracy Daniel Connors

The Nonprofit Handbook, Second Edition: Volume II—Fund Raising by Jim Greenfield

The Nonprofit Manager's Resource Dictionary by Ronald A. Landskroner

Nonprofit Mergers and Alliances: A Strategic Planning Guide, by Thomas A. McLaughlin

Nonprofit Organizations' Business Forms: Disk Edition by John Wiley & Sons, Inc.

The NSFRE Fund Raising Dictionary, by The National Society of Fund Raising Executives

Planned Giving: Management, Marketing, and Law by Ronald R. Jordan and Katelyn L. Quynn

Planned Giving Simplified: The Gift, The Giver, and the Gift Planner, by Robert F. Sharpe, Sr.

Private Foundations: Tax Law and Compliance by Bruce R. Hopkins and Jody Blazek

Program Related Investments: A Technical Manual for Foundations by Christie I. Baxter

Reengineering Your Nonprofit Organization: A Guide to Strategic Transformation by Alceste T. Pappas

Reinventing the University: Managing and Financing Institutions of Higher Education by Sandra L. Johnson and Sean C. Rush, Coopers & Lybrand, LLP

The Second Legal Answer Book for Nonprofit Organizations by Bruce R. Hopkins

Special Events: Proven Strategies for Nonprofit Fund Raising by Alan Wendroff

Strategic Communications for Nonprofit Organizations: Seven Steps to Creating a Successful Plan by Janel Radtke

Strategic Planning for Nonprofit Organizations: A Practical Guide and Workbook by Michael Allison and Jude Kaye, Support Center for Nonprofit Management

Streetsmart Financial Basics for Nonprofit Managers by Thomas A. McLaughlin

A Streetsmart Guide to Nonprofit Mergers and Networks by Thomas A. McLaughlin

Successful Marketing Strategies for Nonprofit Organizations by Barry J. McLeish

The Tax Law of Charitable Giving by Bruce R. Hopkins

The Tax Law of Colleges and Universities by Bertrand M. Harding

Tax Planning and Compliance for Tax-Exempt Organizations: Forms, Checklists, Procedures, Second Edition by Jody Blazek

The Universal Benefits of Volunteering: A Practical Workbook for Nonprofit Organizations, Volunteers and Corporations by Walter P. Pidgeon, Jr.

The Volunteer Management Handbook by Tracy Daniel Connors

THE VOLUNTEER MANAGEMENT HANDBOOK

Edited by Tracy Daniel Connors

John Wiley & Sons, Inc.
New York • Chichester • Weinheim • Brisbane • Toronto • Singapore

Copyright © 1995 by John Wiley & Sons, Inc.

This publication is designed to provide accurate and authoritative information in regard to the subject matter covered. It is sold with the understanding that the publisher is not engaged in rendering legal, accounting, or other professional services. If legal advice or other expert assistance is required, the services of a competent professional person should be sought.

Library of Congress Cataloging-in-Publication Data:
The volunteer management handbook / editing by Tracy Daniel Connors.
   p.   cm.—(Nonprofit law, finance, and management series)
Includes index.
ISBN 0-471-10637-2 (cloth : acid-free paper).—ISBN 0-471-37142-4 (paper)
1. Voluntarism—United States—Management.   2. Nonprofit
organizations—United States—Personnel Management.   I. Connors,
Tracy Daniel.   II. Series.
HN90.V64V65   1995
361.3'7'068—dc20   95-12108
                                                                CIP

Printed in the United States of America
10 9 8 7 6 5 4 3 2 1

For Andrew, Catherine, and Marie

About the Editor

President of the BelleAire Institute in Bowie, Maryland, a management communications and publishing organization, Tracy D. Connors has served in a variety of management positions in business, government, and philanthropic organizations. Since 1979 the largest, most comprehensive management handbooks in print for nonprofit organizations have been those he prepared. A captain in the Naval Reserve, he was voluntarily recalled to active duty six times since 1985, the first Naval Reserve officer to serve as director of Congressional and Public Affairs for the Space and Naval Warfare Systems Command and the Naval Sea Systems Command in Washington, D.C., and as Deputy Director of the Navy's Command Excellence and Leader Development Program. Other recent Navy assignments have included duties on the staff of the Chief of Naval Operations, where he served as the first Total Quality Leadership Public Affairs Officer, and at Naval District Washington. Other positions have included Director of Satellite Learning Services for the U.S. Chamber of Commerce; Congressional administrative assistant; corporate communications manager for a major electronics corporation; vice president of a national publishing corporation; and as an officer, board member, or professional staff director of numerous nonprofit organizations. He attended Jacksonville University, graduated from the University of Florida, and earned a Master of Arts Degree from the University of Rhode Island. He is also the editor of the *Nonprofit Management Handbook: Operating Policies and Procedures, Nonprofit Organization Handbook, Financial Management for Nonprofit Organizations*, the *Dictionary of Mass Media and Communication*, and *Flavors of the Fjords: the Norwegian Holiday Cookbook*.

About the Contributors

Jeanne H. Bradner is nationally renowned author, consultant, and speaker on public affairs and nonprofit management. Among her clients is the Illinois Commission on Community Service and the Americorps program. She served as first vice president of the International Association for Volunteer Administration and was public issues chair. In 1990, Ms. Bradner was appointed by President Bush as Regional Director of ACTION, and served in that capacity until January 1993. From 1984 to 1990, she directed the Illinois Governor's Office of Voluntary Action.

Jeffrey L. Brudney, MA, Ph.D., is professor of political science and director of the Doctor of Public Administration Program at the University of Georgia. He serves on the editorial boards of leading journals in nonprofit sector studies, and his book, *Fostering Volunteer Programs in the Public*, received the John Grenzebach Award for outstanding Research in Philanthropy for Education. He was Fulbright Fellow at the Voluntary Sector Management Program at York University in 1994.

Joseph E. Champoux, Ph.D., is professor of management at the Robert O. Anderson Schools of Management of the University of New Mexico. His research activities include Total Quality Management, the organization and management effects of modern manufacturing, job design, and the relationship between work and nonwork.

Peter J. Eide, JD, is Manager of Human Resources Law and Policy at the United States Chamber of Commerce. He is responsible for developing and effectuating business community positions on legislation and regulations affecting the utilization and management of human resources. Prior to joining the Chamber of Commerce, Mr. Eide practiced law with the firm of Akin, Gump, Strauss, Hauer & Feld in Washington, D.C.

Ellen J. Estes, LL.B., is president of Estes Associates, a firm offering developmental consulting for nonprofit organizations. She is an adjunct professor at the New School for Social Research, where she has taught planned giving to master's degree candidates at its School of Management and Urban Professions. A prominent lecturer, she has spoken before audiences sponsored by CASE, NSFRE, AHP, the American Council on Gift Annuities, and the National Conference on Planned Giving.

Linda L. Graff, MA, is president and senior associate in the nonprofit management consulting firm of Graff and Associates in Dundas, Ontario. She is a policy development specialist and the author of seven books, including *Volunteer/Page Staff/Union Relations, Volunteer for the Health of It,* and the best-selling *Policies for Volunteer Programs.* She now spends her time presenting workshops on volunteer program management issues throughout North America.

Frances Ledwig, owner and director of Volunteer Development Associates, is a consultant, trainer, and facilitator in volunteer management, helping staffs and volunteers to work together as a team. She has over thirty years experience as a volunteer leader and follower in community, church, and school organizations.

Suzanne Lulewicz is a consultant specializing in the development of educational programs that enhance productivity in the workplace. She was previously staff vice president of education for the Community Associations Institute and Curriculum Director for the U.S. Chamber of Commerce. She has served as president and second vice president for programming and professional development for the Metropolitan Washington, D.C., Chapter of American Society for Training and Development.

Nancy Macduff is an internationally recognized authority in the management of volunteer programs. She was the executive director of a nonprofit corporation for fourteen years, and has written several books, including *Building Effective Volunteer Committees.* She regularly contributes to such publications as *Voluntary Action Leadership* and has worked with such diverse organizations as the American Red Cross and Points of Light Foundation. Ms. Macduff also teaches courses on volunteer management at Lewis and Clark College.

Milena M. Meneghetti, CHRP, is the senior advisor, organization and human resources development at Canadian Occidental Petroleum Ltd. She is a certified human resources professional with over 12 years' internal and external human resources consulting experience. She is also the vice-president of M4i Information Industries Inc. She has served on the executive of several not-for-profit boards, including as director of ethics for the Human Resources Institute of Alberta and as the vice president, support services for the Canadian Red Cross Society. Ms. Meneghetti was involved in the development and implementation of Canadian Occidental's Corporate Integrity Program.

Kenneth L. Murrell, DBA, is presently on the faculty of management at the University of West Florida and president of Empowerment Leadership Systems. He has extensive experience in organizational development and management development in improving organizational effectiveness and is working with numerous nonprofit agencies. In addition, he is a management consultant working independently and with internationally recognized consulting organizations.

E. Brian Peach, Ph.D., is an associate professor at the University of West Florida in Pensacola, Florida. His primary teaching areas include strategic management and international business, and he has published in the areas of volunteer motivation, small group performance, performance incentives, and executive pay. He has consulted in the areas of organizational redesign, strategic reorientation and incentive-based compensation. He works with not-for-profit and volunteer organizations as well as for-profit firms.

Carolyn A. Quattrocki is a lawyer at the Office of the Attorney General, State of Maryland. Previously, she worked as an associate at the Washington, D.C., law firm of Arnold & Porter and has clerked on the United States District Court for the District of Maryland.

Keith Seel, M.A., is principal and founder of M41 Information Industries Inc. His work touches on ethics, value-based decision making, community partnerships between business and charitable sectors, and dynamic computer simulations for clients working to understand the complexity of management situations. Mr. Seel instructs not-for-profit and ethics classes at Mount Royal College and has an international reputation as an author, workshop leader, and presenter.

Arlene Stepputat, MA, has been an educator, volunteer manager, trainer, counselor, and consultant for more than 20 years. She created Integrity International, whose mission is to assist, guide, and support individuals, groups, and organizations toward living a life of authenticity. She also teaches volunteer management at the Center for Public Service at Seton Hall University, South Orange, NJ.

Jon Van Til, Ph.D., is Professor of Urban Studies and Community Planning at Rutgers University and is a co-founder of its graduate program of public policy. Mr. Van Til serves as editor-in-chief of *Nonprofit and Voluntary Sector Quarterly* and is the author of many books, including *Mapping the Third Sector*. Dr. Van Til has published in journals such as *Urban Affairs Quarterly*. In 1994, he received the Award for Distinguished Research and Service from the Association for Research in Nonprofit Organizations and Voluntary Action.

Katharine Vargo, MBA, president of Risk Management Services Co., is a risk management and insurance consultant based in Indianapolis, Indiana. She has fifteen years experience in insurance and risk management, including five years as risk manager for the Presbyterian Church (USA). Ms. Vargo is a frequent lecturer and has conducted seminars addressing liability and insurance issues and the various techniques of risk management.

Steven A. Yourstone, Ph.D., is an Associate Professor of Management at the Robert O. Anderson Schools of Management of the Unviersity of New Mexico. He has published in articles *Decisions Science*, Wiley Interscience Publications, *Quality and Reliability Engineering International*, *IEEE Transactions on Engineering Management*, and Marcel Dekker, Inc.

Contents

FOREWORD   xvii

PREFACE   xix

PART 1: VOLUNTEER DEVELOPMENT

CHAPTER 1: METAPHORS AND VISIONS FOR THE VOLUNTARY SECTOR   3

Jon Van Til, Ph.D.

CHAPTER 2: MOTIVATING PEOPLE TO VOLUNTEER THEIR SERVICES   12

Milena M. Meneghetti, CHRP

CHAPTER 3: PREPARING THE ORGANIZATION FOR VOLUNTEERS   36

Jeffrey L. Brudney, Ph.D.

CHAPTER 4: RECRUITMENT, ORIENTATION, AND RETENTION   61

Jeanne H. Bradner

CHAPTER 5: TRAINING AND DEVELOPMENT OF VOLUNTEERS   82

Suzanne J. Lulewicz

**CHAPTER 6: TRAINING VOLUNTEERS IN QUALITY MANAGEMENT
TECHNIQUES AND Tools**   103

Joseph E. Champoux, Ph.D.

Steven A. Yourstone, Ph.D.

PART 2: VOLUNTEER MANAGEMENT

CHAPTER 7: POLICIES FOR VOLUNTEER PROGRAMS   125

Linda L. Graff

CHAPTER 8: ADMINISTRATION OF VOLUNTEER PROGRAMS   156

Arlene Stepputat

CHAPTER 9: EPISODIC VOLUNTEERING   187

Nancy Macduff

CHAPTER 10: VOLUNTEER AND STAFF RELATIONS   206

Nancy Macduff

CHAPTER 11: REWARD AND RECOGNITION SYSTEMS FOR VOLUNTEERS   222

E. Brian Peach

Kenneth L. Murrell

CHAPTER 12: THE ROLE OF VOLUNTEERS IN FUND-RAISING   244

Ellen G. Estes, LL.B.

CHAPTER 13: MANAGING CORPORATE AND EMPLOYEE VOLUNTEER PROGRAMS   259

Keith Seel

PART 3: VOLUNTEERS AND THE LAW

CHAPTER 14: GENERAL LIABILITIES AND IMMUNITIES   293

Carolyn Quattrocki

CHAPTER 15: BOARD MEMBER LIABILITY AND RESPONSIBILITY   309

Katharine S. Vargo

CHAPTER 16: RISK MANAGEMENT STRATEGIES   322

Katharine S. Vargo

CHAPTER 17: VOLUNTEERS AND EMPLOYMENT LAW   **339**

Peter J. Eide

CHAPTER 18: NATIONAL SERVICE: TWENTY QUESTIONS AND SOME ANSWERS   **361**

Jon Van Til, Ph.D.

APPENDIX: SAMPLE FORMS AND DOCUMENTS FROM STATE VOLUNTEER PROGRAMS   **379**

INDEX   **395**

Foreword

As organizations throughout the country face the uncertainties of government cut-backs and the financial challenges that follow in their wake, the need to leverage all available resources to their maximum capacity and efficiency is greater than ever. In this environment, volunteers become an increasingly important resource for non-profit organizations of all types and sizes. The reason is simple: Nothing can replace the impact hands-on community service has as people work together to find a common solution, organize themselves, and reach out helping hands to those in need.

New York Cares responds to this new volunteering atmosphere by building bridges between those in need and those who want to help. In 1987, a group of young, concerned, working New Yorkers were looking for ways to volunteer their time and energy to help the city they called home. Only eight years later, New York Cares is New York's fastest growing volunteer organization, and it has inspired more than 25 other organizational "cousins" in cities all across the country. The New York Cares approach to community service succeeds on three levels: community organizations receive much-needed volunteer support, the constituents of these agencies receive essential services, and community-minded citizens find their volunteer niche.

Until now, we and other nonprofits had to find out the hard way—by trial and error—that garnering the energies of today's volunteers means answering their special needs. That's where *The Volunteer Management Handbook* comes in, with help-ful, practical, and proven solutions to the often overlooked problems of effectively managing volunteer efforts. Volunteers are not staff—and should never be treated as such—but they can and should be managed professionally.

Volunteerism, community, sharing—these concepts are not dead but they have changed. And nonprofit organizations seeking to make these values a reality need to adjust as well. To help them get acclimated, volunteer servicing must be objectively studied, analyzed, and evaluated. This handbook does that and more, by providing specific information and recommendations on volunteer recruitment, training, and retention. Its prescription for volunteer management comes from practices and strategies that have already proven successful out in the field, where it counts. As managers of nonprofit organizations, we call all learn from one another how to build coalitions, enhance the volunteer commitment, and answer the challenges that we all face. Sources like this handbook make that dialogue even more productive.

I wish us all luck as we move forward to create better communities and a brighter future.

Kathleen Behrens
Executive Director
New York Cares

Preface

The nonprofit sector in the United States consists of nearly one million tax-exempt organizations, hundreds of thousands of which depend on participation by volunteers to provide much of their service to clients or community. Independent Sector reports that nonprofit organizations now employ over ten percent (14.5 million) of American workers, including 8.7 million paid employees and 5.8 million volunteers. Millions of Americans volunteer each year. More than half of all American adults volunteered for various causes and organizations representing over $175 *billion* per year.

Due to changing demographics and a treacherous legal environment, nonprofit organizations are hard pressed to stay abreast of rapid changes in volunteer development, management, and liability. Changes in volunteerism mirror the rapid changes in our society. Identifying, motivating, recruiting, training, orienting, and retaining volunteers is a constant challenge. Even more challenging is staying on top of developments and trends in the volatile world of liability and risk management for volunteers. Organizations using volunteers must protect themselves and their leaders from the increasing threat of successful lawsuits and legal actions. Ignorance of risk avoidance and risk management has been disastrous for many nonprofit and public service organizations.

Part 1, Volunteer Development, provides the reader with a comprehensive introduction to the dynamic area of volunteerism. Beginning with an overview of trends and issues of major significance to leaders of nonprofit organizations that use volunteers, this section then covers those topics, issues, and policies of importance from the time the organization sets out to recruit volunteers until it has trained them for their roles within the organization.

In "Metaphors and Visions for the Volunteer Sector," Dr. Jon Van Til presents two powerful metaphors and two compelling visions to help inform the work of those who manage the efforts of volunteers. He presents a comprehensive overview that is simultaneously chilling and inspiring. The Third Sector, he points out, "is coming of age." Those who have "the chance to lead volunteers in the years ahead no longer find themselves in the backwaters of society."

"Motivating People to Volunteer Their Services" by Milena Meneghetti provides a useful overview of the theoretical underpinnings of motivational theory, followed by highly relevant linkages to volunteer management, including how to motivate professional who volunteer their services. Of particular interest will be her perspectives and pointers on multicultural volunteers and what motivates those representing different cultures in our pluralist society.

Before volunteers can be successfully integrated into the plans and operations of any organization, some essential concepts and practices must be understood. Dr. Jeffrey L. Brudney takes the reader from expectations to job descriptions in "Preparing the Organization for Volunteers."

"Recruitment, Orientation, and Retention" by Jeanne H. Bradner leads the reader phase by phase through the complete cycle of volunteer participation. Of particular usefulness to readers are the many checklists and forms she provides to assist them at whatever stage they may be in the volunteer cycle.

An effective training program is essential to any organization using volunteers as service providers. Suzanne J. Lulewicz reflects on many years of experience in her chapter, "Training and Development of Volunteers." After outlining the fundamentals and distinctions between training, education, and development, she explains how to build effective training programs and profiles the types of programs most often used by nonprofit organizations.

Quality management approaches and techniques are being applied with promising results by a growing number of nonprofit organizations. Long-term commitment to continuous quality improvement in services or products differs from what most organizations have done in the past, and offers benefits that do not accrue from other approaches to management and leadership. "Training Volunteers in Quality Management Techniques and Tools" by Dr. Joseph E. Champoux and Dr. Steven A. Yourstone provides a valuable overview of quality management fundamentals for nonprofit organization and offers a training plan and program for organizations making the transition into quality management.

Part 2, Volunteer Management, outlines the policies and personnel procedures that are advisable using the analogous fields of employment or labor law.

In "Policies for Volunteer Programs," Linda L. Graff begins with the fundamentals of what and why policies are needed, then takes us through the process of writing policies specifically for volunteer programs. Of particular importance are her recommendations relating to policy formulation and compliance issues.

The administration of volunteer programs is now a career field of its own. Arlene Stepputat, "Administration of Volunteer Programs," provides an essential overview and guide to the entire continuum of volunteer administration, from volunteer policy implementation through program evaluation, and closes with her assessment of what's ahead for volunteer administrators.

The nature and importance of short term volunteering is explained by Nancy MacDuff in "Episodic Volunteering." She identifies barriers to short term volunteering, and then explains the essential factors needed to recruit and sustain these volunteers, whose numbers are growing.

MacDuff follows up with "Volunteer and Staff Relations," in which she outlines the characteristics of the effective volunteer–staff team and the causes of poor volunteer–staff relationships. She concludes with a dozen proven tips on ways to enhance relationships between these two vital human resources.

Effective reward and recognition systems are essential to sustaining volunteer management programs. How the work within the context of human behavior and how they contribute to organization productivity, morale, retention, and esprit de corps are explained by Dr. Kenneth L. Murrell and Dr. E. Brian Peach in "Reward and Recognition Systems for Volunteers." After they reveal why most reward and recognition systems fail to achieve their full potential, the authors outline techniques that work and describe how to plan a system that can be adjusted to changing conditions.

Fund-raising is a highly technical field, in fact, it is a career field in its own right. Ellen G. Estes, in "The Role of Volunteers in Fund-Raising," does a masterful job of explaining the fundamentals even as she outlines the specific roles and responsibilities volunteers can play in successful campaigns. After outlining specific steps to create a volunteer fund-raising corps, she explains how to obtain support from board members. She concludes with an assessment of what volunteers expect when they become involved in fund-raising, and offers common-sense pointers for successful participation by volunteers in fund-raising programs.

"Managing Corporate and Employee Volunteer Programs" by Keith Seel addresses an area of great potential for nonprofit organization—employees as a significant volunteer force. Such programs also present unique needs and expectations to leaders of volunteer programs. Traditional approaches may not be effective in cases where the company adds its expectations or objectives to the mix. Seel explores and explains the full range of issues and potentials relating to establishing and sustaining an effective employee volunteer program, including evaluation techniques.

Part 3, Volunteers and the Law, provides an overview of the general liabilities and immunities of volunteers under various state laws. This section outlines the legal liabilities of both volunteers and the agencies they serve, including the scope of typical state laws that protect volunteers from civil suits that may arise from acts of ordinary negligence.

Understanding the legal responsibilities of volunteers and agencies to injured parties is the first of many vital areas covered by Carolyn Quattrocki in "General Liabilities and Immunities." After explaining the types and extent of liability of individual volunteers, she addresses the potential liabilities faced by nonprofit organizations as a result of actions by their volunteers. Just as important, she then outlines the various types of immunities and defenses from suit and liability, including both statutory and nonstatutory legal defenses that are available to volunteers.

Leaders on nonprofit organizations are, in many ways, held to an even higher standard in their responsibilities to their nonprofit organizations than those with comparable duties in a for-profit organization. Katharine S. Vargo, in "Board Member Liability and Responsibility," provides a comprehensive review of guidelines that board members and officers of typical charitable organizations should follow to avoid errors and omissions that may lead to legal liability. Following a discussion of the types and potential for liability by board members, she outlines board members' responsibilities. Specific examples are provided to help readers develop policies and procedures for their own organizations.

Avoidance, retention, non-insurance transfers, loss control, and insurance are all important techniques nonprofits use to manage risk. Which risk management technique to use is just one vital answer Ms. Vargo provides in "Risk Management Strategies." Later, she covers a wide variety of insurance coverages available to nonprofit organizations, including how to evaluate potential coverage of areas from property damage to director's liability.

Under what circumstances or conditions are volunteers workers for the purpose of law, and when are nonprofits using the services of volunteers considered employers? In "Volunteers and Employment Law," Peter J. Eide explains how these determinations are made and how they impact nonprofit organizations under the provisions of various Federal statutes and regulations, ranging from the Fair Labor Standards Act to the National Labor Relations Act. He follows this discussion with an equally important review and assessment of various Federal laws that were legislated to protect Americans from employment discrimination, explaining how they apply to nonprofit organizations. Of particular interest to nonprofits is his determination that the Civil Rights Act of 1866 applies to volunteer services. If an individual's right to provide volunteer services is hampered based on race (as broadly defined), the nonprofit organization could be found to be in violation of Section 1981 of the Civil Rights Act.

An important contemporary movement in volunteer management is the provision of national service—governmental support of the performance of voluntary action by citizens, usually young people. In "National Service: Twenty Questions and Some Answers," Dr. Jon Van Til and Frances Ledwig explain the potential represented in this important new national initiative. They address the values underlying the program and operational considerations for volunteer managers, and they suggest practical policies for nonprofit organizations.

Wherever possible, contributors have offered practical guidelines, tips, and sample materials designed to help leaders of nonprofit organizations understand the growing variety of subjects and areas of expertise that affect volunteer program management. We have tried to provide a solid base of necessary information and forms helpful to nonprofit leaders as they prepare their own Volunteer Management Policy Manual. Of particular usefulness to them are the specific guidelines and procedures outlined to help limit liability and to provide solid risk management strategies for volunteer programs.

Professional staff members of all nonprofit organizations—particularly those having responsibilities involving volunteers—will find this work useful. For the first time, they will have available in one volume the fundamental principles of volunteer management, which are explained and illustrated using examples and case studies specific to nonprofit organizations.

The contributors have planned *The Volunteer Management Handbook* as an important new resource to allow professional staff members of nonprofit organizations to:

◆ Review or learn the fundamentals of volunteer development, management, and liability and risk avoidance;

◆ Understand the typical pitfalls and barriers within most organizations that prevent them from gaining the full benefits of an effective volunteer management program, or that put them at inordinate risk of liability;

◆ Help design and conduct assessment and planning initiatives within their organization;

◆ Understand the new model of how these three philosophies work together and influence each other, and how to apply that new model to their organization;

◆ Gain key understandings and tools they can apply in their organization.

Volunteer leaders should also find this work highly useful. Those without previous background in volunteer management will appreciate the grounding it provides in fundamentals. Those with previous background will appreciate the additional focus the work provides, and the fact that it highlights and explains proven approaches in such areas as risk management and liability protection. In addition, it provides many forms, samples, and checklists that offer time-saving tools.

The contributors to *The Volunteer Management Handbook* have brought an unprecedented range of experience and national leadership to this work—combining fundamental concepts with practical application—that we believe will serve as the first truly comprehensive handbook on all important aspects of volunteer management for leaders of nonprofit organizations.

Tracy D. Connors
Bowie, Maryland
July,1995

PART

VOLUNTEER DEVELOPMENT

CHAPTER 1
Metaphors and Visions for the Voluntary Sector

CHAPTER 2
Motivating People to Volunteer Their Services

CHAPTER 3
Preparing the Organization for Volunteers

CHAPTER 4
Recruitment, Orientation, and Retention

CHAPTER 5
Training and Development of Volunteers

CHAPTER 6
Training Volunteers in Quality Management Techniques and Tools

CHAPTER ◇ 1

METAPHORS AND VISIONS FOR THE VOLUNTARY SECTOR*

Jon Van Til
Rutgers University

1.1   First Metaphor: A Society Needs Four Wheels to Run

1.2   Second Metaphor: The Voluntary Sector Is Like an Elephant

1.3   First Vision: Community Is at the Heart of it All

1.4   Second Vision: Voluntarism in a World at the End of Work

1.5   Conclusion: What a Field to Be a Part Of!

     References

*Portions of this chapter originally appeared in my regular column in the *NonProfit Times*.

Ultimately, it is by metaphor and shared vision that we understand the world. This introduction presents two powerful metaphors and two compelling visions to inform the work of those who manage the efforts of volunteers. In presenting these images, it is my hope that volunteer managers will be assisted in understanding why their work is important and what role voluntary organizations play in helping bring about a better society.

1.1 FIRST METAPHOR: A SOCIETY NEEDS FOUR WHEELS TO RUN

My first metaphor is a simple one: Society is like a car. Think of it as having four wheels, each of which must be properly attached to the body of the car, each tire correctly inflated, if it is to proceed smoothly. In talking about society, we call these wheels *sectors* (cf. Van Til, 1988). The first sector, *business,* is where most of us make our living. This sector provides four of every five dollars earned in society, and simply by dint of its great size is a central force in society. The second sector, *government,* guides our democratic society. It also provides 14 percent of all employment and is an important steering wheel. The third sector, sometimes called the *voluntary* or *nonprofit sector,* consists of a wide range of organizations, both small and large, that are neither oriented toward profit nor mandated by government. This sector also provides almost 7 percent of all employment, and plays an important role in sensing the proper direction for the societal car to pursue. Finally, the fourth sector, often identified as the *informal sector,* is comprised of many vital but unpaid institutional forces: the family, neighborhood, and community.

The curious thing about this societal automobile is the way in which people become attached to its various wheels. Some argue that the first sector is all that counts, that the "business of America is business," as Calvin Coolidge is thought to have remarked. Others, though not very many in these days of privatization, contend that government is the most important sector, and should be asked to do more rather than less. Yet others are third-sector chauvinists, holding to the view that voluntary organizations can step in and replace government and business in the provision of many goods and services. And a final group holds that the family is the basic institution of society, without whose strength all others will fail. The lesson I draw from this metaphor is that society is indeed like a car: It cannot run unless all four of its wheels are properly attached and aligned, capped as well with properly inflated tires. We need all four sectors, each working as they should, if we are to solve the pressing social issues of our time.

Readers of this volume, those particularly interested in the third sector, are properly warned about the dangers of sector chauvinism. Your work is important, but so is the work of those who toil in business, government, family, and community. You will not solve all problems in society by your efforts. You will need to work as a member of a societal team, in partnerships with many different people and organizations, if your goals are to be met.

1.2 SECOND METAPHOR: THE VOLUNTARY SECTOR IS LIKE AN ELEPHANT

That brings me to my second metaphor, a somewhat more elegant and familiar one: the parable of the blind people and the elephant. You surely know how it goes—one grabs a tusk and says "it's something smooth and sharp," another gets the tail and says "it's like a rope," and so on. Observers of the nonprofit world are quick to tell us that voluntary associations are like these elephants: Some find them insufficiently oriented to their charitable goals, others that they have abandoned their roots in voluntarism, and still others that they have become too much like businesses or are excessively political. Critic after critic grabs onto one part of the nonprofit elephant, and announces confidently, "This is what voluntarism has become!"

A recent plenary presentation by German historian Rudolph Bauer explains rather succinctly why the nonprofit elephant feels so different to those who come face to face with it. Speaking to an international conference in Barcelona, Bauer (1993) observed that voluntary organizations are experienced very differently depending on the role a person holds in relation to these organizations. Bauer began his comments by noting the ways in which the nonprofit sector is closely linked to the other major sectors of society: (1) to the economy in that many services are provided in return for fees, and others are supported by corporate donations; (2) to government in that nonprofits support many services by means of governmental contracts and must apply to government for tax-exempt status; (3) to the community in that nonprofits are called upon to meet many community needs and to use volunteers from the community. Then Bauer presented his resolution of the elephant problem. The reason that nonprofits seem so different to different folks, he explained, is that the roles provided within them offer very different visions of organizational reality to participants. In particular, he argued, these organizations look very different from the points of view of clients, volunteers, board members, and staff.

Volunteers and clients, Bauer observed, tend to see the organization in terms of the quality of the charitable or membership service it provides. For the volunteer, how the organization serves those it seeks to help—its clients or members—is the basis of judging it. Board members, on the other hand, tend to see nonprofits as political organizations, set in a web of competing interests. For the board member what is most important about the organization is that it play a respected role in the world of other organizations in the community or society. Meanwhile, voluntary sector staffers take as their primary perspective on the organization that it is a business and focus on the way in which the organization provides them a secure and adequate living. Their attention tends to become most focused when issues of compensation and working conditions come to the fore.

In a real sense, then, Bauer argues that a third-sector organization tends to take on the coloration of a business (through its employees), a political association (through its board), and a community group (through its clients and volunteers). It all depends on an observer's point of view, which itself is determined by his or her role within the organization. What it all means for the manager of a voluntary organization is that if you've ever felt like an organizational schizophrenic, surrounded by people making vastly different meanings out of the same actions, you are right.

Your staff is going to view you as a business manager; your board will want to see your actions in terms of their political savvy; and your volunteers will wonder any time you direct your attention toward anything but serving the best interest of your agency's clients.

Faced with these contrasting viewpoints of their organizations, voluntary sector managers must be adept in understanding each others' positions. The most adept among them will be those who themselves are comfortable with the traditions of charity and service that underlie the third sector but can also understand when it is necessary to be politically skillful or decidedly businesslike. Clearly, for a manager to lose sight of the organization's purpose is to lose control of his or her position, but it is also necessary to be able to understand and deal with every important interest on its own ground.

The problem that voluntary sector managers face is how to keep the agency mission in view while being politically adept and mindful of the bottom line. That's not a job definition that anyone can meet, but it does describe what a successful voluntary sector manager is required to do. The job is not an easy one because it requires understanding where a lot of different people are coming from, people who are themselves marching to a lot of different music. To do the job well, the manager must be attuned to these different songs and skilled in working in the different worlds of service, interest accommodation, and economic viability.

Need an image? The best voluntary sector managers do find a way to ride their elephants—their flanks guiding the beast's direction, their eyes wary of the probing tusks, their hands alert to the waving trunk, their hearts remembering why they originally climbed on board, their voices speaking soothingly into the ears of their charges. Nothing to it, you say? Ride on!

1.3 FIRST VISION: COMMUNITY IS AT THE HEART OF IT ALL

What if the work that is done in the third sector were suddenly thrust into national prominence? What if a president of the United States were elected who began to articulate the merits of voluntarism, philanthropy, and nonprofits? What if a new image of caring began to spread throughout the land?

This may sound fanciful, and some of it surely is. But the development of *communitarian theory* in recent years by a group of intellectuals and activists spearheaded by George Washington University professor Amitai Etzioni is bringing part of this fantasy into reality. Through his book, *The Spirit of Community* (Etzioni, 1993), and the journal he edits, "The Responsive Community," Etzioni is calling attention to core values of the third sector. One of Etzioni's close colleagues, William Galston, signed on as a top domestic policy advisor on the White House staff; Vice President Gore has actively participated in a communitarian teach-in; and President Clinton employed communitarian phrases in his inaugural address and other statements. Let us recall some of Clinton's address. In it, he said:

> It is time to break the bad habit of expecting something for nothing from our Government or from each other. Let us all take more responsibility not only for ourselves and our families but also for our communities and our country. . . . I challenge a new generation of young Americans to a season of

service; to act on your idealism by helping troubled children, keeping company with those in need, reconnecting our torn communities. There is so much to be done. Enough, indeed, for millions of others who are still young in spirit to give of themselves in service, too. In serving, we recognize a simple but powerful truth: We need each other and we must care for each other.

Communitarians combine liberal and conservative themes, seeking to find a new balance between individual and social rights and responsibilities in modern societies. Their key policy statement is called the "Responsive Communitarian Platform: Rights and Responsibilities." It articulates a new and compelling vision of societal organization, in which the third sector can play a vital role.

Key to this vision is the recognition that all of us are members of many communities and that the rights that we cherish can only be sustained in the context of these communities. The Responsive Communitarian Platform states that:

◆ A communitarian perspective recognizes both individual human dignity and the social dimension of human existence.

◆ A communitarian perspective recognizes that the preservation of individual liberty depends on the active maintenance of the institutions of civil society.

◆ A communitarian perspective recognizes that communities and polities, too, have obligations—including the duty to be responsive to their members and to foster participation and deliberation in social and political life.

The platform recognizes the pervasive character of voluntary action. On the one hand, its drafters value the bright side of the voluntary tradition, pointing to its valuing of community problem solving through the working of "innumerable social, religious, ethnic, workplace, and professional associations." Communitarians extend this tradition when they express the value of "some measure of caring, sharing, and being our brother's and sister's keeper."

The voluntary tradition, like the communitarian perspective, also values a locality-centered approach to problem solving. As the Responsive Communitarian Platform expresses it, problems should be dealt with as close to the community as possible. "This principle holds for duties of attending to the sick, troubled, delinquent, homeless, and new immigrants. . . ." Moreover, partnerships are important in both the communitarian and voluntary traditions, and such policy initiatives as national service are valued by both.

On the other hand, communitarians are also aware of the dark side of the voluntary tradition. Regarding voluntary associations, they "ask how 'private governments,' whether corporations, labor unions, or voluntary associations, can become more responsible to their members and to the needs of the community." Moreover, communitarians "do not exalt the group as such, nor do they hold that any set of group values is ipso facto good merely because such values originate in a community."

In a recent statement in *The Responsive Community*, political scientists Jeffrey Hayes and Seymour Martin Lipset (1993/1994) explain that "[associations]—including churches, civic organizations, school boards, and philanthropic volunteer groups—are the lifelong training grounds of moral citizenship. They strengthen moral bonds as they encourage belief in liberal principles. They foster an ethos of civic engagement and understanding of democracy." Communitarians seek to expose the false promise of radical individualism, as Charles Taylor has powerfully observed: "Ironically, it is just this pattern of hanging loose that makes us less capable of seeing the social costs of our way of life, and makes us look on the public sector as a barely necessary evil. So, as we increase the need for public sector activity, we decrease our own readiness to assume the burden" (Taylor, 1994). Neither the retrenched state nor the consumer society will provide us what we seek, for both are based on the denial of community as the basis of human growth and satisfaction.

As Etzioni envisions it, a communitarian society carries out a *multilogue,* or national town meeting, which is itself inspired by third-sector social movements. "In it, millions of citizens—over beers in bowling alleys, at water coolers at work, and over coffee and at cocktail parties—discuss and debate the issues flagged by sit-ins, demonstrations, boycotts, and other such dramatizations. The multilogue is further extended in radio call-in shows, letters to the editor, sermons in churches and synagogues. Gradually a new consensus emerges."

What the nonprofit sector can provide here is a commitment to what I like to call *responsible voluntarism.* Such activity might take the form of a particular dedication to work, or whistle-blowing within a governmental or corporate bureaucracy, or working with neighbors to care for elders, install a stop sign, or restrain illicit drug sales within a neighborhood. Voluntary and nonprofit associations form one important set of institutions in the organizational world of contemporary society. From Tocqueville to the present, students of society have found in such associations a source of participation, political competence, and legitimation. It would seem altogether appropriate to hold such associations to tests of effectiveness and responsibility.

After all, if voluntarism is a force that includes the helping act of the altruist, the workings of the Red Cross organization to assure disaster relief, and the terrorist tactics of the Ku Klux Klan, it would certainly seem appropriate to be able to distinguish between responsible and irresponsible voluntarism. Responsible voluntarism is an active, spontaneous, and challenging force in society. Its development might serve, therefore, as an organizing principle for the development of an active and communitarian democracy in an era better known for its complacency.

1.4 SECOND VISION: VOLUNTARISM IN A WORLD AT THE END OF WORK

In an important new book, futurist Jeremy Rifkin (1995) examines the loss of paid work in the nations of the Western world. He documents the impact of the new technology revolution brought by automation and microchip-based information processing. This revolution offers a choice between liberation from long work hours on the one hand, and an increasing social division between the over- and the underemployed on the other. Rifkin believes that we are in the process of making the wrong choice, and that future generations will be faced with dwindling prospects for steady employment of any sort. While fortunes are being made by those who own the patents on technological innovations, most members of the middle classes are on their way to dwindling incomes, threats to whatever jobs they are able to secure, and an inadequate financial base to assure a comfortable retirement.

For voluntary organization managers, Rifkin's message is clear:

1. First of all, wake up and smell the economy. Stop blaming things on "the recession" or "difficult economic times." The last recession ended in 1992 and cannot be blamed for today's troubles. As for difficult economic times, if Rifkin is right, we ain't seen nuthin' yet.

2. Rethink your faith that government will bail you out. When employment shrinks, so does the tax base and the willingness of citizens to support social programs. Up goes the police budget, and down goes everything else, including taxes. Among the most delectable budgetary items to trim: subcontracts to nonprofits.

3. Don't expect anything but less from corporations and corporate philanthropy. Corporations, too, are in long-term decline, particularly as sources of employment. As the virtual corporation takes form, there are fewer places that can be identified with them. And out the window go conceptions of giving based on commitment to a particular community or region, as well as the employment base upon which federated giving has traditionally rested.

4. Ditto for individual giving. Where budgets seek to sustain old expectations on new paychecks, charitable giving begins to look like a discretionary item that can be reduced. Just because lower-income people have traditionally given five percent of their income (although almost all goes to their churches) does not mean that the dispossessed middle classes will follow suit.

So where does this leave us? Rifkin, having painted us into a corner, is not without hope. He sees two ways out: (1) by developing public policies that share the available work by shortening the workweek and thereby redistributing income, and (2) by developing governmental programs "to provide alternative employment in the third sector—the social economy—for those whose labor is no longer required in the marketplace."

Go back and reread that last sentence. Right, what Rifkin is saying is that the third sector has a crucial role to play in the reconstruction of twenty-first-century society! And he is saying this in a book that will have an initial print run of 50,000, a national media tour by its author, and featured attention at a number of policy conferences. This is not another book with the usual third-sector sales of 1,500, if you're lucky. This is the big time!

Rifkin offers three basic policy prescriptions:

1. Address the worldwide crisis in the availability of work by sharing the available work, shortening the workweek to 30 hours.

2. Expand the provision of work by offering a social wage for a wide range of positions throughout the nonprofit sector.

3. Encourage the expansion of volunteering as a leisure-time activity by offering a tax credit to those who volunteer with appropriate nonprofits.

Question: Will it be possible to construct a coalition both strong and stable enough to bring these policies to fruition in a single package? Or, as is so often the case, will separate coalitions be required to advance each issue upon the policy stage? To answer this question, we need to recognize the principal actors capable of shaping the contemporary nonprofit arena. I would suggest that there are five of these:

1. *The new men of power in Washington* (Gingrich, Armey, and company). These folks, while they show little experience with volunteering or nonprofits, sure do give a lot of lip service to the importance of volunteering. But as they talk the talk, will they also learn to walk the walk? Or will they simply provide the sector with warmed-over Reaganism—platitudes about the need to help out coupled with massive budget cuts in contracts with nonprofits?

2. *Evangelical church–related organizations* (focusing on family values). Here too comes a time of test. Are these organizations really serious about strengthening families? Or do their real interests lie in keeping women out of the workplace and breaking up fatherless families by means of orphanages and declining welfare payments? If they really want to preserve the family, that goal would be much advanced by finding ways to reduce the employment hours of working parents, thereby freeing up time to spend at home with the kids.

3. *The nonprofit establishment* (such sector-serving organizations as Independent Sector and the 40 or so university-based centers). These organizations hardly have been a policy force in recent years, largely spending their capital on exhortations to expand diversity in nonprofit organization leadership. Important as this theme may be, it is certainly not as important as finding a central role for the sector in a changing social economy. As for the academic centers, they have not yet begun even to look for a role for themselves on such issues.

4. *Labor unions* (at least those that are still breathing). Unions will need to find something to do in the years ahead, or they will simply vanish into the recesses of American history. What better time to bury their fears of volunteers and join with the sector in addressing the major social issues of our age?

5. *What's left of the progressive advocacy organizations* (the women's movement, the civil rights' organizations, environmental groups, and specifically focused social change organizations). As these pillars of the sector become the new Washington "outs," their membership and financial base can be expected to increase. After all, if their side is no longer in power, the old use of the third sector as a counterforce in society will come into play. They will remain significant players in this new age of one-term governments.

Which among these interests are least likely to support the shorter workweek? The New Republicans, with their desire to liberate business from restrictions. But this view is countered by their adherence to family values. Can they be won over by a common argument from the evangelicals and the progressives that the family can best be strengthened if parents stay at home more?

Which among these interests are least likely to support paid community service? Again, the New Republicans, with their sense that volunteering should remain pure and their fear that young people are likely to favor radical change. Here the sector servers may be most useful in reminding them of the limits of Reaganite volunteering and the need to support nonprofit organization with both rhetoric and cash.

Which among these interests are least likely to support the tax credit for volunteering? Probably the progressive advocacy organizations, with their recollections of the Reagan administration's efforts to remove them from this list of acceptable charities for donation purposes by federal employees. Here the sector servers and the New Republicans may be most helpful in assuring the fairness of any system to be constructed.

At stake here is a society in which work can be assured to all who wish it, and a central role in this process for nonprofit organizations. The development of a broad and unexpected coalition around the policy prescriptions of Rifkin's new book may do much to advance these goals during the coming years of unpredictable social and political developments.

1.5 CONCLUSION: WHAT A FIELD TO BE A PART OF!

Those who have the chance to lead volunteers in the years ahead no longer find themselves in the backwaters of society. The third sector is coming of age, in American society and in most nations of the Western world. Even in Central Europe, Africa, Asia, and the rest of the Americas, voluntarism as a principle increasingly is being explored as a way of dealing with the exhaustion of our planet and its resources. Readers of this book will find many adventures ahead of them as they pursue their chosen line of work. To them all, may they enjoy good luck and many successes. The world has never before been in so great a need of the work of volunteers and of the many voluntary organizations sustained by voluntary commitments.

REFERENCES

Bauer, Rudolph. 1993. Comments to conference, "Well-being in Europe by Strengthening the Third Sector," Barcelona, Centre d'laiciatives de l'Economia Social, May.

Etzioni, Amitai. 1993. *The Spirit of Community*. New York: Crown Publishing.

Hayes, Jeffrey, and Seymour Martin Lipset. 1993/1994. "Individualism: A Double-edged Sword." *The Responsive Community* 4 (Winter): 69–80.

Rifkin, Jeremy. 1993. *The End of Work: The Decline of the Global Labor Force and the Dawn of the Post-market Era*. New York: G.P. Putnam's Sons.

Taylor, Charles. 1994. "The Modern Identity." Pp. 55–71 in Markate Daly (Ed.), *Communitariansim: A New Public Ethics*. Belmont, Calif.: Wadsworth.

Van Til, Jon. 1988. *Mapping the Third Sector: Voluntarism in a Changing Social Economy*. New York: The Foundation Center.

CHAPTER 2

MOTIVATING PEOPLE TO VOLUNTEER THEIR SERVICES

Milena M. Meneghetti, CHRP
Canadian Occidental Petroleum Ltd.

2.1   Introduction

2.2   Altruism as a Motivator

2.3   Instrumentality Theory

2.4   Reinforcement Theory

2.5   Maslow's Need Hierarchy

2.6   Herzberg's Two-factor Theory

2.7   McClelland's Learned Needs Theory

2.8   Contemporary Issues in Motivation

2.9   Connecting the Motivation Theories

2.10 A Final Consideration

      References

2.1 INTRODUCTION

One of the fundamental questions related to volunteer development is: What motivates people to commit their personal resources, emotional energy, and time to volunteering? This chapter will provide the manager of volunteers with a theoretical basis for understanding human motivation—for what instigates, drives, and accounts for the way people behave, particularly as it relates to volunteering.

Theories of motivation can be divided into two broad types. Process-based theories focus on the mechanism of *how* behavior arises and is sustained. Content-based approaches, on the other hand, focus on the specific *needs or factors* that give rise to behavior (Gibson, Ivancevich, and Donnelly, 1982). This chapter will focus on two process-based theories—reinforcement theory and instrumentality theory—and three content-based theories—Maslow's hierarchy of needs, Herzberg's two-factor theory, and McClelland's learned needs theory. In each case the literature and research that supports the theory will be reviewed and implications for volunteer motivation will be outlined. Although it is not articulated as a theory, the altruistic motive is particularly relevant to volunteer motivation, and it, too, will be discussed.

2.2 ALTRUISM AS A MOTIVATOR

Altruism is defined in the *Compact Oxford English Dictionary* (1991) as "devotion to the welfare of others . . . as a principle of action." The word's first known use was in the late nineteenth century, and people have been citing altruism as the motivation behind such apparently unselfish behavior as volunteering ever since.

There is research support for the existence of altruism (Myers, 1983). For example, some sociobiological theories contend that it is an evolutionary advantage for members of a species to act altruistically. These theories propose a sort of natural selection favouring altruistic behavior. Social norm theories have identified and provided scientific support for the existence of the *social responsibility norm*. This norm influences us to help needy, deserving people, even if they cannot reciprocate.

Colloquially, many of us have come to label people as altruistic only if they do something without anticipating anything in return. The dictionary does not place this limitation on the definition of altruism: The fact that a person derives some benefit from acting to promote the welfare of another should not disqualify that action from being altruistic.

(a) Altruism and Volunteering

Whether or not we accept the existence of unconditional altruism, volunteers often cite the desire to help others as at least one reason for choosing to volunteer. In one study (Ross and Shillington, 1989), 92 percent of the respondents said that helping others was a very important or somewhat important reason for volunteering. Another study, looking at the characteristics of college student volunteers (Fagan, 1992), found that students who volunteered emphasized altruistic motives.

(b) Belief in Your Cause

When we ask people to volunteer their services, we are appealing, on at least one fundamental level, to their belief in our cause. For example, the volunteer coordi-

> *In the course of the interview, Hirsko continually mentioned that she was volunteering in order to bring about "good" in somebody else's life. When asked if she expected to "feel good" by doing so, she confirmed her altruistic intentions by saying "That's not what really matters here. . . . I'm here for somebody else, not me."*
>
> Din Ladak

nator for a pro-choice pregnancy counseling agency may be looking for volunteers to help organize a fund-raising event. Those who agree with a pro-choice perspective are more likely to say yes to such a request than are those who oppose abortion.

One study of board member participation (Widmer, 1985) confirmed the relevance of belief in the cause: A large majority was motivated by the contribution each person could make to the important work the agency did in the community. In other sectors, pride in and passion for the service provided by an organization is being recognized more and more as a volunteer motivator (Bianchi, 1993).

> *Tony mentioned that helping another child was really important to him at a belief-system level. You see, as a child who had grown up in foster homes, he firmly believed in the cause of helping other children.*
>
> Din Ladak

(c) Altruism and Your Agency's Image

To the extent that altruism is a primary initial motivator for an individual, the mission of your agency and its *perceived* alignment with the goal of helping others will affect your success in attracting that person's resources (time, services, or money). An example of this principle is reflected in the fact that institutions generally have a harder time raising money for administrative and general operational funds than they do attracting dollars to specific projects. Perhaps this is because with project-specific fund-raising, the link to the good being done by the money is more direct—it is tied to a specific project that can be judged by the giver as worthwhile. Many managers of volunteers would agree that an agency's record of success in helping others will attract volunteers. Nothing can replace a good public image in this regard.

(d) Is Altruism Alive and Well?

As was mentioned earlier, not everyone agrees that altruism is a primary motivator for volunteering. One concept, the *social exchange theory,* claims that, in fact, human interactions are transactions that aim to maximize a person's rewards and minimize the costs. In effect, the theory suggests that altruism in the colloquial sense (that is, unconditional altruism) does not truly exist.

While there is a body of literature that clearly cites altruism as an important volunteer motivator (e.g., Ross and Shillington, 1989; Story, 1992; Van Til, 1985), much of the more recent literature on volunteer motivation expresses a kind of careful skepticism about the possibility that human beings can be so other-centered. For example, out of a general listing of 43 reasons why people volunteer provided by one publication, only three would fit in the altruistic category (McCurley and Vineyard, 1988, p. 12). The goal of much current research appears to be to establish the nature of other important motivators, which we discuss later in this chapter. Perhaps this is because these other motivators can be more directly influenced by specific volunteer management techniques. The issue, then, is still open to healthy debate. In general, however, it can be said that most of the current literature acknowledges altruism as at least one component in the motivation to volunteer.

Flashman and Quick do an excellent job of considering altruism as it relates to volunteer behavior in a chapter entitled "Altruism is Not Dead" (Moore, 1985). They propose adopting some valuable conceptual guidelines (pp. 166–167), including:

1. Altruism is a primary motivational factor in volunteer behavior.
2. The artificial division between egoistic and altruistic motivation must be healed. We need to realize that we live in a unified system where the well-being of each of us affects the well-being of all of us.
3. As a creative response to the many challenges facing the world, our entrance into the twenty-first century will be marked by a parallel rise in both altruism and voluntary activity.

2.3 INSTRUMENTALITY THEORY

Put simply, instrumentality theory predicts that people will be motivated to act if they believe that doing so will eventually help them get something they value. These theories suggest that people are not driven by a desire to help others; rather, they act only if they are likely to get something in return. With some variation on emphasis, most instrumental theories consider *valence, instrumentality,* and *expectancy* (VIE) as critical components in motivation. The theory assumes that people will ask themselves whether or not (Landy and Trumbo, 1980):

1. A certain action has a high probability of leading to an outcome *(expectancy)*.
2. That outcome will yield other outcomes *(instrumentality)*.
3. Those other outcomes are valued *(valence)*.

(a) VIE and Volunteering

What would VIE theories say about people who are considering volunteering their services? Put simplistically, a person's reasoning might go something like this:

1. *Should I volunteer at the Immigrant Women's Center?*
2. *What can I expect the immediate outcomes to be? (Expectancy)* I will receive training on immigrants women's issues; I will work with immigrant women.
3. *What will happen as a result of this? (Instrumentality)* It is highly likely that after being trained and working directly with immigrant women, I will learn more about immigrant women.

4. *How much do I value this outcome? (Valence)* I value this learning very highly.

5. *Decision:* I will volunteer with the Immigrant Women's Center.

Essentially, according to VIE theories, a person attempts to predict "what's in it for me?" when making the decision as to volunteering. The more likely it is that a valued outcome will result, the more likely a particular volunteer activity will be selected.

Many high school graduates will choose to volunteer to gain some career-related experience, or to obtain references to apply for a certain program. "I hope that through volunteering I can put in the fifty hours of volunteering that I need to apply to the social work program at the college."

Din Ladak

(b) So, What Do People Value?

Instrumentality theories suggest that the volunteer manager will be most effective at motivating volunteering if volunteers believe that they will attain something they value in return for their efforts. So the central question becomes: What do volunteers value? The answer to this question depends to some extent on the person involved (Sundeen, 1992). There are differences in personal goals and attitudes among volunteers. However, Clary, Snyder, and Ridge (1992) do provide a useful, scientifically sound *volunteer functions inventory* (VFI) of the motivations underpinning volunteer work. This inventory effectively synthesizes much of the general research on reasons for volunteering into six broad areas. These *valued outcomes* fall into the following categories: social, value, career, understanding, protective, and esteem. Exhibit 2–1 provides examples of valued outcomes and reasons for volunteering within each of the categories identified by Clary and his colleagues.

(c) VIE in Practice

An instrumental, or economic, approach to motivation appears to be favored in some of the more recent literature on volunteer motivation (e.g., Greishop, 1985; Zahrly and Brown, 1993). If one chooses instrumentality theory as a basis, motivating people to volunteer means providing support for and managing each step in the decision-making process described above. Some suggestions include:

1. *Working with the volunteer to determine the valued outcomes.* Often, a person comes to an agency to volunteer without having fully explored the reasons for doing so. Getting to the core of what the volunteer hopes to gain will ultimately benefit both the agency and the volunteer.

2. *Acting on the specific valued outcomes of individual volunteers.* The expectations of a potential volunteer should be taken into account when deciding which assignment or project is most suitable.

3. *Being clear and direct about what the volunteer can and cannot expect in the short, intermediate, and long term.* Some of the expectations of the volunteer may not be realized in the short term or by any one assignment. It is best to be honest about what volunteers can expect for their effort.

◆ **EXHIBIT 2–1   Outcomes Valued by Volunteers**

Motivational Concerns	Reasons for, and Valued Outcomes of, Volunteering
Social	My friends volunteer. People I'm close to volunteer. People I know share an interest in community service.
Value	I am concerned about those less fortunate than myself. I feel compassion toward people in need. I feel it is important to help others.
Career	I can make new contacts that might help my business or career. Volunteering will help me succeed in my chosen profession. Volunteering will look good on my resume.
Understanding	I can learn more about the cause for which I am working. Volunteering allows me to gain a new perspective on things. I can explore my own strengths.
Protective	Volunteering helps me work through my own personal problems. Volunteering is a good escape from my troubles. By volunteering I feel less lonely.
Esteem	Volunteering makes me feel important. Volunteering increases my self-esteem. Volunteering makes me feel needed.

2.4 REINFORCEMENT THEORY

Put very simply, reinforcement theory contends that consequences influence behavior. If positive consequences follow certain behavior, a person is more likely to repeat that behavior. If, on the other hand, a behavior has a negative consequence, that behavior is less likely to be repeated. The theory predicts that a volunteer manager can thus influence behavior by rewarding desired performance.

Positive reinforcers that have been used in organizations include (Hamner and Hamner, 1976):

1. Praise
2. Recognition
3. Earned time off
4. Feedback

Critics of reinforcement theory feel that by ignoring the impact of attitudes, beliefs, and other cognitive processes, the theory reduces human behavior to the same level as that of laboratory rats. They suggest that it is these cognitive processes that contribute to the sometimes unexpected results found in some studies of reinforcement theory.

(a) Behavior Modification and Volunteering

Despite some of the criticisms leveled at reinforcement approaches, many volunteer managers would say that they have practical proof of their value.

Everything an organization puts out is a product of that organization and speaks volumes about the organization. Sound volunteer programs will have policies about volunteer recognition—the crux of volunteer retention. Many volunteer managers have commented that it's not the recruiting that is difficult—it is the retention that is really challenging. Reinforcement theory provides different ways of responding to this challenge.

Din Ladak

Volunteer managers often find that recognizing and rewarding—positively reinforcing—a volunteer's efforts is a practical and relatively straight forward way to encourage continued involvement. Conversely, managers realize that volunteers who have had several bad experiences in their agencies are highly likely to discontinue volunteering there. They may even come to generalize these negative consequences to volunteer opportunities with other agencies and discontinue volunteering all together for a period of time. Such a volunteer has been aversively conditioned. These are examples of reinforcement theory at work. As with other process-based theories of motivation, the focus for the volunteer manager eventually becomes: Which things act as rewards and thereby serve to promote volunteering?

(b) Meaningful Rewards

There are a variety of ways to recognize a volunteer's contributions. The following provides you with some guidelines for providing meaningful recognition.

1. Specific feedback from a coordinator about a particular project or task the volunteer has undertaken can be a very powerful motivator. This feedback should occur as soon as possible after the specific task has been completed, and details about what was most valued should be provided. For example, rather than saying "Thanks for your help with the fund-raising campaign," a more meaningful reinforcer is the comment: "I really appreciated the way you followed up with each of the donors. The letter you developed was very well written and timely." This type of recognition shows volunteers that their particular involvement was special and important to the organization.

2. When possible, the most meaningful recognition is a sincere thank you from a client or client group—those most directly affected by the work the volunteer does. The volunteer manager can facilitate this kind of recognition by

ensuring that opportunities exist for regular positive communication between clients and volunteers.

3. Remember that not everyone likes to be recognized in the same way. Some people prefer to be acknowledged publicly, while others may consider this overly showy and not at all rewarding. Some may like to receive formal recognition in the form of a plaque or pin, whereas others prefer a hand written note from the volunteer manager. Therefore, do your best to ensure that your formal recognition programs are flexible enough to account for these different preferences. *There is nothing more inappropriate than to apply a "we know best" mentality to providing recognition. The reward should be perceived as such by the receiver, or its value is negligible.*

2.5 MASLOW'S NEED HIERARCHY

Maslow's is one of the oldest and most widely known theories of human motivation. It was first presented in 1942 to a psychoanalytic society in an attempt to bring together aspects of Freud, Adler, Jung, Levy, and Fromm's approaches to understanding human behavior (Maslow, 1943). Despite limited research support, it is still regularly referred to in the literature. It identifies and then arranges human needs in priority order, starting from the most basic physiological needs and moving to the more complex self-actualization needs. The theory asserts that a person first will act systematically to satisfy basic needs and then move to more complex needs. Exhibit 2–2 is a diagram of the needs, and their order of priority as they have been described in Maslow's more recent work (1970).

Maslow believed that the first two categories of needs were the most powerful, because they had to be met before other needs could be attended to. The next three needs related to personal growth and the development of personal potential. Maslow believed that these needs motivated behavior, but only after the physiological and safety needs had been fulfilled. Maslow's later conceptualization of his theory (1970) emphasizes several important things:

1. The hierarchy is not rigidly fixed. There may be reversals in the order of priority, particularly between the love and esteem needs.

2. Not everyone moves up the hierarchy and reaches the self-actualization need level. Some people operate at, and are motivated solely by, the most basic needs.

3. Needs that have been consistently satisfied for a long period of time initially will be undervalued as motivators. Only once they cease to be satisfied for an extended period will they again become salient. So, "a man who has given up his job rather than lose his self-respect, and who then starves for six months or so, may be willing to take his job back even at the price of losing his self-respect" (p. 52).

4. No need is ever met completely, and therefore never completely ceases to influence behavior. "Within the sphere of motivational determinants, any behavior tends to be determined by several or *all* of the . . . needs simultaneously rather than by only one of them" (p. 55).

◆ **EXHIBIT 2–2   Maslow's Hierarchy of Needs**

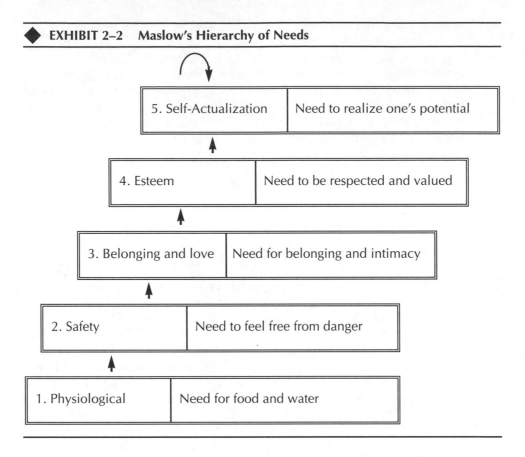

Maslow's theory has much intuitive appeal. It makes sense that people are not likely to be concerned with winning an Olympic gold medal or writing the definitive work on some important scholarly topic if they are having trouble putting dinner on the table.

(a) Volunteer Motivation and Maslow's Hierarchy of Needs

Most research in the volunteer motivation literature does not test Maslow's theory but presupposes its truth. Researchers use Maslow's theory as a paradigm from which to analyze or explore the issues related to volunteer motivation (e.g., Knowles, 1972). This has resulted in some very interesting and practical work. Sue Vineyard, in a book dedicated to volunteer program marketing issues (1984), discusses the implications of Maslow's theory for volunteer motivation. The connections she makes between unmet needs and volunteer management are summarized in Exhibit 2–3.

Another study explores the consequences of structuring volunteerism around the need for self-actualization, rather than the most basic needs such as love and safety (Knowles, 1972). If this were the case, the author conjectures:

◆ Volunteer activities would be defined, at least partially, by their ability to provide learning and growth opportunities to volunteers.

◆ **EXHIBIT 2–3   Unmet Needs and Volunteer Assignments**

The Potential Volunteer	Type of Volunteer Assignment	Unmet Need That May Be Fulfilled
Has gifts that are unused	Opportunities to use unused gifts	Self-actualization
Feels unrecognized, undervalued, or anonymous in other settings	Opportunities to be rewarded, openly recognized, and spotlighted	Esteem
Feels lonely	Opportunities that allow meeting and getting to know other people	Love
Is fearful of losing job	Chances to build new skills, gain new experiences, or expand resumes	Safety
Has a fixed or lower income	Opportunities that happen to have a free meal attached to them or offer them a winter-heated or summer-cooled site in which to work	Physiological

◆ Volunteer centers would target their recruiting efforts to matching volunteers with volunteer opportunities that promoted self-development.

◆ High turnover or what Knowles refers to as "maximum mobility" in the volunteer population would become the accepted norm as people naturally outgrew particular volunteer experiences.

◆ Volunteerism would be seen as part of a nation's educational, rather than welfare, enterprise.

Thus, Maslow's theory has provided a conceptual framework, useful for structuring and ordering observations. This has led to some interesting writing, which is not without practical application. However, despite the intuitive appeal of the theory, it has its limitations. Maslow himself admitted that the experimental research generally does not support his theory (Maslow, 1970), and was hoping that future studies—done in real life rather than laboratory contexts—would eventually lend more support. Unfortunately, this has not generally been the case. Some experts in motivation theory today have concluded that "Maslow's theory is of more historical than functional value" (Landy and Trumbo, 1980). Perhaps the most apt description of the theory is that of Coon (1991): "Rather than being a scientific theory, Maslow's hierarchy represents a philosophical viewpoint." Volunteer managers who wish to truly understand this viewpoint are strongly encouraged to read Maslow's second edition of *Motivation and Personality* (1970).

2.6 HERZBERG'S TWO-FACTOR THEORY

A useful conceptual model for understanding motivation in the context of work is Herzberg's two-factor theory (1959). Essentially, this theory sees motivation and demotivation as two separate issues: The factors that tend to satisfy people are not the same factors that cause dissatisfaction when they are not present. Many of us have experienced this in our own working lives. A dirty, noisy, cold work environment may dissatisfy us, but working in a pleasant one is not necessarily enough to motivate us to be productive and satisfied in our jobs.

Based on a study with engineers and accountants, Herzberg distinguished between *dissatisfiers* and *satisfiers,* or extrinsic and intrinsic conditions, respectively. The *dissatisfiers* tended to be conditions that were extrinsic, or apart from, the work itself, and resulted in dissatisfaction when they were not present. In this study, they included:

1. Salary
2. Job security
3. Working conditions
4. Status
5. Company procedures
6. Quality of technical supervision
7. Quality of interpersonal relations among peers, with superiors, and with subordinates

The *satisfiers* tended to be conditions that were intrinsic to the work and resulted in satisfaction when they were present. In the original study, these included:

1. Achievement
2. Recognition
3. Responsibility
4. Advancement
5. The work itself
6. The possibility of growth

(a) The Two-factor Theory and Volunteer Motivation

As noted above, the original supporting research for the two-factor theory was based on surveys of paid employees. The contention that unpaid workers generally derive satisfaction from things that are intrinsic to the work and dissatisfaction from things extrinsic to the work may be questionable. Smith and Berns (1981) conducted a national survey of recruitment and motivation techniques and attained a relatively high (31 percent) response rate. Their conclusion was that there are "differences in what volunteers and paid workers find satisfying and consider to be most important" (p. 6). In general, they found that volunteers were in fact motivated by conditions that were both intrinsic *and* extrinsic to the job:

> Comparing the top five job factors in importance in each group, paid employees valued self-fulfillment, growth and plenty of freedom on the job. Volunteers on the other hand are looking not only for opportunities to satisfy esteem and self-actualization needs, but also for a chance to build relationships and to satisfy love and belonging needs as well. (Smith and Berns, 1981)

Indeed, most of the literature on volunteer motivation tends to confirm their finding. For example, the "social" and "protective" categories in Clary, Snyder, and Ridge's (1992) VFI are extrinsic conditions and include items such as "My friends volunteer" and "By volunteering I feel less lonely."

Many volunteer managers do believe, however, that motivation to volunteer is multidimensional: It appears that the things that initially motivate people to volunteer and that keep them productive are not the things that will cause them to quit. The research discussed above regarding valued outcomes (Omoto and Snyder, 1993; Puffer, 1991; Widmer, 1985), combined with other literature that cites reasons for satisfaction and dissatisfaction of volunteers (e.g., Howell, 1986; Ilsley, 1990; Schindler-Rainman and Lippitt, 1971) supports this belief. For example, we all know of volunteers who continue to enjoy the work itself but have decided to leave because of poor interpersonal relationships. If we agree that satisfaction and dissatisfaction with volunteer work are two separate issues, it is clear that to motivate volunteering we need to manage both the satisfiers and the dissatisfiers.

(b) Volunteer Satisfiers

One must remember that Herzberg's theory is based largely on the results of a survey of engineers and accountants. These results were extended to the population as a whole without a great deal of additional supporting research. The same criticism can be leveled at many of the lists of reasons for volunteering that have been developed in the volunteer literature. It is likely that the specific satisfiers for one volunteer will not necessarily match those for another (Sundeen, 1992). As a result, whenever it is practical, the volunteer manager should seek to identify and confirm each person's unique satisfiers. This will be more useful to the volunteer manager than treating volunteers as a homogeneous group.

Here is one recommended method for determining a person's unique set of satisfiers:

1. *Ask potential volunteers to complete a motivation inventory or profile during the recruitment phase.* The inventory should be previously tested and have a good theoretical or research basis (e.g., Clary, Snyder, and Ridge, 1992; Francies, 1985).

2. *Use the results of the inventory as the basis for a discussion on motivation in an interview.* Follow-up questions that are related to the results—for example,

"Tell me more about how you think volunteering here may help you succeed in your career"—are very valuable. Confirming probes, such as "What did you particularly enjoy about your last volunteer assignment?" or "What skill sets do you hope to use or develop in your next assignment?" are also useful.

3. If you have been provided with a resume or volunteer application form, *notice the type of previous volunteer assignments they have been involved in,* including the length of their tenure in those assignments and their nature and scope. This will give you some initial insights into what has appealed to a particular person in the past.

(c) Volunteer Dissatisfiers

Perhaps your organization has a tendency to get bogged down in procedural details (a dissatisfier) and is located in a part of the city that is perceived as unsafe by potential volunteers (a dissatisfier). Maybe the quality of supervision provided by your volunteer managers and coordinators needs some improvement (another dissatisfier). Under these circumstances, the Herzberg theory suggests that even the most interesting, challenging volunteer assignment will fail to motivate people to volunteer their services. As a result, it is important to identify and then deal with potential dissatisfiers in your organization.

One way to determine the things present in your organization which are or have the potential to be dissatisfiers is to gather information from departing volunteers. There are two primary vehicles that can be used for obtaining information from past and departing volunteers: the exit interview and post-turnover survey. The exit interview is also discussed in Chapter 4, but a cursory review here will be helpful.

(i) The Exit Interview and Post-turnover Survey

The true exit interview is not a perfunctory good-bye discussion with a volunteer. It has the specific purpose of providing valuable information about the basic cause of a volunteer's departure and the volunteer's perspective on his or her experience with your agency. The two main elements of an exit interview are discovery and communication: discovering the true cause for a volunteer's departure, and communicating these reasons to a person in a position to act on them. Both elements are critical to a useful exit interview program.

Some organizations employ a post-turnover survey as a substitute for or a complement to the exit interview. The survey takes the form of an anonymous questionnaire that is mailed to the volunteer several months after his or her departure. It has the theoretical benefit of eliciting more valid and truthful opinions, because respondents may feel that their comments are more likely to be truly anonymous. On the other hand, response rates do not tend to be high and rarely approach the level necessary to ensure completely valid interpretation.

Timing There is good reason for delaying some part of the post-turnover information gathering. In one study, volunteers were given a first exit interview at the time of their departure and another 11 months later. There was a 40 percent difference between the reasons given at these two interviews. If you wait a few months, it is argued, the volunteer has likely found a new assignment and thus will be less concerned about the consequences of honesty. In addition, the sometimes emotionally charged environment at the point of departure can distort (and perhaps invalidate) the information gathered regarding dissatisfiers at that time.

Confidentiality The advice regarding confidentiality is unequivocal: The results of post-turnover information gathering should be considered anonymous but not confidential. In other words, results should be pooled so that no comments can be traced back to their source. The results must be shared with management and line supervisors if they are to be useful—and then, of course, the pooled and analyzed results obviously are not confidential.

Summary Exit interviews and post-turnover surveys can be viewed as the internal equivalent of external customer surveys. They can be conducted with volunteers of all types: people finishing short-term volunteer assignments and those leaving committee or board positions after their terms have ended, as well as those choosing to discontinue their volunteer efforts sooner than expected. Post-turnover information can help identify both dissatisfiers and satisfiers related to management practices, staff–volunteer relations, volunteer placement, training and development, and recognition programs.

(ii) Dealing with Dissatisfiers

Once potential dissatisfiers have been identified, it is critical that they be attended to. The first option for dealing with dissatisfiers is to eliminate them. In the examples mentioned at the beginning of this section, this would mean simplifying the onerous procedures, seriously planning to relocate to a safer area of the city, and instituting a training program for all those who supervise volunteers.

It is not always possible to eliminate a dissatisfier immediately. The second option for dealing with potential dissatisfiers is to address them when orienting the volunteer. Research suggests that organizational turnover decreases when employees know what challenges to expect. Using the same examples, this would mean admitting to a potential volunteer that some of the procedures may appear cumbersome, and then explaining why they are in place; asking whether the volunteer has any safety concerns, and addressing each one based on the actual experience of volunteers' problems; and advising the volunteer in advance that supervision may be limited, and why.

(d) The Volunteer Assignment

The final step in a motivation process based on Herzberg's two-factor theory is to make a decision regarding the potential volunteer's assignment. The volunteer manager may be able to offer an assignment that includes things that have been identified as satisfiers, and that minimizes the likelihood of dissatisfiers being present (Exhibit 2–4). On the other hand, the particular configuration of satisfiers and dissatisfiers that have been identified for a potential volunteer may suggest that there is no appropriate opportunity for the person at this time. In this case it is best for all involved if the volunteer manager and potential volunteer discuss what seems to be an inappropriate motivational fit. In the end, there may be an agreement to wait until a more appropriate assignment arises.

◆ **EXHIBIT 2–4**   Managing *Satisfiers* and *Dissatisfiers*

Motivation Profile	Exit Interviews

Motivation Profile

↓

Identify Volunteer

Satisfiers

↓

Develop Volunteer Recruitment

and Motivation Strategies

↓

Take into account primary

    Satisfiers

Exit Interviews

↓

Identify Volunteer

Dissatisfiers

↓

Develop Volunteer Retention

    Strategies

↓   ↓

Eliminate OR Address

    Dissatisfiers

↓

Determine whether there is an appropriate assignment, based on a good "motivational fit."

2.7 McCLELLAND'S LEARNED NEEDS THEORY

McClelland's theory of motivation focuses on the influence of learned, culturally based needs on behavior (1962). Primarily by asking people to write "stories to pictures" and then scoring those stories, McClelland identified three needs: the need for achievement, the need for affiliation, and the need for power. He proposed that a person will act to satisfy the need that is strongest at any given time. Although one need will tend to predominate, the interaction of the needs will also affect behavior.

(a) Need for Achievement *(n Achievement)*

Perhaps the most researched of the three needs, the need for achievement refers to the desire to accomplish goals, to grow through challenges, and to improve oneself. People who score high in n Achievement have been found to have some interesting tendencies:

1. They prefer to set moderate goals—those that are neither too easy nor too difficult to attain. This increases their likelihood of success while maintaining the challenge necessary to motivate them.

2. They are particularly interested in feedback, since this helps them measure their success. The feedback has to be focused on actual job-specific performance rather than on the ability to work with the team, for example.

3. They are more restless and need to avoid routine. To feel that they have achieved and thus stay motivated, they need to move on to other tasks or challenges.

(i) High n Achievement and Volunteering

Based on the characteristics of people with high n Achievement, assignments that have specific outcome targets, provide a new challenge or are likely to lead to growth and self-improvement are most likely to attract those trying to satisfy achievement needs. These assignments include:

1. Fund-raising
2. Membership campaigning
3. Researching and analyzing
4. Reporting
5. Chairing committees or occupying leadership positions
6. Filling executive directorships
7. Doing nitty-gritty work (McCurley and Vineyard, 1988)

(b) Need for Power (n Power)

The need for power is the desire to have influence or authority over others. Power itself is not good or bad—it is the way that power is expressed that will make it so. Despite this neutrality of power, McClelland (1987) proposes that individuals scoring high in n Power are forced to find socially sanctioned ways of fulfilling this need. He believes this is because traditional North American socialization causes people with high n Power to feel that their need is wrong, and this results in discomfort. This discomfort is reflected in the finding that people who score high in n Power tend to select negative adjectives, such as "rebellious," "resentful," and "cynical," rather than positive adjectives, to describe themselves (1975).

One sanctioned way for people with high n Power to fulfill their need is through the attainment of prestige. These people will surround themselves with things that suggest power and place themselves in situations that confer status in order to satisfy their need. For example, people with high n Power are more likely to own prestigious possessions than those with a low n Power score. They are also more likely to call attention to themselves in meetings and social gatherings.

Another socially acceptable way to fulfill n Power is to select an occupation that is consistent with this need. McClelland cites studies (1975) which show that students planning for an occupation in teaching, psychology, the ministry, business, or journalism (rather than law or medicine) have significantly higher n Power scores. All of these professions traditionally have involved exercising some degree of influence or authority over others.

Interestingly, n Power appears to be influenced by a person's social and emotional maturity. McClelland believes that high n Power leads to greater participation in *some* power-related activity, although which activity depends on . . . the level of his maturity. The n Power may also be expressed quite differently in men and women, perhaps reflecting traditional sex-role stereotypes. There is some evidence that women are more likely to express n Power by helping people; they wish to have resources to give to others. Men, on the other hand, express the need by being more assertive or argumentative. (McClelland, 1975 p. 49)

(i) High n Power and Volunteering

Based on the research, people who volunteer in order to satisfy their need for power are likely to enjoy assignments that confer prestige and status or that allow them to exercise influence. These assignments include (McCurley and Vineyard, 1988):

1. Public speaking
2. Fund-raising, either one on one or to a group
3. Writing newspaper articles
4. Being a CEO
5. Chairing events that bring public attention to a cause
6. Managing many people

(c) Need for Affiliation (n Affiliation)

Affiliation motive can actually be seen as a drive with two distinct manifestations: the need for affiliation and the need for intimacy. The need for affiliation refers to the desire to form alliances and partnerships with individuals or groups. People who have a high n Affiliation score learn social relationships more quickly, like to engage others in conversation, prefer work teams that consist of friends rather than subject-matter experts, and will actively avoid conflict and competition (McClelland, 1975).

The fact that people who have high n Affiliation "are anxious about their relations with others, fear disapproval, and spend time seeking reassurance from others" (p. 356) leads them to have some surprising characteristics:

1. They are perceived by others to be approval seeking and egotistical. This has been explained by the fact that people who seek affiliation have a strong fear of rejection, which results in approval seeking.
2. They are seen to be self-confident, assertive, enthusiastic, and expressive.
3. They are apprehensive of being evaluated by others.
4. They tend to be less popular.

The more positive side of n Affiliation is the need for intimacy. This need is the desire to form meaningful relationships where psychological growth results, and where a feeling of commitment and concern for another develops. Compared to people with an n Affiliation, those who have a high intimacy motive are distinct in several ways:

1. They are judged by others to be more warm, sincere, appreciative, and loving.
2. They are seen to be less dominant and self-centered.
3. They get involved in deeper relationships.

It seems clear that the need for intimacy and n Affiliation are expressed differently. In the first case, a person may simply crave being in the presence of other people or want to interact with others on any level. In the latter case, a person may be motivated to seek selective and deep friendships. It may be tempting to judge all extroverts in a group as having very similar motives. The existence of both an affiliative motive and an intimacy motive suggests that this may not be an accurate assessment.

(i) High n Affiliation and Volunteering

The following assignments that involve social interaction with others are likely to appeal to people who have a high n Affiliation score (McCurley and Vineyard, 1988):

1. Ushering
2. Task force membership
3. Hospitality committee
4. Banquet committee
5. Senior center worker
6. Social activity worker

People seeking to fill a need for intimacy will prefer assignments where the opportunity to develop deep personal relationships is more likely:

1. Recognition events where they know the people being recognized
2. Case worker
3. Friendly visitor (McCurley and Vineyard, 1988)
4. Counselor

(d) McClelland's Learned Needs in Practice

The tests that McClelland and others have used to measure the various learned needs require professional training to administer. Although it would be ideal if a volunteer manager could directly identify which need predominates in any particular volunteer, this is not absolutely necessary. The volunteer function inventory (VFI) described earlier as useful in determining a person's valued outcomes, or something similar, can also be of assistance here.

People who have a high n Affiliation score or a high need for intimacy could be predicted to select social and perhaps value and protective motivational concerns more often than others. Similarly, volunteers with high n Power will probably select items related to esteem. Finally, it can be anticipated that those with strong n Achievement will select items found in the areas of career and understanding. By making this connection between the VFI and McClelland's learned needs, the volunteer manager can begin to better tailor volunteer assignments to volunteer needs.

2.8 CONTEMPORARY ISSUES IN MOTIVATION

(a) Professionals Who Volunteer

As budget-tight volunteer agencies rely more and more on volunteers for their expertise in human resource management, law, accounting, and finance, the motivation of professionals who choose to volunteer their services becomes increasingly important. In general, professionals who volunteer are much like the general population of volunteers. A taxonomy of valued outcomes specific to professionals can be found in a study of the motives and incentives of professionals who volunteer (e.g., Puffer, 1991). For the most part, it replicates the framework of Clary and his colleagues (1992) using different terminology; with "normative," "rational," and "affiliative" in place of Clary's "social and value," "career and understanding," and "protective and esteem" motives (see Exhibit 2–1).

There are some important additions, though, to the motives of volunteers who have full-time careers. A notable addition to the Puffer taxonomy is the category "status motives," which includes such things as "to be respected for doing worthwhile work" and "to be regarded as someone who cares about my community." These valued outcomes seem to reflect a desire by professionals who volunteer to be perceived by others in a positive, respectful way.

Other studies indicate that motives for professionals who volunteer also include more material incentives, such as developing transferable skills that may assist in acquiring or advancing within a job (Widmer, 1985). Compared to other volunteers, then, it is probably true that the valued outcomes of professionals who volunteer seem to differ with regard to status and to work-related transferability of skills. As a result, this particular group of volunteers may respond particularly well to approaches suggested by instrumentality theory, which focuses on the outcomes volunteers can expect for their efforts.

(b) Seniors Who Volunteer

Seniors (people aged 55 and older) who choose to volunteer are much like other people who do. Seniors cite "helping others," "sympathy with the cause," and "use of skills" as primary reasons for volunteering and being "too busy" as a reason for not doing so (Volunteer Centre of Calgary and Calgary Parks and Recreation, 1991). In at least one important way, however, the senior volunteer is unique. In a recent survey on volunteer activity distributed to seniors (Volunteer Centre of Calgary and Calgary Parks and Recreation, 1991), when asked "Was there anything that particularly motivated you to volunteer?," 29 percent of respondents gave "feeling useful" as their first answer. This response generally does not appear on lists of outcomes valued by volunteers.

As the baby-boom generation gets older, it is likely that the pattern of seniors' volunteer behavior and the motives that underlie it will change. There is some support for the belief that individuals who have a history of meaningful volunteer experiences will continue such involvement for as long as they are able. Seniors may be a minority of current volunteers, but once baby-boomers grow older we should not be surprised if they become the majority.

(c) Multicultural Perspectives in Volunteering

People who come to North America from other parts of the world often view the concept of volunteering quite differently than do native North Americans. Cross-culturally, we can see differences in the underpinnings of the motivation to volunteer. Project Kaleidoscope (Volunteer Centre of Calgary, 1992) asked, among other things, the question: "What are the attitudes to volunteerism in distinct communities?" and discovered some valuable perspectives on volunteering.

Motivation for volunteering ranged from a sense of duty to an ingrained belief in the value of volunteerism for spiritual enhancement. In three out of seven communities, volunteerism was viewed apprehensively by some segments, because of past political or class connotations. Volunteerism was actively promoted and practiced by all generations in three of the distinct communities.

- For the older Chinese generation, volunteer work is done out of courtesy and obligation to a community member. Their primary motive for volunteering is to maintain a link with culture. As the term *volunteering* is associated with social work, the older generation prefers to speak in terms of "giving a helping hand." The younger generation participates in volunteerism primarily to gain work experience and to have fun.

- In the Filipino community, the work for volunteer is *bayanihan,* which means community spirit or involvement. Volunteering is informal, built on trust and friendship. "When this trust is taken away or betrayed, you cannot win this back."

- Within the Ismaili community, there are no generational differences in attitudes. "So highly ingrained is volunteering in our faith, everyone is involved, and therefore it is part of our daily living."

- For Latin Americans, volunteering was an activity of rich people and thus an indication of class. In Chile or Argentina, volunteerism is associated with socialist tendencies. Volunteering, or helping, is seen as a private value and not to be advertised in a resume—"the left hand does *not* need to know what the right hand is doing."

- The Aboriginal community refers to "lend a helping hand" when asked. Volunteering, as a means to learn new skills or to promote the Aboriginal culture, is very acceptable.

- The majority of young new Polish immigrants come from a country where people were forced to volunteer to promote the government ideology, hence there is a negative attitude toward volunteering. The older established community members volunteer primarily within their distinct community.

- The Sikh word for volunteering is translated as "service." Their third religious commandment is "to help others." In India, Sikhs are also engaged in community volunteer work. (Volunteer Centre of Calgary, 1992)

There is a fascinating array of perspectives to volunteering found among ethno-specific communities, many of them rooted in tradition. The volunteer manager should be certain to consider these differences when motivating these diverse volunteers.

2.9 CONNECTING THE MOTIVATION THEORIES

The process- and content-based theories described in this chapter each stem from various psychological traditions. Each of these traditions takes a different perspective on what influences human behavior. If there is any true basis for what instigates, drives, and accounts for human behavior, then these diverse perspectives would be expected to link in some fundamental way. In fact, the theories of motivation are related. Psychologists steeped in the scientific method will note that these linkages do not all have scientific research support. However, these connections seem theoretically, if not intuitively, appealing. They also help the volunteer manager synthesize what psychologists have to say about motivation, and what that means in relation to their volunteer management approaches.

Within this framework and for this purpose, let us conjecture about the ties between Maslow's, McClelland's, and Herzberg's (content-based) theories and the reinforcement and instrumentality (process-based) theories. These relationships are illustrated in Exhibit 2–5. When the chart is read horizontally across the page. Using the need for achievement as an example, the relationships could be understood as follows:

1. By definition, a person with a high n Achievement score is motivated by a need for self-actualization.
2. If someone volunteers for the purpose of self-actualization, it is likely that the intrinsic conditions of achievement, responsibility, and growth in a volunteer assignment will influence that person's satisfaction with the assignment.
3. For such a person, achievement, responsibility, and growth would act as strong rewards in the behaviorist model. This is also consistent with the contention that satisfiers are motivating when present.
4. The stronger the perceived likelihood that these rewards will actually evolve, the more motivated this person will be.

Substituting the need for affiliation for the need for achievement, the relationships would follow the same pattern of relationship:

1. By definition, a person with a high n Affiliation score is motivated by a need for belonging.
2. If someone volunteers for the purpose of belonging, it is likely that the intrinsic condition of strong interpersonal relationships in a volunteer assignment will influence that person's satisfaction with the assignment.
3. For such a person, good interpersonal relations would act as a reward in the behaviorist model.
4. The stronger the perceived likelihood that such a reward would actually result, the more motivated this person will be.

Although they have not been discussed in this chapter, McClelland does propose the existence of *avoidance* motives. These would relate in a similar fashion to safety and physiological needs, to Herzberg's dissatisfiers, and to aversive conditioning.

2.10 A FINAL CONSIDERATION

Thus, the wide body of knowledge related to motivation comes together into a meaningful whole. In the preface to the last edition of *Motivation and Personality,* Maslow appropriately notes that "after all, the cosmos is one and interrelated; any society is one and interrelated; any person is one and interrelated. . . . " (1970, p. xi). So, too, are the conceptions of what drives us to behave in particular ways.

◆ EXHIBIT 2–5 Connecting the Theories of Motivation

Content Theories			Process Theories	
McClelland / **Maslow**	**Herzberg**		**Reinforcement**	**Instrumentality**
n Achievement — Self-Actualization	**Satisfiers** Achievement, Responsibility, Growth		Reward	Valence ← Instrumentality ← Expectancy
Esteem	Recognition, Advancement	Status	Behavior ←	
n Power			Behavior →	
Love and belonging		Interpersonal relations		
n Affiliation			Punishment	
Safety		Job security, Salary, Working conditions, **Dissatisfiers**	→	
Physiological			No behavior	

REFERENCES

Bianchi, Alessandra. 1993. "True Believers: Pride in, and Passion for, a Business's Product or Services Is One of the Most Powerful Workplace Enhancers Around." *The Best Small Companies to Work for in America* 15(1) (July): 72(2).

Clary, E. Gil, Mark Snyder, and Robert Ridge. 1992. "Volunteers' Motivations." *Nonprofit Management and Leadership* 2 (4) (Summer).

Coon, Dennis. 1991. *Essentials of Psychology,* 5th ed. St. Paul, Minn.: West Publishing.

Fagan, Ron. 1992. "Characteristics of College Student Volunteering." *Journal of Volunteer Administration* 5 (Fall).

Francies, George R. 1985. "The Motivation Needs Profile." In Larry F. Moore, (Ed.), *Motivating Volunteers.* Vancouver, British Columbia, Canada: Vancouver Volunteer Centre.

Gibson, James L., John M. Ivancevich, and James H. Donnelly. 1982. *Organizations.* Dallas, Texas: Business Publications.

Gough, H.G., and A.B. Heilbrun, Jr. 1975. *The Adjective Checklist Manual.* Palo Alto, Calif.: Consulting Psychologists Press.

Grieshop, James I. 1985. "How Art Thou Motivated? Let Me Count the Ways." In Larry F. Moore (Ed.), *Motivating Volunteers.* Vancouver, British Columbia, Canada: Vancouver Volunteer Centre.

Hamner, W. Clay, and Ellen P. Hamner. 1976. "Behavior Modification on the Bottom Line." *Organizational Dynamics* (Spring).

Herzberg, Frederick, B. Mausner, and B. Snyderman. 1959. *The Motivation to Work.* New York: Wiley.

Howell, Albert. 1986. *Why Do Volunteers Burnout and Dropout?* Calgary, Alberta, Canada: Research Unit for Public Policy Studies, University of Calgary, Canada (December).

Ilsley, Paul J. 1990. *Enhancing the Volunteer Experience.* San Francisco: Jossey-Bass.

Knowles, Malcolm S. (1972). "Motivation in Volunteerism: Synopsis of a Theory." *Journal of Voluntary Action Research* 1(2).

Landy, Frank J., and Don A. Trumbo. 1980. *Psychology of Work Behavior.* Homewood, Ill.: Dorsey Press.

LeFrancois, Guy R. 1980. *Psychology.* Belmont, Calif.: Wadsworth.

Maslow, Abraham H. 1943. "A Theory of Human Motivation." *Psychological Review* (July).

Maslow, Abraham H. 1970. *Motivation and Personality,* 2nd ed. New York: Harper & Row.

McClelland, David C. 1962. "Business Drive and National Achievement." *Harvard Business Review.* (July–August).

McClelland, David C. 1975. *Power: The Inner Experience.* New York, NY: Irvington Publishers Inc.

McClelland, David C. 1987. *Human Motivation.* Cambridge: Cambridge University Press.

McCurley, Steve, and Sue Vineyard. 1988. *101 Tips for Volunteer Recruitment.* Downers Grove, Ill.: Heritage Arts Publishing.

Moore, Larry F. 1985. Motivating Volunteers, Vancouver Volunteer Centre.

Myers, David G. 1983. *Social Psychology.* New York: McGraw-Hill

Omoto, Allen M., and Mark Snyder. 1993. "AIDS Volunteers and Their Motivations: Theoretical Issues and Practical Concerns." *Nonprofit Management and Leadership* 4(2) (Winter).

Pike, Sue. 1992. *Why People Volunteer.* Ottawa, Ontario, Canada: Volunteer Centre Ottawa–Carlton, Voluntary Action Directorate.

Puffer, Sheila M. 1991. "Career Professionals Who Volunteer." *Nonprofit Management and Leadership* 2(2) (Winter).

Ross, David P., and E. Richard Shillington. 1989. *A Profile of the Canadian Volunteer.* Ottawa, Ontario, Canada: National Voluntary Organizations.

Schindler-Rainman, Eva, and Ronald Lippitt. 1971. *The Volunteer Community.* Washington, D.C.: Center for a Volunteer Society.

Smith, Nan H., and Gregory T. Berns. 1981. "Results of a National Survey of Recruitment and Motivation Techniques." *Volunteer Administration* XIV(2).

Snyder, Mark, and Allen M. Omoto. 1992. "Who Helps and Why? The Psychology of AIDS Volunteerism." In S. Spacapan, and S. Oskamp (Eds.), *Helping and Being Helped: Naturalistic Studies.* Newbury Park, Calif., Sage Publications.

Story, D.C. 1992. "Volunteerism: The 'Self-regarding' and 'Other-regarding' Aspects of the Human Spirit." *Nonprofit and Voluntary Sector Quarterly* 21 (1)(Spring).

Sundeen, Richard A. 1992. "Differences in Personal Goals and Attitudes among Volunteers." *Nonprofit and Voluntary Sector Quarterly* 21 (3)(Fall).

Van Til, Jon. 1985. "Mixed Motives: Residues of Altruism in an Age of Narcissism." In Larry F. Moore (Ed.), *Motivating Volunteers.* Vancouver, British Columbia, Canada: Vancouver Volunteer Centre.

Vineyard, Sue. 1984. *Marketing Magic for Volunteer Programs.* Downers Grove, Il.: Heritage Arts.

Volunteer Centre of Calgary. 1992. *Project Kaleidoscope: Cross Cultural Partnerships in Volunteerism.* Calgary, Alberta, Canada: Volunteer Centre of Calgary (February).

Volunteer Centre of Calgary and Calgary Parks and Recreation. 1991. *Senior Volunteers: The Report of the Senior Volunteer Program Committee.* Calgary, Alberta, Canada: Volunteer Centre of Calgary.

Widmer, Candance. 1985. "Why Board Members Participate." *Journal of Voluntary Action Research* 14 (4)(October–December).

Zahrly, Jan, and Eleanor Brown. 1993. "Self Benefit as a Motivating Factor in Recruiting and Retaining Volunteers." In *1993 Conference Proceedings of the Association for Research in Nonprofit Organizations and Voluntary Action (ARNOVA),* Ontario Institute for Studies in Education (OISE), Toronto, Ontario, Canada, October 28–30.

CHAPTER ◇ 3

PREPARING THE ORGANIZATION FOR VOLUNTEERS

Jeffrey L. Brudney, Ph.D.
University of Georgia

3.1   Introduction

3.2   Setting Reasonable Expectations for Volunteers: Weighing the Benefits and Costs of Volunteer Participation

3.3   Making Volunteer Involvement Matter: Establishing the Rationale and Goals for the Volunteer Program

3.4   Smoothing the Way Toward Effectiveness: Involving Paid Staff in Designing the Volunteer Program

3.5   Housing the Volunteer Program: Integrating Volunteer Participation into the Organization

3.6   Providing Responsibility and Direction for the Volunteer Program: Creating Positions of Leadership

3.7   Sharing the Workplace: Developing Job Descriptions for Volunteer Positions

3.8   Preparing for Volunteers: Developing Systems and Supports for Participation and Management

3.9   Conclusions

        References

3.1 INTRODUCTION

Volunteers play a vital role in the activities and services of hundreds of thousands of nonprofit and governmental agencies. As demands on these organizations have increased and the financial resources available to them have declined, the use of volunteers has become even more critical. National surveys commissioned by the Independent Sector, a nonprofit coalition of some 900 organizational members concerned with documenting, recognizing, and promoting philanthropy and voluntary action, bear out the scope of this remarkable phenomenon. According to the results of a survey conducted by the Gallup Organization in 1994, about one-half of adult Americans (47.7 percent) volunteer for an average of 4.2 hours per week, a rate of volunteering that has remained fairly stable for a decade. In all, they contribute over 15 million hours to recipient organizations, the equivalent of nearly 9,000 full-time employees. If these institutions had to pay for the labor that is now donated, the price tag would have reached a staggering $182.3 billion (Hodgkinson and Weitzman, 1992, p. 23).

The key to tapping the vast pool of energy, talent, and goodwill captured in these arresting figures lies in preparing for volunteer activity. The leaders of many nonprofit and public agencies have taken the appropriate steps to institute a sound volunteer program, and their organization, clients, and volunteers all benefit as a result. Other programs, however, founder on the lack of knowledge or effort necessary to provide the essential groundwork for the participation of nonpaid workers. Problems such as uncertain volunteer recruitment, ineffectual assignment, paid staff resentment, or worse, a disbanded program, often stem from initial failures to plan for and accommodate an unconventional workforce. With a modicum of forethought and commitment to volunteer involvement, however, these maladies are preventable.

Strategies that organizations can use to lay the foundation for an effective volunteer effort are discussed in this chapter. The focus is on *service volunteers,* people who donate their time to help other people directly, rather than on *policy volunteers,* citizens who assume the equally vital role of sitting on boards of directors or advisory boards of nonprofit organizations. (Other chapters in this book deal with policy volunteers.) The strategies discussed in this chapter counsel agency leadership to:

1. Set reasonable expectations concerning volunteers.
2. Establish an explicit rationale and goals for a volunteer program.
3. Involve paid staff in designing the program.
4. Develop job descriptions for the tasks to be performed by volunteers.
5. Implement one of several options for housing the volunteer program and integrating it into the organization.
6. Create positions of leadership for the program.
7. Develop systems and supports to facilitate citizen participation and program management.

3.2 SETTING REASONABLE EXPECTATIONS FOR VOLUNTEERS: WEIGHING THE BENEFITS AND COSTS OF VOLUNTEER PARTICIPATION

The leadership of any organization that enlists volunteers or contemplates their introduction needs to have realistic expectations concerning just what nonpaid workers can achieve, as well as the difficulties they may occasion. Volunteers cannot "save" an organization that may suffer from other problems, and they can even make matters worse. Although well intentioned, an agency that puts out a call for citizen volunteers without due consideration of the additional demands thus created for orientation, training, management, and evaluation quickly learns that it has increased rather than lessened its burdens. Without sufficient preparation prior to volunteer involvement, organizational leadership courts disaster.

The first step in placing the volunteer program on a firm footing is to set and communicate reasonable expectations. The appraisal should be candid in evaluating both the accomplishments and the challenges envisioned from the program. Organizational members must realize that like any other resource, this one entails a mix of disadvantages and advantages.

(a) Potential Disadvantages of Volunteer Involvement

Potential drawbacks to a successful volunteer program fall into three general categories: inadequate funding for the program, possible liabilities of volunteers as workers, and political or labor tensions that might be generated.

(i) Funding the Volunteer Program

The first potential problem is that of funding an ongoing volunteer effort. Although the labor donated by citizens to nonprofit and governmental agencies is not compensated monetarily—a factor that is, in fact, one of the strengths of the approach—the support structure essential to making productive use of this labor does require resources and expenditures. Given popular but misleading conceptions of volunteers as a free resource, agency leadership may not be prepared financially or psychologically to underwrite necessary program investments. For example, reimbursing volunteers' work-related expenses, purchasing liability insurance protection, providing orientation and training, and initiating a recruitment campaign all entail costs for the organization. Another hidden cost is paid staff time, nearly always at a premium, that must be devoted to the administration and management of volunteers.

(ii) Volunteers as Workers

A second set of possible difficulties concerns the perceived shortcomings of volunteers as workers. Familiar criticisms accuse volunteers of poor work, high levels of absenteeism and turnover, and unreliability in meeting work commitments. The decision to seek volunteers presupposes that a sufficient supply of willing citizens exists to meet the demands of organizations that desire useful labor. With the growing dependence of the public and nonprofit sectors on volunteers, however, actual recruitment, rather than dedication and commitment to a task, may well pose the most serious obstacle to the approach (Brudney, 1990a). In some service domains, volunteers have become so difficult to locate and recruit that hiring paid personnel can turn out to be a more attractive option (Brudney and Duncombe, 1992).

(iii) Political and Labor Tensions

Third, volunteer programs may precipitate political and labor tensions that threaten to undermine the benefits of the approach. For example, if top organizational officials or department heads and supervisors lend only weak support to the program, they send the wrong message to both paid staff and volunteers about the legitimate role and value of the citizen participants. Lack of support can exacerbate apprehensions of paid staff, jeopardize working relationships crucial to program success, and trigger objections from unionized personnel. Employees may also fear that organizational use of volunteers may inadvertently fuel popular misconceptions regarding the number of paid staff needed simply to meet work obligations, let alone to perform with full effectiveness.

(b) Potential Advantages of Volunteer Involvement

Despite potential problems, the introduction of volunteers can offer substantial compensating benefits to public and nonprofit organizations in four primary areas: achievement of cost savings or cost effectiveness, expansion of organizational capability, improvements in community relations, and enhancement of service quality.

(i) Achievement of Cost Savings or Cost Effectiveness

Most notably in the public sector, the advantages of volunteer involvement that have stimulated greatest attention focus on possible budgetary savings and gains in cost effectiveness. In this domain especially, organizational leaders should take care not to overstate expectations. Because a volunteer program necessitates expenditures of its own (see above), popular claims that the approach can remedy budget deficits appear highly exaggerated. In fact, unless cuts are identified and exacted elsewhere in the agency budget, the addition of volunteers to an organization can marginally increase monetary outlays.

Nevertheless, a well-designed and -managed volunteer program offers definite economic advantages to public and nonprofit organizations. The total cost to an organization of introducing volunteers (including wages, fringe benefits, and program support) is relatively modest, especially when compared to the cost of paid employees. While displacing paid personnel with volunteers is not an ethical or recommended strategy, by adding volunteers to its existing workforce an organization can boost the amount or quality of the services it delivers for a fixed level of expenditure, or limit the expenses necessary to achieve a given quantity of services (Karn, 1983; 1982–1983). Although practitioners often refer to this advantage as *cost savings,* a more apt term is *cost effectiveness.*

(ii) Expansion of Organizational Capability

A second advantage of volunteer involvement is the potential to augment agency capacity. Applied creatively, the labor, skills, and energy donated by citizens can enable organizations to provide services that would otherwise not be possible, increase the level or types of services or programs offered, maintain normal operations in emergency and peak-load periods, and test new initiatives or innovations. A well-designed volunteer program also facilitates more productive use of paid staff time: Volunteers can relieve highly trained service providers of routine duties, freeing them to concentrate on the tasks and responsibilities for which their professional background and expertise best quality them. In this way, volunteers increase organizational capability to do more with the resources available.

(iii) Improvements in Community Relations

A volunteer program can also yield substantial benefits to the community. Citizen participation within an agency can build the job skills and work experience of volunteers, promote greater awareness of the pressures and constraints faced by service organizations, and generally improve relations within the community. In the public sector, volunteers have often proven to be gifted advocates of agency interests, who help to further organizational missions and win increased appropriations (e.g., Brudney, 1990b; Marando, 1986; Walter, 1987). A study of literacy programs in California found that library administrators who enlisted volunteers were successful in their strategy to expand their base of activities, develop and consolidate political support among elected officials and the larger community, and enhance the credibility and attractiveness of library programs (Walter, 1993). Volunteer involvement offers additional approaches to strengthen ties with the community through such activities as soliciting advice and guidance from citizen participants. As one volunteer states, "frontline volunteers . . . know what's going on and are more willing to tell you what is as distinguished from what you might prefer to hear" (Williams, 1993, p. 11). Because most volunteers live reasonably close to where they donate their time and possess some familiarity with local resources and formal and informal helping networks, they facilitate organizational outreach and case finding in the community.

(iv) Enhancement of Service Quality

Finally, the involvement of volunteers holds the potential to raise the quality of services offered by nonprofit and public agencies. Targeted volunteer recruitment may identify citizens with specialized skills not possessed by employees (for example, legal, computer, accounting, and engineering) who can improve agency services and programs. In addition, many volunteers find rewarding personal contact with service recipients; in national surveys, the motivation expressed most frequently for volunteering is to do something useful to help other people (e.g., Hodgkinson et al., 1992). By devoting detailed attention to agency clients—time that employed personnel frequently lack—volunteers help personalize and enhance the delivery of services. Several scholars argue that volunteers help to humanize organizational services, lending them a more individual and informal quality conducive to maintaining client self-esteem and confidence (e.g., Clary, 1987; Naylor, 1985; Wineburg and Wineburg, 1987).

(c) Realistic Expectations for Volunteer Involvement

Ideally, research would long ago have settled the issue of just how frequently each of these advantages and disadvantages is realized by organizations that incorporate volunteers. Armed with that information, organizational leadership could readily anticipate the likely pitfalls and benefits of the approach and plan accordingly. Unfortunately, scant research has attempted to answer this question. Only two studies have systematically evaluated the effects of volunteer involvement across large, representative samples of organizations; both of them derive from the public sector. In the mid-1980s, Sydney Duncombe (1985) administered a survey to a national sample of 534 localities that enlist volunteers in the delivery of services. More recently, Jeffrey L. Brudney (1993) expanded Duncomb's questionnaire in a survey administered to 250 Georgia localities that use the approach. While Duncombe questioned cities on only four potential benefits of volunteer involvement and six reputed problems, Brudney probed a much more extensive inventory of 14 advantages and a similar number of disadvantages (all discussed above). Exhibits 3–1 and 3–2 present the findings.

◆ **EXHIBIT 3–1   Perceived Disadvantages of Volunteer Involvement in the Delivery of Services**

Perceived Disadvantage	Georgia Sample (N=250, 1990)	National Sample (N=534, 1985)
Funding the Volunteer Program		
Providing insurance for volunteers	22%	21%
Lack of adequate funding for volunteer program	20%	-
Lack of funds for reimbursement of volunteers' expenses	19%	-
Lack of paid staff time to train and supervise volunteers	16%	38%
Volunteers as Workers		
Getting enough people to volunteer	39%	56%
Absenteeism by volunteers	17%	16%
Unreliability of volunteers in meeting work commitments	14%	-
High turnover of volunteers	12%	-
Poor work by volunteers	5%	6%
Political and Labor Tensions		
Volunteers lead to misconceptions about number of paid staff needed	8%	-
Lack of support from department heads and supervisors for volunteer program	7%	16%
Lack of support from top organizational officials for volunteer program	5%	-
Poor working relationship or mistrust between volunteers and paid staff	3%	-
Union objections to volunteer involvement	0%	-

◆ **EXHIBIT 3–2   Perceived Advantages of Volunteer Involvement in the Delivery of Services**

Perceived Advantage	Georgia Sample (N=250, 1990)	National Sample (N=534, 1985)
Cost savings or Cost effectiveness		
Cost savings to organization	82%	82%
Expansion of Organizational Capability		
Capability to provide services otherwise could not provide	64%	–
Capability to do more with available resources	48%	–
Increases in level of services and programs	28%	–
Expansion of staff in emergencies and peak-load periods	27%	–
Enlargement of kinds of services or programs offered	22%	–
Improvements in Community Relations		
Improved community relations	48%	–
Increased public support for programs	46%	25%
Job skills and experience gained by volunteers	31%	–
Greater public awareness of pressures and constraints on organization	28%	
Program advice and guidance from volunteers	24%	–
Enhancement of Service Quality		
Availability of specialized skills possessed by volunteers	34%	40%
Improved quality of services and programs	32%	–
More detailed attention to clients	8%	45%

(i) Disadvantages Realized

For the most part, the two surveys reveal very comparable results regarding the costs and benefits accruing from the participation of volunteers in the delivery of services. As Exhibit 3–1 shows, by a substantial margin, the most common drawback reported by officials is recruitment ("getting enough people to volunteer"), cited by more than half of the national respondents (56 percent) and the largest number of the Georgia sample (39 percent).

The set of problems encountered next most frequently pertain to funding the volunteer program. Approximately one in five of the Georgia officials listed as disadvantages the purchase of liability insurance for volunteers, a general lack of funding for the program, and inadequate funds for reimbursement of the work-related expenses of volunteers. Nearly as many pointed to insufficient time for paid staff to train and supervise volunteers (16 percent), a problem much more widespread in the national sample (38 percent).

If these organizations offer any guide, the shortcomings sometimes attributed to volunteers as workers seem to arise less often. Just 5 percent of the Georgia sample mentioned poor work by volunteers (6 percent in the national survey); 12 percent cited high turnover, and 14 percent listed unreliability in meeting work commitments. Problems with volunteer absenteeism seem a bit more common, cited by 17 percent of the officials (16 percent in the national survey).

Among local governments in Georgia, the political and labor difficulties sometimes associated with volunteer involvement occur very infrequently. A scant 8 percent of the sample reported that use of volunteers had led to misconceptions by the citizenry regarding the number of paid staff actually needed. About the same number acknowledged problems emanating from lack of support for the program from department heads or supervisors (7 percent versus 16 percent in the national survey) or from top elected or appointed officials (5 percent). Remarkably, just 3 percent mentioned poor working relationships or mistrust between paid and nonpaid staff members; none of the Georgia localities cited union objections to volunteer workers.

(ii) Advantages Realized

Exhibit 3–2 presents the data from the two surveys relating to the advantages of volunteer involvement. Without doubt, the most common benefit perceived from the approach is cost savings, reported by 82 percent of the officials in both the Georgia and national samples. High percentages also cited advantages in expanding the capability of their organization: 64 percent of the Georgia local governments reported that volunteers had enabled them to provide services that otherwise would not be possible, and almost half (48 percent) indicated that volunteers had allowed them to do more with available resources. Fewer officials (approximately one in four) felt that use of volunteers had led to an increase in the level of services or programs offered by their organization, expansion of staff in emergencies and peak-load periods, or enlargement of the types of services or programs provided.

The participation of volunteers in these organizations appears to have a positive effect on relations with the community. About half of the Georgia officials stated that volunteer involvement had led to improvements in community relations in general (48 percent) and greater public support for their programs (46 percent versus 25 percent nationally). Mentioned less frequently by the Georgia sample, volunteers raised public awareness of the pressures and constraints on the agency (28 percent) and provided useful advice and guidance on programs (24 percent). Approximately one-third indicated that volunteers had gained valuable job skills and experience (31 percent).

Volunteers also contributed to perceived enhancements in the quality of services. Almost half of the national sample (45 percent) reported that volunteers allowed more detailed attention to agency clients (8 percent in the Georgia study). Other benefits in this category include the specialized skills brought by volunteers (cited by 40 percent in the national survey and 34 percent in Georgia), and overall improvements in services and programs (32 percent in Georgia).

(iii) Mix of Advantages over Disadvantages

Given the findings from these two large surveys, what can organizational leadership reasonably expect from volunteer involvement? Although particular results may vary from one organization to the next, the findings support two general conclusions. First, leaders might anticipate the greatest difficulty in recruiting volunteers and securing necessary resources for the program, including both monetary support and paid staff time. Obtaining liability insurance can present a problem. Before introducing volunteers, organizations are well advised to undertake a risk management process to determine the extent of exposure to injury or legal action, and possible remedies (Liability issues are addressed in other chapters.) By contrast, the benefits reported most frequently from volunteer participation include gains in cost-effectiveness and expansion of organizational capability. Perceived improvements in community relations and overall service quality also seem reasonable expectations.

Second, as suggested by this conclusion and demonstrated more convincingly in Exhibits 3–1 and 3–2, the benefits of volunteer involvement appear to outweigh the costs. Citizen participation in the delivery of services certainly has its limitations (and detractors), but these drawbacks seem to be encountered with much lower frequency than the anticipated benefits. The great similarity in results from two distinct surveys (with very different samples, items, and time points) reinforces this interpretation. Nevertheless, because the potential benefits of volunteer involvement are not realized universally, and disadvantages sometimes occur, organizational leaders must work toward an optimal mix. To begin, they should establish a persuasive rationale for the volunteer program.

3.3 MAKING VOLUNTEER INVOLVEMENT MATTER: ESTABLISHING THE RATIONALE AND GOALS FOR THE VOLUNTEER PROGRAM

A nonprofit organization may be eager for fresh input and innovation and enthusiastic about the potential contribution of citizens. However, no matter how overburdened it may be, or how constrained in its human and financial resources, its efforts to incorporate volunteers must not begin with recruitment. In fact, Susan J. Ellis (1994) titles the opening chapter of her book on this subject "Recruitment Is the Third Step." The first step, treated in this section, is to determine why the organization wants volunteers; the second, discussed in a section below, is to design valuable work assignments for them (Ellis, 1994, pp. 5–6). Before it is ready to begin recruiting volunteers, an agency must lay the groundwork for their sustained participation.

The foundation for a successful volunteer program rests on a serious consideration by the agency of the rationale for citizen involvement and the development of a philosophy or policy to guide this effort. The organization should determine the purposes for introducing the new participants into the organization. The basic motivations can be separated into two major categories: economic and noneconomic.

(a) Economic Motivations

As Exhibit 3–2 demonstrates, volunteers assist organizations in achieving a variety of objectives. Especially during periods of fiscal stringency, top organizational officials may fix too narrowly on cost savings as *the* rationale for volunteer involvement. As mentioned above, this aspiration is misleading. First, while the labor of volunteers may be donated, a volunteer program requires expenditures for recruitment, orientation, training, insurance, reimbursement, materials, and other items. Second, for volunteers to create cost savings, cutbacks must be made in the agency's budget. If the cutbacks come at the expense of paid staff, the results are lamentable and predictable in the form of resentments and antagonisms that have subverted volunteer initiatives in the past.

From an economic perspective, what volunteers offer an organization is the capacity to realize more productive application of existing funds and person-power. With a relatively small investment of resources, volunteers have the potential to increase the type, level, and quality of services that an agency can deliver to clients and to facilitate the work of paid staff members. Although costs are not spared in this situation, to the degree that volunteers improve the return on agency expenditures they extend the resources available to meet pressing needs for assistance and services.

(b) Noneconomic Motivations

Noneconomic motives may also drive a volunteer program. The leadership of a nonprofit organization may enlist volunteers to interject a more vibrant dimension of commitment and caring into its relationships with clients; or the goal may be to learn more about the community, nurture closer ties to the citizenry, stimulate useful feedback and advice, and strengthen public awareness and support. An agency may seek volunteers to identify and reach clients inaccessible through normal organizational channels. Volunteers may be needed to provide professional skills, such as computer programming, legal counsel, or accounting expertise, not possessed by paid employees. The purpose may be to staff a pilot program otherwise doomed to fiscal austerity, expand services to a broader clientele, or upgrade programs or other assistance. Enhancing responsiveness to client groups and the larger community may offer still another rationale.

Volunteers also enjoy a well-earned reputation for success in soliciting donations to causes and organizations. Because the public regards them as neutral participants who will not directly benefit from monetary or in-kind contributions, agencies very frequently enlist citizens for this purpose. In a 1989 national survey, about one-half (48 percent) of all volunteers reported assignments in fund-raising (Hodgkinson et al., 1992, p. 46).

(c) Rationale for Volunteer Involvement

That the list of possible purposes for establishing and maintaining a volunteer program is lengthy attests to the vitality of the approach. Each agency will have somewhat different reasons that should be formalized in a general statement of policy or philosophy to guide volunteer involvement. Although no single rationale can apply

---

◆ **EXHIBIT 3–3   Examples of Statements of Organizational Philosophy Guiding the Involvement of Volunteers**

- ◆ This agency welcomes volunteers to provide a human touch and individual dignity in all dealing with clients.
- ◆ Volunteers extend agency resources to serve a broader clientele.
- ◆ This agency seeks volunteers not only to further our mission but also to make the work of paid staff more productive.
- ◆ Volunteers represent this organization in the community.
- ◆ This agency values volunteers for the work they perform as well as the advice and guidance they offer.
- ◆ Volunteers bring distinctive skills to this organization that would otherwise be beyond its means.
- ◆ Volunteers help this organization to do its job with greater efficiency, quality, and compassion.

---

to all organizations, some useful examples of these statements can be found in Exhibit 3–3. Organizations typically combine several such statements in the policy.

An explicit statement of goals advances several important components of program design and functioning. First, it begins to define the types of volunteer positions that will be needed and the number of people required to fill these roles. Such information is at the core of eventual recruitment and training of volunteers. Second, it aids in delineating concrete objectives against which the program might be evaluated, once in operation. Evaluation results provide essential data to strengthen and improve the program.

Finally, a statement of the philosophy underlying volunteer involvement and the specific ends sought through this form of participation can help to alleviate possible apprehensions by paid staff that the new participants may intrude on professional prerogatives or threaten job security. Clarifying the goals for voluntary assistance can dampen idle, typically negative speculation and begin to build a sense of program ownership on the part of employees, especially if they are included in planning for the volunteer program.

3.4 SMOOTHING THE WAY TOWARD EFFECTIVENESS: INVOLVING PAID STAFF IN DESIGNING THE VOLUNTEER PROGRAM

In most organizations, designing and implementing a volunteer program entails changes in standard practices and routines. For example, funds must be found and committed to the effort, linkages formed to integrate the program into the organization (see below), job positions and working relationships modified, and policies devised and approved to accommodate the citizen participants. Because these changes are ambitious and require ratification by those at higher levels of the organizational hierarchy, the involvement and support of top officials is crucial to the creation and vitality of a volunteer program (e.g., Ellis, 1986).

This group is not the only one that should play an active role in defining the mission, philosophy, and procedures governing the volunteer effort. Paid staff members, and if they are already known to the agency or can be identified, volunteers, should also be included in program planning and implementation.

(a) Participation by Paid Staff Members

A touchstone in the field of organizational development is to include individuals or groups who will be affected by a new policy or program (stakeholders) in its design and achievement. Participation adds to the knowledge base for crafting policy and inculcates a sense of ownership and commitment instrumental to gaining acceptance for innovation.

Because the incorporation of volunteers into an agency can impose dramatic changes in the jobs and working relationships of employees, the involvement of paid staff is especially important. (If employees have a bargaining agent or union, their representatives should be included.) The sharing of needs, perspectives, and information among agency leadership, employees, and prospective volunteers that takes place in pivotal. In the joint planning process, the parties work to overcome differences and reach agreement on how the volunteer program can be most effectively designed, organized, and managed to pursue its mission and goals. Participation by paid staff members helps to alleviate any concerns they might harbor concerning a volunteer initiative and its implications for agency clients or the workplace.

A central purpose of the joint planning meetings and discussions is to develop policies and procedures governing volunteer involvement that are endorsed by all parties. These guidelines should address the major aspects of the volunteer program and work-related behaviors; Exhibit 3–4 presents a list of these areas. This informa-

---

◆ **EXHIBIT 3–4   Aspects of the Volunteer Program That Should Be Addressed in Agency Policy**

- ◆ Application procedure
- ◆ Provision of orientation and training
- ◆ Probationary acceptance period and active status
- ◆ Rights and general standards of conduct
- ◆ Task assignment and reassignment
- ◆ Attendance and absenteeism
- ◆ Performance review
- ◆ Benefits
- ◆ Grievance procedures
- ◆ Requirements for record keeping
- ◆ Reimbursement of work-related expenses
- ◆ Use of agency equipment and facilities
- ◆ Requirements for confidentiality
- ◆ Suspension and termination

---

tion should be readily available in a booklet or manual distributed to all volunteers and employees.

Although some observers may question the need for published standards of organizational conduct as somehow inimical to the spirit of help freely given, this step is a positive one for the agency as well as for the volunteers. In one study, for example, organizations that distributed notebooks with all written policies, formal job descriptions, and training manuals to citizen participants had the lowest rates of turnover; by contrast, the organization with the highest turnover provided none of this information (Pearce, 1978, pp. 276–277). Explicit policies show that the agency takes seriously the participation of volunteers, values their contribution to the organizational mission and goals, and wants to maintain collaborative working relationships. Equally important, formal guidelines greatly help in defusing potential conflicts, handling problem situations on the job, protecting volunteer rights, and managing for consistent results.

(b) Comparable Guidelines for Employees and Volunteers

Steve McCurley and Rick Lynch (1989, p. 23) advise administrators of volunteer programs that agency guidelines for volunteers should be comparable to the respective policies for employees: "If you have a question about the content of a policy or procedure, refer to the agency policies and procedures for paid staff. The rules should be as similar as possible: 'when in doubt, copy'." A seasoned volunteer administrator concurs: "One should not have different qualifications for staff than one has for volunteers doing the same work" (Thornburg, 1992, p. 18). By setting standards as high for volunteers as for paid staff, an agency engenders trust and credibility, increased respect and requests for volunteers from employees, a healthy work environment, and perhaps most important, high-quality services (McCurley and Lynch, 1989; Wilson, 1984). This course helps to preclude treatment of volunteers as second-class citizens.

(c) Empowerment of Volunteers

Because volunteers may not be known to an agency prior to inception of a program, they may miss the initial discussions concerning planning, design, and implementation. Once this effort is launched and in operation, however, they should definitely have input into decisions affecting the volunteer effort. Just as for paid staff, citizens are more likely to accept and endorse organizational policies and programs, and to generate useful input regarding them, if they enjoy ready access to the decision-making process. Participation is key to *empowerment* of volunteers. The term connotes a genuine sharing of responsibility for the volunteer program with citizen participants; more attentive listening to volunteer ideas and preferences; and greater recognition of the time, skills, and value provided to organizations through this approach. Empowerment is thought to result in increased feelings of personal commitment and loyalty to the volunteer program by participants and hence greater retention and effectiveness (Naylor, 1985; Scheier, 1988a,b, 1988–1989).

3.5 HOUSING THE VOLUNTEER PROGRAM: INTEGRATING VOLUNTEER PARTICIPATION INTO THE ORGANIZATION

For the benefits of volunteer involvement to be fully appreciated and achieved by an organization, the volunteer program must be linked to the structure of the agency. A nonprofit organization may be able to accommodate a few volunteers informally or episodically on a case-by-case basis as the demand for them or interest in them arises. Integrating larger numbers of volunteers in an ongoing working relationship, however, requires adaptations in organizational structure. Nonprofit agencies can select from among several alternative structural configurations for this purpose, according to their needs. In order of increasing comprehensiveness, these arrangements encompass ad hoc volunteer efforts, volunteer recruitment by an outside organization with the agency otherwise responsible for management, decentralization of the program to operating departments, or a centralized approach. Each option presents a distinct menu of advantages and disadvantages.

(a) Ad Hoc Volunteer Efforts

Volunteer efforts may arise spontaneously in an ad hoc fashion to meet exigencies confronting an organization, especially on a short-term basis. Normally, citizens motivated to share their background, training, skills, and interests with organizations that could make good use of them are the catalyst. Fiscal stress, leaving an agency few options, may quicken the helping impulse. The Service Corps of Retired Executives (SCORE), an association of primarily retired businesspeople who donate their time and skills to assist clients of the U.S. Small Business Administration (SBA), began in this manner in the early 1960s. Retired business executives approached the SBA to offer assistance in meeting the demands of a huge constituency (Brudney, 1986). The responsiveness and alacrity with which an ad hoc effort can be launched and operating is inspiring: Within six months of its inception, SCORE supplied 2,000 volunteers to the SBA. Crisis and emergency situations can provoke an even more spectacular response, mobilizing huge numbers of volunteers in a remarkably short time.

Spontaneous help from citizens can infuse vitality (and labor) into an agency, alerting officials to the possibilities of volunteerism. Offsetting these advantages, however, is the fact that only selected parts or members of the organization may be aware of an ad hoc citizen effort and thus be able to avail themselves of it. In addition, because energy levels and zeal wane as emergencies are tamed or fade from the limelight of publicity or attention, the ad hoc model of volunteer involvement is very sensitive to the passage of time. A volunteer *program* requires a sustained rather than a sporadic commitment from citizens. The organization must develop a support structure to nurture the contributions of citizens and to make them accessible to all employees. Unless the agency takes steps to institutionalize participation, it risks squandering the long-term benefits of the approach. Almost from the start, the SBA and the SCORE volunteers worked to develop an appropriate structure. The partnership has served the agency well, generating a continuous stream of volunteers to the SBA and assistance to over 1 million small businesspersons.

(b) Reliance on Other Organizations

A second option sometimes open to nonprofit and public agencies is to rely on the expertise and reputation of an established organization, such as the United Way and its affiliates, or a volunteer center or clearinghouse, to assist in recruiting volunteers. The agency retains internally other managerial responsibilities for the program. Since recruitment is the most fundamental function and, arguably, the most difficult (see Exhibit 3–1), regular, professional assistance with this task can be very useful, particularly for an agency just starting a volunteer program. Some private business firms seeking to develop volunteer programs for their employees have extended this model: They have contracted with local volunteer centers for help not only with recruitment but also with other central program functions, such as volunteer placement and evaluation.

When an agency contracts out for the provision of a function, maintaining quality control presents a necessary caution. Relying on other organizations to assist with the volunteer program is no exception. Agencies responsible for recruiting must be familiar with the needs of the organization for voluntary assistance, lest volunteers be referred who do not meet the desired profile of backgrounds, skills, and interests. A recruiter may also deal with a number of client organizations, so that the priority attached to the requests of any one of them is unknown. More important, trusting recruitment exclusively to outsiders is a deterrent to developing the necessary capacity in-house, which itself is a central element of a successful volunteer program. By all means, organizations should nurture positive relationships with agencies in the community to attract volunteers and for other purposes. But they must avoid total dependence on external sources and endeavor to build managerial competencies internally.

(c) Decentralized Approach

Volunteer involvement can also be decentralized to individual departments within a larger organization, each bearing primary responsibility for its own volunteer effort. The primary advantage offered by this approach is the flexibility to tailor the program to the needs of participating organizational units and to introduce volunteers where support for them is greatest. Yet duplication of effort across several departments, difficulties in locating sufficient expertise and resources to afford multiple volunteer programs, and problems in coordination—particularly, restrictions on the ability to shift volunteers to more suitable positions or to offer them opportunities for job enrichment across the organization—are significant liabilities.

In the public sector, lamentably, the decentralized approach can unwittingly generate disincentives for managers to introduce volunteers. Top agency officials may mistakenly equate nonpaid work with "unimportant" activities to the detriment of a department's (and a manager's) standing in the organization, or they may seize upon the willingness to enlist volunteers as an excuse to deny a unit essential increases in budget and paid personnel. One purpose of involving top management, employees, and volunteers in designing and implementing the volunteer program is to avoid such misunderstandings (see above).

Despite these limitations, the decentralized approach may serve an agency quite well in starting a pilot or trial program, the results of which might guide the organization in moving toward more extensive volunteer involvement. Alternatively, a lack of tasks appropriate for volunteers in some parts of the agency, or, perhaps, strong opposition from various quarters, may confine voluntary assistance to selected departments.

(d) Centralized Approach

The final structural arrangement is a centralized volunteer program serving the entire agency. With this approach, a single office or department is responsible for management and coordination of the program, while volunteers are actually deployed and supervised in line departments of the organization. The office provides guidelines, technical assistance, screening, training, and all other administration for volunteer activity throughout the agency. The advantages of centralization for averting duplication of effort, assigning and transferring volunteers so as to meet their needs as well as those of the organization, and producing efficient and effective voluntary services are considerable. The program demands broad support across the organization, especially at the top, to overcome any concerns that may be raised by departmental staff and possible limitations in resources. When such backing is not forthcoming, the other structural arrangements may serve an agency quite well.

3.6 PROVIDING RESPONSIBILITY AND DIRECTION FOR THE VOLUNTEER PROGRAM: CREATING POSITIONS OF LEADERSHIP

(a) Director of Volunteer Services

Irrespective of the structural arrangement by which the volunteer program is integrated into agency operations (ad hoc method, reliance on other organizations, decentralized model, or centralized approach), this component requires a visible, recognized leader. All program functions, those discussed in both this chapter and in the rest of the book, benefit from the establishment and staffing of a position bearing overall responsibility for leadership, management, and representation of the volunteers. The position goes by a variety of names, such as *volunteer administrator* or *volunteer coordinator;* these titles can leave the mistaken impression that the position is not paid. To avoid misunderstanding, and more important, to indicate the significance of the role, here it is called *director of volunteer services* (DVS).

(i) Staffing the DVS

The manner by which the DVS position is staffed sends a forceful message to volunteers and employees alike regarding the significance of the program to the agency and its leadership. Organizations have experimented with an assortment of staffing options for the office, including appointment of volunteers, employees from the human resources department or section, personnel with other duties, and combinations of these officials. No other staffing method so manifestly demonstrates a sense of organizational commitment to the program and its priorities as does a paid DVS position. A paid position lodges accountability for the program squarely with the DVS, presents a focal point for contact with the volunteer operation for those inside as well as outside the organization, implements a core structure for program administration, and rewards the officeholder in relation to the success of the volunteers.

(ii) Positioning the DVS in the Organizational Hierarchy

Establishing this office as close as possible to the apex of the agency's formal hierarchy conveys a similar message of resolve, importance, and purposefulness. The DVS should enjoy prerogatives and responsibilities commensurate with positions at the same level in the organization, including participation in relevant decision and policymaking, and access to superiors. In this manner the incumbent can represent the volunteers before the relevant department(s) as well as the organization as a whole, promote their interests, and help to ensure that officials appreciate their value and contributions to the organization.

(iii) Responsibilities of the DVS

In their performance-based certification process for administrators of volunteer programs, the Association for Volunteer Administration (AVA) recognizes four functional areas in which this official should demonstrate competence. Much like any other manager in the nonprofit or governmental sectors, she or he should be skilled in program planning and organization; staffing and directing; controlling; and agency, community, and professional relations. James C. Fisher and Kathleen M. Cole (1993, pp. 22–24) add a fifth area, budgeting and fund-raising.

The breadth and significance of these functions substantiate the need for a dedicated DVS position. Among the chief job components, this official is responsible for promoting the program and recruiting volunteers—critical tasks demanding active outreach in the community and highly flexible working hours. The incumbent must communicate with department and organizational officials to ascertain workloads and requirements for voluntary assistance. Assessing agency needs for volunteers, enlarging areas for their involvement, and educating staff to the approach should be seen not as a one-time exercise, but as ongoing activities of the DVS. The DVS interviews and screens applicants for volunteer positions, maintains appropriate records, places volunteers in job assignments, supports employees in supervising volunteers, and monitors performance. The office coordinates the bewildering array of schedules, backgrounds, and interests brought by volunteers to the agency and matches participants with the particular areas in which their labor, skill, and energy can be used to mutual advantage.

The DVS is the in-house source of expertise on all facets of volunteer involvement and management. She or he bears overall responsibility for orientation and training, as well as evaluation and recognition, of volunteers. Because employees frequently lack previous experience with volunteers, training may be necessary for them as well to make citizen involvement most effective. Finally, as the chief advocate of the program, the DVS endeavors not only to express the volunteer perspective but also to allay any apprehensions and facilitate collaboration between paid and nonpaid staff.

Fisher and Cole (1993, pp. 15–18) find that the responsibilities of the director of volunteer services vary depending on whether the organization adopts a personnel management or a program management approach to volunteer involvement. In the personnel management approach, the organization deploys volunteers across many functions and departments, and their principal accountability is to the paid staff member to whom they have been assigned. Hospitals, museums, zoos, social service agencies, theater companies, schools, and other organizations where volunteers have many different responsibilities often use this approach. Here the DVS does not supervise or evaluate the volunteers but supports the efforts of the paid staff members who work directly with them. The DVS assists staff in developing volunteer training and in learning and applying appropriate techniques for supervision, record keeping, performance review, and problem solving.

In the program management approach, volunteers are concentrated in one function or department of the organization, usually central to the agency mission. For example, many institutions create volunteer auxiliaries for fund-raising and other purposes, or deploy volunteers in a single organizational unit, such as community relations, client counseling, or intake services. In this approach the DVS performs all of the volunteer management tasks, including training, supervision, record keeping, and evaluation. Regardless of whether an organization uses the personnel management or the program management approach to volunteer participation, the DVS is responsible for job design, recruitment, interviewing, screening, placement, orientation, and recognition.

(b) Other Positions of Program Leadership

Given the scope and importance of the job responsibilities discussed above, as a volunteer program increases in size, the burden on one official to provide all aspects of management and leadership can become onerous. Secretarial support for the director of volunteer services is almost always advisable. In addition, organizational officials should consider creating and establishing other positions to assist the DVS.

One option is to employ paid staff for this purpose. Another fruitful option is to design career ladders for volunteers, a succession of positions for citizens leading to increased opportunities for personal growth and development (Fisher and Cole, 1993, pp. 65–66, 74–76). As one prominent example, highly committed and experienced volunteers might assume greater responsibility for major facets of the program, such as orientation, training, mentoring, and resource raising. This method not only facilitates program leadership but also carries motivational benefits for volunteers.

3.7 SHARING THE WORKPLACE: DEVELOPING JOB DESCRIPTIONS FOR VOLUNTEER POSITIONS

The essential building block of a successful volunteer program is the job description. It is the primary vehicle for recruiting volunteers, reassuring employees, and meeting organizational and client needs. "The importance of a volunteer job description cannot be overstated. The job description is the agency's planning tool to help volunteers understand the results to be accomplished, what tasks are involved, what skills are required, and other important details about the job" (McCurley, 1994, pp. 515–516). The essential volunteer management processes— recruiting, interviewing, placing, supervising, training, and evaluating—are based on the information contained in the job description.

Despite the importance of this program element, no intrinsic basis exists to create a position, or classify an existing one, as paid or volunteer. Even among agencies that have the same purpose or mission or that work in the same substantive or policy domain (for example, child welfare, culture and the arts, adult recreation, and so forth), a given position can be categorized differently. For example, while one social service agency may have all client counselling done by peers (unpaid citizens), in a second agency paid employees handle this function. An environmental protection agency may hire a paid computer programmer; another nonprofit organization in the same policy field may use a well-qualified volunteer for this task. Similarly, some nonprofit organizations employ receptionists or secretarial personnel, while others have willing volunteers to staff these positions.

Since no firm basis exits to classify a position as paid or volunteer, agencies sometimes employ both personnel for a given job. For instance, community-supported day-care centers often have on staff a mixture of paid and unpaid attendants for the children; local fire departments, too, commonly use both paid and volunteer firefighters. Without access to organizational records, it may not be possible to determine who is paid and who is not. Within an agency, moreover, job definitions can change over time, so that volunteers give way to paid employees for some positions, and gain responsibility from them in others. In sum, whether a position is paid or unpaid at a given time depends on organizational needs and history, not on an inherent distinction between these categories.

(a) The Job Design Process

Because no inherent basis exists to classify a task or position as paid or nonpaid, the *process* by which work responsibilities are allocated in an agency is the crucial element in job design. As elaborated above, the most enduring foundation for an effective volunteer program is for top agency officials and employees (and if possible, volunteers) to work out in advance of program implementation explicit understandings regarding the rationale for the involvement of volunteers, the nature of the jobs they are to perform, and the boundaries of their work (Ellis, 1986; Wilson, 1976). The result should be a general agreement that designates (or provides the foundation for distinguishing) the jobs assigned to volunteers and those held by paid staff.

The next step in the job design process consists of a survey of employees, or personal interviews with them, to ascertain key factors about their jobs and to make them aware of the potential contributions of volunteers. Surveys or interviews should seek to identify those aspects of the job that employees most enjoy performing, those that they dislike, and those for which they lack sufficient time or expertise. The survey or interview should also probe for areas in which employees feel the organization should do more, the needs of clients remain unmet, staff support would be most welcome, and novel or different organizational missions could be undertaken were greater time and skills available. Since employees often lack background information regarding the assistance that volunteers might lend to them and to the agency, the survey or interview (or alternatively, in-service training) should provide resource material regarding volunteers, such as a listing of the jobs or functions that nonpaid staff are already performing in their agency or in similar organizations (cf. Ellis, 1994, pp. 11–12; McCurley and Lynch, 1989, pp. 27–28).

This process should help to dispel popular stereotypes regarding volunteers. For example, volunteer positions are not necessarily in supportive roles to employee endeavors, and paid staff can facilitate and support the activities of volunteers rather than the reverse. Volunteer jobs do not signify menial work: Many organizations rely on donated labor for highly technical, professional tasks such as accounting, economic development, and computer applications. Volunteer jobs yield economic value: Incumbents provide skills that might otherwise be unattainable to an agency.

The delegation of tasks among paid and nonpaid staff members should take into account the unique capabilities that each group might bring toward meeting organizational needs and goals. To allocate work responsibilities, Ellis (1986, pp. 89–90) recommends that the agency reassess the job descriptions of all employees. Prime candidates for delegation to volunteers are tasks with the following characteristics:

1. Those performed periodically, such as once a week, rather than on a daily or inflexible basis
2. Those that do not require the specialized training or expertise of paid personnel
3. Those that might be done more effectively by someone with special training in that skill
4. Those for which the position occupant feels uncomfortable or unprepared
5. Those for which the agency lacks in-house expertise

The culmination of the task analysis should be a new set of job descriptions for employees and a second set for volunteers that are sensitive to prevailing organizational conditions. Paid staff are primarily assigned important, daily functions, and volunteers handle tasks that can be performed on a part-time basis or that make use of the special talents and skills for which they have been recruited. The goal is to achieve the most effective deployment of both paid and nonpaid personnel. The respective tasks should be codified in formal job descriptions not only for paid but also for nonpaid workers, with the stipulation that neither group will occupy the positions reserved for the other.

◆ **EXHIBIT 3–5   Model Job Description for Volunteer Positions**

- ◆ Job title
- ◆ Purpose of the position
- ◆ Benefits of position to occupant
- ◆ Qualifications for position
- ◆ Time requirement (e.g., hours per week)
- ◆ Job site or location
- ◆ Proposed starting date (and ending date, if applicable)
- ◆ Job responsibilities and activities
- ◆ Authority invested in the position
- ◆ Reporting relationships and supervision

(b) Volunteer Job Descriptions

The International City/County Management Association advises local governments that "volunteer job descriptions are really no different than job descriptions for paid personnel. A volunteer will need the same information a paid employee would need to determine whether the position is of interest" (Manchester and Bogart, 1988, p. 59). That advice applies equally to nonprofit organizations seeking volunteers. While a variety of attractive formats are possible, the information contained in the job description is fairly standard. Exhibit 3–5 presents a model that might be used in any organization.

(c) Note on Volunteer Recruitment

The most persuasive recruitment mechanism is the availability of nonpaid positions that appeal to the needs and motivations of prospective volunteers. In this context, much of the literature concentrates on the motivational aspects of challenge and accomplishment, personal growth and development, interesting and meaningful work, and career exploration and advancement. Surely, officials might endeavor to design positions for nonpaid—and paid—staff alike with these factors in mind.

Such a preoccupation can easily leave the impression, however, that *every* volunteer job must present close contact with clients, ample opportunity for self-expression, access to program planning and decision making, ready means for acquisition of job skills, and so on. That implication is erroneous. For example, the aversion of many volunteers to positions of greater authority and responsibility is documented with depressing regularity. A more fitting conclusion is that like employees, volunteers are richly diverse in their needs and goals. As a consequence, nonprofit and public organizations will enjoy success in recruiting them to the degree that agencies offer a range of jobs to appeal to a diversity of motivations. An organization should no more allocate exclusively routine, repetitive tasks to volunteers than it should place them solely in highly ambitious work assignments. Volunteer recruitment is discussed more fully in Chapter 4.

3.8 PREPARING FOR VOLUNTEERS: DEVELOPING SYSTEMS AND SUPPORTS FOR PARTICIPATION AND MANAGEMENT

A pioneer in the development of volunteer administration as a field for professional practice and research, Harriet H. Naylor counseled, "Most of the universally recognized principles of administration for employed personnel are even more valid for volunteer workers, who *give* their talents and time" (1973, p. 173, emphasis in original). McCurley and Lynch (1989, p. 23) agree that the volunteer program will need to develop basic personnel-related systems, and operate with essential forms for intake, management, evaluation, record keeping, and so on. "The systems and files developed should match those of paid staff, and can often be the same forms." The job descriptions for volunteer positions discussed above offer a good example. An organization must have other systems and supports in place to build and sustain a thriving volunteer program.

(a) Application and Placement Systems

The application and placement process further illustrates the parallels between administration for paid and nonpaid personnel. Citizens attracted to a volunteer position should be asked to complete an application form; the organization must develop the forms and have them readily available. The director of volunteer services or appropriate official reviews the application and schedules an interview with the candidate. The primary purpose of the interview is to ascertain relevant competencies, skills, and interests, as well as pertinent background and qualifications of citizen applicants, and to evaluate an appropriate matching to the needs of the organization (as specified in the volunteer job descriptions). Should a match look promising for both volunteer and organization, the applicant is often invited for a second interview, this time with the prospective department head or supervisor. If all goes well, a placement should result for the volunteer. If not, just as for paid employees, the organization maintains the applications on file for other openings. Agencies will often stipulate a probationary period for incoming personnel to evaluate the success of a placement.

(b) Education and Training Systems

Members new to an organization, whether paid or nonpaid, cannot be expected to possess great knowledge about the agency initially: They require an orientation. The organization should arrange for orientation activities for volunteers and employees to address such topics as the overall mission and specific objectives of the agency; its traditions, philosophy, and clientele; operating rules and procedures; the rationale, policies, and standards governing volunteer involvement; and the roles and interface of paid and nonpaid staff members. As mentioned above, distributing a booklet or manual containing the pertinent information during orientation sessions is very helpful.

Some volunteer positions do not require training, or perhaps only brief on-the-job instruction (for example, scheduling appointments, filing documents, or cleaning facilities). Many others have a great need for formal education (for example, drug abuse counselor, dispute mediator, or computer specialist). In the latter case, the organization must ensure through the application and placement process that the volunteer possesses the requisite competency, or provide for the training needed, either in-house or in conjunction with an educational institution.

(c) Management and Record-Keeping Systems

Just as for paid personnel, an organization should have record-keeping systems for its volunteer workers. These systems log important information about the volunteer, including personal background, areas of interest and competency, education and training, and preferred assignments. An agency will also need to maintain records with regard to the volunteer's connection, experience, and performance with the organization, for example, the initial visit, entry interviews, job assignments, performance evaluations, and other feedback. Computer software has been developed expressly for this purpose that can not only relieve the director of volunteer services from much of the paperwork burden but also facilitate and enliven the management function. Utilization can aid enormously in keeping track of the skills, preferences, and availability of volunteers and matching them with suitable opportunities for placement and personal growth and development in the organization.

(d) Evaluation and Recognition Systems

Organizations that rely on the assistance of volunteers may be reluctant to appear to question through performance evaluation the worth or impact of well-intentioned helping efforts. The fears of organizational leadership notwithstanding, volunteers have good reason to view assessment in a favorable light.

A powerful motivation for volunteering is to achieve worthwhile and visible results; performance appraisal can guide volunteers toward improvement on this dimension. No citizen contributes her or his time to have his or her labor wasted in misdirected activity or to repeat easily remedied mistakes and misjudgments. That an organization might take one's work so lightly as to allow such inappropriate behavior to continue is an insult to the volunteer and an affront to standards of professional conduct underlying effectiveness on the job. For many who contribute their time, moreover, volunteering presents an opportunity to acquire or hone desirable job skills and/or to build an attractive resume for purposes of paid employment. To deny constructive feedback to those who give their time for organizational purposes, and who could benefit from this knowledge and hope to do so, is a disservice to the volunteer.

Several mechanisms are feasible for the performance evaluation. Frequently, the supervisor to whom the volunteer reports conducts the review, or the responsibility may rest with the director of volunteer services, or with both of these officials. To complement the agency-based perspective, volunteers may also prepare a self-assessment of their experience, accomplishments, and aspirations in the organization. The assessment should tap their satisfaction with important facets of the work assignment, including job duties, schedule, support, training, opportunities for personal growth, and so on. Regardless of the type of evaluation, the goal should be to ascertain the degree to which the needs and expectations of the volunteer and the agency are met, so that job assignments can be continued, amended, or redefined as necessary.

Not only does the volunteer program require systems for evaluation but it also demands a way to recognize volunteers. Recognition should follow naturally from performance appraisal. Agency officials might recognize and show their appreciation to volunteers through a great variety of activities: award or social events (luncheons, banquets, ceremonies), media attention (newsletters, newspapers), certificates (for tenure or special achievement), expansion of opportunities (for learning, training, management), and, especially, personal expressions of gratitude from employees or clients. A heartfelt "thank you" can be all the acknowledgment that many volunteers want or need. Others require more formal recognition. The director of volunteer services should make letters of recommendation available to all volunteers who request them. Recognition is a highly variable activity that, optimally, should be tailored to the wants and needs of individual volunteers.

3.9 CONCLUSIONS

In their eagerness to reap the benefits of volunteer participation, organizational leadership may overlook the groundwork necessary to create and sustain a viable program. Although understandable, this tendency can jeopardize the potential advantages of the approach and increase problem areas. To prepare the organization for volunteers, officials should set reasonable expectations for the program, establish a rationale and goals for this effort, involve paid staff in program design, develop job descriptions for volunteer positions, select and implement a structural arrangement to house the program, create leadership positions, and develop systems and supports to facilitate participation and management. To the degree that leadership undertakes these activities, the organization should avoid the potential pitfalls and generate the considerable benefits of volunteer involvement.

REFERENCES

Brudney, Jeffrey L. 1986. "The SBA and SCORE: Coproducing Management Assistance Services." *Public Productivity Review* 40 (Winter): 57–67.

Brudney, Jeffrey L. 1990a. "The Availability of Volunteers: Implications for Local Governments." *Administration and Society* 21 (February): 413–424.

Brudney, Jeffrey L. 1990b. *Fostering Volunteer Programs in the Public Sector: Planning, Initiating, and Managing Voluntary Activities.* San Francisco: Jossey- Bass.

Brudney, Jeffrey L. 1993. "Volunteer Involvement in the Delivery of Public Services: Advantages and Disadvantages." *Public Productivity and Management Review* 16(3): 283–297.

Brudney, Jeffrey L., and William D. Duncombe. 1992. "An Economic Evaluation of Paid, Volunteer, and Mixed Staffing Options for Public Services. *Public Administration Review* 52 (September–October): 474–481.

Clary, E. Gil 1987. "Social Support as a Unifying Concept in Voluntary Action." *Journal of Voluntary Action Research* 16(4): 58–68.

Duncombe, Sidney 1985. "Volunteers in City Government: Advantages, Disadvantages and Uses." *National Civic Review* 74(9): 356–364.

Ellis, Susan J. 1986. *From the Top Down: The Executive Role in Volunteer Program Success.* Philadelphia: Energize Associates.

Ellis, Susan J. 1994. *The Volunteer Recruitment Book.* Philadelphia: Energize Associates.

Fisher, James C., and Kathleen M. Cole. 1993. *Leadership and Management of Volunteer Programs: A Guide for Volunteer Administrators.* San Francisco: Jossey- Bass.

Hodgkinson, Virginia A., and Murray S. Weitzman. 1994. *Giving and Volunteering in the United States: Findings from a National Survey.* Washington, D.C.: Independent Sector.

Hodgkinson, Virginia A., Murray S. Weitzman, Christopher M. Toppe, and Stephen M. Noga. 1992. *Nonprofit Almanac, 1992–1993: Dimensions of the Independent Sector.* San Francisco: Jossey-Bass.

Karn, G. Neil 1982–1983. "Money Talks: A Guide to Establishing the True Dollar Value of Volunteer Time, Part I." *Journal of Volunteer Administration* 1 (Winter): 1–17.

Karn, G. Neil 1983. "Money Talks: A Guide to Establishing the True Dollar Value of Volunteer Time, Part II." *Journal of Volunteer Administration* 1 (Spring): 1–19.

Manchester, Lydia D., and Geoffrey S. Bogart. 1988. *Contracting and Volunteerism in Local Government: A Self-help Guide.* Washington, D.C.: International City/County Management Association.

Marando, Vincent L. 1986. "Local Service Delivery: Volunteers and Recreation Councils." *Journal of Volunteer Administration* 4(4): 16–24.

McCurley, Steven 1994. "Recruiting and Retaining Volunteers." Pp. 511–534 in Robert D. Herman and Associates, *The Jossey-Bass Handbook of Nonprofit Leadership and Management.* San Francisco: Jossey-Bass.

McCurley, Steven, and Richard Lynch. 1989. *Essential Volunteer Management.* Downers Grove, Ill.: VMSystems and Heritage Arts Publishing.

Naylor, Harriet H. 1973. *Volunteers Today: Finding, Training and Working with Them.* Dryden, N.Y.: Dryden Associates.

Naylor, Harriet H. 1985. "Beyond Managing Volunteers." *Journal of Voluntary Action Research* 14(2–3): 25–30.

Pearce, Jone L. 1978. "Something for Nothing: An Empirical Examination of the Structures and Norms of Volunteer Organizations." Doctoral dissertation, Yale University.

Scheier, Ivan H. 1988a. "Empowering a Profession: What's in Our Name?" *Journal of Volunteer Administration* 6(4): 31–36.

Scheier, Ivan H. 1988b. "Empowering a Profession:" Seeing Ourselves as More Than Subsidiary." *Journal of Volunteer Administration* 7(1): 29–34.

Scheier, Ivan H. 1988–1989. "Empowering a Profession: Leverage Points and Process." *Journal of Volunteer Administration* 7(2): 50–57.

Thornburg, Linda 1992. "What Makes an Effective Volunteer Administrator? Viewpoints from Several Practitioners." *Voluntary Action Leadership* (Summer): 18–21.

Walter, Virginia A. 1987. "Volunteers and Bureaucrats: Clarifying Roles and Creating Meaning." *Journal of Voluntary Action Research* 16(3): 22–32.

Walter, Virginia A. 1993. "For All the Wrong Reasons? Implementing Volunteer Programs in Public Organizations." *Public Productivity and Management Review* 16(3): 271–282.

Williams, Rianna M. 1993. "Advice to Administrators: Get Out of Your Office." *Leadership* (January–March): 11.

Wilson, Marlene 1976. *The Effective Management of Volunteer Programs.* Boulder, Colo.: Johnson Publishing.

Wilson, Marlene 1984. "The New Frontier: Volunteer Management Training." *Training and Development Journal* 38(7): 50–52.

Wineburg, Catherine R., and Robert J. Wineburg. 1987. "Local Human Service Development: Institutional Utilization of Volunteers to Solve Community Problems." *Journal of Volunteer Administration* 5(4): 9–14.

CHAPTER 4

RECRUITMENT, ORIENTATION, AND RETENTION

Jeanne H. Bradner
Consultant and Director of Programs,
Illinois Commission on Community Service, State of Illinois

4.1 Recruitment

4.2 Interviewing and Screening Volunteers

4.3 Orientation

4.4 Retention

4.5 Recognition

4.6 Summary

References

4.1 RECRUITMENT

(a) Overall Considerations

(i) Be Ready

Volunteer recruitment is not the first step to take when setting up a volunteer program. Prior to developing a plan for volunteer recruitment, a program must have accomplished the following:

- *Developed a strong and compelling mission statement.*
- *Conducted a needs assessment,* involving staff and board, so that both see volunteers as valuable resources—as important as dollars—to be developed to implement the mission of the agency and improve the community.
- *Created a climate of agency readiness for volunteers.* This includes designing policies covering the involvement and risk management (good volunteer management is good risk management) of volunteers as important—albeit unpaid— staff members. It should include a budget for the management of volunteers, including training, reimbursement for expenses, insurance, and recognition.
- *Written appropriate job descriptions for the volunteer positions the agency has in mind.* These job descriptions should include the mission of the job, the time and energy commitment required, the skills needed to perform the job and any requirements (for example, a valid driver's license, automobile insurance, criminal records check, probation period, health tests, and/or the need for confidentiality). These requirements should be no harsher than for paid staff who do similar work, but as with paid staff, risks of the job should be analyzed ahead of time and methods identified to lessen those risks.

(ii) Understand Values Exchange

The closer a manager of volunteers can come to meeting the needs of the volunteers while *at the same time* meeting the needs of the program, the more successful he or she will be. Therefore, starting with the development of recruitment strategy, the successful volunteer recruiter tries to match the needs of the program with the needs of the volunteer. Questions the recruiter must keep in mind continuously are: What can a volunteer get out of the volunteer experience? Who are the people most likely to find satisfaction in the opportunity? How can the program give them a motivational paycheck that will keep them interested?

    If the manager worries only about the needs of the program, the volunteers are likely to feel unappreciated and quit. But equally important, if the manager worries only about the needs of the volunteer, the program will suffer. Balancing these needs is essential to good volunteer management.

(iii) Strive for Quality and Measurable Outcomes

It is better management to start with a small quality program that is welcomed by staff and meaningfully involves a few volunteers than to aim for large numbers. For example, programs that seek to involve classroom volunteers have better luck when the manager chooses two or three classes headed by teachers who are ready for volunteer involvement, who have specific duties in mind, and who welcome the volunteers' participation. The wise manager will recruit carefully for these situations to try to guarantee as much success as possible. Soon, when the positive effect of these volunteers is noted, other teachers (many of whom at first resisted the notion of an outsider in their classrooms) will say, "I want a volunteer, too." And thus the school will have a growing volunteer program.

The success of programs cannot be demonstrated solely by such measurements as numbers of volunteers and number of hours contributed. Computing hours and affixing a dollar amount (minimum wage, fair market value, or the Points of Light/Gallup Survey figure) is a useful device to include in monthly financial statements to demonstrate to a board of directors and the CEO the approximate dollar value of in-kind human resources—frequently greater than the actual dollars raised during a given period. This measurement is also useful when approaching funding sources to show that the organization is reaching out to the community and that the community is involved and supportive.

A much more significant demonstration, however, is outcomes measurement: How did the program fulfill the mission of the agency and improve the community? A wise manager should think through: What are the changes we want this program to make in the community? How will we know if these changes have happened? How will we measure their impact? This is more difficult to do because it takes advance planning and developing program-specific measurement devices rather than just keeping records of time and hours. However, such information is invaluable in proving the impact of a program to funders, board, staff, and the volunteers themselves.

(b) Where to Find Potential Volunteers

Volunteers are found everywhere. The Gallup Organization survey *Giving and Volunteering in the United States* for the year 1991 (Independent Sector, 1992) states that 51 percent of the people interviewed volunteer, and that volunteerism embraces both sexes, all ages, and all ethnic, racial, cultural, educational, and income backgrounds. Often, people think that volunteerism is limited to middle-aged people; however, the survey shows significant volunteer involvement from ages 12 to 75 and over. For example, about three-fifths of young people 12 to 17 volunteer. With the growth of school and university/college service learning programs, where the experiential learning from service is regarded as valid education for good citizenship, more and more young people are being encouraged to volunteer. The Learn and Serve America programs of the Corporation for National and Community Service should have a positive impact on youth program development. Forty-eight percent of young people 18 to 24 are volunteering and 53 percent of those 25 to 34.

Forty-five percent of people 65 to 75 volunteer; 27 percent of those over age 75 volunteer. As America's aging population grows and, as expected, doubles during the next 30 years, programs have a great natural resource to involve experienced people who are living longer and are healthier and better educated than any other time in our society. Edgar Cahn, in his book *Retirement Reconsidered,* quoted by Marc Freedman (Public/Private Ventures, April 1994), issues a challenge to senior volunteer recruitment: "When a society has vast unmet needs at the same time when there are large numbers of healthy, energetic productive human beings for whom the society can find no use—even though they would like to be useful—then something is wrong."

Sources from which to recruit volunteers include:

- Volunteer centers, which will try to match prospective volunteers with an agency and job description appropriate to their talents
- Retired and senior volunteer programs, which involve almost half a million people age 55 and above in volunteer opportunities
- School, college, and university service learning and community service programs
- Service clubs, such as Rotary, Kiwanis, and Altrusa
- City Cares programs, which involve young professionals in projects in major urban areas
- Corporate, business, and labor volunteer programs
- Senior centers and retirement homes
- Religious groups
- Professional organizations (e.g., accountants, lawyers)
- Executive Service Corps for management volunteers
- National Retiree Volunteer Coalition (groups of retired employees who volunteer under the auspices of their former employer)
- American Association for Retired Persons
- Alumni groups
- Sororities and fraternities
- Stipended programs (e.g., VISTA, AmeriCorps, Foster Grandparents, Senior Companions)
- Open houses
- Volunteer fairs

(c) Developing Strong and Diverse Volunteer Support

(i) Ask Them

The Gallup Survey tells us that people of all ages are three times as likely to volunteer if someone asks them . . . particularly someone they know. Fund-raisers have known for years that "you don't get if you don't ask," and a person the potential donor respects is the most effective person to do the asking.

In his 1966 book *Designs for Fund-Raising* (so effective that it was reprinted in 1988 by the FundRaising Institute), Harold Seymour posits two hypotheses that are equally important for managers of volunteers, who, after all, are also in development work:

1. The most universal and deep-seated fear that people have is xenophobia—fear of the stranger.

2. We all aspire to be sought out and to be worthwhile members of a worthwhile group.

This is why person-to-person recruitment works so well. Because someone who is known to potential volunteers is doing the asking, volunteers are assured that they are not getting involved in something strange or unsavory. Volunteers also know that the group must be worthwhile because the person doing the asking is worthwhile.

(ii) Plan for Cultural Diversity

In our society, however, person-to-person asking sometimes breaks down when programs want, as they should, to involve a cross section of the community and need to recruit for ethnic, racial, age, and economic diversity that is not already present in the program. Here setting up an advisory group made up of leaders from the groups the program wishes to involve can be helpful in learning whom and how to target. Sometimes cultural sensitivity training is necessary for both current paid staff and volunteers.

Many programs fail to be as effective as they might because recruiters or volunteer managers have a limited notion of whom to involve. In addition to the diversity mentioned above, think about involving:

◆ Clients
◆ People with disabilities
◆ Unemployed people
◆ Ex-clients
◆ Families of clients
◆ Donors
◆ Interns
◆ Offenders sentenced to community service
◆ Displaced homemakers

When recruiting any groups, however, one must again think of what they need from the program. Clients, people with disabilities, unemployed people, ex-clients, and displaced homemakers, for example, might like to work as volunteers for a limited period of time in exchange for some job training, a personnel file, and a letter of recommendation. Donors might enjoy hands-on experience and some involvement with people rather than always being viewed as writers of checks. Interns might work for a college credit or for experience in the area in which they have concentrated. Offenders, while required to serve, might consciously or unconsciously be looking for something they can care about.

(iii) Plan for Diversity of Commitment

As managers think about their needs, they are likely to think that those needs can only be met between the hours of 9:00 A.M. and 5:00 P.M. on weekdays. This can seriously limit volunteer resource potential and, more important, the potential to help the community.

Volunteers today can be short term or long term; they can work every Tuesday for a year or more; or they can handle a project that lasts just a few weeks or even just a day. Some might prefer a project they can do at their offices, others will want to do something with their families; some want to work in the evenings, some want to work on the weekends; some want to do something in their area of expertise, some want to develop a new skill, and others want to do something from home.

Although it may not be possible to meet all of these personal desires in any particular program, a wise manager will evaluate whether the job can be done under circumstances different from those envisioned originally.

(iv) Plan for Diversity of Special Volunteer Needs

Besides understanding the need for cultural diversity and the volunteers' diversity of commitment, managers must understand the special needs that may make it impossible for people to volunteer. Some volunteers may be able to help if the agency can provide child care. A busy program during the day at a Champaign, Illinois, hospital provides baby sitting while young mothers satisfy their needs for affiliation and outreach by working together at the hospital. Families can offer their help on weekend and evening projects if their younger children can be taken care of.

Programs should offer to reimburse volunteer out-of-pocket expenses: car fare, for example. Many volunteers will not turn in their expense lists, but for some, car fare may be the difference between involvement or staying at home. Transportation or parking for volunteers can also be helpful. A hospital parking lot for volunteers at a Connecticut hospital carries a sign "Volunteer Lane."

People with disabilities also have abilities that can benefit programs, but the agency needs to make "reasonable accommodation" for the disability—perhaps supplying a tape recorder for someone who is legally blind or understanding that people with mental retardation are pleased to be involved as volunteers. A program in Chicago involves young adults with mental retardation as ushers in neighborhood theaters.

Concerns about liability are a deterrent to some people. Many states have statutes limiting liability of volunteers to acts that are willful and wanton. In addition, agencies need to make sure that their umbrella liability coverage extends to volunteers, and many programs purchase inexpensive liability, accident, and excess automobile insurance specifically for their volunteers.

(d) Types of Volunteers

(i) Types of Service

Generally, volunteers fall into two broad categories: policy making and direct service. Policy making can be binding as from a board of directors, or not binding as from an advisory board. Direct service can be given to clients in many forms or to the organization through administrative work, advocacy, and/or fund-raising.

(ii) Types of Motivation

Gallup Survey results show that most people volunteer to be helpful and become involved as a direct result of their religious beliefs. However, there are many additional reasons: need to be needed, desire for sociability, interest in a particular area, curiosity about a particular program, job experience, and boredom with a paying job . . . the list can go on and on.

For the purposes of volunteer management, one of the most valuable tools on motivation is the work done by David McClelland and John Atkinson referred to by Marlene Wilson (Volunteer Management Associates, 1976). McClelland and Atkinson conclude that all people are motivated by three things, but most strongly by one more than the others. These motivations are:

1. *Affiliation:* the need to be with other people and enjoy freindship
2. *Achievement:* the need to accomplish goals and do one's personal best
3. *Power:* the need to have influence on others

In 1970, McClelland defined power as having two faces:

1. *Positive power:* socialized power: I win/you win
2. *Negative power:* personalized power: I win/you lose

People motivated by socialized power internalize the *raison d'être* for volunteerism: We can't change the world by ourselves, but if we can involve enough other people in socialized power, we can change the world (or a community or a block). Socialized power people understand that when we improve a community for others, we also improve it for ourselves. A wise volunteer manager can use affiliation, achievement, and power (negative or positive) to understand volunteers and to match them with the right assignment.

(a) Recruitment Techniques

To be successful and to protect the agency, client, and volunteer, recruitment techniques need to be matched to the challenges, complexities, and risks of the job.

- ◆ *Generic* (for mass events and low-risk and unskilled jobs). "Volunteers Wanted" on posters, newsletters, and public service announcement can be effective for assignments that anyone and everyone can do. For example, Hands Across America, a 1986 campaign to raise consciousness about hunger and homelessness by a unbroken line of Americans holding hands, was something in which everyone would be involved. It took no special skills, and the only limitation, for some, was transportation to a site. Therefore, an open invitation was all that was needed.
- ◆ *Specific* (for medium- or high-risk and skilled jobs). Targeted recruitment is usually the more effective method since "volunteers wanted" does not work when the recruiter has specific skills in mind, just as "paid staff wanted" would not work when an agency wants to hire someone with the ability to do a specific job.

The recruiter should review the job description and ask: What is the mission of the job (why is it important); what is the commitment (long term, short term, evenings, at home, in the office, or ongoing); what skills would the volunteer need;

what will be required of the volunteer; what benefits, psychic and tangible, will the volunteer receive from the assignment; and finally, who might have the necessary skills and be attracted by the mission, commitment, and benefits? (See Exhibit 4–1.)

(b) Offering the Opportunity

After this exercise, the volunteer manager will begin to focus on a recruitment strategy; targeting individuals and groups who might be interested in the program. The manager will then ask: "How can I reach them, and what should the message be?"

There are many ways to reach prospective volunteers, but the wise recruiter needs to decide which might be most effective for the job in mind:

- ◆ Soliciting names of individuals from current volunteers, board members, and staff and having the most credible person ask them to be involved
- ◆ Contacting volunteer centers or organizations (religious, professional, educational) that include the targeted population
- ◆ Distributing targeted flyers (consider multilingual material)
- ◆ Distributing targeted brochures
- ◆ Giving speeches to targeted organizations (most successful when given by a volunteer who is a member of that organization)
- ◆ Putting public service announcements on television or radio on stations to which the targeted population listens
- ◆ Placing classified ads in newspapers that prospects might read (include free shoppers and neighborhood papers)

It is important that the promotional message emphasize the need your program hopes to remedy: "Two million people in this state can't read above a fourth-grade level"; "One out of every three children in this country is living in poverty." People want to do worthwhile work, and even though the job may be administrative in

---

◆ **EXHIBIT 4-1 Targeted Volunteer Recruitment Analysis**

What do I need? (Skills and commitment required. Would the ideal person be motivated by affirmation, achievement, or power?)

Who could do this job? (Flexibly evaluate the times and places the commitment could be fulfilled, the training you will offer, and the diversity of volunteer resources available to you.)

What do they need and want from me? (Training, child care, flexible time commitment, experience, affiliation, achievement, power?)

How can I reach them? (Where do they live, work, go to school, worship?)

What should be my message? (Consider program mission and the motivation of potential volunteer.)

© Jeanne H. Bradner

nature, prospective volunteers will be more involved if they share the mission that the work is advancing.

The promotional message should also speak to the needs of the people who could potentially be most effective in the job: If they are affiliators, being with others and helping others will be motivating; if they are achievers, concrete accomplishments will be enticing; and if they are power people, a task that has significant impact will attract them. Remember, affiliators are concerned about relationships; achievers look for goals and objectives; and power people demand them. If the program doesn't have them, they will create them or leave!

4.2 INTERVIEWING AND SCREENING VOLUNTEERS

(a) The Application Form

Prospective volunteers should fill out an application form. Exhibit 4–2 is a sample, but many agencies use the same form that they use for their paid staff. The application form should include information relevant to the work that is to be done. It should ask for at least two references (not relatives); and it should require the driver's license number and insurance source for volunteers who will drive in the course of their duties. If the volunteer will be working with vulnerable populations, it should ask for permission to do a criminal records check. If health or drug tests are required, it should so state.

A confidentiality agreement may also be required in certain agencies. For example, agencies who work with people with disabilities will require this. Some people who do not understand that volunteers are unpaid staff will suggest that volunteers cannot keep information confidential. That, of course, is nonsense. It is the personal integrity of a person, not a salary, that determines his or her ability to keep a pledge. Agencies for whom confidentiality is important will often state in their policies that a breach of confidentiality is regarded as a reason for dismissal.

(b) The Interview

(i) Ask Open-ended Questions

As the volunteer director interviews potential volunteers and works to make sure that the job and the volunteer are a good match, McClelland's affiliation, achievement, and power are extraordinarily helpful. Open-ended questions—What are your goals? What do you hope to get out of your volunteer involvement? What kind of work environment do you like? What job have you had that you enjoyed the most?—can all help the interviewer understand the prospective volunteer and make an effective match.

The volunteer manager should clarify that:

- ◆ An interview is necessary to make a proper placement.
- ◆ Both volunteer and the program should benefit from the match.
- ◆ This is an opportunity for the manager and the prospective volunteer to explore whether the job is appropriate for the volunteer's skills and interest.
- ◆ Everyone who is interviewed is not appropriate for the program.

◆ **EXHIBIT 4–2   Application for Volunteer Position**

Name:

Current address:

Telephone Number: Home: Work:

Current employment:

Volunteer experience, current and past:

Skills:

How did you learn about our program?

Educational background: High school graduate:___Some college:___College degrees:___

Have you had any previous experience working with our cause (or population)? Give specifics:

References: (List two people whom we may contact, and include addresses and telephone numbers. These should not be relatives but should be teachers, employers, or other community members)

When (days, hours, seasons) would you prefer to volunteer?

In case of an emergency, whom should we notify?

For high-risk programs, add any of the following that are appropriate:

Since driving is part of the volunteer job for which you are applying, we need your driver's license number and your proof of insurance

License number: Insurance carrier:

State: (Please attach a copy of your certificate)

Since the volunteer job requires working with children, people with disabilities, the dying, or the frail elderly, we will need to do a criminal records check. Permission granted ___yes ___no

All volunteers (and paid staff) are required to sign a confidentiality agreement. By signing on the space below, you agree that you will keep confidential all information you learn about clients or families if you perform, volunteer duties for this agency.

Signature _____

When interviewing, remember that the same rules apply that cover equal employment practices. Questions about race, religion, sexual preference, national origin, age, and marital status should not be asked.

(ii) Tailor Depth of Interview to Risk of Program

Programs that serve vulnerable populations and where the volunteer is directly involved with clients—children, people with disabilities, the homebound, and the dying—will want to explore the motivations of the volunteer for the interest in this particular population; and a second interview, after applications are processed and references checked, may be required.

Although good interviewers listen more than they talk, they know that the interview is the time to review the job description and to pay particular attention to policies that cover agency attitudes and volunteer behavior. It affords an opportunity to listen and observe carefully and to assess volunteers' reactions to these policies. Cover all items appropriate and necessary for the program: confidentiality, contracts, probation, health and drug tests, and criminal records checks.

While it is only fair to ask the same questions and make the same general statements to all prospective volunteers, the less comfortable the interviewer is with the volunteer's reactions to policies, the more the interviewer should emphasize the policies in order to probe the volunteer's attitudes.

Interviews should also cover required training. Some agencies that offer intensive and often-sought-after training (for example, negotiation skills, HIV prevention, or crisis intervention) ask prospective volunteers to commit to six months or more of volunteerism once training is completed.

(iii) Explore Volunteers' Special Needs

During the interview, managers should be sensitive to accommodations that the agency might make to the volunteer (for example, transportation, parking, car fare, planned leave of absence, flex time, shared jobs, or disability-related accommodations). Exhibit 4–3 is a sample form on which to record interview impressions.

(a) Screening

(i) The Interview

Preliminary screening starts with the application and the interview. At the end of the interview, three things may happen:

1. The manager of volunteers is convinced that the job is not appropriate for the prospective volunteer and suggests another assignment in the agency or refers the volunteer to a local volunteer center or an agency with a more compatible program.

2. The potential volunteer realizes that the job is not appropriate and says so. It is helpful to the manager to say at the end of the interview, "Are you still interested in this job?" This gives the prospective volunteer a graceful exit, if desired.

3. The interview is satisfactory enough that it leads to the next step. . . .

◆ **EXHIBIT 4–3　Interviewer's Report Form**

Name of prospect:　　　　　　　　　　　　　　　　　Date:

Background relevant to placement:

Does this person have a special reason for wanting to be involved with your population or cause?

Did the person understand your requirements: probation, training, contract, confidentiality, criminal records check, health tests? (Use those appropriate to program and add others.)

Times available for volunteer job:

Strengths of the person:

Weaknesses you perceived:

Special needs:

References checked:　　　___Satisfactory　　　　　___Unsatisfactory

　　　　Date:

(If appropriate, add space for receipt and status of health or drug tests and/or criminal records check.)

Second interview to be scheduled? ___yes　　　___no

　　　　If "yes," date:

Accept ___yes　　　___no

Person notified: Date_____

© Jeanne H. Bradner

(ii) The Reference Check

The reference check should be conducted, and Exhibit 4–4 is an easy way to contact the references. If the references are satisfactory, the manager will proceed. If not, the manager will follow suggestion (i)1 above.

(iii) Special Requirements

The volunteer manager institutes the criminal records check. There are usually two forms this check can take: a check of conviction records based on date of birth and

◆ **EXHIBIT 4–4   Volunteer Reference Form**

The person named below wishes to become a volunteer in our program. This person has indicated that you would be able to evaluate his/her qualifications. This form is confidential and voluntary; but we would appreciate having it returned as soon as possible.

Name:

How long have you known this person?

In what capacity have you known the person?

In your opinion, is this person responsible?

In your opinion, can this person work well with others?

Are you aware of other volunteer work in which this person is involved? (If so, please name it.)

Please tell us about any special talents you believe this person has.

Additional comments:

Your name: Address:
       Phone:

MANY THANKS FOR YOUR HELP

© Jeanne H. Bradner

name or a more expensive but surer check based on fingerprints. The latter is recommended for especially sensitive cases, such as screening for possible pedophiles.

If the volunteer is required to have a health test (for example, a tuberculosis test is required for some schools, and drug testing for some correctional facilities), the volunteer should take responsibility for making sure that the manager receives the results.

(iv) Second Interview

In especially sensitive work, a second interview is usually required; and sometimes it is needed in other instances just to verify impressions. If (iii) and (iv) are not satisfactory, the next step is rejection.

(d) Rejecting Applicants

Managers of volunteers should remember that in all personnel work, the most important decision made is whom to hire. This is no less true for volunteer jobs. To involve someone about whom one has real misgivings is not fair to the person and not fair to the program. Refer them to another job, another agency, or a volunteer center. It is good to pay a sincere compliment to the prospective volunteer, such as, "You have wonderful writing skills, but as I mentioned to you, our needs are limited in that area. I would like to keep you in mind for the future, but meanwhile, you might call. . . ."

4.3 ORIENTATION

The volunteer has been invited to join the program and has been accepted. The next steps are important to maintain enthusiasm and momentum.

(a) Sign a Contract

The simplest form for a contract is the job description, which the volunteer manager shared at the interview. Any additional items agreed upon can be added to the job description (length of probation period, for example), and then it can be dated and signed by the volunteer and the manager. The manager can also make the program policies or code of behavior part of the contract.

This contract is an important risk management tool. States that have laws limiting the liability of volunteers usually hold them responsible for acts that are willful and wanton. A contract clarifies the assingment for the volunteer and is a protection for the agency if the volunteer should do something that is willful and wanton—that is, with a deliberate intention to cause harm.

The contract can be signed before, during, or after the orientation. The volunteer should be given a copy and the original should go in the office personnel file. (See Exhibit 4–5 for a sample job description and contract.)

(b) What the Volunteer Needs to Know

Orientation to the program is a process to familiarize volunteers with the broad mission and function of the agency so that the volunteer sees his or her job as an important part of that mission. Orientation can be individual, in small groups, or in large groups. Large-group orientations usually happen when a significant number of volunteers are brought into a program at almost the same time. But whether the orientation is held in a classroom setting with videos and speeches, a small group around a conference table or individually through appointments with relevant personnel, the agenda must be set to meet the volunteer's need to know.

Don't bore them with information that may be important to agency operations but is not necessary for them to know to perform their duties. However, do share with them exciting plans for new buildings, new programs, breakthroughs in technology, and recognitions of agency excellence. These make the volunteers feel that they are respected new members of the staff and are learning some things that only "insiders" would know. Exhibit 4–6 is a sample agenda for one person or a large- or small-group orientation.

(c) Questions

A special packet should be prepared for volunteers. It should include a welcoming letter, an annual report, newsletters, an organizational chart, a list of staff and board, and any other information that might be helpful. If the agency is holding a

◆ **EXHIBIT 4–5   Volunteer Job Description and Contract**

Job title:

Supervisor: Location:

Objective: (Why is this job necessary; what will it accomplish?)

Responsibilities: (What specifically will the volunteer do?)

Commitment: (Short term; long term; hours)

Qualifications: (What special skills are needed? Can all ages do it? Does the job require any particular educational background?)

Policies: (e.g., confidentiality, criminal records check, code of behavior, prohibited activities)

Training provided:

Benefits: (Transportation, insurance, parking, expenses)

Trial period (probation):

References required:

Other:

Signatures to be added at time of mutual agreement

Date:

Signature of volunteer:

Signature of supervisor:

© Jeanne H. Bradner

large-group orientation, make sure that it is lively, friendly, and energetic. Ask only those people who are enthusiastic and mission driven to make presentations. Start with coffee and cookies, have attractive name tags (perhaps permanent ones that the volunteer can use consistently), make sure in advance that audiovisual equipment works, and encourage questions, participation and evaluation. Send out invitations a month in advance and follow up with phone calls.

◆ **EXHIBIT 4–6   Sample Orientation Agenda**

   I.   Greetings from the boss: the executive director or board president, who acknowledges how integral volunteers are to agency operations.

  II.   A review of the history and organizational structure of the agency. This could be a role for a staff member who has been with the agency a long time, or perhaps the agency has a good video.

 III.   Introductions of staff to volunteer(s).

 IV.   An overview of the population or cause for which the volunteers are working. Experienced and enthusiastic program persons who do not use acronyms and jargon can do this.

  V.   Expectations of volunteers: a review of important policies and behaviors.

 VI.   Volunteer expectations of agency (e.g., benefits, insurance, parking, expenses, training).

VII.   A presentation from an enthusiastic volunteer about what the agency has meant to him or her.

VIII.   A tour of the facility.

© Jeanne H. Bradner

4.4 RETENTION

One hundred percent retention of volunteers is an unrealistic goal. As with paid staff, there are sometimes people who *need* to be outplaced (yes, volunteers can be dismissed when they consistently do not honor their contract). In addition, new jobs, moves, lifestyle changes, and new interests are bound to take their toll on the volunteer program. However, volunteer managers can and must take steps to help their volunteers grow, learn, and build self-esteem to maintain their interest in the program. Some ways to do this are outlined below.

(a) Opportunities for Evaluation

There should be opportunities for mutual evaluation of the volunteer experience. Evaluation can take a very informal tone. Ask "How's it going?" and if the response or body language is negative, invite the volunteer in for a chat. Certainly evaluation is required at the end of a probation period, and managers should provide a chance for discussion about the volunteer commitment at least twice a year. Questions that can be asked are:

◆ What do you like most about your job?

◆ What do you like least?

◆ Was your training sufficient?

- ◆ Are there other programs in this agency in which you would like to be involved?
- ◆ What can we do to make your time here more fulfilling for you?

In addition, the volunteer manager needs to provide honest feedback on the volunteer's contribution.

(b) Volunteer Vacations and Leaves of Absence

Sometimes good volunteers like to take the winter off, they may become deeply interested in another volunteer assignment, their paying jobs may become overwhelming, or they suffer from burnout. Offer them a volunteer leave of absence or vacation rather than losing them. Keep in touch with them; send them newsletters, an annual report, and a birthday card; and if you don't hear from them, call and invite them back.

(c) Volunteer Promotions

Few people want to do the same job endlessly, even when they are good at it. Consider offering good volunteers a promotion—perhaps as a manager. Be creative about restructuring your program to make the most of their talents. How about a volunteer as an assistant to the volunteer manager, or as an assistant fund-raiser or marketing person? The possibilities are endless, depending on the talents of the volunteers and the needs of the community.

(d) In-service Training

In-service professional training can be a great reward for a volunteer. For example, volunteers who serve in hospice care treasure the opportunity to meet with social workers and psychiatrists to learn more about grieving. While they are helping others, the volunteers learn things of value to their own lives. When a conference or training of interest comes up, the wise manager thinks about involving the volunteer as well as the paid staff. Volunteer management conferences can also be of interest to volunteers.

(e) Staff Meetings

Include volunteers at staff meetings; if this isn't possible, create team meetings. Volunteers need to have a voice in their own assignments, and they can contribute good ideas. Good ideas are not restricted to those who get paid for their work.

(f) Presentations

Invite volunteers who are involved in interesting projects to make presentations at a board meeting. The enthusiasm and interest of the unpaid staff person can frequently be more inspirational than that of a paid staff member.

Also, involve volunteers in radio and television interviews. It is tempting for staff to want to take center stage, but volunteers speak engagingly about a program since they are involved only because they want to be.

(g) Advocacy Opportunities

Invite volunteers to advocate with governmental agencies. Volunteers are often much more credible witnesses, simply because they are not paid to advocate.

(h) Volunteer Advisory Council

Form a volunteer advisory council to discuss the policies and procedures of the program; develop new ideas for volunteer recognition; and assess additional needs for volunteer involvement. Rotate the membership among the volunteers by having terms of office, and always include some members of the board of directors so that policymaking and direct-service volunteers have a chance to interact.

(i) Expense Reimbursement

Volunteers should be reimbursed for out-of-pocket expenses such as car fare or parking. Volunteers are not free, but a very small budget yields remarkable cost benefit.

(j) Benefits

Volunteers need a cup of coffee or a soda; a safe working environment; and liability, accident, and excess automobile insurance (if they drive as part of their volunteer job description). They also need to be regarded as an important part of the staff.

(k) Personnel File

A volunteer should have a personnel file that contains a record of involvement. This is very useful when the volunteer needs a reference or the manager has to be reminded of good performance to be recognized.

(l) Grievance Procedures

It is good for volunteers to know that there is a process for settling grievances—perhaps first with the manager of the program, second with the advisory committee, and finally with the executive director.

(m) Interesting Tasks

Volunteers want to do interesting and meaningful work. Routine tasks have to be done sometime, but vary the work that volunteers are given.

(n) Respecting Volunteers

No one is "just a volunteer"; volunteers are unpaid staff and deserve respect and work that takes advantage of their skills and interest. If one agency isn't right for them, they should be referred to another.

(o) Vision

Managers should work with board and staff to develop a vision of how to involve volunteers. The volunteer manager should be involved in agency strategic planning with an eye to renewing the agency, its mission, and its volunteer involvement. Change is a constant, and a leader always tries to keep pace with it.

(p) Professionalizing the Program

Volunteer managers are professionals in the area of human resource development. They must respect their own professional development. They must regard their volunteers as professionals, too, and expect professional behavior from them. The more respect volunteers receive, the more they will contribute. Think every day: "There is no job in this agency that the right volunteer can't do."

(q) Volunteers as Trainers

Volunteers can be very helpful in training other volunteers, and they will appreciate being tapped for this kind of responsibility.

(r) Volunteer Socialization

Create opportunities for volunteers to celebrate successes.

(s) Staff Appreciation

Recognize and commend staff who work particularly well with volunteers. When staff see that their management skills are recognized, they are much more apt to welcome volunteers as part of their team.

4.5 RECOGNITION

Recognition is something that starts the minute a volunteer enters the program when the program in all that it does recognizes its volunteers as worthy unpaid staff, doing significant work in an effective way; the manager sets high standards and encourages and supports the volunteers.

Recognition is remembering people's names, their birthdays, their needs, and their motivations, and giving them honest compliments for their good work. Recognition can be formal or informal, public or private; it can be tailored to suit the person's individual need for affiliation, achievement, or power. For example:

- ◆ Recognition for people motivated by affiliation
  - Public: Balloons tied to their desks
  -                 A recognition lunch, tea, or dinner and a corsage or coffee mug
  -                 Their pictures on the bulletin board
  - Private: A personal note
  -                 A birthday card
  -                 An invitation to have coffee, one on one

- ◆ Recognition for people motivated by achievement
  Public: A report with their byline
                  A letter to their boss recognizing their achievements
                  A promotion
  Private: A letter from the executive director
                  A letter from the chair of the board
- ◆ Recognition for people motivated by personalized power
  Public: Their pictures in a metropolitan newspaper
                  An interview on radio or television
                  Their picture with the president, governor, or mayor
  Private: A letter from the president, governor, or mayor
- ◆ Recognition for people motivated by socialized power
  Public: Acknowledgment that some important legislation wouldn't have passed without their lobbying power
                  Acknowledgment that the fund-raising goal wouldn't have been reached without their organizational skill
  Private: Observing that they are developing other leaders in the organization besides themselves
                  Encouragement and respect of peers.

Many agencies give annual dinners for their volunteers and find that all volunteers don't attend. That's simply because that kind of recognition doesn't appeal to everyone: It doesn't meet their needs.

Pins, mugs, and certificates are all pleasant ways to recognize volunteers, but there is a great deal of debate about recognition that takes the form of choosing "the best volunteer." Those in favor of choosing an outstanding volunteer say that it is an inspiration to other volunteers and gives them something to strive for. It also can create good media coverage, particularly if the best volunteer is honored by the president, governor, or mayor.

Those opposed to such awards say that it is impossible to choose the best volunteer and that for every volunteer that is happy to be chosen, at least 20 who believe they are just outstanding feel hurt and unappreciated. They suggest that it is better to choose the "most exciting new idea," the "most interesting project," the "best team"—or, don't worry about the "best"; just celebrate the program and treat everyone equally. If a program does decide to give "best" awards, it should choose an objective committee so that the decision is not attributable to anyone who manages the program or the agency.

4.6 SUMMARY

The recruitment, orientation, and retention of volunteers is a continuum, but it is a continuum that must constantly be evaluated and improved, based on community needs and the evolving mission of the agency. Needs for volunteers change as the needs of the community change. The needs of the volunteers themselves change as their lives change. Yesterday's strategies for volunteer involvement may not work

◆ **EXHIBIT 4–7   Measuring the Effectiveness of the Program**

1. Are volunteers doing work that is meaningful to them and the community? (Measurement devices: needs assessments, community response, volunteer evaluations)

2. Does staff regard volunteers as partners in accomplishing goals? (Measurement devices: staff meetings; input from staff; staff requests for volunteers; staff/volunteer management relationships)

3. Are any volunteers performing middle-management or management jobs?

4. Is the volunteer program diverse including people of both genders and all ages, races, economic backgrounds, and educational backgrounds?

5. Is the program flexible about time commitments, flex time, and assignments that can be performed off site?

6. Does the board view volunteers as important? (Measurement devices: budget for program, planning for volunteer involvement, attendance at recognition events)

7. What specific impacts have the volunteers had on:
   a. Improving the community?
   b. Improving agency operations?
   c. Improving staff capacity?

©Jeanne H. Bradner

today, and today's strategies may not work tomorrow. However, the closer we can come to matching the needs of our agency today with the needs of today's volunteers, the more successful we will be in improving the community. It is a challenging assignment and one that can change the future for all. Exhibit 4-7 may be helpful in measuring the impact of today's program so that it can be improved tomorrow.

REFERENCES

Freedman, Marc. 1994. *Seniors in National and Community Service: A Report Prepared for The Commonwealth Fund's Americans Over 55 At Work Program.* Philadelphia: Public-Private Ventures.

Gallup Organization. 1992. *Independent Sector: Giving and Volunteering in the United States.* Washington, DC: Gallup Organization.

Seymour, Harold J. 1988. *Designs for Fund-Raising,* (Second ed.). Ambler, PA: Fund-Raising Institute.

Wilson, Marlene. 1976. *The Effective Management of Volunteer Programs.* Boulder, CO: Volunteer Management Associates.

TRAINING AND DEVELOPMENT OF VOLUNTEERS

Suzanne J. Lulewicz

5.1 Overview

5.2 Training, Education, and Development

5.3 Building an Effective Training Program

5.4 Commonly Used Training Programs

5.5 Emerging Trends

5.6 Conclusions

References

5.1 OVERVIEW

Today's volunteers are among the busiest and least likely to have an abundance of time to devote to their chosen organizations. It is not unusual today to hear leaders of nonprofit organizations, both large and small, express the difficulty they have in recruiting, retaining, and developing an adequate pool of volunteers to accomplish organizational goals and objectives. Yet those who do volunteer are generally highly motivated and bring to the organizations they choose to work with a wide range of education, knowledge, skills, compassion, and commitment.

Despite the personal difficulties they face, over 94.2 million adults volunteer 20.8 billion hours of time outside their homes and offices either to contribute to the goals and objectives of organizations they care about or to demonstrate care and compassion as they help their neighbors in times of need and trouble. Volunteers contribute an average of 4.2 hours per week, with 51.1 percent of all adults 18 years of age or older volunteering. Those who volunteer more than 4 hours a week are more likely to have had some college education, volunteer to help others, attend religious services regularly, have a higher average household income, and volunteer to explore their strengths (Independent Sector, 1994, pp. 1–2).

American's volunteers come from a variety of economic and cultural backgrounds. Men and women of all ages, from senior citizens at one end of the spectrum to teenagers at the other end, make important contributions to the nonprofit workforce and the organizations they represent. Motivating this broad and diverse volunteer base through training, education, and development is of vital importance to the life of a nonprofit. It also creates one of its biggest challenges.

A nonprofit organization relies heavily on its volunteers to implement goals and objectives. Therefore, plans for the training and development of the organization's volunteers must be included at every stage of the organizational planning process. Volunteer training bridges the differences between what a volunteer understands an assignment to be, their own expectations on how well they can perform that assignment, and what their performance level actually is when given the opportunity to perform.

Effective training programs for volunteers are developed when specific job and task requirements are clearly identified, and organizational and volunteer needs are recognized and brought into the development of the training program. Identifying what job knowledge needs to be acquired, what skills need to be developed, what organizational values need to be transmitted, and what volunteer motivations can be built upon or enhanced are the foundations of an effective volunteer training program.

5.2 TRAINING, EDUCATION, AND DEVELOPMENT

Learning to develop human resources is generally categorized into three major areas. Leonard Nadler (1984, p. 1.16) identified them as:

- Training (learning that is related to one's present job)
- Education (learning to prepare a person for a different but known job)
- Development (learning for growth of the individual but not related to a specific present or known future job)

With the development of the *learning organization* and *open space* technology, the word *training* has fallen on difficult times. For some, the word may carry with it an underlying mechanical, Pavlovian implication—an assumption that knowledge is being transmitted to an inert, passive subject, who, when appropriately trained, will go out and perform exactly as taught. The distinction many educators make these days is that whereas some animals can be trained, people *learn*.

Nonprofit administrators however want to capitalize on the concrete benefits and results that training can provide. However, the very nature of the volunteer commitment and the organization's drive for change make it necessary for sponsoring organizations to be aware of and capitalize on the broader motivations, expertise, and knowledge base their volunteers bring with them. For nonprofit staff who work with training volunteers, the differences between training, education, and development do not usually reflect clear and distinct categories.

In many instances, training for particular volunteer positions not only enhances volunteers' education but also helps advance their personal growth, development, and recognition of values. For example, training provided to people who volunteer for a crisis hotline or to provide care for the elderly that may relate directly to how successfully they will perform in these volunteer positions may include developing attitudes of patience and calm, learning how to negotiate and balance another's personal wants and needs, and developing the art of active listening and flexibility in dealing with stressful situations. All of these skills also help further develop personal growth and discovery in the volunteers.

Because of the quality of the work that most volunteers do for organizations, the term *learning* has much more resonance and is more appropriate to what nonprofits engage in with their volunteers than the word *training*. The current emphasis on learning as opposed to training in the training and development field is discussed in Section 5.5.

(a) Staff Training versus Volunteer Training

In the staff-driven training world, jobs are analyzed and subdivided into specific task components. Training is designed to show observable improvement in performance in specific task areas that can be measured in terms of productivity and the bottom line. While some nonprofits have successfully incorporated measurements within their training programs to better identify the return on the organization's investment, a nonprofit's product or service does not often lend itself to measuring productivity in dollars.

According to Peter Drucker (1990, p. 54), "the nonprofit institution neither supplies goods or services nor an effective regulation. Its product is a changed human being." Thus, when training, education, and development of volunteers become organizational goals, innovative ways need to be found to measure a training program's success beyond the traditional measures of productivity and profit. The nonprofit product that Drucker identifies casts the training, education, and development that a nonprofit organization provides its volunteers in a deeper, much more motivational light. Internal corporate staff training focuses on how to do a better job. Volunteer training, on the other hand, is about how doing a better job helps and changes others, or how they live their lives, for the better.

Training, education, and development in the context of the nonprofit is extremely important. It serves as an additional factor in the search for individual and organizational discovery, growth, and change. Knowledge about how an organization functions, about its mission and vision, where its strengths and weaknesses lay, develop for the organization a perspective of advocacy that helps volunteers better serve the wider community or more effectively canvass for change. It may include raising money to implement much needed community programs, educating the community on the purpose and goals of the organization, or advocating support for a perspective that is supported by an organization's constituency.

Training and the planning-for-training programs are areas that nonprofits must recognize as presenting win–win situations for all concerned. The volunteer benefits by being more successful and by learning new and additional information and skills. The organization benefits by getting the energies and services of volunteers who are committed, motivated, and more focused on achieving an organization's objectives. The members or people who receive the added value as a result of trained volunteers benefit by being a part of an organization that brings them together with volunteers who have achieved a level of competency and effectiveness that generates loyalty, warmth, understanding, and success.

The broad categories and population diversity that were identified during the Independent Sector's Gallup survey underscore the need for every organization to know who its volunteers are: their values, motivations, and lifestyles. In addition, they must be able to identify and assess the skills, knowledge, and attitudes of their volunteers and match them to the assignments the organization asks them to undertake. Volunteers who staff a crisis hot line or care for an elderly person under the hospice program not only must have caring and compassionate attitudes but clearly need information on what contingencies to expect. They must have an opportunity to gain the expertise that will enable them to react with the confidence and skill required by the situation.

A volunteer who is working a fund-raising telethon may require different training from a person staffing a religious counseling program. Although advocacy and commitment are needed in both, the special techniques that provide competency must become the focus of their training. A different range of skills are needed by volunteers who are learning to be leaders than by someone learning to be a literacy tutor or career counselor. As training programs must be designed with the specific needs of both the organization and its volunteers in mind, fundamental questions for any nonprofit volunteer training program will include:

1. What is the problem the program needs to overcome or what are the goals of the program?
2. What are the standards for volunteer performance?
3. What skills do the volunteers currently possess?
4. Is training an appropriate solution or method?
5. If so, what learning objectives will drive the training program?
6. What are the best training methods to bring about those outcomes?
7. What volunteer and organizational needs must be acknowledged in order to develop a training program?
8. What organizational resources will be required?
9. What volunteer resources will be required?

10. Will the expenditure of resources to train volunteers provide the expected results?

11. Once again, is training an appropriate solution or method?

Answers to these questions need to be factored into an organization's strategic and operational planning processes. Only if such questions are raised and answered during strategic and operational planning can an organization effectively identify and allocate the resources needed to deliver the quality of programs that will advance its mission and goals. The success of any program will depend, in large part, on where the organization has identified current and potential resources and how it matches them appropriately to opportunities for both long- and short-term training. Planning in this way can make the difference between an organization's success or failure with volunteer-driven programs

Recognizing the difference between where an organization is now and where it wants to be is critical to identifying the type of training resources needed to help bring an organization's vision to reality. Knowing the planned outcome of training programs and how they fit into the organization's overall goals and objectives enables volunteer administrators to build, through training, the volunteer expertise necessary to support the organization's outreach and advocacy goals.

5.3 BUILDING AN EFFECTIVE TRAINING PROGRAM

Steps to plan an effective volunteer training program include:

1. Identify organizational goals in the strategic planning process.
2. Identify volunteer-driven programs needed to achieve organizational goals.
3. Identify organizational resources needed to achieve program goals.
4. Identify volunteer resources needed to achieve program and organizational goals.

Once organizational, programming, and volunteer goals have been identified, job position descriptions and standards of performance for each program and the varying volunteer assignments within each program will need to be developed. These need to be done before any identification of volunteer needs and resources can be accomplished. Once this work is completed, a review of volunteer applications and interview results will help determine a volunteer's most appropriate position in the organization and helps define the volunteer's appropriate training and development path toward leadership or ever-expanding opportunities within the organization.

Appropriately identifying all the resources and needs necessary to accomplish program goals helps the volunteer manager identify cases when individual goals may be in conflict with organizational goals (for example, when the person is not suited to the volunteer opportunity). In such circumstances, the usefulness of training to the organization becomes minimal and may, in fact, waste valuable resources. When a person is not suited for a job based on the specifics of expected performance and training does not appear to be an appropriate solution, reassignment may be more appropriate and should be considered.

According to Cole and Fisher (1993), the precise design of a learning program for a particular job depends on the number of volunteers to be trained, the amount of time available, and the background of the volunteers. Greater numbers of trainees make individualized instruction more difficult; more experienced trainees require less time. However, the complexity of the task to be learned is probably one of the most critical elements. For example:

◆ Does the task need to be handled in exactly the same way by every volunteer?

◆ How much flexibility is built into the outcome?

◆ Can the volunteer exercise judgment in determining what activities to perform and at what level?

Demonstrations of skills, combined with practice sessions to meet performance standards, not only help establish baselines of acceptable performance, but help build confidence in a volunteer's performance. According to Cole and Fisher learning to exercise judgment requires having volunteers make decisions in situations that are as close as possible to those they will encounter in their program.

(a) Good Training Depends on Good Volunteer Management

All effective volunteer training programs are based on a sound volunteer management program. An application process and prescreening interviews are important activities to be incorporated in any volunteer program. Sometimes a need for resources can color a nonprofit's perspective of its volunteers. They believe them to be a cost-free labor resource. In reality the nonprofit–volunteer connection is not cost-free and should be designed as a mutually beneficial relationship.

Volunteers often gain added confidence as a result of commitment to a cause beyond themselves. They also gain an opportunity to grow, discover, and develop in a larger world. They will be able to add professional skills to their repertoire or have opportunities provided to practice skills they cannot always exercise elsewhere. In turn, the organization gains the needed help to reach out and benefit its constituency, or the public at large, through more effective programs that provide help and goodwill.

(i) Application Process

When a volunteer is interviewed—and every volunteer for all nonprofits should be interviewed—the volunteer administrator should learn what skills and education this particular volunteer brings to the organization. Questions need to be raised to identify the person's motivation in volunteering at this time and what will keep the volunteer satisfied. It is up to the nonprofit administrator to discover the volunteer's numerous talents and abilities, to nurture them, and to identify potential areas of growth.

The application process provides the organization with the opportunity and the means to identify the skills and abilities of the would-be volunteer. This process also helps the potential volunteer determine what this organization can offer them through their participation in its service program. Information important to the volunteer training manager that a volunteer administrator needs to obtain during the volunteer application and interview process includes:

◆ *Employment status.* Volunteers who work full time, part-time, or are unemployed have differing time commitments, availabilities, and motivations.

◆ *Education.* This provides the organization with important information to target future training materials. The prospective volunteer may already possess the requisite knowledge or educational background. This information can also help guide the training developer on the methodology to be used when designing the training program.

◆ *Special skills and interests, past volunteer work and other experience, volunteer task preferences, time and days available for volunteering, home address.* All provide helpful information for planning the time, length, and location of training activities as well as who may need to be involved. The items identifying special skills and interests, along with preferences, can be expanded further during the interview process. This information will help an organization understand a volunteer's commitment and plan an educational and/or a leadership track for that volunteer, if appropriate. Thus, an organization has an opportunity to develop and possibly expand its leadership ranks, and the volunteer has an opportunity to grow, develop, and possibly provide leadership expertise.

(ii) Interview Process

The interview is as important as the job description to the success of a volunteer training program. The interview allows the organization's representative to find out more about volunteers' qualifications and why they want to work with a particular organization. It is also an opportunity for prospective volunteers to gain information about the organization and to discover what specific volunteer opportunities are available. Volunteers can learn about any special requirements time commitments that may accompany any of the volunteer assignments, and any concerns can be answered in a personal way. The interview provides the organization's representatives with an opportunity to talk with prospective volunteers and learn their preferences, needs, and interests—all important elements in implementing organizational goals successfully.

Interviews can identify the volunteer's strengths and weaknesses. It can help match the right volunteer to the right assignment, closing the gap as much as possible between qualifications needed to perform the job successfully and those that the volunteer already brings to the organization. The interview process also exposes the real-time motivational issues and values of the prospective volunteer. An effective nonprofit will use that information as a foundation for its future training programs. Organizations that rely heavily on keeping their volunteers competent, focused, and performing will integrate a person's personal motivations and values into the training process.

(iii) Job Descriptions

Job descriptions, as mentioned earlier, are another vital component of a volunteer training program. Why are they important? Because they identify clearly for all concerned the assignment the volunteer is expected to perform and the standards of performance. They also identify the qualifications that volunteers performing the assignment must exhibit to be successful. An ideal job description includes the job title, how it relates to the work of the organization, a list of specific responsibilities and accountabilities, standards of performance, what education and/or experience qualifications are needed to perform the job successfully, attitudes or values that may be necessary, the time commitments (include training, meetings, and orientations), the location of the assignment, the supervisor of the assignment, and a brief description of that supervisory relationship. Finally, the job description is used to outline the benefits of this assignment for the volunteer.

(iv) Needs Analysis

It is important to conduct needs analysis of volunteers on a regular basis. The application and interview process can provide volunteer administrators with the necessary data to analyze volunteer training needs. When this information is either unavailable or no longer up to date, a separate training needs analysis is essential to the design of a training program. A well-designed analysis will identify for the nonprofit, to the extent possible, the learning and training needs of its volunteers. The success of a volunteer training program will depend on whether it has matched the program's design with the kind of quality education and training that its volunteers require to work successfully and to sustain motivation.

There are three reasons to conduct a needs analysis.

1. It will identify whether volunteers have the qualifications the organization has identified as necessary for competent job performance.
2. It will identify new volunteer needs that have occurred as a result of changes that may have taken place. (Identifying the cause of these changes—as residing in the organization, the volunteer program, or the volunteer—will not always be possible, but the need will be evident.)
3. A needs analysis will identify the gap between volunteer performance and expectation. This is most important for a successful training program, because the volunteer-perceived need for training is identified. Learning new skills really takes place only when the volunteer is an active participant in the learning process.

In addition to improving productivity, a well-developed needs analysis can help a nonprofit measure and demonstrate the worth of its volunteers. Once volunteer behaviors and skills have been identified and measured in relationship to organizational assignments, the training and development of volunteers through effective program design can be accelerated. When combined with other information, such as program performance objectives, data gathered from needs analysis can offer feedback on volunteer performance and development that is reliable. It provides needed information to volunteer managers who are continuously developing ways to improve volunteer performance, and it can provide evidence of behavior and productivity changes.

Successful volunteer needs analysis consists of the following steps:

1. Define the goals or purpose of the needs analysis process. If a nonprofit organization wants information of a general nature about its volunteers, the questions will reflect that. More specific goals will require developing needs analysis questions that seek specific information. As a result, the data gained will directly reflect the goals laid out at the very beginning of the project.

2. Determine the methodology to be used. A needs analysis can be conducted by reviewing applications and prescreening interview information, conducting telephone or face-to-face interviews, observing the volunteers in action, and compiling surveys or questionnaires. The method used depends not only on the time, skill, and financial resources of the organization but also on the driving purpose of the needs analysis.

Sampling techniques can be used effectively for training programs as long as the samples are representative of the volunteer group that the nonprofit is targeting through this analysis process. Sampling focuses on carefully selected individuals rather than all of the targeted audience. As Nadler states (1987, p. 88), by questioning this carefully chosen sample, a nonprofit can make highly accurate predictions regarding the larger group of volunteers. This technique requires a set standard of criteria to be followed and should be used with caution.

Other research tools and tactics beyond the use of the surveys and questionnaires include focus groups and observation. Use of both of these tools must be directed by a person experienced in the techniques who can deal with designing and implementing an objective analysis using these means.

3. Design the questions. The purpose behind the needs analysis is especially important here. Questions asked of volunteers to get at the needed information must be clear, direct, and uniformly understood by all who read or hear the questions.

Whether using a survey, focus group, interview, or questionnaire, question design can start simply by writing down the questions that need to be answered to design a training program. Questions can be developed so that each category of skills identified with a job description aligns with the training being planned or currently provided. More sophisticated designs use small groups that provide basic skills and behaviors from which professional question writers develop the questions to be used in the needs analysis process. Once again the purpose of the needs analysis and the availability of organizational resources determine which method will be used.

4. Organize the data. The information collected from the surveys, interview, applications, and questionnaires must be compiled and organized. If a simple survey or questionnaire is used, there are cost-effective, easy-to-use software programs that can assist a nonprofit's staff or volunteers to organize the information collected. If a more complex questionnaire or the inclusion of other sources of data is called for, an outside professional may need to be involved in designing and developing the analysis. The details on the organization of these data must be included when contracting for or designing the needs analysis. How the data will be organized and analyzed needs to be included in the design of any instrument.

5. Review the findings. The data collected create the foundation upon which a nonprofit organization will build its training programs. However, the volunteer administrator should regularly refer to the initial assessment goals or purpose so that the information gleaned fro the assessment process relates directly to those goals. Information that is secondary to those goals should be considered peripheral (McClelland, 1992). Further, when the review and analysis of findings should be done as objectively as possible.

6. Develop training recommendations. All training recommendations should be substantiated by information gained during the needs assessment process. Choices the volunteer administrator makes on what type of training program to design—the length, breadth, and depth—should all be supported in the data gathered.

   7. Repeat the process on the same skills and behaviors 6 to 12 months later. This step is also one that will give valuable information on whether training programs actually work (Ludeman, 1991). By assessing the volunteer's skills before the training program is begun and then measuring them again 6 to 12 months later, the organization can obtain valuable information on the volunteers' progress in skill development and job performance. Ludeman states that pretraining assessments make it easy for participants to see the areas in which they need to improve and help them to set appropriate goals and cites extensive research that showed a significant correlation between learning and goal setting in the training process. The more clearly training goals are defined in the needs analysis process and communicated throughout the program, the more successfully will volunteers learn.
   An assessment should include the following characteristics:

1. Be easy to use and practical to implement
2. Create guidelines to develop needs analysis questions
3. Build the organization's skill priorities into the questions
4. Organize questions into job categories and competencies, organizational values, or potential training topics
5. Build a pool of hundreds of questions from which to select for the surveys
6. Analyze current volunteer skills and compare them to what the organization needs
7. Identify a volunteer's various strengths and areas to develop
8. Link this needs analysis with a volunteer development process that relates to the nonprofit environment

The needs analysis provides a useful tool for the nonprofit staff not only to show productive changes in volunteer skills and behaviors, but also to provide quantifiable data that show an organization's leadership how competently trained volunteers are necessary to implement strategic organizational goals successfully.

(b) Defining Learning Objectives

Once the information gathered from the assessment process is reviewed, design is begun on the program, adjusting the materials to the specific level of education, experience, skills, attitudes, and personal motivations of the targeted audience. Training needs are weighed against reality and the constraints of time, money, facilities, and resources. At this stage the specific and measurable learning objectives this training is designed to achieve must be developed.
   Learning objectives are found in the gap between what volunteers can do and what an organization needs them to do. These objectives identify what additional knowledge, performance skills, and/or attitude changes need to occur at the conclusion of the training program if it is to be considered successful. This segment is especially important because it ties together whatever learning the participants have gained. These objectives define the areas the trainer will focus on and what skills and/or information the volunteer will have gained by the end of the program. The objectives should include information relating to specific conditions that must be in place to achieve the program's learning objectives. In other words, does there need to be prior knowledge to accomplish the objectives; or are certain tools, such as

computers, necessary and available to the volunteers to enable them to achieve any of the program's learning objectives? Further, the conditions that enable volunteer trainees to achieve these objectives and thus need to be replicated on the assignment should be identified. Any time constraints that will affect success in achieving the objectives also should be included. For example, does the volunteer have adequate time to carry out the steps identified in the training?

The quality of the result also must be addressed in these objectives. How well does the volunteer need to perform the steps described in the delivery of this training for the results to be acceptable? A typical learning objective might look as follows:

Upon completion of this program, the volunteer will be able to:

◆ Establish a team structure for the board.
◆ Perform the duties of a team mentor, enabling the team to perform efficiently and effectively, and contribute to the achievement of board milestones and member satisfaction.
◆ Given a problem in performance, identify when to form a new team to resolve this performance problem and develop potential timetables for specific performance problems.
◆ Describe the components of an effective team and be able to write a clear mission statement.

Note: All objectives begin with a verb unless the objective also qualifies a condition of prior knowledge, with limitations on performance, time, or acceptable quality identified. These objectives should be completely self-explanatory, providing the facilitator or instructor with all the information necessary to determine what volunteers take away with them at the conclusion of the program. Everything taught in this program is based on these objectives, which determine the success of the program.

(c) Curriculum Development

Next comes the development of the curriculum. Bring together instructional or learning objectives, methods, media, training content, examples, exercises, and activities, and organize them into a curriculum that supports adult-learning theory and provides a blueprint for developing the training program. Have a volunteer task force of subject matter experts review and approve the design document at every stage of development.

(i) Select an Instructional Strategy to Complement the Training Material

The selection of an instructional strategy is as important as the selection of the material. The strategy selected will give the training presentation purpose and direction. Time is needed to make certain that the strategy selected fits the material and the purpose. The following is a representative selection of instructional strategies from which a course designer can choose depending on the program and the organization.

- *Buzz Group.* Divide the group into smaller groups (two to six people) for a short period of time to discuss topic or perform a task. The group's representative will report decisions to the entire gathering. This strategy encourages participation and, if used with a lecture, will encourage concentration.

- *Brainstorming.* Arrange for the volunteer participants to participate in discussions designed to provide a number of ideas and solutions to a problem. All ideas and solutions are recorded, no matter how impractical or strange the idea may appear. The key is to encourage thought and to discourage inhibition. At the conclusion, the group is free to analyze all ideas and solutions and, if possible, to develop courses of action.

- *Guided discussions.* Ask the group questions that draw upon their knowledge of the subject. The trainer may wish to start with general questions and proceed to more specific ones. The key is to remain flexible and to allow for free-flowing discussion while controlling the group through questions.

- *Discussion groups.* Divide the large group into smaller groups that will seek, identify, and explore solutions to problems and develop plans of action. The trainer should allow the participants to control the discussion. The trainer's role is to guide and mediate the discussion. This approach requires that volunteer participants have considerable prior knowledge on the subject.

- *Lectures.* Deliver the material through carefully planned oral presentation. Although the lecture is a method that allows the trainer to control the situation, it does not allow for much audience participation. The lecture is best when used in conjunction with another strategy.

- *Lecture-discussions.* Deliver the material through a carefully planned oral presentation that is followed by group discussion. Begin with a lecture over which the trainer has total control. Then move to the group discussion, where the trainer directs but does not control the subject matter. The direction in the latter part of the session is designed to give the trainer the opportunity to emphasize the key points of the lecture.

- *Case studies.* Use an incident or situation—real or fictitious—that allows the group to gain new perspectives on the subject being covered. Allow time for the group to discuss and develop solutions. Present the case through either printed materials or role-playing.

- *Role-playing.* Ask the group to improvise behavior of assigned roles to demonstrate or experience a selected condition or objective. The trainer can use role-playing to demonstrate a single purpose or to cover a series of situations. This technique works best with small groups where individuals will not feel inhibited.

- *Exercise.* Assign the group tasks that will make them apply the information trainer has provided. The trainer should control these exercises to make certain that specific information is understood. Exercises are helpful because they allow the group to participate actively and to use the information the trainer has given them.

- *Questions and answers.* Give the participants the opportunity to ask questions about the information the trainer has given them. This method will help the trainer and participants clarify the material delivered in the presentation. Question-and-answer periods usually work best at the end of a session.

- *Demonstrations.* Schedule a visual presentation along with a lecture or discussion. Such a demonstration will show volunteer participants the appropriate method for completing an act or procedure. The pace is flexible and the class will probably accept a new idea if they see it demonstrated. Upon completion of the demonstration, the trainer should allow the group to repeat the act or procedure themselves.
- *Panels.* Organize a panel to take full advantage of the experience and expertise of visitors or of the program participants themselves. The trainer can approach the use of a panel from two directions. First, let each panel member deliver short remarks and then let program participants ask questions. Second, let all the panel members discuss a specific topic and then let the program participants ask questions. The latter method requires a moderator.
- *Debates.* Consider this as a last alternative. Debate is not usually used in adult education sessions because it is too formal. It does, however, allow for the presentation of contrasting viewpoints and it demonstrates how differing opinions are analyzed and addressed.

In summary, remember these key points when selecting trainer instructional strategy:

Select an instructional strategy that will enhance the presentation.
Select an instructional strategy that the trainer will find comfortable.
Use the instructional strategy alone or in any combination.

Training materials and manuals must be written clearly. Course designers and developers must ensure that they blend directly into the program's learning objectives. *Keep training materials as simple as possible.* Although state-of-the-art technology is nice and attractive, it can be costly. Before designing a course with costly technology, it is wise to make sure that there is financial support for developing, maintaining, and upgrading the technology. Once the curriculum is designed, the program is tested using a representative audience to introduce and validate the training. Final revisions are based on the results of the pilot.

(ii) Conduct the Training

No longer are instructors in the business of lecturing or being the sole expert on how things are to be done; they are moving toward facilitating experiential activities, with participants actively involved in group process. The instructor's role is to identify, explain, and model the skills, watch the learners perform, and help them understand the training points.

(d) Evaluation Process

Kirkpatrick's four types of evaluation are still the standard used to measure a training program's effectiveness:

1. Participants' reaction to the program. This type of evaluation informs program administrators how relevant the training was for participants and how they felt about the training. It provides answers on whether the training was clear and if it met stated organizational and learning objectives. This information can be gathered through reactionnaire forms or posttraining interviews.

2. What participants learned from the program. This particular evaluation acknowledges whether participants have gained the skill and knowledge defined by the training program's learning objectives. This can be accomplished by testing the participants knowledge or skill base. Tests can include a paper-and-pencil test for knowledge comprehension or incorporate role-playing or simulations that ask learners to replay situations in which the newly developed skills can be observed. For example, if the objectives for a training program focused on learning the series of steps that go into learning how to negotiate, an activity that allows the participant to test this skill would tell observers whether the training goals were achieved.

3. Participants' changed behavior. This type of evaluation focuses on whether the knowledge, skill, or attitude is being used successfully on assignment. Often called *transfer of training,* this is one of the more difficult evaluation techniques to implement. Interviews, on-the-job observations by volunteer supervisors or mentors, participant questionnaires, follow-up phone calls, and focus groups are all techniques to help administrators find out if the training program actually improved a volunteer's performance. Once again, specialized experience is necessary to develop questions and checklists that support all of the techniques needed to evaluate at this level.

Seeking the answers to this evaluation measure requires having completed the previous measure: what participants learned from the training program. This is necessary to isolate the cause of a volunteer's failure to implement the learning while on assignment. Since the environment in which the volunteer works could have something to do with the training not being implemented successfully, it is important to know the skill level the volunteer achieved at the time the training ended. Training administrators need to take into account possible factors in the volunteer's environment that could prevent the application of newly learned knowledge and skills. If proper organizational reinforcement of what a volunteer learns is not there, the investment in training is wasted.

4. How the change in behavior affected the organization. Krein and Weldon (1994) state that this type of evaluation probably has the greatest value to the nonprofit organization and is the most difficult to measure. Evaluating a training program at this level provides information on what effect the training program has on such organizational measures as reduced costs, improved quality, increase in favorable comments from customers, decrease in number of grievances filed, and increased profitability and productivity. Important business items are usually measured at this level because evidence of training as the sole cause is hard to isolate. Some business areas are easier to measure than others. Budget items (such as increased profits or reduced costs) can be identified through pre- and post-tracking systems. However, for the most part, specialized knowledge and skill go into developing evaluation strategies. Careful development of design studies using experimental and control groups that recognize what other variables may contribute to the behavior change requires specialists and may be costly.

5.4 COMMONLY USED TRAINING PROGRAMS

A variety of training programs used successfully in many organizations focus on learning beyond the formal classroom or skill-based training sessions. These include orientation programs, observation, volunteer handbooks and/or manuals, succession/leadership programs, mentoring and shadowing programs, on-the-job training, and networking. The use of such educational activities depends on the nature of the job to be learned and how much of it volunteers already know or can do. Such programs offer a combination of formal and informal volunteer learning encounters with the organization. As a result of these contacts, new volunteers can learn how the organization operates and how they can participate.

(a) Orientation

Orientation programs are just the beginning of the planned learning opportunities that acquaint volunteers with an organization. The advantage to a nonprofit in delivering orientation programs to its interested or newly recruited volunteers is that the organization then will have volunteers who have accurate and up-to-date information about the organization—its purpose, its programs, and its current needs. Orientation programs also include information on the current issues confronting the organization. Providing volunteers with this information allows them to represent the organization in the best possible light.

An orientation program will generally cover information on the organization's philosophy, how it began and where has it been, and background regarding major traditions that it has built over time. A discussion of its mission, organization, funding, operations, and financial policies and procedures is also included, as well as how the staff and volunteers work together to achieve the organization's goals. An organization would include all information that would enable a volunteer to understand and develop a relationship with an organization and feel that they are making a major contribution to its membership and goals. They will feel that they are part of a team.

(b) Organizational Handbooks

Manuals or handbooks can be another way of supplementing the orientation process. Providing material in a handbook that contains all relevant and current information discussed in the orientation program does a great deal to reinforce the information with the volunteers. It provides an easy source of data as questions occur and memory fades. It can also keep volunteers from being overwhelmed with information. However, care must be taken to update written materials continually as the nonprofit grows and changes and develops new systems and programs. Also, as Cole and Fisher (1993) state, a handbook can protect against liability by providing tangible evidence that information on organizational policy and behavior was provided.

The orientation process sets the stage for a successful volunteer organization relationship. Other items that need to be addressed during the orientation process include what an organization expects from its volunteers and the conduct, responsibility, and accountability that it requires. Decisions on how and when volunteers will donate time depend on their understanding of what the organization expects from them.

According to Cole and Fisher (1993), when volunteers deal with the terminally ill, disabled, or incarcerated, people from different cultural or socioeconomic backgrounds, or abused people, an explicit examination of the emotional demands involved and of the attitudes and values that potential volunteers may bring is necessary. Some organizations use orientations to confront potential volunteers with the challenges such as these that are inherent in the program. Networking during this orientation is extremely important to help volunteers feel welcome. It is an opportunity for them to meet both new and experienced staff and other volunteers. It can help develop a feeling of belonging: that they are part of a team and have a role in the organization.

(c) Mentoring

Mentoring programs are important tools to help organizations build and reinforce volunteer skills. In Greek mythology, Mentor was Odysseus's wise and faithful friend, a counselor and advisor. Today's mentors play basically the same role. According to Rogers (1992), mentoring has been used as an early identification program for high-potential and talented individuals, who are selected by their future mentors. As brought out by Rogers, mentoring can be viewed as an educational tool to train and track new talent, or it can be viewed as a flawed program that does not allow for diversity when administered in a traditional one-on-one approach.

In her article, Rogers tracked the success of a mentoring circle at a corporation that found this a successful approach. In response to the fact that few women were in high levels of the organization, thereby restricting opportunities for women in the mentoring process, this organization developed a mentoring circle to allow more women to build and expand their networking system. This could not have happened under the more traditional one-on-one mentoring system. This mentoring circle used a consciousness-raising group format as a model, with members invited to participate and meet once a week, outside work hours. Circles had a maximum of 12 participants and a minimum of 8 participants. Two-thirds of the participants were people to be mentored, and the remaining third were would-be mentors from more senior levels within the organization. A facilitator monitored the first meetings. According to Rogers, this mentoring circle can work better than mentoring on a one-on-one basis. There is more exposure to more people, and instead of having one person to go to, you now have many—your network has expanded.

(d) Shadowing

Shadowing provides another opportunity for learning. It provides not only on-the-job training but gives a person an opportunity to learn from the experience of another. The length of time a person remains as a shadow, and the depth to which that experience is carried out, remain very much a function of the job at hand. Clear planning and the same orientation to goals and objectives performed for all other activities are necessary.

(e) Networking

Effective networks can ease communication across functions within an organization as well as outside it and increase effective problemsolving. Although networking is not usually a stated goal in most training programs, it is an extremely important communications tool to assist in the learning process. Networking is based on trust and the building of relationships within a nonprofit's volunteer ranks. On-the-job training generally proceeds from the more formal training activities to help volunteers better understand the task assignment and be able to perform it. Mentoring and coaching techniques frequently help people interpret their experience and build on their failures and successes.

Volunteers learn best by experience. According to Cole and Fisher (1993), volunteers with little or no formal training are able to master a job as they perform it. However, that does not guarantee that volunteers can analyze their experience and learn from it. As a result, a program can fail due to poor performance, and the goals of the organization go unrealized because volunteers failed to make the necessary connection between what they need to know and their current experience. Volunteers can interpret being left on their own as the organization's placing a low priority on quality performance, according to Cole and Fisher. The program may suffer damage from inadequate performance and the goals of the organization may never be realized due to the fact that the volunteers fail to learn from their own experiences. On-the-job training provides administrators with an opportunity to observe how volunteer trainees perform their new assignment.

(f) Succession Planning/Leadership Programs

Seasoned volunteers may also need opportunities for growth and development through increases in their volunteer responsibilities. Succession planning and leadership development provide ideal mutually beneficial ways for any organization to keep its experienced volunteers challenged, interested, and committed to the organization's future. Therefore, it is extremely important for nonprofit organizations to recognize their role in developing leadership programs for their volunteers. The health and vibrancy of nonprofits will be maintained only as long as succession planning is an important keystone to their volunteer program. However, because of the fluid nature of volunteers themselves, some structure needs to be given to the succession planning process. While specific individuals may bubble up to the surface, too many get lost if a specific program is not in place.

According to James P. Gelatt (1992, p. 209), committees are living laboratories for leadership development. Once you watch a committee it becomes clear very quickly which members are most willing to work, which are always coming up with ideas, and which the others listen to. Individual committee assignments provide another way to find potential leaders. Not every leader is a skilled speaker, but given the task they may be able to be successful at it. This can then give them the confidence to take on additional responsibilities that can enhance their leadership skills.

Leadership development could include service on committees that have broad-based goals and objectives. Work on these committees will give volunteers the same broad-based access to the work of the organization. Membership, financial, and fund-raising committees are good examples of these types of committees. Committees may serve as seeding grounds to bring new volunteers into a leadership path. Those seasoned volunteers able to express a clear and broad view can be extremely valuable to a nonprofit as it seeks to implement its vision. Observation and/or mentoring by board members of committee chairs and observation and/mentoring of committee members can help steer future leaders into effective placement within the organization.

Beyond leadership positions, volunteers familiar with the organization who have volunteer experience can be identified as having the potential to be membership and volunteer recruiters or trainers and supervisors of volunteers. They also make ideal representatives of the organization in the community or serving on committees. Offering development programs is also a way to reward the more experienced volunteer for his or her contribution as well as to identify the steps for those who wish to become leaders. A succession plan can provide a structure whereby potential leaders can be identified and selected for further development of leadership-related skills. Orientations in addition to leadership and board training can help ground seasoned volunteers in an understanding of organizational policies and procedures as well as providing one-on-one mentoring by current organizational leaders. They can also prepare the organization for smooth transitions of leadership as boards and committees transfer from one term to another. Seminars, workshops, conferences, and self-directed learning activities also provide opportunities to reward, re-commit, and prepare volunteers for leadership.

(g) Personal and Professional Development

When learning and training activities are designed to promote personal growth, both the volunteer and the organization profit. Therefore, each organization must consider what and how it develops, recognizes, and enriches its volunteer staff as it helps to compensate them for their contributions. Cole and Fisher (1993) have discussed how volunteers often view their volunteer activity as a form of self-development and that learning opportunities are an important factor in the satisfaction as well as the retention of volunteers.

Programs that help volunteers enhance and develop their own self-confidence, increase their knowledge, or learn more about the expertise of others improve their growth as people. Through these types of programs, seasoned and experienced volunteers can be given opportunities to grow in their knowledge of themselves and of topics of interest to them, and to build a stronger relationship with the organization.

(h) Training of Members of the Board

New leaders within the organization need care and attention, as do all organizational volunteers. Their commitment to and knowledge of the organization needs to be deepened to enhance their decision making as they serve their term on the board. According to Cyril Houle (1989, pp. 47–53), an effective orientation to the board will address feelings of concern and self-doubt. As he says in his book *Governing Boards* (1989), "Everybody really knows what to do; they just don't take the time to do it." Initial orientation for new board members needs to consist of:

1. Welcome to the organization and an offer of assistance
2. Interview or conference with a new board member to talk about the work of the organization and its programs
3. Details on their role on the board
4. An opportunity to see some of the programs in action
5. Regular orientations on a continual basis to provide a complete introduction to the various volunteer and the programs and the role of the chief executive and the staff
6. Time for questions and an opportunity for follow-up sessions to exchange additional or needed information

7. Opportunity for new board members to get to know other board members
8. Information about who to turn to as questions arise

(i) Continuing Education of Boards

Board members are generally engaged in the process of understanding and perfecting their skills on a continuing basis. Much of their experience on the board enables them to draw lessons that tap their deepest sense of learning. Not only do they need formal opportunities for learning—seminars, conferences, local, state, and national organization memberships—but also additional opportunities to help the organization fulfill its mission. As Houle (1989) states: "It is important to take advantage of the fact that human beings are capable of continuous intellectual growth." Neither the selection of the board members nor the increase of their knowledge should be left to chance.

5.5 EMERGING TRENDS

Training and development in the future will incorporate the development of learning as a goal and vision. This is as true for the individual volunteer as it is for the nonprofit organization. A great deal of discussion, debate, and dialogue is now taking place around the concepts of learning as the major authors and thinkers of our time wrestle with the identity, formation, development, and results of the inspired organization, the *learning organization*. Leading-edge authors such as Peter Senge *(The Fifth Discipline)*, Harrison Owens *(Riding the Tiger* and *Open Space Technology)*, Margaret Wheatley *(Leadership and the New Science)*, and Chris Argyris *(Action Science)* emphasize continually that there is an evolutionary shift currently going on from the traditional definitions of training and development of human potential to something called *deep learning* or *high learning*.

As Owen (1991) describes it, "Our learning concerns are not just the facts and figures of everyday life, but rather the high learning indicative of real creativity: making something where nothing existed before. And also the deep learning where we come face to face with what we really are, our essence so to speak." In the workplace of the future, "every moment becomes a learning moment, as the distinction between learning and doing progressively disappears." Creative chaos replaces control; interactive and inspired organizations replace the current reactive, responsive, and proactive organizations. Learning in organizations will manifest the evolution of human consciousness. The fundamental function of intelligent and creative organizations will be to facilitate that human process.

The discussion that follows is a brief review taken from the 50th anniversary issue of *Training and Development,* (ASTD, 1994) of the future of learning in the workplace and the development of human potential as envisioned by major training and development thinkers and authors. Patterns that emerge from their thinking highlight the entrepreneurial foundation that will be the basis for future organizations. To build and maintain that entrepreneurial foundation will require the development of workplace skills that focus on group communications systems and processes and the development of effective teams needed to arrive at truly creative solutions.

The reader should note that throughout the following summary, the term *organization* is used repeatedly. Use of the term in this context applies just as easily to nonprofit as to corporate or other professional organizational structures. No distinction is needed.

Chris Argyris is the father of *action science* or *double-looped learning*. This learning rests on a mode of questioning and/or inquiry that is designed to generate organizational or social knowledge that is both valid and useful. Argyris emphasizes the importance of creating new solutions by setting aside the assumptions we so often bring to decision making and problem solving. He describes two basic types of questions that will drive learning in the workplace. The first question is "How do I change things when I see an error?" This means changing behaviors and processes. The second question is "Is the way I frame reality and the organization frames reality in need of change?" Learning in these terms becomes the process of detecting and correcting error.

To build on this, we hear from Ken Blanchard that most of the training in organizations to date has focused on training in the areas of knowledge and attitudes. "We're finding that wherever we go now, people are asking if the training we deliver will make a difference. They want to know how we will tie learning into changes in behavior and performance and bottom-line results."

Peter Block expands on these perspectives by identifying learning and performing as becoming one and the same thing. Learning and performance will depend upon the individual, the entrepreneur, working to build community and participation. The hard part will be to identify the connection between training and learning because our current orientation and focus on training rests on the external techniques, coming from outside the volunteer's universe. Therefore, we feel we have a need for teachers and technology to impart information and answers.

William Bridges, author of the classic *Transitions*, sees the long-run future of training and development as the "radical reinvention of our organizations—something which is currently going on." People will need to learn to work in and for an organization in a new way. Training will thus need to provide people with the help to learn how to work in these new conditions. Organizations will need people with entrepreneurial skills.

As Margaret Wheatley explains, those skills needed by the fluid, rapidly shifting organization are skills in discernment, sense-making, and interpretation that are not widely distributed in today's organizations. These skills and the ability to learn continually will be the essential characteristics in our ability to prosper in business. Designers of training and learning experiences will need to create learning experiences that are not "rigidly structured or confined by classroom boundaries."

To Rosabeth Moss Kanter there will be a growing emphasis on learning in the workplace, but not necessarily on training. "Learning involves no only absorbing existing information, but also creating new solutions to not yet fully understood problems." Although training cannot occur in the absence of students, learning, according to Kanter, "can take place in the absence of teachers. It is an ability of the person, the group and the organization."

5.6 CONCLUSIONS

Chaos, complexity, and new mental models all affect the way that nonprofit organizations and volunteers will have to deal with their future. While change continues to assault all of today's workers, volunteers, and leaders, volunteers more than any other element of today's workforce hold the hope of positively transforming organizations and thus the society at large. Their passion, commitment, and loyalty to their chosen organizations are the spark needed to help realize organizational change. Volunteer training must include opportunities to develop skills in facilitation, dialogue, Socratic thinking and questioning, and scenario building. If a nonprofit seeks and is able to help its volunteers acquire these skills successfully, the organization will build an important strategic base for itself in implementing a positive interactive, possibly inspired, strategic vision. In Kanter's words, "Organizations will want to insure that people can learn together. That they share a common vocabulary, common analytic tools, communication channels, and commitment so that they can solve problems jointly."

REFERENCES

ASTD. 1994. "The Future of Workplace Learning and Performance." *Training and Development* 48(5): S36–S47.

Cole, Kathleen M., and James C. Fisher. 1993. *Leadership and Management of Volunteer Programs: A Guide for Volunteer Administrators.* San Francisco: Jossey-Bass.

Drucker, Peter. 1990. *Managing the Nonprofit Organization: Principles and Practices.* New York: HarperCollins.

Garavaglie, Paul L. 1993. "How to Ensure Transfer of Training." *Training and Development 47(10): 63–68.*

Gelatt, James P. 1992. *Managing Nonprofit Organizations in the 21st Century.* Phoenix, Ariz.: Oryx Press.

Houle, Cyril O. 1989. *Governing Boards.* San Francisco: National Center for Nonprofit Boards/Jossey-Bass.

Independent Sector. 1994. *Giving and Volunteering in the United States: Findings from a National Survey.* Washington, D.C.: Independent Sector.

Krein, Theodore J., and Katharine Weldon. 1994. "Making a Play for Training Evaluation." *Training and Development* 48(4): 62–67.

Ludeman, Kate. 1991. "Measuring Skills and Behavior." *Training and Development* 45(11): 61–66.

McClelland, Sam. 1992. "Systems Approach to Needs Assessment. *Training and Development* 46(8): 51–53.

Nadler, Leonard. 1984. *Handbook of Human Resource Development.* New York: Wiley.

Nadler, Leonard. 1987. *Designing Training Programs: The Critical Events Mode.* Reading, Mass.: Addison-Wesley.

Owen, Harrison. 1991. *Riding the Tiger: Doing Business in a Transforming World.* Potomac, MD: Abbott Publishing.

Rogers, Beth. 1992. "Mentoring Takes a New Twist." *HRMagazine on Human Resources Management* 37(8): 48–51.

CHAPTER ⬦ 6

TRAINING VOLUNTEERS IN QUALITY MANAGEMENT TECHNIQUES AND TOOLS*

Joseph E. Champoux, Ph.D.
The Robert O. Anderson Schools of Management
The University of New Mexico

Steven A. Yourstone, Ph.D.
The Robert O. Anderson Schools of Management
The University of New Mexico

6.1   Introduction

6.2   Summary of Total Quality Management

6.3   Total Quality Management and Nonprofit Organizations

6.4   Continuous Improvement in Total Quality Management

6.5   The Process Focus of Total Quality Management

6.6   Training Plan and Training Program

References

*Part of this chapter appeared originally in J.E. Champoux and L.D. Goldman, "Building a Total Quality Culture," in T.D. Connors (Ed.), *Nonprofit Organizations Policies and Procedures Handbook* (New York: Wiley, 1993), pp. 54-55. Copyright©1993 by John Wiley & Sons, Inc. Reprinted by permission of John Wiley & Sons, Inc.

6.1 INTRODUCTION

This discussion of quality management tools and techniques and ways of training volunteers in their use begins with a brief overview of total quality management and its application to nonprofit organizations. If you have a good background in the ideas and processes of total quality management, you can skip to Section 6.4. From that section on, the subject is the continuous improvement emphasis of TQM, process analysis, and process analysis tools. The chapter closes with an outline of a plan and program to train paid staff and volunteers to do process analysis.

6.2 SUMMARY OF TOTAL QUALITY MANAGEMENT

Total quality management (TQM) is a philosophy and system of management built on work dating back to the 1920s (Garvin, 1988). TQM includes a set of principles, tools, and techniques that help organizations manage for quality services, products, processes, and relationships. Although its roots are in manufacturing, it is a management system that can result in major improvements for any organization.

The goal of TQM is the management of quality. Although long-term cost reductions and increased profit often result, quality management is the focus of TQM. It applies readily to the management of service organizations, nonprofit organizations, and the internal processes of any organization or group. TQM focuses an entire organization on continuous improvement in its product or service.

TQM forces a total systems view of management that reaches well beyond the boundary of the organization. It uses an understanding of interdependence with outside people, outside organizations, and groups within the organization to improve its quality management. The list of those stakeholders—groups with an interest in the organization's activities—is long. It includes employees, vendors, suppliers, donors, board members, volunteers, clients, customers, patrons, constituents, members, the community surrounding the organization, coalitions of which the organization is part, professional or trade associations, chapters of the organization, and competitors for the same funds or clients.

TQM can bring many benefits to organizations that do not result directly from other approaches to management. Managers (executive directors, managers, program directors, administrators, development directors) can expect lower costs of providing a service, doing research, starting a social issue campaign, or manufacturing a product. Service processes will function more dependably. Research will be more focused and cost-effective. Issues can be targeted and communicated more effectively. Products will have higher reliability.

Employee, board, and volunteer commitment to continuous quality improvement will increase. The result can be more loyalty to the organization, improved funding potential, easier volunteer and board recruitment, and more lasting social change. TQM's assumption of high interdependence among many system parts to get continuous quality improvement can lead to better cooperation and clarity with outside contractors, suppliers, vendors, coalition partners, and the community.

TQM differs from other systems of management in specific ways. It is a way of managing that differs from what most organizations have done in the past. TQM emphasizes a long-term commitment to continuous quality improvement. TQM stresses that quality is everyone's job, not only the job of a hospital's quality assurance department, the executive director of a refugee services center, or the administrator of a cooperative pottery studio. It is intensely client focused, a focus it requires of all members of the organization.

TQM emphasizes cooperation among people in any unit that has adopted TQM and with people outside the unit. TQM also emphasizes high involvement in the work process. It assumes that people want high involvement in their work or that managers and supervisors can create that involvement.

TQM emphasizes communication in all directions: top-down, bottom-up, and lateral. This feature follows directly from the requirements of cooperation and high involvement. It is also a way TQM generates large amounts of information in the system. Many organizations already have such communication systems. Some examples are those with experience using cross-departmental task forces; participative decision making; multicultural staffs, boards, volunteers, or clients; community and client involvement in policy development; and those with a decentralized organization design.

Managers who adopt the TQM philosophy develop a long-term orientation, a view to the future. It is not the here-and-now that is important. The decisions made today by anyone in the organization must focus on the future. Being good now is not enough. Being great is the goal—a passionate pursuit of continuous improvement.

6.3 TOTAL QUALITY MANAGEMENT AND NONPROFIT ORGANIZATIONS

Peter Drucker's analysis of high-performing nonprofit organizations (Drucker, 1989, 1990) suggests they have many features that support a move toward TQM. The strongest supportive features are a mission focus, a client focus, and self-motivated volunteers.

A mission focus gives people in the organization a clear sense of direction and reason for being. A strong client focus keeps the nonprofit organization focused on client needs. Both foci can remind members of the organization of the need for constant improvement in what they offer to their environment. Self-motivated volunteers are a key way in which nonprofit organizations attain their mission. They already want to do well. TQM can show them how to do better continuously.

Drucker's observations for high-performing nonprofit organizations should have reminded you of the description of TQM above. If your organization is not performing as well as it can, then TQM can help improve its performance in the following ways.

TQM's emphasis on continuous improvement of all processes in an organization will let nonprofit organizations do more with fewer, equal, or new dollars (Kotler and Roberto, 1989). The agitation to do more for a nonprofit organization's clients is consistent with the philosophies of those organizations and the philosophies of staff and volunteers. Involvement of everyone in continuous improvement can add challenge to employees' and volunteers' jobs. The long-run effect for a nonprofit organization is a highly committed corps of people with an impassioned focus on mission and client.

6.4 CONTINUOUS IMPROVEMENT IN TOTAL QUALITY MANAGEMENT

The continuous improvement emphasis of TQM does not accept satisfaction with current performance in meeting customer needs, desires, and expectations. This focus wants people to continually examine an organization's processes to get error-free performance. Meeting customer expectations remains a continual focus while improving processes with process analysis.

The continuous-improvement focus of TQM is sometimes strange to people. It becomes clearer when it is compared to a more common way of dealing with problems—fixing them after they happen. For example, a failed machine in a manufacturing process gets the immediate attention of the maintenance staff. Employees work overtime to fix errors discovered in posting accounts payable. Delays caused by errors in a report can require sending the report by overnight mail to meet a deadline.

Continuous improvement is driven by the motto: "Get it right the first time." Eliminating the root causes of problems becomes important to let an organization meet immediate customer needs while pursuing continuous quality improvement. The long-run approach of TQM urges people to work relentlessly at process analysis to "get it right the first time."

6.5 THE PROCESS FOCUS OF TOTAL QUALITY MANAGEMENT

A process is a sequence of repeated activities with measurable inputs and outputs. Activities in the process transform the inputs into the outputs. A key question from TQM is whether those activities have any non-value-adding steps that introduce poor quality into the output. The process analysis tools described later help find such steps.

The process focus of TQM views organizations as a series of process flows. There is a chain of customers and suppliers, some inside and some outside the organization. The work of the organization happens within processes that can snake through many functions and departments. The process focus of TQM contrasts sharply with the more common functional and hierarchical view of an organization. TQM views organizations as a set of process flows, not hierarchical relationships.

Exhibit 6–1 is an example of a process view of an organization. It shows how many insurance companies process a life insurance application (Hammer, 1990). The part of the process involving the customer happens outside the organization. Other parts clearly happen inside the organization.

(a) Process Variability

All processes vary in the quantity and quality of their output. TQM focuses on eliminating defects by identifying root causes of variability and continuously reducing them over time. It views variability as an enemy of quality and seeks continuous quality improvement by systematically reducing or removing root causes (Montgomery, 1991, ch. 4).

◆ **EXHIBIT 6–1   Life Insurance Application Process**

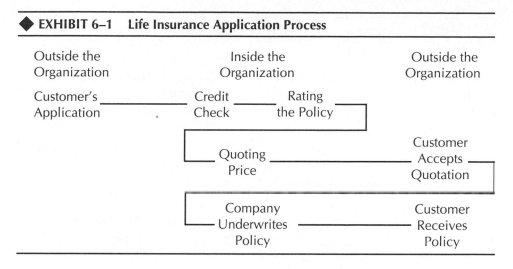

Process variability comes from two main sources: chance (or random) causes and assignable (or special) causes. *Chance causes* are sources of normal variability of a process (Shewhart, 1931). They are not attributable to a specific person, machine, or action. If chance causes are the only source of variability, the process is behaving properly. *Assignable causes* are sources of abnormal variability that are attributable to a specific person, machine, or action. Bad raw materials, incorrect machine adjustments, poor systems, and people errors are examples of assignable causes.

Both sources of variability are targets for continuous quality improvement, but the methods used to reduce the sources are different. Variability from assignable causes produces poor-quality product or service now. Managers and employees in the process must respond quickly to remove assignable causes so that product or service returns to desired quality levels. For example, a power surge creates computer errors while people use word processors to prepare forms. Putting surge protectors between the computers and the power source can remove that assignable cause.

Chance causes of variability are the targets of efforts to squeeze process variability to lower and lower levels. Although the process yields a quality level that is acceptable, continuous improvement says "keep trying to get better." There are two approaches to squeezing chance causes of process variability to lower and lower levels. One approach designs products, processes, and services to be robust. Robust design lets a product, process, or service react less to sources of variation from people, methods, materials, temperatures, and so on (Lochner and Matar, 1990).

The second approach uses process analysis to find process improvements that reduce chance causes. Process analysis helps reduce many sources of chance variation. Cutting some process steps, redesigning business forms, and so on, help minimize process variability. For example, clerks make errors when entering standard information on forms. Preprinting the standard information on the forms prevents clerks from making such errors.

◆   **EXHIBIT 6–2**   Summary of Total Quality Management Tools and Techniques

---

Checksheet

A structured method of collecting quantitative data about the results of a process. A checksheet helps the user count items, such as number of defects or types of defects in a product.

Pareto Chart

A bar chart that displays the bars in descending order according to height. Each bar represents a problem measured in the same units. Pareto charts let you isolate the major problems from the minor ones.

Control Chart

A line graph that shows the performance of a process over time. The user compares the line showing actual performance to previously computed upper and lower limits of process performance. It quickly shows whether the variability in a process is within or outside the control limits.

Flowchart

A diagram that shows the steps and relationships among steps in a process. The flowchart uses different symbols to show action steps, decision steps, and waiting periods.

Cause–and–Effect Diagram

A drawing that shows the relationship between a problem and its probable causes. The diagram shows relationships among the factors that can affect the variability of a process.

(b) Process Analysis Tools and Techniques

The five process analysis tools are shown in Exhibit 6–2. The five tools are related. It is often necessary to use all the process analysis tools to find the causes of process problems. Each tool gives the user a unique insight into a problem area. When all tools are used together, a complete picture of process problems emerges.

A *checksheet* is a structured method of collecting quantitative data about the results of a process. It lets the user count items such as number of defects or types of defects in a product. It can also assess a service process by counting types of customer complaints or types of customer returns. Checksheets answer the question: "How often are certain events happening?"

Exhibit 6–3 shows a sample checksheet for monitoring mismatches among purchase orders, receiving documents, and invoices in an accounts payable process (Hammer, 1990). Each document usually must match before a company pays an invoice. Matched documents say that payment is requested (invoice) for goods that were requested (purchase order) and received (receiving report).

The checksheet in Exhibit 6–3 shows a record of events in one week. Accounts payable clerks note each mismatch for a day in three expected sources of errors by marking with a "/." The notations on a series of checksheets are basic data for further analysis with a Pareto chart.

◆ **EXHIBIT 6–3   Checksheet: Monitoring the Accounts Payable Process Source of Errors in Mismatches**

Error Source	Day of Week					Total
	Mon	Tues	Wed	Thurs	Fri	
Purchase order		//		/		3
Receiving document	/				/	2
Invoice	/		////	/		5
Total	2	2	3	2	1	10

A *Pareto chart* is a vertical bar chart displaying the bars in descending order according to height. Each bar is a problem measured in the same units. Pareto charts let you isolate major problems from minor ones. They were named for Vilfredo Pareto (1848-1923), an Italian economist who theorized that 20 percent of a society's population held 80 percent of its wealth.

Exhibit 6–4 shows a Pareto chart for the data collected with checksheets. The left axis shows the units of measurement used to collect the data, here as errors in a document. The right axis shows a percentage scale for the percentage of total errors. The line over the bars from the left axis to right axis shows the cumulative percentage of errors.

The Pareto chart in Exhibit 6–4 shows receiving reports as a key source of errors in mismatches. A second source is invoices and a distant third is the purchase order. This chart suggests focusing process improvement attention on preparation of receiving reports. Perhaps it is lack of clarity in writing the receiving information. It also could be the number of copies prepared that does not let the recorded information appear clearly on multiple copies.

Linking Pareto charts can increase their effectiveness. Exhibit 6–4, for example, shows receiving reports as a key source of errors. The receiving reports could be analyzed for their Pareto distribution of errors using different Pareto charts. The errors could be analyzed by when, where, who, what, and how many. Such Pareto analyses could show when the errors occur, where they occur on the form, and who is making the errors.

A *control chart* is a line graph showing the performance of a process over time (Montgomery, 1991, ch. 4). The user compares the line showing actual performance to previously computed upper and lower limits of process performance. The control chart can show quickly whether the variability of a process is within or outside those limits. When the variability is outside the limits, the process has an unacceptable amount of variation.

Exhibit 6–5 shows some control charts. The vertical axis of a control chart is a measure of a quality characteristic of interest. The center line is the average performance of the process for the period shown by the chart. Upper and lower control limits are boundaries that define the area of acceptable process behavior. If observations fall outside the limits, the process is out of control (Exhibit 6–5*b*).

◆ **EXHIBIT 6–4 Pareto Chart: Source of Errors in Mismatches**

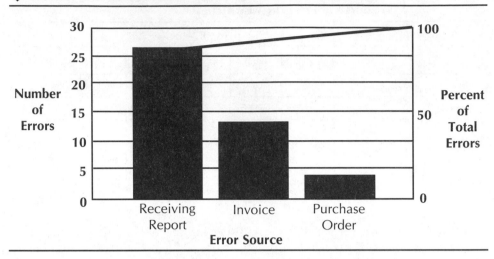

A process is also out of control when observations follow a consistent pattern between the control limits (Exhibit 6–5*c* and *d*). Observations toward the end of the period all clustered below or above the center line. Such patterns do not have the randomness shown in Exhibit 6–5*a*. The three instances of a process out of statistical control are targets for problem solution and process improvement.

Flowcharting is a diagram and technique that lets you understand the steps in a process. It is a simple and powerful tool borrowed from systems analysis and computer programming. Flowcharts show the flows within and across the functional areas of an organization. An analysis of the chart can show non-value-added steps such as waiting, checking, and returning to previously entered functions. The chart can also show places where people can make mistakes. For example, typing information that is common to all forms, such as a company's address, creates repeated chances for typographical errors. Discovering such steps from a flowchart can lead to finding a solution.

Flowcharts are excellent planning tools for control charts. A flowchart can tell a user where to put control charts to monitor defects and time at key process steps. They can show where process redesign or additional training might be needed.

Exhibit 6–6 shows some common flowcharting symbols. Templates and software exist to allow easy preparation of flowcharts. One maps the steps in a process, either individually or in a team, to understand the process. The flowchart becomes a picture of the process that many people can view.

The flowchart should include all parts of a process as it actually operates, including informal processes. A complete picture of how a process works can emerge in a complete flowchart created by those involved in the process. A major benefit of flowcharting comes from its ability to clarify misunderstandings about how a process works. It also becomes the basic document for finding non-value-adding steps in the process and reducing or dropping them. Exhibit 6–7 shows a flowchart for the accounts payable process discussed earlier. It shows movement of documents across various functions, such as purchasing, receiving, and accounts payable. The chart includes the vendor, although it is outside the organization. The vendor obviously plays a key role because of the preparation of invoices.

◆ **EXHIBIT 6-5** Control Chart

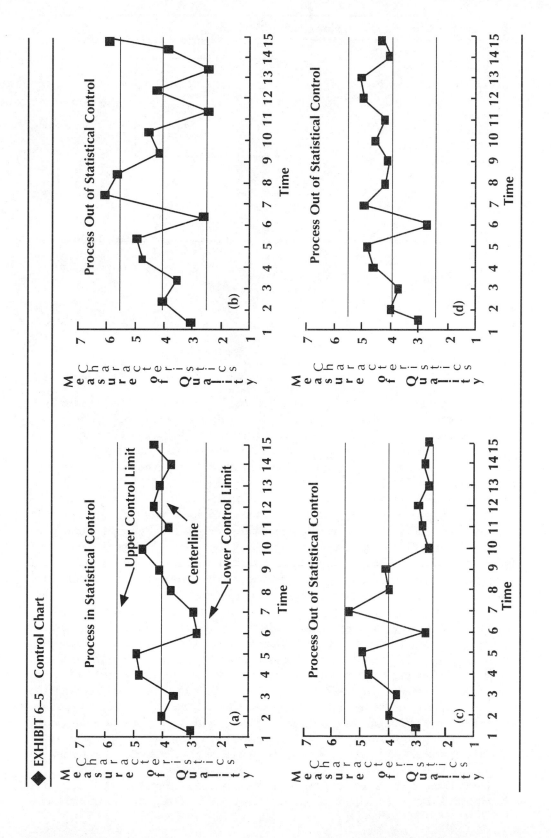

◆ **EXHIBIT 6–6   Common Flowcharting Symbols**

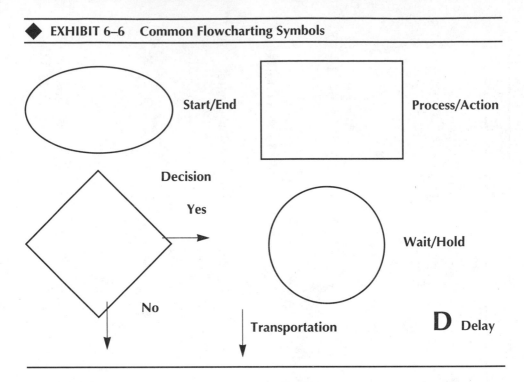

The flowchart of Exhibit 6–7 highlights the flows across functions and efforts toward manual matching of information from different documents. Each person who prepares a document can introduce error. Each document comparison can cause errors when an employee says that a document does not match when they do, or says they match when they do not. The latter could result in paying an invoice for goods not received.

A *cause-and-effect diagram* is a drawing showing the relationship between a problem and its probable causes. It is also called a *fishbone diagram* because of its appearance. Kaoru Ishikawa developed the cause-and-effect diagram to guide people systematically through an analysis of probable causes (Ishikawa, 1982). The diagram shows relationships among factors that can affect the variability of a process. It is a systematic and graphic way of analyzing a process after understanding its steps from a flowchart. Cause-and-effect diagrams are excellent complements to a flowchart.

Exhibit 6–8 shows a simple cause-and-effect diagram for the accounts payable process. Cause-and-effect diagrams group causes of errors into major categories, those in Exhibit 6–8 being the functional areas where mismatches in the accounts payable process can happen. Such diagrams guide users toward sources of errors within each category. Groups can use these diagrams to help in process analysis, and individuals can use them if the program is not complex. Within each category, one speculates about causes. In a group approach with a diagram, the analysis can use a crude brainstorming approach featuring a freewheeling listing of possible causes. As the analysis continues, the probable causes become refined from discussion and agreement.

Linked cause-and-effect diagrams produce a focused analysis. For example, Exhibit 6–8 shows receiving as a causal category. A new diagram can show receiv-

◆ **EXHIBIT 6–7   Flowchart of Accounts Payable Process**

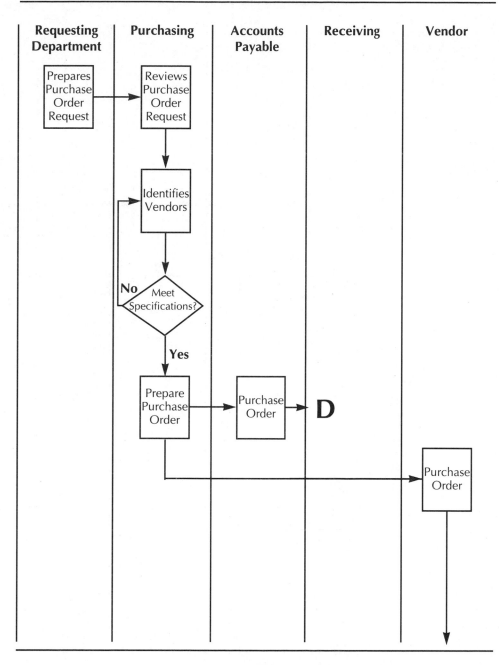

ing as the effect of interest and the causal categories for problems in receiving. The analysis progresses through layers of understanding of the root cause of problems in a process.

Such diagrams can become complex, with many categories, probable causes, and relationships among causes. Their strength lies in the structure they give to the analysis and the picture of the flow of cause and effects in a process.

◆   **EXHIBIT 6–7**   **Flowchart of Accounts Payable Process (Cont.)**

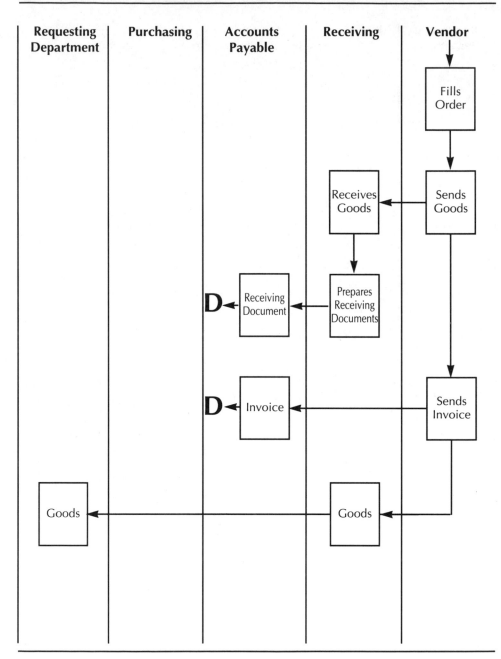

6.6   TRAINING PLAN AND TRAINING PROGRAM

An organization can develop a training plan and a training program to train paid staff and volunteers in quality management techniques and tools. This section outlines the steps for building a training plan. The plan describes the goals of the train-

◆ **EXHIBIT 6–7   Flowchart of Accounts Payable Process (Cont.)**

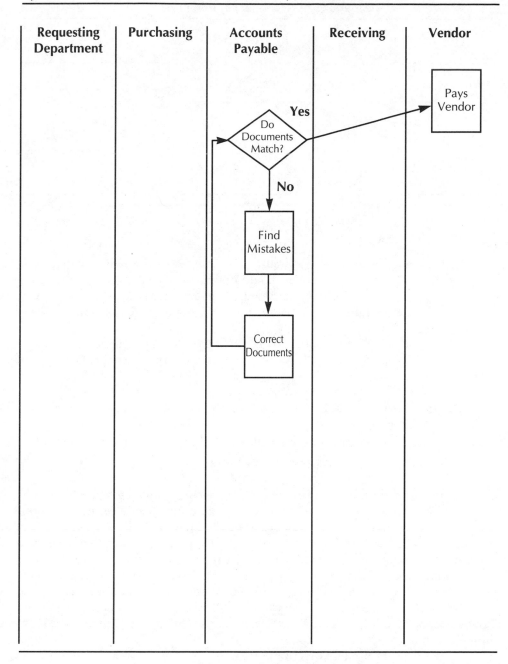

Requesting Department	Purchasing	Accounts Payable	Receiving	Vendor

ing, the training target, its content, training resources, and training media that an organization wants to use in a training program. It also includes a schedule and a cost budget. A later section broadly outlines a training program that an organization can tailor to its specific needs.

◆ **EXHIBIT 6–8**   **Cause-and-Effect Diagram:**
                              Mismatches in Accounts Payable Process

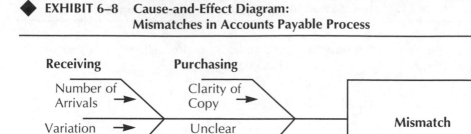

(a) Training Plan

A written training plan helps guide an organization toward a systematic training program for its members. The plan should describe the goals of the training, the people who will receive the training, training resources or media, a time budget, and a cost budget. Exhibit 6–9 outlines the major parts of a training plan as a series of steps.

The training plan first describes the goals of the training. The goals should be specific, reachable, and tied to the major activities of the organization. Examples of goals include:

- Building awareness of TQM among members of the organization, both paid and volunteer
- Developing knowledge of process analysis and of its tools and techniques
- Developing skills in doing process analysis

The training plan next describes the target of the training—the people in the organization who will receive the training. For the training to have the most positive effect on an organization, it should not be limited to volunteers; all paid and volunteer staff should be included. The order in which people are trained then becomes important. We recommend a top-down approach, starting with the director or other senior executive and his or her top staff, followed by people at the next level of the organization. Volunteers and paid staff who are at equal organization levels should be trained at the same time. Other sequences of training can use cross-sections of the organization, especially when building cross-functional continuous improvement teams.

The training plan broadly describes the content of the training. It describes the major topics in the training and some aspects of desired approaches to the training. The major topics of interest in quality management techniques and tools include (1) TQM awareness training, if it has not already been done; (2) process analysis; and (3) process analysis tools and techniques.

The form of the training can include a seminar discussion format, lecture, and activity-based training. Training that actively involves participants in process flow-

◆ **EXHIBIT 6–9 Steps to a Training Plan**

charting, Pareto analysis, and the like will hold interest longer than a lecture format. Using your organization's processes as examples for analysis will also increase the reality and perceived practicality of the training. Short cases drawn from experiences of people in the organization also are highly effective training tools.

Many resources and media exist to do quality management tools and techniques training: print publications, videotapes, audiotapes, and television. A later section serves as a resource for materials to include in a training program.

The training plan then describes the training: when it will happen, where it will happen, and who is scheduled for specific training sessions. The timing is tied directly to the goals of the training and the target groups. For example, TQM awareness training typically precedes training for process analysis. If you use a top-down training approach, people at the top of the organization should be scheduled before people at lower levels.

The last part of the training plan is a cost budget. It obviously is an important part of the plan because of the resource implications for any organization. A cost budge estimates the amount of money needed for each type and phase of training. It also allows an analysis of the benefit expected from specific training and the associated costs.

(b) Training Program

A training program for quality management tools and techniques includes the topical content, the various resources from which the program can draw, and the media of presentation. There is much variety in all those areas, which lets you tailor the program to the needs of your organization.

(i) Training Content

TQM awareness training is a typical starting point of a quality management training program. Such training usually takes three to four hours and should cover the following topics:

- *Total quality management:* its characteristics and its history
- *Continuous improvement:* what it is and how it differs from simply accepting quality as it stands
- *The process focus of TQM:* a description and comparison with more traditional ways of viewing an organization
- *The customer focus of TQM:* understanding customer expectations and meeting or exceeding them

Typical awareness training assumes that participants have no background in TQM other than having heard about it from associates or in press descriptions.

Training in process analysis and process analysis tools and techniques follows the awareness training. Such training usually takes about three full days and should focus on the following:

- A process view of organizations
- The steps in doing a process analysis
- The major tools and techniques of process analysis

The probable tools and techniques that should be the focus of this training were described earlier.

An organization can get maximum benefit from process analysis training when it uses its processes for analysis during the training. For example, hospital volunteers who work in admission and discharge areas could be trained in doing process analysis by focusing on the hospital's admission and discharge processes. The process is real to them and something they interact with regularly. This approach to learning process analysis and associated tools and techniques can show the immediate application of what they are learning.

(ii) Training Resources and Media

There are highly varied training resources available for quality management training. The media of presentation are equally rich in variety and go well beyond the typical classroom approach to such training. Training resources and media include print publications, audiotapes, videotapes, workshops, and television based training.

Exhibit 6–10 lists selected print publications and their sources. Many publishers now have books on TQM, process analysis, and related topics such as team building. Such publications can be used individually by paid staff and volunteers. They serve as useful training resources in the workshops described later. They also can form the basis of discussions within the organization during regular meetings such

---

◆ **EXHIBIT 6–10   Publications**

Berry, Leonard I., and A. Parasuraman. *Marketing Services: Competing Through Quality.* New York: Free Press, 1991.

> Describes a customer-focused marketing orientation for service organizations

Champoux, Joseph E., and Lenore B. Goldman. "Building a Total Quality Culture." In T.D. Connors (Ed.), *Nonprofit Organizations Policies and Procedures Handbook.* New York: Wiley, 1993, Chapter 3.

> Describes total quality management and building quality- and customer-oriented cultures in nonprofit organizations.

Galloway, Diane. *Mapping Work Processes.* Milwaukee, Wis.: American Society for Quality Control Press, 1994.

> Describes procedures for describing or mapping work processes. It shows how to choose a process for mapping, how to do the mapping, and how to use a process map to improve the process.

Garvin, David A. *Managing Quality: The Strategic and Competitive Edge.* New York: Free Press, 1988.

> A solid introduction to managing for quality and using it strategically. Has a good history of the evolution of quality management in the United States and Japan. Excellent bibliography.

Harrington, H. James. *Business Process Improvement.* Milwaukee, Wis.: American Society for Quality Control Press, 1991.

> Describes how to assess customer needs and expectations and deliver the level of service that meets them. It shows you how to decide which processes drive the organization, which ones are working, and which need to be introduced. The book also describes how to create process improvement teams, train team leaders, and how to carry out appropriate changes.

Wilson, Paul F., Larry D. Dell, and Gaylord F. Anderson. *Root Cause Analysis* (with workbook). Milwaukee, Wis.: American Society for Quality Control Press, 1993.

> Describes root cause analysis, a key tool for reaching and maintaining excellence and getting continuous quality improvement. The workbook has four case studies that illustrate the application of root cause analysis tools.

---

as staff meetings.

Exhibit 6–11 lists some audiotapes and their sources. Audiotapes are especially suitable for use by individuals or in a guided discussion group that uses a workshop format. People can listen to such tapes at times that fit their personal learning styles and schedules. Many publishers offer audiotapes on approval or offer preview tapes. The tapes should be reviewed before purchase to ensure that they will fit the organization's needs.

Exhibit 6–12 lists selected videotapes and their sources. There are many sources for videotapes, although the Society of Manufacturing Engineers (SME) and the American Society for Quality Control (ASQC) have especially rich collections. Because of their source, they usually focus on manufacturing or service environments, but their content applies to most organizations. Previewing the titles that interest you, or getting an overview videotape, will help to assess their suitability for your organization.

Workshops are a training medium that allows interaction between the trainer and the participants. They typically are offered by private or academically based consultants, private organizations such as the American Society of Quality Control and the American Management Association, or as credit and noncredit courses by colleges and universities. Quality management workshops might also be offered or sponsored by associations to which you or your organization belong.

Outside workshops usually are held at a facility away from the organization. Hotels and convention centers are typical sites for quality management workshops. Participants come from different organizations with the advantage of offering many viewpoints on quality management issues. Outside workshops can have the disadvantage of not focusing on issues unique to your organization or volunteer management.

In-house workshops can be designed for your organization and the issues important to it. Trainers for in-house workshops usually are academic or private

---

◆ EXHIBIT 6–11   Audiotapes

Building a Customer-Driven Organization™: *The Manager's Role.* CareerTrack Publications, 3085 Center Green Drive, P.O. Box 18778, Boulder, CO 80308-1778. (800) 334-1018.

> Describes how to build a customer focus in an organization. An advanced look at customer service and building commitment to customers in an organization.

Implementing Total Quality Management ™: *How to Make TQM Work in Your Organization.* CareerTrack Publications, 3085 Center Green Drive, P.O. Box 18778, Boulder, CO 80308-1778. (800) 334-1018.

> An introduction to total quality management. Discusses the costs of quality and how to get an organization headed in the right direction.
> A companion to the videotape described in Exhibit 6–12.

Managing Today's Nonprofit Organization. CareerTrack Publications, 3085 Center Drive, P.O. Box 18778, Boulder, CO 80308. (800) 334-1018.

> Discusses the changes in nonprofit organization's environments and the management responses that are needed to meet new challenges. Includes board relationships, fund-raising errors, and writing grant proposals.

◆ **EXHIBIT 6–12   Videotapes**

Implementing Total Quality Management. CareerTrack Publications, 3085 Center Green Drive, P.O. Box 18778, Boulder, CO 80308-1778. (800) 334-1018.

> An introduction to total quality management. Discusses the costs of quality and how to get an organization headed in a quality direction.

Quality and Productivity Improvement through Statistical Methods. Society of Manufacturing Engineers, One SME Drive, P.O. Box 930, Dearborn, MI 48121-0930. (800) 733-4SME.

> Two videotapes, an instructor's guide, and a participant's package that is a course in statistical process control. Presents many process analysis tools described in this chapter. Although this videotape and others from the same source have a manufacturing focus, the underlying observations are the same for nonprofit organizations.

Quality Service: A Commitment to Customer Satisfaction. American Society for Quality Control, P.O. Box 3005, Milwaukee, WI 53201-3005. (414) 272-8575. Running time: 17:35.

> Brief visits with an airline, bank, hospital, electric utility, and hotel. Shows how service operations can pursue continuous improvement.

Total Quality Management—The First Steps. Society of Manufacturing Engineers, One SME Drive, P.O. Box 930, Dearborn, MI 48121-0930. (800) 733-4SME.

> Offers an overview of total quality management. Describes many cases studies of carrying out quality management in major U.S. manufacturing organizations.

Total Quality Management—Creating a Culture of Continuous Improvement. Society of Manufacturing Engineers, One SME Drive, P.O. Box 930, Dearborn, MI 48121-0930. (800) 733-4SME.

Continues from the "The First Steps" videotape described above. Discusses the major reasons that organizations do not reach their goals of managing for quality.

consultants. Such workshops would often only have participants from the paid and volunteer staff of one organization. If there are not enough participants from a single organization, you could try to build a consortium of organizations in your area to get a large enough group. Twenty to thirty people is a good size for most quality management workshops.

Extensive television-based quality management training resources and media are available to many organizations in two forms: satellite television training broadcast from private and public sources, and instructional television from many colleges and universities.

The U.S. Chamber of Commerce in Washington, D.C., offers quality management training throughout the year as part of their Quality Learning Series®. Your local Chamber of Commerce should have information on the topics available, current costs, and locations receiving the broadcasts. The National University

Teleconference Network at Oklahoma State University also offers credit and non-credit courses in quality management and related topics.

Instructional television is offered by many colleges and universities throughout the United States and Canada. This medium broadcasts credit and noncredit courses to receiving sites throughout a specific area. Colleges and universities that offer instructional television often can receive programs from satellite sources and broadcast the program to the local community. Contact the colleges and universities in your area to see whether such televised instruction is available, the courses offered, and the methods of receiving the programs.

This chapter's description of quality management techniques and tools should help guide your thinking about a training program for paid staff and volunteers in your organization. With the rich and varied training resources and media now available, an organization can tailor a quality management training program to its needs and the learning styles of its members.

REFERENCES

Drucker, Peter F. 1989. "What Business Can Learn from Nonprofits." *Harvard Business Review* 67(4) (July–August): 88–91.

Drucker, Peter F. 1990. *Managing the Nonprofit Organization.* New York: HarperCollins.

Garvin, David A. 1988. *Managing Quality: The Strategic and Competitive Edge.* New York: Free Press.

Hammer, Michael. 1990. "Reengineering Work: Don't Automate, Obliterate." *Harvard Business Review* 68(4) (July–August): 104–111.

Ishikawa, Kaoru. 1982. *Guide to Quality Control.* Tokyo: Asian Productivity Organization.

Kotler, Philip, and Edwardo L. Roberto. 1989. *Social Marketing: Strategies for Changing Public Behavior.* New York: Free Press.

Lochner, Robert H., Joseph E. Matar. 1990. *Designing for Quality: An Introduction to the Best of Taguchi and Western Methods of Statistical Experimental Design.* Milwaukee, Wisc.: American Society for Quality Control Press.

Montgomery, Douglas C. 1991. *Introduction to Statistical Quality Control.* New York: Wiley.

Shewhart, Walter A. 1931. *Economic Control of Quality of Manufactured Product.* New York: Van Nostrand.

VOLUNTEER MANAGEMENT

CHAPTER 7
Policies for Volunteer Programs

CHAPTER 8
Administration of Volunteer Programs

CHAPTER 9
Episodic Volunteering

CHAPTER 10
Volunteer and Staff Relations

CHAPTER 11
Reward and Recognition Systems for Volunteers

CHAPTER 12
The Role of Volunteers in Fund-Raising

CHAPTER 13
Managing Corporate and Employee Volunteer Programs

CHAPTER 7

POLICIES FOR VOLUNTEER PROGRAMS*

Linda L. Graff
Graff and Associates

7.1   Introduction

7.2   What Are Policies?

7.3   Why Policies Are Written

7.4   Where Policies Are Needed

7.5   Policy Development Process

7.6   How to Write Policies for Volunteer Programs

7.7   Compliance

7.8   Resistance to Policy Development

7.9   Conclusions

      References

*This chapter is adapted from the monograph *By Definition: Policies for Volunteer Programs* (Graff, 1992), used here with the generous permission of the publisher, Volunteer Ontario.

All of this is a far cry from the days when an agency staff member would pick up the phone periodically and call in some friends and neighbours to help with the task at hand. (Nora Silver, 1988, p. 86)

7.1 INTRODUCTION

There are many excellent reasons to write policies around voluntary action in non-profit organizations. Such policies can be used to establish continuity, to ensure fairness and equity, to clarify values and beliefs, to communicate expectations, to specify standards, and to state rules. There is no more compelling reason for immediate policy development, however, than fear of the consequences of not doing so.

Consider the situation described in Exhibit 7–1. If this happened in your volunteer program, you would probably be wringing your hands, rushing to check your insurance coverage, and wondering where things went wrong. The fact is that this kind of example, and thousands like it, describe accidents waiting to happen in volunteer programs all over North America. And while there is nothing anyone can do to guarantee that injuries and loss will not occur as the result of volunteering, there are many things that agency administrators and managers of volunteers can do to help prevent serious incidents and to minimize harm and reduce liability when they do occur. Policy development is one of the most critical of those. This chapter will define policies and procedures, discuss how policies fit in an overall risk management program, and outline four important types and functions of policies. Included are descriptions of the policy development process, how to write policies, and how to increase compliance with policies.

7.2 WHAT ARE POLICIES?

(a) Definitions of Policy and Procedure

The word *policy* is one with which we are all familiar, yet for most people it is difficult to identify exactly what it means in the context of our agencies and programs.

◆ **EXHIBIT 7–1   Case Study**

Sandy, a volunteer friendly visitor in a program for isolated seniors, arrived for her regular shift at her client's house to find the client quite unwell. The client, Mrs. Fritz, didn't want to make a fuss and tried to keep Sandy from notifying anyone, but finally allowed her to call the family doctor. The doctor said, "Bring her in." While driving wasn't really part of the volunteer job, Sandy thought it important to get help right away and drove Mrs. Fritz over to the doctor's office.

The doctor thought that Mrs. Fritz might have had a mild heart attack, scheduled some tests, and told Sandy to take her home. Sandy objected, but when the physician insisted, Sandy helped Mrs. Fritz into the car and they headed off home. On the way, Mrs. Fritz cried out, put her hands to her chest, and slumped forward. Sandy reached over to hold Mrs. Fritz up, and drove into a tree.

It is difficult to sort out what a policy is, how it differs from a procedure, and the respective roles of each. The very word policy can be intimidating. Few people work with policies on a regular basis. Most do not have the opportunity to understand policy or to feel at ease with it.

There are a variety of perspectives on what policy is or should be. A number of definitions of policy are presented here, because each offers different elements of what policies are and what they can achieve. *Webster's New World Dictionary* (Second College Edition) defines policy as "a principle, plan, or course of action." Two distinct themes emerge from this definition:

1. Policy, in the sense of a principle, implies that some kind of position is being taken, that a value or belief is being stated.
2. Policy, in the sense of a plan or a course of action, would include specific steps, procedures, or perhaps a method.

Both of these aspects of the definition of policies are relevant because nonprofit organizations need to articulate their values and also need to have procedural guidelines in place to instruct staff (paid and unpaid) on what to do or not to do.

Robert Shaw (1990) adds some thoughts on the nature of policies:

◆ They apply to everybody associated with the organization: its directors, staff, volunteers, and clients.

Policies from the top of the organization typically have organization-wide applicability. For example, organizations develop board policy statements on philosophy, values, and beliefs that apply to all aspects of the organization. Here is an example from the Volunteer Centre of Metropolitan Toronto that has implications for both external programming (who is eligible for service) and internal operations (who is hired as paid staff, who is recruited as a volunteer, how promotions are determined):

> The Volunteer Centre of Metropolitan Toronto is committed to ensuring that its mission and operations embrace the community. It actively encourages the community to participate fully and benefit fully from its services. The Volunteer Centre . . . is committed to racial equality and the elimination of racism in Metro Toronto. It strives to reflect the community in its structure (volunteer and staff) and to promote equal access to its services. (Volunteer Centre of Metropolitan Toronto, 1993)

Typically, policies at this level will be the responsibility of senior administration, both paid and unpaid. Input from staff, direct-service volunteers, and other organizational stakeholders may be invited, but the board is the key player in this kind of policymaking.

Many policies are much more specific and much more limited in scope. For example, organizations write policies about whether or not the newsletter volunteers in the home support program must pay for the coffee they drink while on duty. This too is a policy matter, but with limited applicability, influence, and import. Policies of this nature are less likely to receive board and CEO attention. Rather, they are more likely to be the responsibility of departmental staff or program committees, although in smaller organizations, boards will sometimes involve themselves in policy matters of this sort.

7.3 WHY POLICIES ARE WRITTEN

(a) Why Now?

The convergence of several key trends in the voluntary sector is beginning to compel us to develop policies for volunteer programs. Among these trends are the:

◆ Changing nature of volunteering
◆ Increasing degree of risk associated with volunteering
◆ Deficit of organizational and administrative support for volunteer programs
◆ Increasingly litigational nature of our culture

Volunteer work is increasingly responsible, sophisticated, and complex. It constitutes the "real work" of voluntary organizations. In fact, a great many voluntary organizations would see their work grind to a halt without the contributions of volunteers. Volunteers themselves are increasingly skilled and educated, and looking to apply their expertise through voluntary action.

◆ A policy states a boundary: inside the boundary, things are acceptable; outside the boundary, things are not.
◆ It is also in the nature of a policy that violations make one liable for consequences; in that sense, a policy is tough.

Paula Cryderman, who has written a manual on how to write policy manuals, helps clarify the difference between policies and procedures. She says policies tell people *what* to do:

> Policies form the written basis of operation secondary to legislation and the organization's bylaws. They serve as guidelines for decision making; they prescribe limits and pinpoint responsibilities within an organization. Policies can be viewed as rules or laws related to the facility's overall mission, goals and objectives. They are usually broad statements that are general in content. Despite this, policies may be detailed and particular if appropriate to the subject matter. (Cryderman, 1987, p. 10)

On the other hand, procedures tell people *how* to do what they must do. According to Cryderman:

> Procedures give directions according to which daily operations are conducted within the framework of policies. They are a natural outgrowth of policies, supplying the "how to" for the rule. Procedures describe a series of steps, outline sequences of activities or detail progression. Thus the procedure manual is operational and is usually best expressed in a directive tone. (1987, p. 10)

Cryderman says that the terms policy and procedure should not be confused, yet in practice it is often difficult to distinguish between types of policies, or between policies and procedures. The distinction drawn above—policy as *what* and procedure as *how*—seems straightforward, but in reality the distinction blurs.

(b) Levels of Policy

When we think about the term policy we usually think about statements issued from the highest levels of the organization terms that are both general in nature and broad in scope. Proclamations issued from senior administration often take the form of policy statements. In fact, John Carver, who writes about policy governance by boards of directors, says "Conventionally, policy has referred to any board utterance" (Carver, 1990, p. 28). Simply put, the more responsible and complex the work, the greater the risks associated with its completion. If volunteers are rolling bandages, for example, dangers are minimal. But consider these actual examples:

◆ Volunteers providing home support for the disabled are helping to transfer patients in and out of the bathtub without training.

◆ Volunteer counsellors staff a suicide prevention hot line with little training, and they have no professional backup while on duty.

◆ A volunteer friendly visitor drives his client to the grocery store each week to help her do her shopping. If he were to be stopped, his car would be pulled off the road for noncompliance with safety regulations.

◆ A volunteer at the local senior citizen center has some first-aid training and has been helping seniors make some decisions about which of their prescription medications they should and should not bother to take.

◆ An elderly woman who has been a volunteer escort at the cancer treatment center for over two decades is beginning to lose her faculties. Last week she took a patient in a wheelchair to the wrong clinic, where he waited for three hours before staff were able to locate him.

◆ Female volunteers are sent out to deliver parenting education classes to single mothers in low-income housing projects. The volunteers go alone, according to their own schedule, often at night. The agency has no record of who is going where or when.

◆ Volunteers for the local environmental cleanup agency have been disabling the chain brake safety mechanisms on chain saws because the brakes make this already hard work even more arduous.

Rapid change and growth, combined with chronic underfunding of volunteer programs, have produced a gap between the real complexity of volunteer involvement and the ability of organizations to understand and manage the valuable resource they have mobilized. As Nora Silver puts it:

The future of community organizations, and the independent sector as a while, depends on the future of our volunteers. Right now that future is at risk. It is not for want of volunteers. It is not for want of good organizations providing good services. It is for want of the capacity of these good organizations to utilize people well. (Silver, 1988, p.1)

In contrast to the stereotype of volunteering held by the general public, and even by some agency managers (paid and unpaid), volunteering has developed into important work that deserves profound and immediate administrative attention. Unfortunately, administrators in many voluntary organizations do not understand that their attention is needed. Susan Ellis puts it this way:

> After years of training and consulting with so many leaders of volunteers, I have become convinced that many of their concerns stem directly from a lack of substantive support from their agencies' top administrators. This lack of support is not due to malice or unwillingness to be of help, but is rather due to the failure of executives to understand what is really needed from them. (Ellis, 1986; p. 1)

As a consequence, many large-scale, complex volunteer programs operate in a policy void, and, ironically, remain virtually invisible to the very people who will be held accountable when something goes wrong.

That someone will be held accountable for errors, omissions, accidents, injuries, or loss grows more certain every day. In this increasingly litigational culture—the "suit society," according to William Conrad and William Glenn (1976, p. 14), where people "sue anybody for anything"—voluntary organizations, and the good people who are ultimately responsible for the work undertaken in the name of the organization (themselves volunteers), simply cannot afford to ignore such exposure to liability. As Brian O'Connell indicates: "There have been several legal cases where board members were held legally accountable, largely because they had failed to exercise reasonable oversight and objectivity . . . the trustees had not taken responsibility for knowing what was going on" (1985, p. 20).

In the courts, in the press, in the public mind, boards are being held accountable for mistakes, accidents, and negligence on the part of volunteers acting on behalf of the organization. "Not knowing" simply is not a good enough excuse—legally or morally. The matter of policy development for volunteer programs has become urgent. The formula is quite simple: The greater the degree of responsibility of volunteer work itself, the greater the need for rules to govern and regulate its accomplishment; the greater the need for guidelines to ensure safety; the greater the need for policies.

(c) Policy And Risk Management

There is no more pressing reason to develop policies for volunteer programs than the role that policies play in an overall risk management system. There are several simple, straightforward risk management models that managers of volunteers can consult (McCurley, 1993; Minnesota Office on Volunteer Services, 1992; Tremper and Kostin, 1993; Vargo, Chapter 15, this volume). While each of these models is slightly different from the others, a key theme found in all of them is the need for policy development as a critical component of a comprehensive risk management program.

Policies supply rules. They establish boundaries beyond which volunteers should not wander. They specify what is and is not expected, what is and is not safe. To take the case study about Sandy and Mrs. Fritz (Exhibit 7–1), there were several points at which the presence of policies could have prevented the tragedy that occurred. For example:

- What is the agency policy regarding volunteers who are tempted to exceed the limits of their job description?

◆ What is the agency policy regarding volunteers who encounter a situation with which they feel they cannot cope or in which they feel uncomfortable making decisions?

◆ What is the agency policy regarding volunteer backup? Is there someone in authority on call at all times that volunteers are on duty—staff who can take over when the situation exceeds the limitations and responsibilities of the volunteer's role?

◆ What is the agency policy about friendly visiting volunteers driving their clients? Is it allowed? Is there a full set of policies regarding such volunteer transportation service? What is the agency policy regarding insurance coverage for nonowned automobiles?

If policies such as these had been in place and well known to Sandy, the story would most certainly have had a different outcome. The conclusions to be drawn here are obvious: Policies can play a major role in preventing accidents; and policies can serve to minimize the harm that can result from accidents. Although there is nothing that any agency can do to guarantee that accidents will not happen, policies can reduce an organization's exposure to liability in the event that a law suit is launched. For example, there is no better proof that an agency has acted prudently and responsibly in attempting to reduce the likelihood of injury or loss than a full set of current, comprehensive policies and procedures, clearly in place, and consistently communicated to all relevant parties. As Charles Tremper and Gwynne Kostin (1993, p. 11) suggest, "a written termination policy that is carefully and faithfully applied can convince a judge or jury that a supervisor did not treat an employee arbitrarily."

(d) Policies as Empowerment (Gaining Access to the Board)

Volunteer programs are typically underrecognized and underresourced. Boards and senior management have lost touch with the expansion in scale and significance of voluntary action, even in their own organizations. As Nora Silver (1988) points out, a gap has been created between the ability of managers of volunteers to create volunteer programs—to recruit, place, and supervise volunteers—and the organization's development of administrative, communications, and accountability systems to support those volunteer programs. Susan Ellis (1986, p. 1) calls this "benign neglect." Nora Silver (1988, p. 116) calls it "benign indifference." Silver says:

> The Board of Directors provides leadership to the organization: it sets overall agency policy and assumes fiscal responsibility for the organization. As the board is ultimately legally responsible for the agency program, it is also responsible for the volunteer component. The board has the power to authorize the construction of a volunteer program, and it has the responsibility to ensure the effectiveness of that program. The board can—and should—call for program objectives, established policies and procedures, professional management, involvement and recognition of volunteers, and adequate budget for the volunteer program. (Silver, 1988; pp. 115–116)

The question arises: "But how do we get the attention of senior management and boards of directors?" The answer may be: "Policies, in the context of risk management."

When something goes wrong in the volunteer program, the ultimate responsibility will not fall to the manager of volunteers. As Silver notes, the board is ultimately legally responsible for all that occurs under the auspices of the agency, and hence the law suit, when it arrives, will settle on the board table. And board members, in general, are becoming increasingly aware of their own vulnerability to liability:

> Board volunteers are suddenly realizing that not only can the voluntary organization they serve be sued; but there are instances in which *volunteers themselves* can be sued—as individuals. (Conrad and Glenn, 1976, p. 14)

It is suggested, then, that the best way to get the attention of senior management— boards and CEOs—is to alert them to the potential risks and hazards embodied in volunteering. In this view, policy development for volunteer programs is the key to the boardroom door (Linda Graff, 1993). Some would suggest this to be fear-mongering, or manipulation by fear. In fact, managers of volunteers have an obligation to alert their supervisors to risks and liability. Not doing so is irresponsible. Only when risks are fully identified and assessed can they be managed properly.

But alerting management to the dangers is only half of the task. As we have seen, policy development is a key component in risk management. Boards generally concur that policy development is within the realm of board mandate, and they can, therefore, be counted on to pay attention when someone exclaims, "We need a policy on that!" The comprehensive strategy might be to:

- ◆ Identify the risks.
- ◆ Draft policies and procedures that minimize the risk and/or limit the organization's liability.
- ◆ Take these, together, to the board table.

When the board realizes that the activity being undertaken in the volunteer department is significant enough to create liability exposures for both the organization and board members personally, the volunteer program will be seen in a different light. Suddenly it will become a department worthy of board time and attention. From here, the manager of volunteers can build a case for adequate resources (budget, space, staffing), and agency support services (supervision, direction, insurance, policy and procedure development). Here is a concrete tool to accomplish what Ivan Scheier calls on all managers to do: "Insofar as volunteer administration continues to see itself as derivative, passive and dependent, others naturally tend to see us that way too. Beginning to define ourselves as powerful, active and autonomous is the first step in becoming more so" (Scheier, 1988, p. 29).

Policy development via risk management may be the most productive route for managers of volunteers to empower their volunteer programs. As Silver found in her research on organizational factors that engender effective volunteer programs:

> The commitment of the administrative leadership of an organization is necessary to raise the volunteer program to priority status. Without the leadership behind it, a volunteer program—no matter how well organized and potentially viable and valuable—simply will not have the organizational power necessary to progress and develop. (Silver, 1988, p. 117)

7.4 WHERE POLICIES ARE NEEDED

With the possible exception of policies about confidentiality, a great many volunteer programs operate in a complete policy vacuum. Managers of volunteers ask anxiously, "What policies do I need?" and "What if I miss something really important?" The answer to these questions varies from program to program and inevitably hinges on the nature of the volunteer program, the kind of work done by volunteers, the nature and complexity of the organization, and the amount of resources available for policy development. In a recent manual on policy development for volunteer programs (Linda Graff, 1992), sample policies are presented on more than 70 different topics that would be applicable to most types of volunteer programs. Nearly as many again could be added to cover the unique dimensions of any specific program.

(a) Functions of Policies

There is a way of conceptualizing policies according to their function that can be used to determine which policies any specific program needs to develop. There are four general functions served by policies in volunteer programs:

- ◆ Policies as risk management
- ◆ Policies as values and belief statements
- ◆ Policies as rules
- ◆ Policies as program improvement tools

Each is explored in some detail below.

(i) Policies as Risk Management

As discussed above, policies are a critical component in an agency's overall risk management program. Through policies, boundaries can be established to delineate what is and what is not safe. Consider these examples.

On waivers:

> All new clients must sign a liability release form as a standard component of the "application for service" procedure.

On agency backup for volunteers on duty:

> It is important that all direct service volunteers have backup from the agency in the event that they encounter trouble in the course of their volunteer duties. An identified staff member or other agency representative will be on duty and accessible at all times when agency volunteers are on assignment.

On volunteers driving:

> While on duty, volunteer Friendly Visitors for the Acme Home Support Agency will not use their own personal vehicles to transport agency clients.

The procedure to follow such a policy might look like this:

> Should an emergency arise in which a client requires immediate transportation, and time permits, the volunteer will contact his or her manager of volunteers or agency backup at Acme for direction. If the circumstance is more urgent, the volunteer may use his or her own judgment regarding whether an ambulance or other emergency service is required. Immediately after an incident of this sort, the volunteer must notify Acme of the situation and of the actions the volunteer has initiated.

Here is a final example of a policy established primarily for risk management purposes regarding the agency's obligation to inform volunteers of risks associated with volunteering, and the right of volunteers to refuse assignments:

> The safety and well-being of all volunteers serving Acme is of paramount importance, and every effort will be made to eliminate all hazards related to the performance of volunteer duties. In circumstances where some element of risk remains beyond our control, volunteers will be informed, in advance, to the best of our knowledge and ability. This includes, but is not limited to, notification of any hazardous material, practice or process that volunteers may encounter while engaged in Acme business. Volunteers are entirely within their rights to refuse to perform volunteer assignments that appear to pose unacceptable risks.

Using this particular policy function as a guide to determining which policies a volunteer program needs to develop, the manager would:

♦ Look around the volunteer program.
♦ Better still, walk around the volunteer work site(s).
♦ Watch our for risks, hazards, and dangers.
♦ Play the "What if?" game, trying to identify what could go wrong under a series of different circumstances. What would this room look like if it were filled with smoke? How would this activity look from the perspective of a wheelchair? Would this activity be more dangerous in cold temperatures? in high winds? in the middle of an ice storm?

This, in fact, is a common first step in the risk management process. Called *disaster imaging,* it allows the manager to determine where policies might prevent accidents and injuries, to minimize the likelihood of accidents and injuries, and to minimize the harm should an accident happen. For example:

♦ If the manager, in walking around the day care center, spots a skateboard in the toy box, she may very well go back to her desk and issue a policy to the day care staff that prohibits use of skateboards on agency property.
♦ When the trail maintenance supervisor accompanies her volunteers on a shift and notices that they have disengaged the chain saw brake mechanism, she might very well write a new policy about *all* equipment safety features and be

certain that this new policy is highlighted in all volunteer training programs from here on.

This technique is proactive and, of course, takes place under ideal circumstances. In reality, we often cannot foresee accidents. We are alerted to dangers only after an incident or a near miss. So write a policy that requires all staff and volunteers to report all accidents and other serious occurrences to you. Make it a practice to think in detail about policy development whenever a serious incident report arrives on your desk. Accidents are bad enough. Reoccurrences because of inaction are inexcusable.

(ii) Policies as Values and Belief Statements

Every organization builds a web of values and beliefs about the world in which it works, the nature of the problem(s) it seeks to address, and the way in which it operates. Some of these are subtle and rarely discussed. Many are unwritten but nonetheless well known and clearly understood. In addition, agencies often take positions on questions and issues related to their services, as well as to their own internal operations. Policy statements are a mechanism for both articulating and communicating such values, beliefs, and positions. Following are some examples.

On antidiscrimination and affirmative action:

> The Centre will not permit discrimination against applicants or employees (paid staff/volunteers) on the basis of race, religion, age, gender, sexual orientation, disability, socio-economic background or ethnicity. This applies to all areas of employment (paid staff/volunteers) including recruiting, hiring, promotion, assigning of work . . . provided the individual is qualified and meets the requirements established by the Centre for the position. (Volunteer Centre of Metropolitan Toronto, 1993)

> Equal opportunity practices and affirmative action techniques relative to minority involvement, training, development, recognition, and retention will be incorporated in volunteer recruitment efforts. Established affirmative action targets will be met within a specified time frame, tailored to local demographic realities, and include formalized, periodic evaluation. (Adapted from American Red Cross, n.d.)

On the importance of volunteers to the organization:

> The achievement of the goals of this agency is best served by the active participation of citizens of the community. To this end, the agency accepts and encourages the involvement of volunteers at all levels of the agency and within all appropriate programs and activities. . . . (McCurley, 1990, p. 2)

> Volunteers, and the contributions they make through volunteering, significantly enhance the quality of life, community spirit, and leisure time opportunities in Burlington. Volunteers are a valuable human resource requiring and warranting support and encouragement to maintain and develop their skills

and to ensure their continued involvement in the provision of leisure opportunities throughout the City. The Parks and Recreation Department will continue to develop and provide support for volunteers and volunteer groups to ensure their continued involvement in leisure services and to develop this resource to its fullest. (Parks and Recreation Department, Burlington, Ontario)

On the agency's right to fire volunteers:

The agency accepts the service of all volunteers with the understanding that such service is at the sole discretion of the agency. Volunteers agree that the agency may at any time, for whatever reason, decide to terminate the volunteer's relationship with the agency. (McCurley, 1990, p. 3)

Values embodied in acceptable terminology:

. . . greater policy direction be given and attention be paid, in both speech and the written and printed word, to the appropriate and accepted vocabulary in describing the Red Cross work force. This is always "paid and volunteer staff" or "paid and volunteer consultants" or "paid and volunteer instructors," etc., and never "professional staff and volunteers." . . . The entire organization, including volunteers themselves, are to be encouraged to think of volunteers as staff members, with all the organizational support and personal responsibilities which this implies. Such phrases and attitudes as "I am just a volunteer" or "he is just a volunteer" are to be strongly discouraged. (American Red Cross, n.d.)

The technique to identify policies of this sort involves thinking through the values, beliefs, and positions held by the organization. Answer these questions:

◆ What do we hold as important? What do we value that volunteers need to know about? What is our philosophy about volunteers, about the work we do, about how we do business around here?
◆ What positions has the agency taken on issues, questions, or problems?
◆ What does the organization believe regarding good and bad, right and wrong, proper and improper, ethical and unethical?

The answers to many of these questions might be substance around which policies should be written and communicated.

Frequently, the most difficult policies to write—the ones around which there develops the greatest debate—are the policies that derive from values. Often, where disagreement surfaces in policy development, conflicting values will be the cause. In the examples in Exhibit 7–2 policy development will be difficult because the values that underpin the policies are both complex and not necessarily congruent with one another.

These are values in conflict. Profound beliefs that run to the very heart of organizational existence can sometimes be found to clash with one another. In these circumstances, it is first useful to recognize that the source of disagreement is values in conflict. Having identified the problem, the organization must engage in a *values sort,* a process whereby values are prioritized, with those that emerge on top serving as the basis for policy development.

(iii) Policies as Rules

Policies can be employed as rules to specify expectations, regulations, and guides to action. The distinction between policies as rules and policies as risk management often blurs. That is, a policy written to eliminate or reduce a specific risk might sound like a rule. A policy written because a rule is needed to guide a particular action may serve to reduce a specific hazard. The solution to this seeming confusion is this: Don't worry about it, because it simply does not matter. The point is that one develops whatever policies are needed; if some policies serve more than

---

 EXHIBIT 7–2   Examples of Conflicting Values

Values Conflict 1:

✓ We believe that volunteering is about caring for others, about simple motives to do good and help one's neighbors in times of need. It should not be overbureaucratized and overorganized.

✓ We also acknowledge that rules and regulations around volunteer involvement—rules on topics such as application processes, thorough screening, and discipline and dismissal—have become necessary to protect the well-being of both volunteers and clients.

☞ Will the volunteer screening policy require background checks, references, and criminal records checks for all volunteers?

Values Conflict 2:

✓ Like many voluntary organizations, our mission is based on the struggle to obtain and preserve the values of inclusivity, individual rights and freedoms, and antioppression in all of its manifestations. We believe that we have an obligation to extend those values both to our programming (outreach and equality of access, for example) and to our internal operations (hiring and promotions practices, for example).

✓ We also believe that clients have the right to demand from us services of the highest quality. Yet what is our response when a client refuses to accept the services of a volunteer on grounds typically prohibited by human rights legislation (the volunteer is the "wrong" age, the "wrong" gender, the "wrong" color, the "wrong" sexual orientation . . .)?

☞ Will we comply and find another volunteer and thereby collude with beliefs and behaviors that contradict our deeply held values regarding antioppression, or will we stand firm and refuse to reassign a volunteer, thereby failing to fulfill our mission to deliver services?

---

one function, all the better. The following example of a conflict of interest policy is a good illustration of a policy as a rule:

> Any possible conflict of interest on the part of a director shall be disclosed to the board. When any such interest becomes a matter of board action, such director shall not vote or use personal influence on the matter, and shall not be counted in the quorum for a meeting at which board action is to be taken on the interest. The director may, however, briefly state a position on the matter, and answer pertinent questions of board members. The minutes of all actions taken on such matters shall clearly reflect that these requirements have been met. (Conrad and Glenn, 1976, p. 16)

On the use of organizational affiliation:

> Volunteers may not use their organizational affiliation in connection with partisan politics, religious matters, or community issues contrary to positions taken by the organization.

On volunteers and picket lines:

> In the event of a union-initiated work stoppage or legal strike, volunteers will not cross the picket line.

On paid employees as volunteers:

> Paid employees may not serve in governing, policy-making or advisory role while employed by the organization, or within one year of terminating their paid employment with the organization. Paid employees may, however, serve in direct-service volunteer roles which are outside the scope of their paid work within the organization and which take place outside of usual working hours. (Adapted from Canadian Red Cross—Ontario Division, 1992)

On family members as volunteers:

> Family members of employees are allowed to volunteer but they may not be placed under the direct supervision or within the same department as other members of their family who are employees. (Adapted from Canadian Red Cross—Ontario Division 1992)

To determine required policies of this sort, the manager might spend time reviewing existing rules, both written and unwritten. Review past records such as memoranda, volunteer job descriptions, and volunteer performance review documentation to identify where rules have been articulated or directives issued. Also think about advisements or directives issued verbally to volunteers that have never been written down anywhere, but that nonetheless reflect "how we do things around here."

(iv) Policies as Program Improvement Tools

Upon occasion, it may be useful to upgrade an expectation, a protocol, or a standard to the level of a policy, to give it more authority and import. This technique is useful where an activity is important but is perhaps not seen to be important by, or at least warranting the attention of, those expected to comply. Time sheets are an excellent example:

> Volunteers will mail or deliver their activity logs to the manager of volunteers within five working days of month-end.

Sometimes policies can be used to ensure that a program operates smoothly or to improve the effectiveness of a program or service. This policy on expectations of volunteers will enhance the service delivered:

> Volunteers are expected to work within the parameters of their own volunteer job description while on duty with the agency. However, regular contact with clients can allow volunteers to make important observations about changes in the health and well-being of clients. Agency policy requires volunteers to report such observations to the Manager of Volunteers who will take appropriate action.

Implementing a policy that speaks to the operation of the program does not, of course, guarantee compliance, but the weight or import of stating an expectation in the form of a policy can help. It will also provide a basis for pursuing consequences in the case of noncompliance. To pinpoint which policies of this sort are required, the manager can simply consider aspects of the volunteer program that are not operating as effectively or as efficiently as desired. Having identified these, one might consider whether the additional weight of a policy pronouncement would encourage improvement.

(b) Equality or Elitism? Policy for Direct Service and Administrative Volunteers

It is rarely the case in agencies where policies have been written to guide the volunteer component that policies apply equally to direct service *and* administrative (board, committee, advisory) volunteers. In the same way that so many board members refuse to consider themselves as volunteers (is it because they consider the label below them?), board members often think of themselves as outside (above?) the scope of policies written for volunteers. This type of two-tiered elitism among volunteer ranks has left administrative volunteering beyond both the control of, and the protection afforded by, risk management programs and policy development. The consequences of this pattern are dangerous. Consider these examples:

- ◆ Board members are rarely screened; formal application and interview procedures are rarely required.
- ◆ Reference checks on board members are rarely required, even of those board members who have significant financial responsibilities—treasurers and comptrollers, for example.
- ◆ The involvement of board members is rarely monitored, even though their actions and decisions are among the most important and influential in the whole organization.
- ◆ Board members are rarely disciplined or dismissed, even when clear cause exists.

It is recommended that policies written for volunteer programs include, in their scope, *all* volunteers, equally. Exceptions need to be identified clearly, and only with justification.

7.5 POLICY DEVELOPMENT PROCESS

(a) Who Sets Policy?

The precise way in which policies are drafted, reviewed, revised, approved, and implemented varies a good deal from agency to agency. In some agencies, the board will hold within its own mandate anything that even remotely resembles a policy. In other agencies, the executive director (CEO, administrator, or other senior staff member) may determine that drafting policies for board approval is his or her own responsibility. Some agencies may have, or decide to create, a policy committee that will oversee all matters of policy for the agency. In other agencies, senior administration (paid and unpaid) will welcome the research, advice, input, and drafts from front-line staff regarding policies with broad applicability, allowing more specific policies or policies with limited scope to be developed and implemented by department staff. Although none of these development systems is inherently right or wrong, it is probably best if organizations develop an internal culture that welcomes notification of the need for policy development, review, or revision from all agency personnel, paid or unpaid. It is not helpful for front-line workers to think of policy as out of their realm, or somehow "above them." People actually doing the work are often those most likely to identify risks, the need for improvements, or the need for rules or changes in rules.

(b) The Role of the Manager or Director of Volunteers

It is important for the manager of volunteers to determine how policy development is typically handled in his or her organization. The manager will thus be able to determine just what role he or she can play in policy development for the volunteer program. There is no question, however, that the manager of volunteers is primarily responsible for identifying policy issues within the volunteer department and for bringing those to the attention of senior staff and administrators. At a minimum it would be unethical not to report hazards or risks and to do everything possible to ensure the safety and well-being of all volunteers.

With few exceptions, senior administrators, paid and unpaid alike, have little knowledge of the details, the complexities, or the scale of volunteering as it actually occurs within their organizations. This makes getting the attention of senior administrators more difficult, to be sure, but it is all the more reason why the manager of volunteers must take the initiative in policy development for volunteer programs. The process may have to include a good deal of education regarding the true dimensions and significance of volunteer work, and some mention of personal and collective liability exposure will often motivate board members and senior staff to listen more closely.

(c) Ask for Help

As volunteer programs grow larger, as risks and liabilities grow, and as volunteers become engaged in increasingly sophisticated and even technical work, managers of volunteers have more and more complexities to manage. And changes and growth outside the volunteer department create new demands on the manager of volunteers. As Sue Vineyard says:

> All of the trends that surround us as a nation have an impact on the work of directing volunteer efforts. As the rapid pace of change escalates in the wider world, we find ourselves having to adapt to the impact of those changes on our daily work and the roles we play in leading volunteer energies. (1993,179)

It is simply unreasonable to expect any single individual to have expertise in all the areas in which volunteers are engaged, especially in large organizations or organizations with large volunteer programs. Developing policies for volunteer programs can require skills and background in a wide range of fields, including:

Human resource management
Labor law
Contract law
Human rights legislation
Risk management
Statistics
Insurance
Information management
Athletics
Fund-raising
Planning
Occupational health and safety
Systems analysis
Liability
Accounting
Education and training

How many managers of volunteers who do not work in health care settings know enough details about communicable diseases and universal precautions to develop policies and procedures in this area? How many managers of volunteers know enough about liability and insurance to guarantee maximum coverage and protection?

No one can be expected to know enough to develop all policies alone, so ask for help. People from all walks of life are generally willing to volunteer for short-term positions as consultants. Ask them to prepare a draft policy, to work with you and/or other agency representatives to draft a policy, or to review or edit an existing draft. After all, managers of volunteers are experts at volunteer recruitment—they just do not think, as often as they might, about recruiting volunteers to help with their own work.

7.6 HOW TO WRITE POLICIES FOR VOLUNTEER PROGRAMS

(a) Six Principles of Writing Policies

(i) Be Concise

Write as much as is required for the policy to be clear and comprehensive. Remember, however, that the longer the policies and the thicker the policy manual, the more intimidating it will be and the less likely that it will be read and used regularly.

(ii) Be Clear

Policy writers must take great care to ensure that the policies they develop convey precisely and completely what is intended. Do not assume that the people reading and applying policies will understand them to mean what was originally intended. Avoid technical terminology and jargon. Where it is necessary to use technical terms, explain them, either in the text or in an attached glossary.

(iii) Be Directive

Policies should very clearly tell people what is expected. Although one wouldhope for complete compliance with all policies, it is obvious that compliance with some policies is much more important than compliance with others. It is appropriate, therefore, that some policies be more strongly worded and more authoritative than others. For example, there are some policies for which the imperative mood—a command—is entirely proper:

> Volunteers will not give patients anything to eat or drink before patient's surgery.
> Volunteers will not disengage or otherwise tamper with any safety mechanisms on any equipment entrusted to their use.

In all cases, remember that policies are policies. They must be directive and they must articulate, as Cryderman (1987) says, the *what*.

(iv) Round the Edges

Without diminishing the importance of the three preceding principles, one must not lose sight of the fact that the subject of the policy development being discussed here is the work of volunteers. For this reason it is suggested that the tone of many policies in the volunteer department very consciously be softened to be as palatable and inoffensive as possible. Here are some sample policies to illustrate how rounding some of the rough edges of policies can make a big difference in tone.

On conflict of interest:

> No person who has a conflict of interest with any activity or program of the agency, whether personal, philosophical, or financial shall be accepted or serve as a volunteer with the agency. (Steve McCurley, 1990, p. 4)

An alternative might read something like this:

> Many volunteers are very busy people who often have many connections and who sometimes volunteer for more than one organization at the same time. It is, therefore, not unusual for volunteers to find themselves in a conflict of interest situation, regardless of whether they do administrative (board or committee) or direct service volunteering. Any volunteer who suspects that he or she may have a conflict of interest must notify his/her immediate supervisor in order to discuss application of the conflict of interest procedure, a copy of which is available from. . . .

On turning volunteers away:

> The agency reserves the right to decline involvement in its volunteer program by anyone it assesses to be unsuitable. The decision of the agency is final in these matters.

Versus:

> While the agency may need to decline offers of involvement by prospective volunteer applicants, every care must be taken, in turning such applicants away, to leave intact the applicant's sense of self-confidence and dignity. In the process, emphasis must remain on the absence of a match between the gifts that the volunteer has to offer and what the position requires at the present time. Alternate placement opportunities or referral to the Voluntary Action Center will be offered wherever possible. (See also the Anti-discrimination Policy, outlined on page. . . .)

The following series of policy statements regarding volunteer placement also conveys a deep respect for the rights and dignity of volunteers:

> In determining suitable placements for volunteers, equal attention will be given to the interests and goals of the volunteer and to the requirements of the agency and of the position(s) in question.

> No volunteer will be placed in a position for which s/he is not fully qualified or for which the organization could not provide adequate training.
> Volunteers will be fully and honestly informed of the expectations and responsibilities of their volunteer position along with any risk or liability that the position might entail.

> Volunteers will be made to feel comfortable in declining a suggested placement or in requesting changes to the position expectations at any point in their involvement with the organization.

> Volunteers have the right to expect work that is meaningful and satisfying to them.

No position is too high in the organizational structure or too skilled for a volunteer, assuming appropriate background and time commitment.

No position should be considered too tedious or unskilled as long as volunteers are given a clear understanding of the nature and importance of the work to be performed.

(v) Emphasize the Positives

Whenever possible, policies should enable, motivate, and inspire. They should articulate outside limits, leaving as much room as possible for flexibility and creativity. The presence of supportive and enabling policies can provide the encouragement and recognition that volunteers require to maximize their potential. Policies can demonstrate just how important the work is and the very real consequence of error when standards are not attained or guidelines are not followed. As Rick Lynch (1983) points out, *we should never be surprised at the lack of results we get from volunteers if we never give them results to achieve.*

(vi) Illustrate

Do not hesitate to draw pictures, illustrate steps and sequences, or sketch methods or techniques. Diagrams and other graphic additions make the manual more pleasing to read, but more to the point, convey specific details that words sometimes cannot.

(b) Which Policies? Which Ones First?

Policy development for volunteer programs can seem completely overwhelming, particularly for those who are starting with few or no policies. The panicky question, "Oh dear! Where do I start?" is both typical and understandable at this stage. Given that developing a full set of policies for the volunteer department might take two or three years of fairly steady work, the task is to outline the range of possible policy topics and then be certain that the most urgent are developed first. Following is a simple, two-step process that is equally useful to managers of volunteers who are just getting started and to managers who already have many policies in place.

(i) Which Policies?

Developing a list of possible policy topics is the first task. Using the policy checklist in Exhibit 7–3, the manager of volunteers can begin the process by listing all the items that he or she can think of. Consult the table of contents of Linda Graff's *By Definition: Policies for Volunteer Programs* (1992), which lists over 70 generic volunteer program policy topics. The brainstorming process can be prompted at this point by segmenting the policy checklist into separate sections for risk management policies, values and belief statement policies, policies as rules, and policies that will enhance the program's effectiveness. See Section 7.4 for guiding questions.

Since this is a brainstorming exercise, no possibility should be ruled out at this point. It is also appropriate to include on this list those policies that are already in place. As possible policy topics arise, list them in the left-hand column. Complete

◆ **EXHIBIT 7–3 Policy Checklist**

POLICY TOPIC	DEVELOPED: Date Of Last Review	IN PROGRESS	TO DO	NOT APPLICABLE
1. Volunteer Screening			✓	
2. Recruitment			✓	
3. Anti-Discrimination			✓	
4. Crossing Picket Lines			✓	
5. Probation			✓	
6. Recruitment of Minors			✓	
7. Volunteer–Paid Staff Relations			✓	
8. Confidentiality	January '92			
9. Sexual Harassment		✓		
10. Conflict of Interest	September '90			
11. Discipline			✓	
12. Dismissal			✓	
13. Immediate Dismissal		✓		
14.				
15.				
16.				
17.				
18.				
19.				
20.				

Additional Policies Our Organization Should Develop

1. Professional Development/On-going Training for Volunteers
2. Police Checks
3. Volunteer Recognition
4.
5.
6.
7.
8.

the other columns for each topic as appropriate, indicating whether the policy exists, is in progress, or needs to be developed. It is suggested that the manager of volunteers begin this process by listing the policies identified initially. More than one page may be required to contain the growing list of topics. When the manager has listed all that he or she can think of for the moment, the checklist can be circulated so that others—staff, volunteers, clients, supervisor, board members, colleagues, outside consultants—may add to the list. They use the bottom portion of the checklist, and since they are less likely to know what does and does not already exist, they do not need the additional columns. There should be no censoring at this point, although the right-hand column does allow anyone to register an opinion on the applicability of any policy topic(s) already on the list. The manager of volunteers can pursue these notations in more detail with the people involved.

(ii) Which Ones First?

If this process generates an enormous list there is no reason to panic. Remember that the goal is to prioritize so that the most urgent and/or most important policies are being developed at any given time. What needs to be done is to rank each prospective policy topic on an urgency scale, from which can follow the list of policies in order of greatest to least urgency. To assess urgency and importance, the manager of volunteers can again refer to the questions itemized in Section 7.4 on functions of policies. Each policy can be rated on its importance within each function. Exhibit 7–4, the priority scale, can be used to facilitate the process and record the results. To use the priority scale, transfer the policy topics that were itemized on the policy checklist (Exhibit 7–3) to the left-hand column of the priority scale. Taking each policy topic in turn, assess its urgency on a scale of 1 to 5 (1 meaning not very urgent, it can wait; 5 meaning very urgent, needs development immediately) with respect to each of the four possible functions: risk management, values and belief statements, rules, and program improvement aides. Follow through this illustration on volunteer screening, asking the following questions about the urgency of need for policy statements:

Risk Management

- ◆ Are there risks associated with volunteer screening?
- ◆ Do we expose ourselves, our clients, or the organization to liability by not having a volunteer screening policy?
- ◆ Are our screening policies and procedures thorough enough to screen out dangerous candidates?
- ◆ Are our screening policies and procedures so extensive that they infringe on the privacy and/or the legal rights of prospective volunteers?
- ◆ How great are those risks?

Allowing for some variance depending on the nature of the work done by volunteers, the vulnerability of clients, and so on, it is likely that the risks surrounding volunteer screening will be quite high because of the need to strike a proper balance between agency responsibilities and the rights of volunteers. Consider the implications of a violent offender or a pedophile being recruited into a day care center because "He was such a *nice* man!" or the ramifications of accepting an expert in fraud as the treasurer for the board of directors. Consider as well the indignation of

◆ EXHIBIT 7–4 Priority Scale

POLICY TOPIC	← ASSIGN RATINGS* →						
	Level of Risk	Need Value Statement	Need Rules	Need to Improve	Other	Totals	
1. *Volunteer Screening*	5	4	5	3	—	17	
2. *Recruitment*	2	4	3	1	—	10	
3. *Anti-Discrimination*	3	5	4	0	—	12	
4. *Crossing Picket Lines*	5	5	5	2	5	22	*Strike Imminent*
5. *Probation*							
6. *Recruitment of Minors*							
7. *Volunteer-Paid Staff Relations*							
8. *Confidentiality*							
9. *Sexual Harassment*	3	5	5	5	5	23	*Incident Reported Last Week*
10. *Conflict of Interest*							
11.							
12.							
13.							
14. *Enabling Funds*	1	4	4	2	4	15	*Funder Demands Clear Policy*
15.							
16.							
17. *Free Coffee For Volunteers*	0	2	3	0	—	5	
18.							

*Rate on a scale of urgency/importance: 1 = can wait ..... 5 = needs immediate attention a well-meaning candidate when confronted with unnecessarily probing questions. To complete the priority scale for the policy on volunteer screening, the score under the heading "level of risk" would be 5 for most programs.

Values and Belief Statements

◆ Do we have values or beliefs about volunteer screening that need to be articulated?

There are always certain beliefs and positions held by organizations about volunteer screening that may seem self-evident to those in the field but that are completely unknown to the general public. For example, many citizens still believe that seeking to do good unto others is the only criterion one must meet to become a volunteer. Being refused would be a shocking offense. It is therefore quite important for the agency to be clear about its beliefs about volunteer screening, including messages about the agency's right to decline offers of involvement; the belief that the screening interview is an opportunity for mutual information exchange and assessment; that antidiscrimination and affirmative action principles will guide assessments of suitability. The score for volunteer screening in the "need value statement" column would also be high: 4 or 5.

Rules

◆ Do organizations need to identify rules around the volunteer screening process?

Rules regarding background checks, police checks, and references are very important. Additionally, agencies need to state their policies that detail what will be done with, and who can gain access to, confidential information obtained through the screening process; what constitutes grounds for nonacceptance; and what the prohibited grounds are for nonacceptance. The score in this column, headed "need rule 4," would be 5 for most programs.

Program Improvement Tools   Each agency needs to assess its own functioning in this regard, but here is an example of a policy that could serve to improve the recruitment success rate: Undue delay in following up with volunteers after the screening interview regarding their acceptance, is both disrespectful and potentially damaging to volunteers' motivation. A policy that commits the organization to contacting the volunteer within a specified number of working days of the screening interview could significantly alter the proportion of volunteers who are still willing to volunteer when the agency is able to confirm acceptance. How well the screening program is currently functioning will be a major determinant of how high the score will be in this column for screening policy.

To summarize, screening would rate high to very high in all four columns. It is a policy topic that requires thorough attention. To illustrate, by contrast, the range in urgency scores that various policy topics might receive, the policy on whether volunteers should or should not pay for their own coffee while on duty is an example of a policy issue that would rate fairly low on the urgency scale.

The fifth column on the priority scale, "other," is there for use at the manager's discretion. There may be additional reasons for work on a specific policy to begin sooner rather than later: the organization just had a serious incident in an area where policy could prevent reoccurrence; the funder is insisting that all its member agencies implement a specific philosophy of service; the manager's supervisor just came back from a course on safety in the workplace and is requiring immediate policy development on sexual harassment. This column allows the manager to assign urgency bonus points in these kinds of circumstances.

To complete the priority scale, rate each policy topic in each of the five columns, add across each row to obtain a total score for each topic, and place that total in the right-hand column. Those topics with the highest scores need to be dealt with first. Those with lower scores can wait. Transfer the list of policy topics to a separate list in order from highest to lowest score, and consider this the "policy to do list" for the foreseeable future.

(c) Tracking Drafts and Input

Once the policy development agenda has been established, the manager can actually begin the process of researching, drafting, and revising policies. Some policies will be relatively easy to write; others will be extremely complex; some will demand input from outside experts; others will involve lengthy processing and values clarification. Work on a wide range of policies can proceed simultaneously, particularly if a policy development team, a policy committee, or a collection of consultants/re-source persons is recruited to assist with the task. Depending on the number of policies needing to be drafted and the number in progress at any given time, tracking where each policy is in its development may become cumbersome.

Exhibit 7–5 can be used as a tool to track the progress of policies as they are being researched, drafted, revised, and approved. Use one of these forms for each policy that needs to be tracked. Track development by indicating who needs to be involved and/or consulted and who is responsible for each stage of the policy's evolution. The form allows the manager to note due dates and completion dates for various activities. Use the two blank lines at the bottom to add other policy development activities that may need to be accomplished: external reading and editing; vetting by head office, staff, or union.

(d) Editing Policies

Careful review of policies after they have been drafted is a critical step that is often overlooked. It is recommended that at least four people read newly drafted policy. Readers and editors from both within the field of volunteer management and from outside it will round out the editing team. Different readers can be asked to attend to different aspects of policies. For example, legal counsel or insurance advisors can be asked to review from their professional point of view. Other readers may be asked to concentrate on meaning; others may attend to mechanics and sequencing or terminology and grammar.

7.7 COMPLIANCE

A great deal of time and resources can be wasted on policy development if policies are not understood and followed. Although there is nothing one can do to guarantee absolute compliance, there is a good deal that one can do to increase the likelihood of compliance. Here are some suggestions.

◆ **EXHIBIT 7–5   Tracking Policy Development**

POLICY ISSUE: _____

POLICY NUMBER: _____

WHO WILL BE INVOLVED?

❑ Manager of Volunteers	❑ Board of Directors
❑ Staff Department Head	❑ Executive Director
❑ Staff_____	❑ Policy Committee
_____	❑ Legal Counsel
❑ Volunteers_____	❑ Insurance Advisor
_____	❑ Others _____
	❑ Others _____

VERSION	WHO IS RESPONSIBLE	DUE DATE	COMPLETE (✓)
First Draft			
Second Draft			
Third Draft			
Approval			
Review/Revision			

(a) Sensitive Wording

The way in which policies are worded can significantly enhance compliance. As noted above, rounding rough edges of policies can make them both more understandable and more palatable to volunteers who might otherwise be hurt or offended by apparent absence of trust or appreciation (review Section 7.6a(iv) for examples).

(b) State the Way

Including in the policy statement the reason for its existence reminds volunteers that policies do not exist just to make volunteering more bureaucratic for those engaged in it. This is not to say that agencies must justify every sentence of policy they write, or that the rationale for every policy statement must be an integral part of the policy itself. However, the rationale for some policies may not be immediately apparent to volunteers. In such cases, reference to reasons such as the well-being of clients, the importance of efficient expenditure of precious resources, the furthering of the mission of the agency, or the safety of volunteer workers will certainly clarify its purpose and reinforce the importance of volunteers' compliance with it. Here is an excellent example:

> Volunteers in this program are considered as nonpaid, part-time staff and it is expected that volunteer relationships with clients will have the same boundaries as those of paid staff. Our role is therapeutic in nature. It is not appropriate to become friends with clients. This is not to say that volunteers cannot be friendly, caring or supportive. On the contrary. The reason that relationships with clients should not lead to friendships is because the relationship is not equal. Volunteers are privileged to more power by virtue of their position with the organization. Hence, clients are in a more vulnerable role. It is normal for clients to want to establish friendships with volunteers. They perceive volunteers to be caring individuals who pay attention.

> The procedure that accompanies this policy is:

> 1. When "turning a client down" in terms of a friendship role, volunteers will do this in a supportive manner giving the basis of this policy as a reason.
> 2. Volunteers will notify the Coordinator of Volunteers whenever the nature of the friendship with a client is in question. (Psychiatric Day Programme, 1992)

This policy clearly outlines the "why." It is unlikely that a shorter version of the same policy that reads, "Volunteers are prohibited from developing social or friendship relationships with clients" would engender the same level of compliance, simply because it does not communicate sound reasons for doing so.

(c) Make Compliance Easy

The preceding sections notwithstanding, the shorter, more concise, more clear, and more straightforward that policies are, the greater the likelihood of compliance. Policy writers need to strike a balance between policies that are short and to the point, and policies that are more involved and detailed. Without trying to be facetious, the lesson here might be: Write as many and as much as you need to ensure understanding and compliance, and not one policy or one word more.

(d) Make Policies Accessible

Produce policies in a format that makes them easily accessible to volunteers. For example, produce a complete manual of policies and procedures for the volunteer program and make it available to all volunteers. Extract the most critical of all policies for reproduction in a smaller handbook for each type of volunteer position or for volunteers in each department. Print that subset of the most critical policies in a pocket- or purse-sized summary for day-to-day use. Distill these even further and print the policies about emergency situations on a card the size of a credit card, have it laminated, and ask volunteers to post it near the phone at the worksite, carry it in their wallets, and/or carry it in the glove compartments of their automobiles.

(e) Communicate Policies at Every Opportunity

Create and take every opportunity to communicate with and remind volunteers about policies and procedures.

- ◆ Begin to make reference to policies in volunteer recruitment publicity by mentioning agency efforts to make volunteering safe and satisfying.
- ◆ Notify volunteers at the initial screening interview that there are policies—rules, beliefs, and ways of doing things—that are integral to volunteering with your agency.
- ◆ Include detailed coverage of agency policies and procedures in volunteer training and ongoing training sessions.
- ◆ Be certain to assess compliance with policies and procedures as a regular component of volunteer supervision and evaluation sessions.
- ◆ Post relevant policies and procedures as reminders around the worksite.
- ◆ Write articles about policies and procedures in newsletters and other communication vehicles, giving background, rationale, and implications.

(f) Signed Contract

As part of their acceptance into service with the organization, require volunteers to sign a contract. This type of document, alternately called an *agreement* or a *memorandum of understanding* to soften its image, requires volunteers to sign their commitment to following policies and procedures. Signing such a contract lends greater significance to the promise of compliance. Typically, the commitment to compliance with agency policies and procedures is one of several items included in an initial volunteer/agency contract. The sample drafted by Steve McCurley (1988, p. 10) includes other agreements: to serve as a volunteer, to perform volunteer duties to the best of his or her abilities, to meet time and duty commitments or provide adequate notice, as well as a section on adherence to rules and procedures. It is suggested that a paragraph such as the following be included in the signed agreement:

> I, _____, affirm that I have read, understood, and agree to comply with the policies and procedures of the (name of agency) as they are outlined in the attached job description, and in the volunteer handbook/policy manual . . .

An optional paragraph such as the following may be considered:

> I understand that compliance with these policies and procedures is important to preserve the quality of service offered to our clients, and critical to the safety and well being of (agency) volunteers, clients, staff, and the general public. Further, I understand that any breach of agency policies and procedures will be taken seriously, and could be cause for discipline, suspension, or even dismissal.

(g) Follow Through

Consistently monitor compliance. Ensure that compliance with policies is a routine aspect of the volunteer performance review system. Offer speedy reinforcement, including awards for superior performance. Write newsletter articles about positive outcomes that have resulted from volunteers following policies and procedures. Act quickly when policies are breached. Clarify what the consequences of failure to comply will be (for example, reminders, verbal or written warnings, suspension, dismissal, immediate dismissal). Do not hesitate to follow through on their implementation.

7.8 RESISTANCE TO POLICY DEVELOPMENT

Near the end of a recent workshop on risk management and policy development in which most administrative leaders of an environmental conservancy organization had begun to recognize the full range of risks being undertaken by volunteers in service to their organization, a participant stood up and exclaimed: "I just don't see why we have to worry about all these things now. We've been operating this organization since 1953 and not one single person has ever been seriously hurt!" The kind of resistance to policy development embodied in this remark is prevalent throughout the voluntary sector. Susan Ellis anticipated similar resistance to her call for senior management to recognize their own responsibilities in volunteer program success:

> Some readers may be feeling a bit uncomfortable in the suspicion that I am going to suggest lots of structure to bureaucratize volunteerism. The fact is that successful volunteering does not come from spontaneous combustion. Most of our organizations today are already rather complex and, unless we develop clear ways for volunteers to participate in our activities, people really do not know how to become involved. This is true whether the organization is an "agency," an "institution," or an all-volunteer association. (Ellis, 1986, p. 3)

By clinging to outdated stereotypes and myths about volunteering, people—staff and volunteers alike—have lost touch with the reality of volunteering as it really is as we approach the twenty-first century. It is understandable to wish to preserve a simpler time when volunteering to help your neighbor required only that you show up with the desire to do good. But denying the complex, sophisticated, demanding, and risky nature of volunteering as it is today exposes both organizations and individuals to liabilities that are simply too great to bear.

It *is* important to preserve what we can of volunteering's essential quality of altruistic helping others. But as long as we expect volunteers to do real work, volunteers deserve real management. Nora Silver puts it this way:

> Coming into their maturity, volunteer programs are being challenged to socialize their volunteers into increasingly complex organizations, to formalize their policies and procedures and yet to maintain a humane and personalized character . . . to construct a volunteer program that is at the same time highly organized and highly flexible. (1988, pp. 99-100)

The challenge is to craft policies and procedures for volunteer programs that ensure the safest, most satisfying, and most productive experience without kicking the heart out of volunteering. And while continuing to ignore the need for policies in volunteer programs might put off for a little bit longer the realization that volunteering now is not what volunteering was 40, 30, 20, even just 10 years ago, we run the risk of allowing endless accidents, injuries, and tragedies, to transform volunteering into a movement people are simply too afraid to join. How you decide to manage *that* risk is up to you.

7.9 CONCLUSIONS

Now is the time to engage in policy development for volunteer programs. Because our expectations of volunteers have become more complex and more demanding, the practice of voluntary action involves more risks and creates greater exposure to liabilities both for volunteers and for the voluntary agencies through which they volunteer. Policy development is a crucial risk management tool that simply cannot be put off any longer. In addition, policies help volunteer programs to communicate values and beliefs to guide action, articulate rules, and develop guidelines that increase service effectiveness.

The development of a comprehensive set of policies for a volunteer program may take two to three years of concentrated effort. It is not unusual for mangers of volunteers to feel overwhelmed by the magnitude of the task or by the fear that crucial policies will be missed. This chapter has outlined useful techniques for segmenting the policy development process into a manageable plan, including guidelines for determining which policies are required. Concrete suggestions have been offered regarding how to write policies and how to increase compliance with policies. Readers are urged to overcome resistance to policy development since further delays can only mean increased risks and dangers for volunteers, clients, staff, agencies, and the general public.

REFERENCES

American Red Cross. No date. *Volunteer 2000 Study.* Washington, D.C.: The American Red Cross Society.

Canadian Red Cross - Ontario Division. 1992. *Human Resources Policies & Procedures Manual.* Mississaugo, Ontario, Canada.

Carver, John. 1990. *Boards That Make a Difference: A New Design for Leadership in Nonprofit and Public Organizations.* San Francisco: Jossey-Bass.

Conrad, William R., and William E. Glenn. 1976. *The Effective Voluntary Board of Directors.* Athens, Ohio: Swallow Press.

Cryderman, Paula. 1987. *Developing Policy and Procedure Manuals,* (rev. ed.) Ottawa: Canadian Hospital Association.

Ellis, Susan J. 1986. *From the Top Down: The Executive Role in Volunteer Program Success.* Philadelphia: Energize Associates.

Graff, Linda L. 1983. *Volunteer/Paid Staff/Union Relations: A Discussion Paper.* Hamilton, Ontario, Canada: Volunteer Centre of Hamilton and District.

Graff, Linda L. 1992. *By Definition: Policies for Volunteer Programs.* Etobicoke, Ontario, Canada: Volunteer Ontario.

Graff, Linda L. 1993. "The Key to the Boardroom Door: Policies for Volunteer Programs." *Journal of Volunteer Administration* XI (4) (Summer).

Lynch, Richard. 1983. "Designing Volunteer Jobs for Results." *Voluntary Action Leadership.* (Summer): 20–23.

McCurley, Steve. 1993. "Risk Management Techniques for Volunteer Programs." *Grapevine* (September/October): 9–13.

McCurley, Steve. 1990. *Volunteer Management Policies.* Downers Grove, Ill.: VMSystems and Heritage Arts Publishing.

McCurley, Steve. 1988. *Volunteer Management Forms.* Downers Grove, Ill.: VMSystems and Heritage Arts Publishing.

Minnesota Office on Volunteer Services. 1992. *How to Control Liability and Risk in Volunteer Programs.* St. Paul, Minn.: Minnesota Office on Volunteer Services.

O'Connell, Brian. 1985. *The Board Members' Book: Making a Difference in Voluntary Organizations.* New York: The Foundation Center.

Parks and Recreation Department, Burlington, Ontario, Canada. No date. *Brochure.*

Psychiatric Day Programme. 1992. *Volunteer Policy and Procedure Manual.* Hamilton, Ontario, Canada: Psychiatric Day Programme, St. Joseph's Hospital.

Scheier, Ivan. 1988. "Empowering a Profession: Seeing Ourselves as More Than Subsidiary." *Journal of Volunteer Administration* (Fall): 29–34.

Shaw, Robert C. 1990. "Strengthening the Role of the Voluntary Board of Directors." Excerpts reprinted in Ginette Johnstone (Ed.), *Boards of Directors' Resource Binder.* Etobicoke, Ontario, Canada: Volunteer Ontario.

Tremper, Charles, and Gwynne Kostin. 1993. *No Surprises: Controlling Risks in Volunteer Programs.* Washington, D.C.: Nonprofit Risk Management Center.

Vineyard, Sue. 1993. *Megatrends and Volunteerism: Mapping the Future of Volunteer Programs.* Downers Grove, Ill.: Heritage Arts Publishing.

Volunteer Centre of Metropolitan Toronto. 1993. *Administrative Manual.* Toronto, Ontario, Canada: Volunteer Centre of Metropolitan Toronto.

CHAPTER  8

ADMINISTRATION OF VOLUNTEER PROGRAMS

Arlene Stepputat
Director of Marketing, Advocacy Press

8.1 The Changing Role of Volunteer Administration

8.2 The Unique Role of the Volunteer Administrator

8.3 Volunteer Policy Implementation

8.4 Recruitment

8.5 Application, Interview, and Screening Process

8.6 The Process of Becoming a Volunteer

8.7 The Volunteer Application

8.8 The Interview and Screening Process

8.9 Orientation and Training

8.10 Volunteer Placement

8.11 Supervision and Evaluation

8.12 Recognition

8.13 Retention

8.14 Record Keeping

8.15 Program Evaluation

8.16 Advocacy and Education

8.17 Professional Development

8.18 The Future

Suggested Readings

8.1 THE CHANGING ROLE OF VOLUNTEER ADMINISTRATION

America has a strong and unique history founded on volunteerism. Whether at a barn-raising or a town picnic, Americans have long joined together to support each other as well as to further a cause in which they believe. A simple review of major nonprofit organizations reveals roots in volunteerism. More often than not, it is the vision and commitment of one person or a small group of leaders addressing an unmet need that is the genesis of a nonprofit organization. Clara Barton's legacy of the Red Cross is just one example of how one visionary willing to commit deeply to meet a need can change our lives permanently.

Most nonprofit organizations have their foundations in the inspired leadership and motivation of people committed to meeting a pressing need or filling a gap they saw in society. Although these organizations usually begin with the grass-roots activism of volunteers who share the founders' vision, an organized, structured approach to the use of their talents individually is often overlooked once the agency is established with paid staff members. No successful organization would consider operating without having skilled professionals in finance, program development, or personnel management, yet creating a full-time or even part-time position for a manager of volunteers may be considered a low priority. Too many nonprofit organizations are still not utilizing the full potential of the volunteer community, simply because they have not appreciated the need for a professional in that area. However, as volunteer management continues to demonstrate its invaluable contribution to organizational success, the need for trained professionals is better recognized and appropriated.

In recent years, American volunteerism has achieved a visibility and credibility previously unknown. In part, this change is a political action or reaction to the funding cuts in critical human service areas made in the 1980s. The Reagan administration launched the initial call to service and involvement, but it was George Bush's reference to volunteerism as "a thousand points of light" that underscored the enormous contributions volunteers make to our nation's overall quality of life.

Alarmed at the cutbacks in critical services, many citizens stepped forward rather than see agencies close their doors. Although there was much controversy about the fact that the private sector and the general public were expected to plug the holes left by spending cuts, the fact remains that people did come forward. Independent Sector launched its "Give Five" campaign in the spring of 1987 to encourage citizens to give five hours a week to volunteerism and 5 percent of their incomes to nonprofit organizations they believed in. The success of the campaign can be measured by the results. In 1994 it was reported that nearly 48 percent of all Americans volunteer at least four hours a week.

Other factors also opened hearts and doors. The AIDS pandemic motivated many people to respond to the crisis. Some of the most compassionate created programs. Often, these developed out of a sense of frustration at the gap between services needed and services provided. The number of people requiring assistance is growing exponentially.

During the 1980s, when symbols of affluence seemed to be in vogue, many came to realize that the acquisition of a BMW or Rolex watch was a short-lived experience of fulfillment. Many baby boomers began to rethink their value systems and looked for a more rewarding way to experience success.

Homelessness, illiteracy, domestic abuse of spouses and children, environmental crises, and international turmoil all became prevalent issues to which many felt compelled to respond. Even celebrities created concerts and records, and volunteered publicly to offer their talents as a way to help the causes most dear to them.

The creation of the National and Community Service Act of 1990 put federal funds and support behind creating meaningful community service opportunities and making them available to everyone regardless of income, race, or background.

Clearly, volunteerism now strives to include everyone. The days when the typical volunteer was a retiree looking for a meaningful way to contribute to society or a married woman who stayed home to care for the children and gave some hours while the kids were in school are gone. Women's entrance into the workforce, the need for double-income families, the rise in divorce, the improved health and more discretionary time of many older adults are all factors that have changed the face of the typical volunteer. Alternative sentencing, offering community service in lieu of jail time, has also brought new volunteers and new challenges. Increasingly, schools require students to participate actively in the community as prerequisites for graduation—for example, the state of Maryland requires it.

The net result of all these changes is the critical need to increase the numbers of professional volunteer administrators who are able to serve as a link between the needs of an organization or agency and the skills and availability of the volunteers who want to contribute their time and talent. Leading an effective, efficient volunteer administration program over time is a critical factor for the volunteer administrator and a true measure of success. There are several key areas in volunteer management that comprise a well-founded program (Exhibit 8–1). They are often interrelated, as further discussion will indicate. The successful volunteer manager must address each of them consistently on an ongoing basis.

8.2 THE UNIQUE ROLE OF THE VOLUNTEER ADMINISTRATOR

The role of the volunteer administrator is unlike any other position within an organization. First, it is a role that many nonprofit professionals still do not understand or value completely. Part of this is due to the fact that it is only within the last decade or so that institutions of higher learning began to offer courses in volunteer administration. All too often, volunteerism was mentioned in a survey class covering nonprofit organizations but was not given the in-depth attention necessary to provide those interested in the field of nonprofit management a clear understanding of the complex role the volunteer administrator plays within an agency as well as in the community at large.

A survey of those employed as volunteer administrators for five years or more would probably reveal that most have no formal education in the management of volunteers. Many learned by trial and error, called on their own experiences as a volunteer, and sought to network with others for information and support. Other volunteer administrators fell into their positions, usually because they had superb people skills, were dedicated and well organized, and had years of leadership experience, often as volunteers.

Volunteer management is now a profession and commands the respect it deserves. This is due in large measure to the efforts of the Association for Volunteer

---

◆ **EXHIBIT 8–1   Core Elements of Volunteer Administration**

The elements of a volunteer program include:

Recruitment - the methodology by which the organization extends itself into the potential volunteer pool of the community to get its needs met.

Application, interview, and screening process - the initial process by which an organization evaluates and selects feasible volunteer candidates.

Orientation and training - the preparation and education of volunteers to familiarize them with general knowledge about policy and procedure and to develop specific skills for services they will perform.

Volunteer placement - matching the skills and availability of the volunteer with the needs of the organization to ensure the most effective use of the individual volunteer.

Supervision and evaluation - regular performance-related monitoring and feedback provided to volunteers, both informally and formally.

Recognition - methods used to express appreciation to volunteers, both formally and informally, as well as to communicate the value of volunteers to the organization and to the community.

Retention - the number of volunteers who successfully complete their initial commitment to an agency, including those who renew and continue serving the organization.

Record keeping - the system established to store and retrieve information about the individual volunteer, including the ability to generate cumulative data regarding the entire corps.

Program evaluation - the mechanism by which the success of the program is determined as well as a tool for setting long- and short-term goals and objectives.

Advocacy and education - a clear philosophy regarding the vital role of volunteers within the organization and the methods used to ensure that leadership, staff members, and volunteers continually expand their knowledge about volunteerism and its impact on the agency.

Administration (AVA), the international professional association for effective leaders who mobilize volunteers to meet community needs. Its mission is to promote professionalism and strengthen leadership in volunteerism. Membership is open to salaried and unsalaried workers in all types of government in both nonprofit and for-profit settings. Further information about AVA is provided later in the chapter.

Clearly, then, a top priority is educating one's co-workers about the role of the volunteer administrator and how that person must work in cooperation with all functions within the organization and with all levels of personnel, from the executive director to the part-time maintenance person. This means that the volunteer administrator must understand all facets of the organization and must be kept informed about policies and developments.

The volunteer administrator's singular duty is to serve as a bridge: for paid staff and volunteers to understand and support each other; for the community and the agency to cooperate and serve each other; for the volunteers and those who are being assisted to connect with each other; and for any person or situation that may arise in which information, understanding, neutrality, and humor are required to help ensure harmonious cooperation on all levels.

Often, the volunteer administrator has no peer or professional colleague within the organization. Although there may be many staff in the personnel or finance departments, the volunteer administrator is usually alone and is expected to staff the office with volunteers.

Typically, the manager of volunteers gets feedback about all facets of the organization from volunteers. This can be threatening for some staff members unless they are secure in the knowledge that the volunteer administrator is an advocate for the overall good of the organization and does not automatically side with the volunteers.

The volunteer administrator is often responsible for more people than those handled by the personnel department. Usually, he or she has as much contact with the community as anyone doing public relations. Unfortunately, the volunteer department's budget is quite limited because some managers do not understand fully the costs (investments) involved in maintaining a well-run department.

The strength inherent in the role of volunteer administrator is that everybody wins. Volunteers get opportunities to use their gifts, the paid staff gets extra support, the clients are served, and the mission of the organization is advanced. In direct service, volunteers send clients the message that they are cared about simply because they are who they are. Many people who have felt disenfranchised or apart from society are uplifted when others have come forward to serve them simply because they care.

The most positive aspect of being an administrator of volunteers is that the best of humanity is visible daily in the compassionate action that is undertaken.

8.3 VOLUNTEER POLICY IMPLEMENTATION

It is important that a volunteer administrator have a strong personal philosophy about the role of volunteerism, not only in a particular agency but from a much broader base. Within an agency the volunteer administrator has a unique and vital role serving as a bridge and linking pin between all the players in an organization. The volunteer administrator must serve as an advocate for the volunteer corps. In addition, the administrator also must align him or herself with both the administration and the staff to ensure cooperation and careful planning.

The organizational climate, from the board of directors to the staff person hired yesterday, is a key factor in the implementation and ongoing development of a solid volunteer corps. Looking first at the mission statement, one can tell how service oriented the organization is. Also, the history of an organization will help reveal how volunteers are perceived. Although things are changing, unfortunately many nonprofit organizations that use volunteers have not given them the same degree of care, focus, and professionalism that they have given their paid staff. For many organizations, the volunteer manager is not considered with the same level of seriousness and planning as other managers within the agency. One revealing feature is where the volunteer manager is located on the organizational chart and to whom that person reports. The title itself may indicate the value of the position within the organization.

Often, there is a perceived hierarchy within the range of titles accorded the person who handles volunteers within an agency. In smaller agencies, the role is delegated to someone who has other primary responsibilities as well. Someone, perhaps the public relations person, a fund-raiser, a special events coordinator, or a program manager, may be assigned the responsibility for managing volunteers. In agencies where a full-time volunteer manager position exists, the title ranges from volunteer coordinator to volunteer manager to director of volunteers. The word *director* within a title establishes some recognition of power within an organization and signifies that the holder is considered upper management, with other directors as peers.

Even so, the role of volunteer administrator often is not valued to the same degree as that of other administrative positions within an organization in the eyes of management and thus by staff as well. Part of this is due to a lack of understanding about what the role entails. A common viewpoint held by many is that if someone is a volunteer, then that person should be able to manage a volunteer department. This is akin to saying that if a person goes to the dentist, then he or she should be able to fill cavities!

Clearly, one of the most important roles that volunteer managers can play in the development of volunteer policy implementation is to educate their colleagues about the magnitude and scope of responsibility involved in the position. This is done over time and is an ongoing area of focus. The cooperation of the entire staff—from board to housekeeping—is essential to implement some of the volunteer policies set forward. The best way to achieve this is to make an effort to work with all staff members, both individually and departmentally, formally in training and informally in the hallway, to continually develop a partnership with staff and volunteers.

A very important perspective for the volunteer manager to establish is that volunteers are unpaid staff and that everything that must be done to maintain paid employees—from application through retirement—is also required to maintain a vital volunteer department. Although some programs do provide stipends or modified benefits to volunteers, the most common view held by staff is that volunteers and staff members differ because volunteers perform the work "for free." Recognizing and working with the attitudes and belief systems that may flow from this point of view is basic to overall staff–volunteer relationships. For example, staff members may be reluctant to correct volunteers in the performance of their duties because they do not want to hurt someone's feelings or because they believe that it is wrong to do so because volunteers are giving their time. Also, those receiving stipends or other benefits may not be considered pure volunteers because some financial incentive is present. Exploring staff beliefs about who and what makes a person a volunteer is a worthwhile endeavor.

Implementing volunteer policies requires the following elements: (1) a respect and understanding for the role of volunteers within the organization and how that role interfaces with all other departments, and (2) the attitude that volunteers are additional human resources for an organization and require the same level of management as do paid employees. Also required is a clear and consistent method of communicating volunteer policies within the organization to all parties. This can be done in a variety of ways and might include the creation of a handbook or policy manual, participation in staff orientation and training, and regular participation in management meetings.

In any organization, sound policies and procedures are developed with thought, designed for easy and practical application, and have both an ethical and a professional foundation. They also are communicated effectively to all staff members and are implemented in a consistent way. Policies and procedures are evaluated and reviewed periodically to ensure that they continue to serve the organization. The volunteer department is no exception.

8.4 RECRUITMENT

There are two general types of volunteer recruitment: generic and targeted. *Generic volunteer recruitment* includes a general call to the public to become involved in an issue or organization on a broad scale. Usually, these appeals invite people to explore the agency and see how their skills and talents might match up with a wide range of agency needs. There may be many openings and uses for volunteers, or there may just be a need for many people to work on a similar task in order to get it completed. In addition, the task may not require extensive training or screening, just a simple desire to be of service. Working in a soup kitchen is one example of a daily need for a number of people to assist with a variety of tasks that facilitate the smooth operation of feeding large groups. A big factor is volunteers' ability to commit to a specific period of time. They may then be assigned to food preparation, serving, waiting on tables, or socializing and monitoring those standing on line waiting their turn.

Generic volunteer recruitment is the methodology used to inform the community about volunteer opportunities and to invite them to participate. Ways to reach various components of the community are as creative as the volunteer administrator. Public service announcements on radio or minispots on television may attract the largest audience. Appeals to schools, houses of worship, and service organizations may be done via fliers, speaking engagements at meetings, or networking with key members of these groups. Voluntary action centers (usually referred to as VACs) are government funded to serve as clearinghouses to match the volunteer needs of an organization with citizens in the community seeking to offer their time and talents.

The astute volunteer manager looks at every opportunity that presents itself to both recruit and recognize the existing volunteer corps as well. Effective recognition is a recruitment tool because it encourages people to belong to an organization where clearly they are valued.

Targeted volunteer recruitment occurs when an organization seeks to fill a specific need with a qualified volunteer. Suppose that an organization needs a photographer to shoot a special event but does not have the budget to pay a professional. The volunteer manager then seeks to network and recruit volunteers from a select pool of people who may be able to assist. There may be a professional organization of photographers or a fine arts school in the community, or the volunteer manager may simply approach a local newspaper and ask for an in-kind donation of a photographer for the day.

Targeted recruitment can be conducted within an existing volunteer pool. Creating an internal talent bank is the first step in meeting the specific skill needs of an agency. One of the best sources of recruitment is the active volunteer corps the organization should already have. Fun events such as "Each One, Bring One" encourages volunteers to bring friends and family into the organization to explore and develop their own interests. It also provides a wonderful opportunity for both recruitment *and* recognition. An event such as Each One, Bring One is an open house recruitment tool where every volunteer is requested to bring one new potential recruit. This builds esprit de corps among existing volunteers, and provides a unique recognition of the volunteers who already work in the organization. A tour, brief overview of the organization, and refreshments assist in welcoming people recruited by their friends and family. Most people currently volunteer because they were specifically asked to help.

Before any recruitment campaign gets under way, it is imperative that the volunteer manager have a clear process and program designed to utilize those who respond. This takes planning and coordination with management and staff. Involving paid employees in the process of volunteer management from the beginning is an important key to creating a team approach and helping to ensure that departments and/or supervisors "take ownership" for the way volunteers are used in their respective area.

8.5 APPLICATION, INTERVIEW, AND SCREENING PROCESS

Depending upon the unique nature of the organization—the mission, the clients, the services, the facility, the number of paid staff, and the immediate need for volunteers—the process of becoming a volunteer can vary widely. A primary role of the volunteer administrator is to design a timely and effective methodology by which people become volunteers, to include leadership in the developmental plans, and to inform all levels of the organization about the process.

As part of a university class in volunteer management, students were given the assignment to contact three community organizations that use volunteers and find out how prospective volunteers might become involved with the agency. They were asked to track the method, time frame, and response they received. Students are usually surprised at the wide range of responses they receive. All too often, the staff members answering the telephone are unclear about the process of how to become a volunteer. Often, they do not even know the name of the person within the agency who oversees that area. Students discover that many organizations do not even bother to take a name and telephone number. Others have found that an overworked or annoyed person can dampen a potential volunteer's enthusiasm within minutes.

The volunteer administrator must work continuously with all members of the staff (particularly those with "reception" duties) to help them understand their unique role in the organization and how it supports the volunteer effort, particularly in the area of recruitment and response to inquiries.

As the consummate bridge builder in an agency, the volunteer manager should provide the switchboard with written information about events and training; the receptionist with a supply of volunteer literature; and the security guards with background information about the volunteer program, and how to become a volunteer, and dates when potential volunteers will be coming to the agency. Engaging the paid staff at all levels, empowering them with information, and having regular contact with them assists in creating a volunteer-friendly environment when members of the general public make their first inquiry.

Recruitment is an ongoing process. The wise manager works with the funding and development department to make sure that when solicitations and annual campaigns are launched, the option to give via volunteering is included. There is a high correlation between financial donors to an agency and volunteers. Consistently, those who affiliate with an agency as volunteers also become financial contributors, especially after witnessing firsthand how the organization fulfills the mission and the financial constraints that impede.

Working closely with special events coordinators and public relations departments are key factors to ensure that each time the organization is in the public eye, the use of volunteers and the opportunities for participation are a part of the agenda. Agencies that provide public education services have frequent opportunities to invite the public to participate. Written materials and information packages (including an application) are essential tools to help improve success in reaching out to the community.

8.6 THE PROCESS OF BECOMING A VOLUNTEER

All prospective employees seeking work expect to go through a process to determine the fit between their skills and the organization's needs. This includes completing paperwork, interviewing, and exploring with the employer or decision maker their perception of their suitability for the job at hand. Job seekers also expect to receive specific information about the job, including the skills required, working hours, conditions, salary, and benefits. Anyone who has ever sought a job is familiar with this process.

Too often, volunteers do not go through a similar procedure, yet they, too, must be viewed as employees. A step-by-step method to affiliate with the organization must be carefully designed and consistently implemented to ensure that a uniform and positive process is achieved by all applicants. The process and development from application to training design must be carefully planned *before* any recruitment campaign for new volunteers is launched. Nothing is more destructive to the initial enthusiasm of a volunteer than to be met with chaos, unpreparedness, or apathy on the part of the organization that requested volunteer assistance and participation.

There is a mutuality in the process that the volunteer manager must keep in mind. While the agency is determining how the volunteer may best fit into the agency's needs, the volunteer is assessing how the opportunities provided in this volunteer position best meet his or her expectations. Often, volunteer candidates do not have a clear sense of what it is they are looking for, except perhaps to serve. The skilled manager provides information and checkpoints so that continual assessment is part of the process, enabling a volunteer to make a heartfelt and sound commitment. It also provides an opportunity for the volunteer to opt out of a particular experience upon discovering that his or her expectations or abilities do not work with those of the particular agency.

8.7 THE VOLUNTEER APPLICATION

A well-designed volunteer application can be an invaluable tool for a volunteer department, not only for initial interviewing and screening but also as a resource for the talent bank and for links to the community at large. Depending on the size of the organization and the other duties for which the volunteer administrator is responsible, how and when a volunteer receives an application and even an interview may vary. Each manager determines policy and procedure. Sometimes managers can accommodate a walk-in volunteer candidate and may even briefly interview the potential volunteer before receiving an application; at other times this is impossible. It is essential that the staff be trained to create a volunteer-friendly environment so that whether or not the volunteer administrator is available, the candidate receives a welcome and some information.

It is important to realize that applications for employment, whether as paid employees or as volunteers, follow strict guidelines about information that can be legally requested. Questions regarding age, religion, marital status, ethnicity, sexual orientation, or anything that may be considered discriminatory are prohibited.

Some volunteer opportunities may require minimum ages. Hospitals or agencies working with children may have minimum age requirements for specific duties. One child care agency that served young people until the age of 21 required that volunteers requesting direct contact with the youths be at least 23 years of age. This information was clearly stated on the application itself. However, other volunteer options were also listed that had no age criterion.

As the first record of contact and information a volunteer manager may receive from a volunteer candidate, the application design should contain pertinent data such as name, address, employment history, and education (Exhibit 8–2). As a tool, preferably completed before an interview, the application can provide the volunteer manager with important information that will speed the interview and ensure satisfactory placement.

The application can also serve as a tool for the volunteer candidate. Specific questions, such as time availability, special skills, talents, hobbies, and previous volunteer history assist the candidate in beginning to define for him or herself exactly the experience he or she is seeking. The person begins to consider scheduling and commitments as a preferred time slot and day of the week are checked as preferences.

Depending on the nature of the nonprofit organization and the range of activities from which a volunteer may choose, two or three open-ended questions on the application may assist both the administrator and the volunteer in clarifying motivation and expectation. Discovering whether a volunteer candidate has had previous volunteer experience in other organizations is important information. Providing a place to list the organization, the volunteer's role, and the length of service can assist in the interviewing and placement process. If a person is a first-time volunteer, this is also valuable to know.

Many roles for volunteers include working with issues that carry a high emotional content. It is wise to ask a question that may provide some insight into the motivation and/or experience of the volunteer candidate. For instance, a question such as "How has cancer touched your life?" on a hospice volunteer application causes the volunteer to reflect carefully and in the response may provide information worth exploring during the interview. If the response is, "My son died of it eight months ago," this may be an indicator that the candidate is not emotionally ready to assist others. When people choose not to answer these brief questions, this is also worth exploring in an interview.

Whenever possible, if there are certain requirements for the agency, such as driving clients around, it is appropriate to ask for additional information, such as whether the person has a valid driver's license. One question that is useful to ask no matter what organization a volunteer is applying to is, "What do you hope to

---

◆ **EXHIBIT 8–2   Sample Volunteer Application for Youth Shelter**

Name: _____   Telephone: Home_____

Address: _____ Work _____

Zip code: _____ Age: (optional) _____ Birthday: _____

Present employment _____ Employer's name_____

Previous employment history: Indicate jobs that you have held within the past five years. If possible, please include a resume._____

_____

Please circle or check areas of interest for volunteer work.
Note that any work preceded by an asterisk requires that a volunteer be over the age of 23.

*Tutor	Kitchen aide	Reception
*Job counselor	Grounds and maintenance	Computer support
*Recreation/gym	*Escort/driver	Newsletter
*Resident assistant thrift shop		Fund-raising
Other areas not listed		

List any skills or special training that you have (examples: computers, crafts, hobbies, foreign languages, etc.)   _____

_____

List any previous volunteer experience that you have had. Please include the organization, your involvement, and the length of time you volunteered.

_____

_____

1. Briefly describe an experience in your life that has had a great impact on you.

_____

_____

_____

2. What do you hope to accomplish as a volunteer at our agency?_____

_____

_____

_____

Signature _____ Date _____

---

experience as a volunteer in our organization?" This question can help identify realistic or false expectations.

Providing a volunteer candidate with an overview of the options and expectations of the volunteer program is a useful way to assist the volunteer in the self-selection process. A one-page statement that describes how volunteers participate in the organization and includes a summary of the steps required to become a volunteer provides a foundation that is useful to both the potential volunteer and the volunteer manager (Exhibit 8–3). This statement can often accompany the volunteer application. Then time is not spent during the volunteer interview providing information on the program but can be focused more directly on the individual candidate.

Another consideration is a request for references as part of the application process. Particularly in volunteer work, where the volunteer may have access to children, home-bound or incapacitated adults, or people who may have impaired physical, mental, or emotional abilities, such prudence is warranted as part of the screening process.

Although the overwhelming majority of people pursuing volunteer work have pure intentions, sadly there are those who would use such opportunities to take advantage of clients. One incident of any type of abuse can have dire effects on the entire organization. Since such events are well publicized when they occur, most volunteer applicants understand the need to be cautious when the clients being served are vulnerable. The mission of the organization is the first principle for the volunteer manager, and protecting the clients is more important than adding new volunteers about whom the manager does not feel secure.

A simple reference form can be designed and included as part of the application package (Exhibit 8–4). A written document that is to be returned directly to the volunteer administrator is preferable both as a record and as a time saver. Telephoning references listed on an application can be tedious, and the documentation is then based on the manager's recording of the response.

Some states have specific requirements for checking criminal history and/or allegations of abuse if the nature of the work involves minors. It is wise to contact the state governmental body in charge of children's services to ensure that any forms or clearance checks required are also part of the application and screening process.

8.8 THE INTERVIEW AND SCREENING PROCESS

The timing of an interview and what it is to discover are part of the planning process. One useful tool to create is an interview feedback form that assists with structuring a consistent format for each volunteer candidate (Exhibit 8–5). This document is a road map to be utilized in the course of a 30- to 45-minute interview. Afterward, it serves as a written record of information gleaned and becomes part of the volunteer's file.

The purpose of the interview is to further assess whether a match can be made between the organization's needs and the volunteer candidate's skills, talents, and wants. It is also an opportunity to review pertinent information that may be critical in helping both parties determine the suitability of the match.

Prior to scheduling an interview, the administrator must carefully review all the information provided on the volunteer application and, if utilized, on reference

---

◆ **EXHIBIT 8–3   Sample Program Description for a Youth Shelter**

Volunteers are a vital part of our agency and are utilized in every aspect of our program. Currently, we have approximately 150 part-time volunteers.

There are two basic kinds of volunteer work—direct and indirect care. Our need for indirect work is essentially clerical. Although most of the work is done during business hours, we do use this assistance at night and on weekends.

Volunteers are also utilized in our kitchen, in our thrift shop, and in our reception area. Although many people want to work directly with our kids, every volunteer who assists us *is* working for our kids.

People willing to serve indirectly are invited for an interview after we've received and reviewed their application and references. Usually, they can begin service within a week after the interview.

Many people want to have direct interaction with our youth. These people assist counselors, serve meals, offer recreation, tutor, act as van escorts, and are flexible enough to do whatever immediate task is at hand.

To ensure the best possible experience for both our kids and our volunteers, we have a screening and training process.

Volunteers requesting direct care must be at least 21 years of age. We've found that it is better for all concerned if volunteers are older than residents.

After both reference forms attached to the initial application have been completed and returned to the agency, we invite that person for an interview. References can be from an employer, colleague, clergy member, teacher, or anyone who can provide insight into your abilities to work in our setting. Family members cannot provide references. At the interview we schedule a tour of the facility to allow potential volunteers an inside view of what volunteers do here. We match candidates with experienced volunteers for an hour or two to observe the way we work with young people.

Our training program is held in three sessions over the course of two weeks. Most of our volunteers hold full-time jobs, so the training sessions are held weeknights and one full week-end day. Attendance at all three sessions is required.

Our training process takes time. We run sessions about every six to eight weeks and limit each session to 15 people. Please be patient, because we *do* want you here.

When a volunteer has completed these steps successfully, we ask for a consecutive four-hour commitment per week for six months—equaling 100 hours of service. We ask for consistency and reliability.

Volunteering with our kids is an experience that provides growth, challenge, and reward. If you have any questions, please call us at. . . .

Thank you for caring enough to give the gift of yourself.

---

forms. Reading the responses to the open-ended questions may also reveal some areas or "flags" that may need further exploration.

The interview of a volunteer candidate is as important as one for a potential employee and merits the same consideration. The interview must be in a private place with no distractions. This simple fact can be a challenge in small agencies

---

◆ **EXHIBIT 8–4   Sample Reference Form (to be printed on letterhead)**

Volunteer Department

Applicant's Name _____

The person named above has applied to serve as a volunteer at our agency. In that capacity, he or she may work with children and adolescents in our shelter. We would appreciate your candid assessment of the applicant's suitability as a volunteer in our program, which serves homeless youth. Of special interest to us is your assessment of the applicant's ability to work with young people as a role model. Your response will help us to provide a meaningful volunteer experience for the applicant.

_____

_____

_____

_____

_____

_____

_____

_____

_____

_____

_____

_____

_____

Reference completed by _____

Address _____

Telephone _____

Relationship to applicant* _____

*References from family members are not acceptable.   Please return this form to the Volunteer Department.

◆ **EXHIBIT 8–5   Sample Interview Sheet for Volunteers**

CONFIDENTIAL

Name of Applicant _____   Date _____

1. What motivated the applicant to become a volunteer at the shelter?

_____

_____

_____

2. What strengths does the applicant see in him or herself that would assist others?

_____

_____

_____

3. What major concerns or questions does the applicant foresee in dealing with young people who have been homeless?

_____

_____

_____

4. What strengths did the applicant exhibit that suggest suitability for this work? Be specific.

_____

_____

_____

5. Did any part of the interview suggest unsuitability or leave reservations about the candidate? Be specific.

_____

_____

_____

Overall rating: ❑ Recommend with enthusiasm   ❑ Recommend
                     ❑ Recommend with reservations   ❑ Question suitability

Signature of the interviewer _____

---

with shared office space, but it is worth being creative to ensure that the manager and the volunteer candidate have an opportunity to meet uninterrupted.

The interview is to be based on information exchange and mutuality. Too often, the interviewer can do too much talking during an interview and realize afterward that critical points may have been overlooked. It is the manager's role to keep the interview focused.

The reception of the volunteer candidate and the climate of the interview are critical. Warmth and sincerity as well as organization and preparation by the volunteer administrator will assuage any nervousness the candidate may be experiencing. Outstanding people skills are a major requirement of a good volunteer manager, and the interview is often the first face-to-face contact volunteer candidates have with staff people as they begin to explore this new path.

Volunteer candidates must be invited to share information about themselves in the course of the interview. However, it is important to remember that any question that does not relate directly to the ability of an applicant to perform a specific role can be viewed as discriminatory. Therefore, avoid asking about the following:

- Age, height, or weight
- Birthplace, national origin, or English language skill
- Marital status, child care, pregnancy
- Religious affiliation
- Discharge from military service
- Length of residence in the community
- Name and addresses of relatives
- Home or credit card ownership
- Arrest record (If you are interviewing a court-referred community service volunteer, obtain specifics from the parole or probation officer prior to the interview.)

In some situations, the volunteer candidate is interviewed first by the volunteer coordinator, then again by the staff member who is likely to be the volunteer's supervisor.

Preplanning with the paid employees involved will result in a coordinated effort that does not duplicate information or waste anyone's time. If it is feasible as part of the process, having the volunteer candidate meet with a perspective supervisor on the day of initial interview may speed the time of placement for all concerned.

The volunteer administrator may use this time to explain special considerations or policies of the organization that may be critical for the candidate to know as part of his or her own decision-making process. For instance, perhaps a group that advocates sex education for adolescents provides condoms to teens as part of their service, or conversely, perhaps the organization's goal is to promote abstinence as the only feasible prevention method against sexually transmitted diseases and unwanted pregnancies.

It is imperative that volunteer candidates have this type of information initially so that the mission of the organization and the belief systems of the candidates are in alignment. This is all part of the self-screening and selection process. It is a mutual process. The candidate is assessing the organization while the agency is screening the potential volunteer. Both are seeking a fit.

If at any point during the interview a candidate realizes that an agency policy is one with which he or she cannot comply or that the volunteer role is not what was anticipated, it is imperative that the interviewer respond with acceptance and neutrality. The candidate has determined the organization doesn't match the volunteer's expectations. This is not a time to defend or persuade. This is an opportunity to redirect the volunteer to another volunteer option within the community. A person's desire to assist the greater good must not be lost because the avenue that he or she has explored initially does not match his or her personal beliefs. The resourceful volunteer administrator retains a list of volunteer referrals to assist the volunteer candidate in locating a more suitable agency. There may be a local Voluntary Action Center (VAC) that serves as a clearinghouse for volunteer referrals in the community. In any case, the volunteer candidate must not leave the interview feeling dejected because the desire to help did not match the organization.

On occasion, the interview may reveal to the volunteer administrator that the candidate is not suited to the agency even though the candidate wants to become a volunteer. The candidate may have a hidden agenda—in fact, that agenda may be hidden even from the candidate him or herself. An honest, sensitive, and straightforward approach is the best way to handle such a situation. Any volunteer candidate who is denied a volunteer position in an organization deserves to know the reason. This can be the most challenging part of the interview process, yet to falsify reasons or, worse, not to follow up the interview, is unethical, although it may seem easier. Whenever possible, the manager should offer an alternative.

Specific and concrete statements provide the candidate with feedback. "Mr. Robbins, your strong view that AIDS is a punishment from God is inconsistent with our philosophy, and some of the homeless people who come to our shelter are HIV positive. We feel it is better that you not have direct contact with our clients. However, we could use someone to pick up donations from local merchants in the community. Is that something you would feel comfortable with?" This respectful approach attempts to create a win—win situation. However, the volunteer manager must not jeopardize the volunteer department if the person is clearly unsuitable. The feedback form allows room for careful documentation of the interaction and impressions left. Should any repercussions surface, a record is available. The application and paperwork of any candidates who are considered unsuitable should be retained by the volunteer manager.

Volunteers who will have access to children or other vulnerable populations must be carefully screened, and it is better to err toward the overprotection of clients than to risk admitting a person who may harm a client emotionally, psychologically, or even physically. This is a reality that cannot be ignored.

In most cases, the volunteer interview process is a positive experience and aids in the ultimate placement of the volunteer within the organization. Ample time to answer the volunteer's questions must be balanced with not beginning the training process during the interview. The volunteer candidate should leave the interview knowing exactly what the next action step is and who will be taking it as he or she continues to move through the process of becoming a volunteer.

8.9 ORIENTATION AND TRAINING

The types of orientation and training a volunteer needs to perform well in the organization is as varied as the range of duties and responsibilities available. The fact that volunteers do need initial and ongoing training is essential. Although the words *orientation* and *training* are often used interchangeably, here a distinction will be made.

An orientation is a sharing of information that provides volunteer candidates with an overview of the agency, its mission, how the volunteer department supports that mission, and the range of options available to the candidate before he or she commits to becoming a volunteer. An orientation can be viewed as part of the self-selection process. Volunteer candidates are invited to explore the potential for involvement and can pursue next steps as they wish. Orientations are akin to an open house and might even be scheduled on a regular basis so that recruitment is ongoing. A potential volunteer might attend an orientation prior to submitting an application to the agency.

Training is more extensive and occurs after a volunteer applicant has been interviewed, screened, and accepted as a volunteer. Although it may be done on a one-to-one basis, in larger groups, or even in classes, training provides volunteers with the information, skills, and experiences required to perform the task at hand with confidence and quality. A review of the information presented in an orientation such as agency mission and history can be a part of volunteer training.

The volunteer administrator is responsible for ensuring that all volunteers receive adequate training for the roles they are to perform and is the person who plans, with paid employees, exactly how that training is to be delivered. Often, paid employees forget what the organization felt like when they first entered it, when everything was new. Involving them in the process of training volunteers assists them in remembering what being new to an organization feels like. It heightens their sensitivity and also contributes to building staff and volunteer relationships. Providing basic information about organizational procedure as well as the location of such essential places as the supply room, the cafeteria, and the administrative offices is all part of training. Whether done formally or informally, training must be well planned, consistent, and thorough.

Some volunteer roles require extensive training prior to involvement. Although some administrators fear that candidates may be discouraged if training requirements are lengthy, to compromise on the quality of the training provided is to cater to the lowest common denominator. The volunteer administrator must believe that it is a disservice to the organization, to those being served, and to the volunteers themselves when volunteers are not sufficiently prepared to function in the situations they encounter.

Consider a volunteer worker on a hotline. Most programs require extensive training, usually a minimum of 40 to 50 hours, before the volunteer is capable of answering a call independently. Consider the consequences should a volunteer answer a suicide call when he or she is not skilled in the techniques used in such a situation. Yet some volunteer programs that place volunteers in sensitive positions, such as working with young people, the elderly, or other specialized populations, sometimes fail to include critical information and techniques that could support the volunteer in working effectively with these groups. Experienced professionals must remember that volunteers don't always know information that may seem obvious. Training is a critical component to volunteer success.

Training, especially for areas that involve heavy emotional content, can also be a part of the screening process. Using the hotline analogy above, the volunteer candidate perhaps demonstrates during the course of role-playing that his or her listening skills are not at the level required for such sensitive work. It is the volunteer manager's role to examine this problem, working this with the candidate to see what intervention may be necessary.

Volunteers must be told about the training requirements prior to becoming accepted as candidates. Clear guidelines about attendance, competencies, and schedule must be established so that a volunteer realizes how extensive the expected commitment will be. This is part of the information reviewed in the interview.

Some programs have limited spots available for training and thus it is imperative that the volunteer candidate who enters training has the intention of completing the program. With the diversity of the volunteer pool, training times may need to be scheduled in the evening, on weekends, and in the course of the week. If an organization has a training department for employees, it may be helpful for the volunteer administrator to work in collaboration with them.

Adult learners require a range of activities that continue to keep them engaged. Most of the learning that they will retain is experiential, so interactive presentations using such methods as dyads, small group problem solving, and role-plays are useful. Providing training that addresses the visual, auditory, and kinesthetic learning modalities ensures that information gets across to all participants. Videos, written materials, guest speakers, tours of the facility, and the like are all ways to vary the presentation and ensure that information is presented for everyone.

Training is an ongoing part of participation in an organization and it is imperative that in-service training be provided for volunteers. Working in conjunction with the human resources or training department in an organization may simply mean that volunteers are welcome to attend any special training being held for paid employees that improves skills or strengthen knowledge.

Informal training must also be encouraged. Establishing a lending library of books and videos, providing copies of a news article, posting a notice about a new agency policy or staff member, and establishing volunteer buddies where newer volunteers a repaired with experienced ones are all ways to continue the educational process. Periodical feedback sessions or support groups are especially effective in assisting volunteers in gathering new skills and finding solutions to challenges they may be experiencing in their work.

8.10 VOLUNTEER PLACEMENT

Matching the skills and talents of a volunteer with the specific needs of an organization is the marriage everyone is seeking. Each of the components detailed earlier assists in this process. Another extremely valuable tool is the volunteer job description (Exhibit 8–6).

Ideally, every volunteer opportunity within an organization should have an accompanying job description that is written by the department and the supervisor requesting volunteer assistance. Often, the volunteer manager creates a format and may meet with the staff to make sure that the roles and responsibilities are clearly defined. The completed job description should convey all the particulars about the position, including skills required, training offered, and optimal times for which this work is best suited. Also, some tasks are necessary for a limited time period, so someone assisting with the annual campaign, for example, should be advised that the role will be ongoing for a two-month period and then may be complete.

◆ **EXHIBIT 8–6   Sample Format for Volunteer Job Descriptions**

JOB TITLE: Resident Assistant
DEPARTMENT: Program Services
LOCATION: Boys Unit
SUPERVISOR: Martin Allen
TIME COMMITMENT: Six months
OPTIMAL TIME PERIODS: Evenings from 6 to 9, any time on weekends

I. PURPOSE AND GOAL OF THE POSITION—Assist staff in monitoring individual treatment plan goals on a daily basis.

II. MAJOR DUTIES AND RESPONSIBILITY—The resident assistant will work in partnership with child care staff to assist in supervising structured activities, transporting youth to appointments, listening, and assisting residents with problem solving regarding their treatment goals, and providing support and encouragement.
Specific duties may include the following:

- Escorting residents to recreational activities
- Checking in and monitoring progress on treatment plans
- Playing games, reading stories, etc.
- Assisting with cleaning of living space
- Inventorying and ordering supplies
- Accessing and checking rooms
- Filing forms in residents' folders

III. EXPECTED RESULTS:
The resident assistant will support both staff and residents. This volunteer will act as a role model and ensure that the residents' needs are being attended to as expediently as possible. The resident assistant will supervise resident activity and ensure that it complies with the goals of the program.

IV. SKILLS AND QUALIFICATIONS:

- Excellent listening skills
- Ability to use good judgment
- Warmth
- Ability to respond quickly to direction
- Flexibility
- Completion of resident assistant volunteer training program

V. TRAINING PROVIDED
All resident assistants will receive a one-hour orientation to the boy's unit presented by Martin Allen. Ongoing training will be provided. Attendance at case review is encouraged and occurs twice weekly. Case schedules are posted a week in advance.

Even if most volunteers perform similar roles within the organization, creating job descriptions ensures that everyone is working with the same reference point regarding roles and responsibilities. This also makes supervision and evaluation easier.

Establishing a trial period for a volunteer placement can provide the staff, the supervisor, and the volunteer with the freedom to try on the role. The volunteer can assess the role and its suitability based on actual experience. Usually a four- to six-week period (assuming that the volunteer is reporting to work at least once a week for a minimum of three hours) is adequate to assess the effectiveness of the placement.

It is imperative that the volunteer manager monitor the placement for both the volunteer and the staff during this time and seek feedback as early as possible. Sometimes it is clear after an initial experience that the placement is not working. When both volunteer and staff member agree, an alternative placement can be sought. However, if the feeling of unsuitability is one-sided, there is an opportunity for the volunteer manager to trouble shoot for some critical information was not communicated effectively. Speaking with both volunteer and staff will assist in determining how the role might be more accurately presented and perhaps what additional training might be required prior to placement. Volunteers must know that if they are uncomfortable with their volunteer placement, they need to speak with both the staff supervisor and the volunteer manager. Creating a climate in which open dialogue can occur is essential.

Volunteer opportunities and options for a range of skills and abilities allow for a diversity of volunteers to serve an organization. Often, the volunteer manager is the creative resource that tailors aspects of a job description to provide an opportunity for service to all people who wish to contribute in whatever way they can.

8.11 SUPERVISION AND EVALUATION

Providing supervision for volunteers is critical in supporting them to fulfill the role they have assumed within the organization. In some settings, the volunteer manager is the person responsible for all aspects of supervision and evaluation. Optimally, volunteers are supervised by staff members and become integrated into the area or department in which they serve, and the volunteer manager is kept informed of any major developments.

The supervision and evaluation of volunteers can be a challenging issue because often even paid personnel see supervision as "being watched," and evaluations as "being judged." Both processes are designed to be supportive and offer information and feedback to assist people in doing the best possible job. A negative experience with evaluations, which may go back as far as elementary school, can be threatening to an otherwise confident person. Even the most sensitive staff supervisor may require some coaching in the supervision of volunteers.

A common misunderstanding among paid employees is that volunteers cannot be fired from a job. Therefore, no matter how they perform or behave on the job, the agency is stuck with them. This is simply not true—volunteers can be dismissed from an organization, and they should be if they violate policies and standards or are disruptive to an organization. However, as with paid employees, termination should be considered only after a series of corrective actions have been attempted and have failed.

When there is an issue with a volunteer, the staff supervisor should bring the problem to the attention of the volunteer manager. The manager must be certain that all viewpoints are represented and that all information is clear before taking any action.

As with any personnel issue, there are times when immediate termination may be appropriate. It is imperative that information regarding situations that result in dismissal be included in the training materials as a written document and reviewed as part of the volunteer program, so that there will be no doubt that the volunteer was fully informed about consequences for such actions.

However, in most cases a situation can be clarified and resolved by honest dialogue and a mutually acceptable concrete action plan. Any time that such an incident occurs, the volunteer manager must document the meeting, include the plan for change, and provide the volunteer with a copy. Following the organization's steps for progressive discipline is one way to provide an opportunity for a volunteer to continue service while growing in skill, knowledge, and behavior.

Volunteers can also be trained to supervise each other. Thus a senior volunteer with perhaps three or more years of experience with an organization can be used to ensure that newcomers are applying the skills and knowledge they received in their training. Creating such leadership roles within the volunteer corps demonstrates that volunteer experience is valued and trusted. It adds another dimension to the experienced volunteer's role and also conveys to a newer volunteer the self-sufficiency and quality of the volunteer corps. Before creating such a role, clear guidelines and a job description detailing expectations and procedures must be developed for the volunteer supervisor.

Here are some suggestions for supervising volunteers:

1. Be certain that the volunteer understands both *what* the task or role involves and *why* it is important.
2. Offer both positive and corrective feedback.
3. Involve volunteers in planning and decision making regarding the task at hand.
4. Create an environment of partnership with staff, volunteers, and clients.
5. Provide volunteers with authority, not ultimate responsibility.
6. Listen and value volunteers' input.
7. Be accessible, not intimidating or overshadowing. Provide volunteers with information to contact a supervisor if necessary.
8. Anticipate problems and plan for solutions.
9. Acknowledge and appreciate what gets accomplished.
10. Never waste volunteers' time.

Evaluations of volunteers, if done well, can be a very insightful tool for the volunteer, the supervisor, and the volunteer manager. However, it is commonly the area that continually gets neglected for both paid employees and volunteer staff. If a staff supervisor is behind in completing evaluations for paid employees, there will be resistance to providing them for volunteers.

An evaluation process should focus on the value of service performed, but often it is viewed as a report card of what had been done wrong. To alter this perception, the volunteer manager can take several steps. First, set a schedule that shows when volunteers will be evaluated. One suggestion is to evaluate halfway through a volunteer's initial time commitment to afford an opportunity to implement any changes or suggestions that result from the dialogue. Second, design a simple yet meaningful evaluation form that corresponds to duties and criteria of the job description and present this to the volunteer when he or she is placed in the role. This provides the volunteer with information in advance and can stimulate discussion about the job. Short narrative answers to a few key questions, with concrete examples, provide more information than a checklist with a number scale.

One effective method to evaluate volunteers is to ask them to complete for themselves the same form the supervisor will use. Providing this form about a week in advance gives the volunteer an opportunity to reflect on his or her experience. Including questions that also ask the volunteer to evaluate the supervision received and invite feedback about the organization creates a sense of the mutuality of exchanging observations. Like an interview, the evaluation should be done in privacy. Suggestions and plans should be recorded on the form, and at the conclusion both the volunteer and the supervisor should sign the form and each should receive a copy.

It is advisable to evaluate volunteers again, this time at the conclusion of their initial commitments. This process assists them in deciding to recommit for another term and provides an opportunity to assess the next steps in their work with the organization.

8.12 RECOGNITION

Most volunteers would say that the rewards of volunteering are enough and that their motivation in serving is not to be recognized for the work they do, and this is probably true. However, it is the volunteer administrator's role to be sure that the efforts of the volunteer department, both as individuals and as a corps, get the agency and public recognition they deserve. Here again, methods to acknowledge volunteers are limitless. Extraordinary and creative ideas abound, including flying a blimp with a huge "Thank you, volunteers!" illuminated in the evening sky.

Recognition at one level is a daily occurrence. It is calling volunteers by name, greeting them warmly, providing parking spaces for them, and saying a simple yet heartfelt "thank you," to name but a few examples. Volunteers receive recognition from staff, from clients, and from other volunteers.

Formal recognition of volunteer contributions is worth celebrating, and the third or fourth week of April usually is designated as National Volunteer Week. It is suggested that some acknowledgment of volunteers be made within an organization, especially during this period. Ideally, an event that brings staff and volunteers together is a fun way to celebrate the partnership and resulting achievements. Such opportunities build an esprit de corps that strengthens the entire organization.

In addition, cities, states, and the federal government sponsor recognition events to honor the contributions of volunteers to an organization. Usually, the volunteer administrator can nominate a person or group with a narrative explaining the unique and valuable contribution that has been made. Such recognition is a boon to the entire organization because it provides positive exposure to a wide audience.

Budget need not be a deterrent to a demonstration of gratitude. A thank-you letter from the executive director or from the clients is one simple way of appreciating the work of volunteers. Volunteers usually like practical items imprinted with the organization's logo. T-shirts serve both as recognition thank-you items and as a recruitment and public relations tools every time they are worn.

Acknowledging outstanding service, length of service, and other contributions serves to honor not only the volunteers themselves but the staff and the community as well. When a new volunteer attends such a function and sees a dozen people being honored for 10 years of commitment, the message is: This must be a great place to volunteer!

A ceremony to celebrate volunteerism also provides an opportunity to recognize staff members who supervise volunteers and paid employees who may serve as volunteers in other organizations. National Volunteer Week is designed to honor the importance of serving as a basic tenet of our way of life. Other agency events that include volunteers are a natural way of demonstrating that volunteers are valued as an integral part of the organization. Holiday parties, birthdays, and other major events provide an opportunity to recognize volunteers.

The volunteer manager uses careful record keeping to document statistics that often surprise even those who are familiar with the volunteer program. The total number of hours of service contributed by volunteers is worth noting in an annual report and is often a factor used to support grant proposals. These are also ways to assist people in recognizing the value of volunteers.

More than an event, or a gift, or a plaque, volunteer recognition is an attitude that is conveyed by all staff to the volunteers. It is the philosophy that each component—paid staff, volunteers, and those being served—is vital to the total mission of the organization. It is the celebration of the strength that comes from the unity of hands in service to the heart.

8.13 RETENTION

One way to assess the effectiveness of a volunteer program is to track how many volunteers keep the initial time commitment of service that they made to the organization, how many renew their commitment, how many drop out, and why. Despite extensive recruitment, screening, and training, if volunteers are leaving an organization in large numbers there is something amiss.

Emphasizing expectations and time commitments throughout the screening and training process assists volunteers in determining their ability to meet the agency's needs. One method that assists the volunteer manager in creating sense of commitment is to ask volunteers to sign a letter of agreement at the conclusion of a training program. The letter could restate key policies or principles, including maintaining client confidentiality and the expectations for weekly and overall time commitments, and it should explain that an exit interview is part of the agreement if at any time a volunteer discovers he or she cannot fulfill the original time commitment expected.

An exit interview is one of the most valuable tools that a manager can use to gather information about a program. It also provides a graceful out for a volunteer because there is an opportunity to put closure on the experience and not feel guilty if he or she has to leave before the original commitment is completed. If a family emergency arises, for instance, the volunteer can leave the organization having discussed the value of the experience with the volunteer administrator. It also affords the manager an opportunity to acknowledge the volunteer for the service that has been provided. Knowing that there is a process for leaving should the volunteer's experience not be what was anticipated can be reassuring to volunteers. Likewise, exit interviews can often leave the door open for volunteers to return when circumstances shift again.

Volunteers leaving an agency are more apt to provide feedback on issues that they may have left unsaid previously simply because they are leaving. They also have experience and can offer insights about the overall program from a unique perspective.

As part of the general day-to-day operations of the volunteer department, the manager must create a mechanism for monitoring volunteer attendance and participation. This can be challenging if volunteers work in the field, from their homes, or in other situations far away from the main offices, yet it is important data to gather.

Having volunteers set a schedule assists in the smooth coordination of resources and allows the manager to monitor volunteers who begin not to meet their schedules. Requesting that a volunteer call to report an absence to the volunteer department as well as to the department in which they serve makes volunteers accountable and counteracts the stereotypical view that "You can't depend on a volunteer to show up!" If these are standard operating procedures, then a volunteer who misses two to three weeks receives an outreach call. The outreach call lets volunteers know that they have been missed, and lets the manager begin to probe gently into volunteers' problems.

A caring inquiry can provide the manager with important information. Volunteers may have become ill or overtaken by family emergencies: in those cases, the manager can support the volunteers, and assure them that as soon as they are free to return, the organization will welcome them back. Often, this alleviates any guilt the volunteers may be feeling. The manager can also send a card or alert other concerned volunteers and staff about the situation. This is another way to provide volunteers with recognition.

If the outreach calls reveals that there is no obvious reason why volunteers have missed their scheduled times, the manager then begins gently to explore why they have neither come nor called. Often, the volunteers have had upsetting experiences at the organization and have decided to quit rather than go back. The call presents an opportunity for the manager to process the events with the volunteers. After hearing volunteers' stories, the manager may offer some support and options for the volunteers to consider. It is suggested that the manager and volunteer meet in person if the volunteer is agreeable.

Empathetic listening skills are an invaluable tool for the volunteer manager. It is essential that each volunteer feels accepted and that regardless of the decision taken—to return to volunteering or to quit—the manager supports and respects the volunteer's decision.

The reality is that not everyone is happy with the volunteer work he or she has chosen. People cannot anticipate job promotions, illness, or other lifestyle changes that may cause them to quit volunteering. Some people fulfill their initial commitment and then want another experience in another agency. Turnover in a volunteer department is inevitable. Supervision and evaluations will assist in minimizing it. Exit interviews will also serve to provide information on the total program (Exhibit 8–7).

The exit interview serves volunteers by putting closure on their volunteer experience. It also affords the volunteer administrator the chance to acknowledge

◆ **EXHIBIT 8–7   Sample Exit Interview**

Name: _____   Date:_____

Location: _____Supervisor: _____

Starting Date: _____Last date of service: _____

Day and time usually worked: _____Total hours served: _____

1. Why have you decided to leave your volunteer position?

_____

2. Did you receive adequate training for your job?

_____

3. What other kinds of training or advanced training would have been helpful?

_____

4. Do you feel you were properly informed about policies and developments?

_____

5. What didn't we tell you about the job that you would have liked to know?

_____

6. What were the tasks you performed most often?

_____

7. How would you describe your relationship with other volunteers? With
   your supervisor? With the paid staff?

_____

8. Did you receive effective and fair supervision? How could it be improved?

_____

9. Please summarize your volunteer experience.

_____

10. Would you like to return as a volunteer at any time in the future?

_____

Interviewer's comments: _____

_____

_____

Interviewed by:_____

Volunteer's signature _____

Date:_____

Circle one: in person   telephone   mailed response volunteers' service and to assist in working through any negative feelings they may still have about their experience. Ideally the interview is done in person, but a telephone conversation or even a form that is filled out and mailed back can provide a similar sense of completion. Whether the volunteer has been with the organization three months or three years, the information gleaned from this process is invaluable and will assist in retaining a high-quality voluntary corps.

8.14 RECORD KEEPING

As a manager of human resources, the volunteer administrator must keep accurate and confidential records on all volunteers in a locked file. An individual file is created as each volunteer application is received, and this begins the documentation of the volunteer's history with the organization.

Volunteer files should have a checklist on the inside cover indicating the contents. Items to be included are:

- ◆ Completed application
- ◆ References
- ◆ Interview form
- ◆ Health screening (if required)
- ◆ Copy of driver's license (if applicable)
- ◆ Letter of understanding completed at training
- ◆ Evaluation forms
- ◆ Awards or recognition given
- ◆ Notes from any supervisory sessions
- ◆ Exit interview
- ◆ Any other pertinent documentation

As with personnel records, access to this information should be limited. Records of volunteers who are inactive as well as volunteers who were dismissed should be kept separately. It is advised that recommended files be kept for applicants who were denied admission into the volunteer program and for those who dropped out of the program before their training was complete.

In addition to information on individuals, the volunteer manager will want to keep statistical information on various components of the program to chart activity and growth. A wide range of software is available to track individual volunteer skills, hours of service, value of donated service, names and addresses, and training completed, and to create data bases for special needs.

Monthly statistical data provide one way to measure the effectiveness of a recruitment effort, to monitor the number of new volunteers trained in a quarter, and to document any change, in hours of time donated to the agency. Although of course the value of volunteer service to an organization is invaluable, statistical data provide a clear method of measuring goals and objectives that are quantifiable.

A wise volunteer manager uses the information gathered to advocate, to celebrate, to document, and to publicize the impact of the department on the overall agency.

8.15 PROGRAM EVALUATION

The evaluation and effectiveness of the volunteer program constitute an ongoing focus for the volunteer administrator. There are many different sources of information that can assist in the overall measurement of the program. As mentioned previously, an ideal time to solicit volunteers' feedback about the entire program is while they are being evaluated. A simple checklist that also affords ample space for comments can provide information on such subjects as supervision, training, the actual experience of various volunteer roles, how the organization is perceived, and so on. This could be mailed prior to the evaluation.

A similar checklist or questionnaire might be distributed annually to all staff as well, this one designed to elicit their perceptions about the volunteer corps. Both versions should be designed to elicit honest responses and offer the option of anonymity. Often, people feel freer answering an anonymous survey than in speaking in person.

Discussions with other managers, the executive director, and even the board can assist the volunteer manager to ensure that the goals and objectives of the volunteer department support the direction in which the organization as a whole is moving.

Annually, the volunteer administrator should set goals for each quarter, for the year, and for goals three to five years in the future. These goals should be specific, measurable, achievable, realistic, and have target dates that will allow the manager to gauge success.

There are also aspects of the volunteer program that are hard to measure and yet determine its effectiveness. On one level, numbers can reflect how many volunteers reported to work and how many hours they served. What cannot be quantified is the emotional impact—how they served with love and dedication, how this service was received, and how it benefited the recipients. It is not just what is accomplished but the way in which it is being done that determines the true value of a program.

8.16 ADVOCACY AND EDUCATION

One of the primary roles and responsibilities of any volunteer manager is to serve as an advocate for volunteers and volunteerism within the organization and the community. This requires focus, creativity, and vigilance. As he or she participates in the overall operations of the organization each day, the volunteer manager listens for new developments and pays particular attention to how they may affect volunteers. Perhaps the discussion is about developing a new program component. From the onset, roles and ways for volunteers to participate must be planned. A one-day special training session is being offered on-site. Are there slots designated for volunteers to attend? A new procedure is being used for clients. How will this information be conveyed to the volunteers? These are the kinds of questions the manager asks consistently. Soon staff members learn to include volunteers in all phases of the organization.

The volunteer manager also keeps current with issues that affect volunteers on a broader scale. Federal legislation known as the Volunteer Protection Act (H.R. 911) to cover volunteer liability has been pending for 10 years and is reported to be passed in the Spring of 1995. In the interim, it is the volunteer manager's role to raise such issues with the executive director so that a policy is developed before a problem arises.

The field of volunteer management continues to develop and expand. As new theories, philosophies, and practices are generated, it is incumbent upon the volunteer manager to educate staff and volunteers alike to keep the organization current.

8.17 PROFESSIONAL DEVELOPMENT

One way to continue to develop knowledge and skill as a practitioner and professional volunteer administrator is to work with peers. On a local level, working closely with a voluntary action center will provide a sense of community trends and needs. Often, VACs sponsor various types of training pertaining to issues in volunteerism and the nonprofit sector. Belonging to a DOVIA (Directors of Volunteers in Agencies) group is another way to learn about the field and share with other professionals who truly understand the challenges and triumphs of volunteer administration. Working with colleagues to find solutions to common problems is invaluable. The collective experience of the members provides a solid foundation of support. Some states have offices of volunteerism and may even sponsor annual conferences. Larger cities such as New York also have offices of volunteerism that operate through the mayor's office.

Membership in the Association for Volunteer Administration (AVA) is essential to a professional in the field of volunteer management. The mission of this international organization is "to promote professionalism and strengthen leadership in volunteerism." Formed in 1960, this group has done more to advance the status of the field than has any other.

Some of the activities of AVA include serving as a clearinghouse for information about volunteer management, providing information on public issues affecting leaders of volunteers, articulating ethics and standards for professional volunteers, and sponsoring the performance-based certification program that identifies key competencies in volunteer administration. The list of these competencies is included as Exhibit 8–8.

Volunteer administration is being integrated into the curriculum of higher education. Certification programs and accredited courses that may lead to a degree in public administration are being offered increasingly across the country. Thus the opportunity to be a student, an instructor, or both is available for the volunteer administrator.

Professional development is a continuing process. Membership in professional organizations and affiliation with one's colleagues is a vital part of this ongoing growth.

8.18 THE FUTURE

In 1993 the National and Community Service Trust Act established volunteerism and service as key components in the American way of life and provided funding for the creation of AmeriCorps and service learning programs nationwide. The Corporation for National Service is charged with implementing a national program that directs service efforts toward national priorities in four issue areas: education,

◆ **EXHIBIT 8–8   Summary of Competency Statements Included in the AVA Performance Based Certification Program in Volunteer Administration**

I.   PROGRAM PLANNING AND ORGANIZATION REQUIRES THAT THE VOL-
UNTEER ADMINISTRATOR:
   A.   Demonstrate knowledge of the agency/organization including its mis-
sion/purpose, its structure and the policies or regulations that affect its
operation.
   B.   Demonstrate the capability to engage in planning activities, armed with
adequate information about the community and the agency/organization,
which set the course of action for the volunteer program through goals,
objectives and action plans.
   C.   Demonstrate the ability to make decisions.
   D.   Establish structures and procedures to enable the smooth operation of the
program.
   E.   Assign the activities necessary to accomplish the goals and objectives of
the program through delegation and coordination.
   F.   Demonstrate knowledge of the target population, your agency/organiza-
tion serves, including needs, strengths, limitations.
II.   STAFFING AND DIRECTING FUNCTIONS REQUIRE THAT THE VOLUN-
TEER ADMINISTRATOR:
   A.   Demonstrate knowledge and expertise in planning and conducting suc-
cessful recruitment campaigns.
   B.   Demonstrate knowledge and capability in selecting appropriate persons to
fill positions.
   C.   Demonstrate knowledge of the growth and development needs of person-
nel and assure that these needs are addressed.
   D.   Demonstrate the ability to motivate, communicate with, and lead volun-
teers and paid staff.
   E.   Recognize the accomplishment of personnel.
   F.   facilitate the transition of volunteers to other life experiences.
III.   CONTROLLING FUNCTIONS REQUIRE THAT THE VOLUNTEER ADMINIS-
TRATOR:
   A.   Demonstrate the ability to monitor and evaluate total program results.
   B.   Demonstrate the ability to document program results and to apply this
information to future planning.
IV.   INDIVIDUAL, GROUP AND ORGANIZATIONAL BEHAVIOR REQUIRES
THAT THE VOLUNTEER ADMINISTRATOR:
   A.   Demonstrate the ability to work effectively with many different segments
of the population.
   B.   Demonstrate a knowledge of group process and the ability to work with,
and as, a member of groups.
   C.   Demonstrate the knowledge of social organizations, and dynamics of
change.
V.   GROUNDING IN THE PROFESSION REQUIRES THAT THE VOLUNTEER
ADMINISTRATOR:
   A.   Demonstrate knowledge of external regulations affecting volunteerism.
   B.   Demonstrate knowledge of the history and philosophy of voluntary action
and trends affecting volunteerism.
   C.   Demonstrate knowledge of the profession of volunteer administration.

© The AVA Certification Program. Used with permission from the Association for Volunteer
Administration, P.O. Box 4584, Boulder, Colorado 80306, (303) 541-0238.

human needs, public safety, and the environment. Though funding cutbacks may limit the intended impact and design of the initial legislation, the involvement of service as a key component to the American way of life and as a way "to get things done" is still the message for young people. Service learning, the teaching methodology that integrates service with a curriculum is also gaining wide acceptance as a central component to educational reform.

Educational institutions, nonprofit organizations, and the government are engaged in exciting and creative projects to make service a highly visible and valued aspect of American life. The need for professional volunteer managers has never been greater.

The essence of volunteer management is bringing the gifts and talents of each person forward to be in service to others. Techniques and methodologies are important, but it is the loving connection, our very humanity, that binds us together. Volunteer administration is a joyful opportunity to be a catalyst for service that impacts and changes lives in extraordinary ways every day.

SUGGESTED READINGS

Association for Volunteer Administration. 1992. *Volunteer Administration: Portrait of a Profession.* P.O. Box 4584, Boulder, Colo. 80306.

Corporation for National Service. 1994. *Principles for High Quality National Service Programs.* 1201 New York Avenue, Washington, D.C. 20525.

Ellis, Susan J. 1986. *From the Top Down: The Executive Role in Volunteer Program Success.* Philadelphia: Energize Associates.

Independent Sector. 1987. *Daring Goals for a Caring Society: A Blueprint for Substantial Growth in Giving and Volunteering in America.* Washington, D.C.: Independent Sector.

McCurley, Steve, and Sue Vineyard. 1988. *101 Tips for Volunteer Recruitment.* Downers Grove, Ill.: Heritage Arts Publishing.

Pearson, Henry G. 1986. "Interviewing Volunteer Applicants for Skills." *Voluntary Action Leadership* (Summer).

Points of Light. 1993. *Volunteer Center Start-up Kit.* 1737 H Street NW, Washington, D.C. 20006.

Thornburg, Linda. 1992. "Evaluating Volunteers for Positive Results." *Voluntary Action Leadership* (Fall).

Wilson, Marlene. 1976. *The Effective Management of Volunteer Programs.* Boulder, Colo.: Volunteer Management Associates.

CHAPTER ◇ 9

EPISODIC VOLUNTEERING

Nancy Macduff
Macduff/Bunt Associates

9.1   What Is Episodic Volunteering?

9.2   Barriers to Episodic Volunteering

9.3   Recruiting the Episodic Volunteer

9.4   Sustenance: Providing Support for the Episodic Volunteer

9.5   Launching the Episodic Volunteer Program: Field Tests

References

9.1 WHAT IS EPISODIC VOLUNTEERING?

Hundreds of volunteer programs used to attract people who came every Thursday all year round and worked a four-hour shift. They often did this for 20 or 30 years. In 1994, people call and want to know what they can do this weekend. They are prepared to work for several hours or days, not for several years.

A 1989 study by the National VOLUNTEER Center and J.C. Penney Co. asked those not volunteering why they were reluctant to volunteer. Seventy-nine percent of those asked said that they would be more inclined to volunteer if the jobs were shorter (National Volunteer Center, 1989). Many volunteer organizations and programs seek ways to attract the episodic or "short-term" volunteer. The *Oxford-American Dictionary* (Ehrlich et al., 1980) defines the word *episodic* as follows: "Ep-i-sod-ic/, ep e-'sad-ik, 1: made up of separate, especially loosely connected episodes; 2: of or limited in duration or significance to a particular episode, TEMPORARY; 3: occurring, appearing, or changing at usual irregular intervals, OCCASIONALLY." The term is gaining increasing popularity in the volunteer field.

An understanding of the nature of short-term volunteering begins with an understanding of terminology. Not all volunteers who provide short-term service disappear at the end of their jobs. Some volunteers provide assistance annually for events or one-time jobs. They might work at the registration table at a statewide Special Olympics track and field event, serve as auctioneers for a gala fund-raising dinner for a symphony orchestra, or coordinate cookie sales for the local Girl Scout Council. They are reliable long-term volunteers but they do their work in an episodic fashion.

Other short-term volunteers more aptly fit the definition. They may be students who need real-world experience outside the classroom for the subject they are studying, a busy professional person who has an interest in the service provided by the organization but can only work for one Saturday on a special project, or a relative or friends of a staff member who is looking for something to do for a few hours. All of this service is episodic.

To develop effective strategies to both recruit and sustain volunteers, it is essential to understand what episodic volunteering is and how it differs from the type of volunteering that is currently the norm in the field. The dictionary definition outlines the two most predominant types of episodic volunteer opportunities. A *temporary* episodic volunteer gives service that is short in duration, and the *occasional* episodic volunteer provides service at regular intervals for short periods of time. A rule of thumb is that the episodic volunteer is never around longer than six months. Committee members whose group meets once a month all year long are not episodic volunteers; their service is continuous.

Both of these types of volunteering are familiar to the volunteer program manager. Informally, volunteer programs, organizations, and agencies accommodate people who wish to serve in short-term assignments. So why is the notion of an episodic volunteer program such a revolutionary idea?

Traditionally, many volunteer programs organized their jobs and services around the continuous-service volunteer. In the past the person providing this service was likely to be a middle-aged woman not employed outside her home. Increasingly, continuous-service volunteers—those who serve on boards, as docents in museums, as church school teachers; who lead youth clubs and troops; or who provide service each week in hospitals and libraries—are employed, male, or newly retired. Usually, the volunteer recruitment effort is geared to continuous-service long-term volunteers. Jobs are designed for them, training is created to meet their long-term needs, motivational activities are used to enhance their retention over time, and recognition activities occur during National Volunteer Week in the spring.

This strategy is accurate and well conceived but totally inappropriate for the episodic volunteer. In fact, short-term volunteers may question the validity of the job choice if they are forced to sit through an orientation designed for continuous-service volunteers. The volunteer program manager who wants to implement a program designed specifically to attract episodic volunteers must first realize that taking a current job description written for the continuous-service volunteer and applying it to someone serving for a short term is not developing job opportunities for those wishing to give episodic service. A program to attract those who want to give episodic service requires the establishment of a separate program with its own recruiting, screening, supervision, training, recognition, and evaluation. There are no shortcuts to developing an effective and high-quality program to attract those who will serve volunteer programs episodically.

9.2 BARRIERS TO EPISODIC VOLUNTEERING

If people want short-term assignments and organizations are already providing them in an informal and unstructured way, why aren't there more episodic volunteer programs? What are those barriers that keep volunteer programs from implementing what people need and want?

Current volunteers and staff may see little value in the use of episodic volunteers. Undoubtedly, the single largest barrier to starting a formalized episodic volunteer program exists in the current workforce, both paid and unpaid. Volunteers expect other volunteers to have paid their dues or to have the same level of time commitment. Continuous service volunteers expect other volunteers to have gone through the same things that they have gone through, to have made the same regular commitment to a regular schedule, to have endured the same changes in staff and procedures. The episodic volunteer doesn't have to put up with those difficulties, but still is invited to celebrations, is awarded certificates of thanks, and is recognized alongside those who have been there forever. Professional staff often find the supervision of continuous volunteers challenging and the idea of training and supervising someone who is on the job for a short time as inefficient. There has always been tension between staff and volunteers—even continuous volunteers. Volunteers are sometimes seen by staff as potential usurpers of their jobs; staff work can be misjudged by volunteers as being easy and something they could do. These attitudes are by no means universal, but they exist when volunteers and paid staff have worked together for years. Introducing the idea of "office temporary" types of volunteers can be a cause for both anxiety and resistance.

There is a myth that there has been little use of episodic volunteers in the past. Institutional knowledge frequently overlooks the fact that episodic volunteers have been around forever. Those inside the organization tend to remember the people they see on a daily, weekly, or monthly basis. This perception of episodic volunteers as different from continuous-service volunteers can create a lack of confidence in the ability of the organization or agency and its staff and volunteers to cope with a new type of volunteers.

Allegiance to volunteer jobs as they are currently designed is strong. Church and synagogue teachers used to come in the year-long variety. Girl Scout leaders signed on for several years. Ten years ago leaders in youth organizations did not envision shared leadership teams or other ways of delivering their programs to children. Today, those organizations offer and promote a variety of ways to make programs available without adults having to sign on for the rest of their natural lives or the lives of their children. A barrier to developing an episodic volunteer program may be an organization's resistance to changing traditional job descriptions or the way service is delivered. Some volunteer jobs can be divided into smaller pieces, redesigned, or organized to be done by a team rather than an individual. Staff and volunteers need assistance and guidance to develop jobs specifically for those wishing short-term service. Resistance is often due to inexperience or lack of knowledge, not just a desire to be difficult.

Energy and resources are focused on the volunteer who stays. Training sessions for hospice volunteers can be as long as 40 to 80 hours. Formal recognition for most volunteers comes during the spring celebration of National Volunteer Week. For the episodic volunteer the message is clear: The people who count here are those who stay. This is a barrier to attracting those who want to give episodic service but receive a clear message that it is insufficient. Emphasis, and thus the energy of staff and current volunteers, is placed on keeping the continuous volunteer happy, not on meeting the needs of the person with short-term service. This is a double-barreled barrier. It has the potential to immobilize the staff and current volunteers by restricting their focus to one type of volunteer, and it can turn off people who do volunteer for a short service assignment. Those who are unhappy share it with their friends and colleagues. Thus recruiting for episodic positions (and sometimes continuous positions) might become difficult.

Legal liabilities can be a barrier. Some programs require volunteers to complete screening procedures that are costly and time consuming. For example, many hospitals require volunteers with direct patient contact to have a physical examination prior to beginning their work. Because this exam is provided at no cost to the volunteer, recruiting episodic volunteers is expensive when the time and charges for the physical exam are considered. However, exempting episodic volunteers from this requirement could put the organization in a legally tenuous position. Similarly, screening for volunteers who work with children, the developmentally disabled, or the fragile elderly is often extensive. Doing the same type of screening for someone who is giving only four or five hours of service hardly seems worth the effort. The reluctance of many organizations to organize an episodic volunteer program formally is based on the legal liability issues. Addressing the legal liability issues with those in charge of risk management is critical for some programs.

Episodic volunteers can face rejection. Some volunteer managers are reluctant to put volunteers in harm's way. They sense that the person giving short-time service will be treated shabbily by those who work in the program for a longer time, both staff and volunteers. What if the volunteer administrator organizes and episodic volunteer program, recruits new people, and orients them to their jobs, only to have them rejected by staff or continuous-service volunteers? It is easier to avoid the issue by not formally organizing the volunteer program. Episodic volunteers continue to be used informally, thus sidestepping the issue of the acceptance or rejection of those giving short-term service. Allowing this to continue means that a class system of volunteers is created. Those with the highest status are those who give continuous service.

These barriers can be reduced or eliminated by the organization through a formally established episodic volunteer program with clear lines of authority and responsibility. This is best done by involving continuous-service volunteers in the planning process and creating a trained and supervised corps of volunteers to serve as middle managers monitoring the work of episodic volunteers. The process begins with understanding where the organizations stands now in its use of episodic volunteers and how it might better organize that effort.

The development of an episodic volunteer program requires thoughtful consideration by volunteers and paid staff.

9.3 RECRUITING THE EPISODIC VOLUNTEER

Formal or informal episodic volunteer positions already existing in an organization can be the foundation on which to develop a full-fledged episodic program. To do that requires planning and implementing an organized volunteer recruitment and support initiative specifically designed for the episodic volunteer opportunities in the organization. There are six steps in the development of an episodic volunteer program.

(a) The Needs Assessment

Any new program or service begins with a needs assessment. "A needs assessment is an excellent means of involving the public in problem solving and developing local goals. There is a tendency for people to resist change—frequently because they have inadequate information, or because they have not been involved in the decision-making process" (Butler, 1980, p. 3). Increasing the acceptance of current staff and volunteers to the use of episodic volunteers can be achieved by involving them in the needs assessment process. As full participants in identifying potential job opportunities, surveying others about the need for episodic volunteers, determining resources available, and delineating the current use of episodic volunteers, they become owners of the outcomes.

A needs assessment for the episodic volunteer program (Exhibit 9–1) should include but not be limited to (1) identifying the current quality and quantity of service by episodic volunteers in the last three to five years (if applicable), (2) surveys identifying areas in which episodic volunteers might be helpful, (3) resources needed to support episodic volunteers (human and financial), and (4) the perceived need for episodic volunteers in areas where they are not now serving or to increase service in underutilized areas.

The results of the questionnaire are compiled and published, then provided to anyone interested in the development of the episodic volunteer program. It is also a useful document to provide to a board of directors or advisory committee that is considering financial or programmatic support to an episodic volunteer program. When you have competed this self-assessment it is clear whether your program, organization, or agency is ready to move to the next phase in the development of an episodic volunteering program.

◆ **EXHIBIT 9–1   Are We Ready For An Episodic Volunteer Program?**

DIRECTIONS: Organize a group of volunteers and staff to help assess the readiness of the organization for an episodic volunteer program. Begin by using this form to list the current episodic volunteer opportunities available in your organization. Be careful. Remember the definitions!

1. What type of episodic volunteer positions or opportunities do we currently have? List all the different types of episodic positions or jobs that you have accommodated in the last three years. Remember to list those in both categories.

   a. Temporary: short in duration:

   b. Occasional: occurs at regular intervals:

2. In your view, will short-term or episodic volunteers be accepted as members of the volunteer and staff team?

   Why or why not?

3. Are there adequate human and financial resources to launch an episodic volunteer program? How do we know? Who can do it? How long will it take them? Is there financial support for their work? Will management support the work of volunteers and staff to establish an episodic volunteer program?

4. How can you document the need for episodic volunteering in your program, organization, or agency? For example, are there episodic jobs available? Have volunteers and staff been surveyed about the availability of episodic jobs?

5. Is every partner in the equation prepared to support the development of a dual-focused volunteer program? Conceptually, this means thinking in new ways about volunteer programs. For example, the establishment of an episodic volunteer program means promoting continuous-service volunteers into positions of manager or supervisor. Who will train them to carry out the management functions? Who will supervise them? (Macduff, 1985)

(b) The Plan

If an affirmative decision is made, following the needs assessment, to develop and implement a episodic volunteer program, the next step is to establish a plan to accomplish the task. This includes setting an overall goal and smaller objective statements that describe in measurable increments the steps to be taken to implement the episodic volunteer program. This planning process also serves as the foundation upon which an evaluation of the success of the total program is based.

"Planning is a disciplined effort to produce fundamental decisions and actions that shape and guide what an organization is, what it does, and why it does it" (Bryson and Einsweiler, 1988, p. 1). Many episodic volunteer positions or jobs are arrived at by accident. Someone calls and asks for a short assignments, he or she seems sincere, there is an immediate need, so the person participates for two weeks.

Individuals deserve respect for their volunteer service, no matter what its duration. Volunteers feel respected when the organization has a plan that will use their time and talents wisely. Plans address the areas of job or position development, job descriptions, recruitment strategies, screening methods, training plans, supervision strategies, and evaluation and recognition techniques.

A key to the success of the episodic program is the organization and staffing of the planning team. "The best examples of planning . . . demonstrate effective, focused information gathering; extensive communication among and participation by key decision makers and opinion leaders; the accommodation of divergent interests and values; the development and analysis of alternatives; an emphasis on the future implications of present decisions and actions; focused, reasonably analytic, and orderly decision making; and successful implementation" (Bryson and Einsweiler, 1988, p. 1). Assembling the right people to serve on the planning team is the key to achieving the objectives listed above. Success or failure of an episodic program rests initially with this important group of people.

The episodic planning team should include current continuous-service volunteers, paid staff, and former episodic volunteers. It is also useful to include representatives of the support staff. Often, it is clerical or maintenance support staff who observe volunteers' work, have ideas about possible short-term jobs, and are often put in the position of supervising episodic volunteers. However, they are rarely included in the group that makes decisions that affect their jobs.

It is also helpful to have outsiders sit on the committee. These can be people from organizations with experience in episodic volunteering, people who are effective planners, or are interested in the mission of the organization. Outsiders frequently challenge those inside the organization to do their best work. The committee chair should be someone who supports the idea of a formally organized episodic volunteer program and has good leadership skills. The volunteer program manager serves as staff support for this group.

(c) Job Development and Job Descriptions

Frequently, short-term volunteers are assigned tasks that have been done by a continuous-service volunteer. Often they perform poorly or do not complete the task. This has the effect of reinforcing all the barriers and stereotypes mentioned earlier. It is a mistake to take current jobs for continuous-service volunteers and assume that they can be performed by episodic volunteers. A primary task for the planning team is to identify new jobs that can be performed on a short-term basis and/or to redesign traditional volunteer jobs so that they can be more appropriately assigned to the short-term volunteer. Once this job development process is completed, job descriptions are written.

Marlene Wilson refers to this job development stage as "job design." She says that job development is "to plan and fashion artistically and skillfully" (Wilson, 1976, p. 101). Job development includes gathering information from staff and other volunteers about specific tasks that can be accomplished by those giving short-term service. The form shown as Exhibit 9–2 is designed to collect information needed to design positions for episodic volunteers.

Distributing the form to staff and volunteers can help quickly to identify jobs ideally suited for the person wanting to give short-term service. Members of the planning team or the volunteer manager need to be available to assist those who have never completed a job development form.

Another way to develop episodic jobs is to review the jobs or tasks currently done by continuous-service volunteers. It is not necessary to commit 12 years to the Girl Scouts in order to be a Girl Scout leader. The scouting organization has adapted to the needs of the modern volunteer by allowing and encouraging leadership of troops to take a variety of forms. There are teams of parents or adults who work with large groups of more than one troop, but the actual time of service is only two or three meetings per year. In other cases leadership is rotated through the parents of girls in the troop every few months. In some cases the troop meets less often than they used to. These are creative solutions for busy parents and children.

The challenge to altering the way in which volunteer jobs are now developed is the strength of the commitment to the existing way of doing things. If the program is delivered effectively, there is a natural reluctance to change it. However, many continuous-service volunteers can have their service or experience enhanced by the participation of an episodic volunteer. As an example, hospice friendly visitors (the volunteers who visit terminally ill patients) can be assisted by episodic volunteers. The episodic volunteers might make library trips, thus allowing the continuous-service volunteer to spend more time with the patient. Episodic volunteers need clearly defined parameters for their jobs and that might mean not seeing the patient except with staff or a volunteer from Hospice present.

This adaptation of a long-term job requires some flexibility and creativity. The value is to the organization, the person receiving the service or program, and the volunteer who has the opportunity to give without guilt. Their job has clear limitations. They are not expected to provide continuous service. They know the short service they give is needed and provides valuable help.

"All volunteer positions within an organization should have job descriptions. We tell volunteers how we feel about their position by the professionalism we display in regard to that position. If we want to attract energetic, busy, professional people to our organization, we must send a message loud and clear that we take the volunteer role seriously" (Macduff, 1993, p. 93). The haphazard way in which episodic volunteers are often fit into an organization can influence that organization's ability to attract more volunteers. People talk. They tell their friends and colleagues about their experience on a volunteer job. The organization that treats them with respect and professionalism is miles ahead of the one where the volunteer manager says, "Gosh, I'm sure I can find a job for you somewhere. Just give me 10 minutes."

◆ **EXHIBIT 9–2   Episodic Volunteer Request**

DIRECTIONS: Some volunteers like to provide their service to [name of organization or agency] with short-term or episodic service. These are jobs that can be completed in one day, over a short period of time (less than three months), or occur only once in a given year. Complete the following form and deliver the completed copy to _____

DATE: _____   Phone/EXT: _____

Name of Person Making Request: _____

Department or Division: _____

Brief Description of Job:

_____

List briefly the skills or abilities required to do this job:

_____

Who will supervise the work of this volunteer?_____

Has this supervisor worked with volunteers before, and if so, how long?

Yes_____No _____How long?_____

Where will the person work?_____

List the minimum and maximum amount of time you think this work will take. If the volunteer is needed on specific days of the week or times, please list those.

Minimum _____Maximum_____

Any other requirements: _____

When do you need the volunteer to start on this job?_____

Is this a job that could be done by different episodic volunteers on a regular basis?

              Yes _____No_____

Return this form to:_____

The job description should provide basic information about the task and time required and it should be portable. The job requirements for the hospice friendly visitor mentioned earlier would be much longer than those of aide-de-camp, who is only going to work two hours per week for three months. Exhibit 9–3 gives an idea of what an episodic volunteer job description might look like.

The planning team working with the staff can use the job development forms to write a job description. Notice that the job description sample would easily fit on a 5- by 8-inch card. The rule of thumb is KISS—Keep it simple, sweetheart.

◆ **EXHIBIT 9–3   Job Description**

Job Title: *Hospice Aide-de-Camp*   **Supervisor:** *Friendly Visitor*

Description of Duties: run errands for hospice client at the direction of the friendly visitor; includes, but is not limited to, library services, VCR pickup and delivery, mail services, supplies pickup and delivery; incidental grocery shopping, and so on.

Qualifications: Must be 18 and have a valid driver's license and insurance, a reliable vehicle, an interest in the work of hospice, patience, and sensitivity to the needs of those who are critically ill.

Time required: two hours per week for a minimum of two months

Training: 30-minute orientation by the director of volunteers, training as needed by the friendly visitor

---

(d) Recruitment

The recruitment process begins with the needs assessment, a plan, job development, and finally job descriptions. Without this preliminary work recruitment efforts are wasted. The needs of episodic volunteers differ from those of continuous-service volunteers. Information to the episodic volunteer should be aimed at them very directly. In marketing terminology, the product (the volunteer job) is priced (cost of doing the job for the volunteer—financial, emotional, and personal) within reach. Then a promotion strategy (brochures, public service announcements, television ads) is selected to attract those who are probable "buyers" of the product. The promotional material is placed where it can be most easily accessible to the potential customer.

For example, suppose that the organization is sponsoring a fund-raising foot race. Many episodic volunteers will be needed at the various checkpoints along the run. Therefore, flyers asking for volunteers must be placed in stores that carry runners' equipment.

Marketing strategy insists that when you sell you must consider product, promotion, price, and placement. These are the infamous 4 Ps of marketing. They apply in the volunteer sector as well. "Develop the right *product*. Support it with the right *promotion*. Put it in the right *place*. And at the right *price*" (Vineyard, 1984, p. 94).

Vineyard suggests four methods to use for recruitment. First is the one-to-one or in-person method. Studies of volunteers from a variety of sources reinforces the fact that the majority of people become volunteers "because someone asked them" (Pearce, 1993, p. 66). Episodic volunteers who are recruited by other volunteers or representatives of the organization will have a better sense of the needs, develop a relationship with someone inside the organization, and have the opportunity to have their questions answered directly (Vineyard, 1984, p. 106).

The second recruiting technique involves a person asking a group. "The asker explains the need, shares their own commitment, tells the group what they can do to help and what is being asked of them" (Vineyard, 1984, p. 106). Many clubs and organizations are interested in episodic volunteer opportunities for their members.

The group request is an effective way to provide information to a large number of people at the same time.

To be effective, this technique should include such resources as client-oriented audiovisuals, colorful and informational written material, and more than one person to answer questions informally at the end of the presentation.

The third recruiting technique is telephone contact. Consider the possible types of calls:

1. Callers know the people they call, and the people know about the organization.

2. Callers know the people they call, but the people they call know little or nothing about the organization.

3. Callers do not know the people they call, but the people they call know about the organization.

4. Callers do not know the people they call, and the people they call know little or nothing about the organization (Vineyard, 1984, p. 107).

As you might expect, the first type of call is the most likely to be successful, the last type the least likely. It is easier to talk to someone you know about things with which you are both familiar. The chances of recruiting the individual are higher. Colleges have increased the likelihood that the calls made on their behalf will be successful by using students to call alumni during their fund-raising drives. In this case the people don't know each other, but they know the institution.

The fourth method of recruiting is the mass appeal. Broadly defined, this would include such things as flyers, print and media ads, billboards, brochures, window displays, bus/subway cards, handbills, posters, or want ads. This is a passive method of recruiting, and it is the least personal, and therefore it has the least likelihood of success.

All volunteers are making a consumer decision when they agree to do a job. The volunteer job is the product. That product requires them to exchange some of their leisure time to meet a personal need. Despite the fact that the terms are not often discussed, it is an exchange, just as the purchase of a new shirt or a milkshake is an exchange. "Exchange is the act of obtaining a desired object from someone by offering something in return" (Kotler, 1983, p. 9). In the case of a volunteer the object is an intangible need.

Episodic volunteers will not respond favorably to appeals directed at those expected to give long-term service. To build the episodic volunteer program the recruiting effort must treat the potential volunteer with the same respect it gives those giving longer service. By creating and developing recruiting techniques and strategies aimed at the narrow market of episodic volunteers, the organization signals respect for them by telling them emphatically that the work they do is valuable enough for the organization to have expended time and effort in finding the right people for the job. Merely finding places for the episodic volunteer who stumbles into the organization means that the work they do is not very important to the mission. It also sends a clear message about how seriously volunteers should take their jobs and with its responsibilities, including being on time, dressing appropriately, observing safety and health rules, and completing assigned tasks.

(e) Screening

Screening episodic volunteers is similar to screening for long-term volunteers. Screening, both continuous and episodic volunteers, includes written job descriptions, applications, and interviews.

A difference between screening done for an episodic volunteer and a continuous-service volunteer is the extent of the scrutiny (Macduff, 1991, p. 19). For example, hospice friendly visitors are screened closely. They are often asked to complete a "grief or loss history." This is a document that helps them focus on their experiences with loss. Given the sensitivity of the work they do with terminally ill patients and their families, this seems sensible. An episodic volunteer who is running errands for a client at the request of the friendly visitor might not be required to complete such a history. Each organization must decide the extent of the screening absolutely essential for volunteers. It is good practice to review screening procedures every two years.

Another way to deal with the issue of screening is to establish policies regarding the types of jobs that might be performed by episodic volunteers. Suppose that a hospital has stringent screening requirements for volunteers giving continuous service, including an overall requirement that all volunteers complete an expensive health screening. A policy is established that no episodic volunteer position that has direct patient contact can be created. Volunteers work in administrative offices, the volunteer office, or with external educational programs, but they do not work with patients. Thus the screening requirements are targeted at the job being performed and might therefore reduce barriers, costs, and time needed for the potential episodic volunteer.

Once the policies and minimum requirements are established, the three areas of the screening process are put in place.

- *Job descriptions* are a means by which a person can self-screen. If someone calls and says that she has two Saturdays available and would like to volunteer for the organization, the next step is to use the mail service. Send her a description of jobs in her area of interest and an application. A phone call from the organization in a few days may find that she does not meet the requirements or is not interested in what is available. Both her time and the staff's is saved—the potential volunteer has self-screened.

- *Applications* for episodic volunteers should be edited to fit on a 5- by 8-inch card (Macduff, 1991, p. 19). It should contain only essential information. Be sure to have emergency contact phone numbers. A filing system can be a labeled box.

- *Interviews* for episodic volunteers can be conducted by phone. This means that there should be a standardized interview process and script that is the same for every applicant. In some cases it is necessary to interview applicants. This is done most effectively by specially trained volunteers.

Barriers to starting an episodic volunteer program are the potential legal liabilities. Interviews are a more effective way to screen out the volunteer who may be inappropriate for the job. When volunteers are only going to serve for several hours on one day it may seem like a waste of time to interview them. From there it is easy to think the entire idea of short-term volunteers is a big time guzzler. Creativity is demanded to surmount this barrier.

The 1988 Calgary Winter Olympics is a case in point. Some 40,000 volunteers were needed at various locations around the city and in the mountains of Alberta. A paid staff of five trained a score of volunteers to interview the thousands of Albertans who had completed the application process. From those interviews came the corps of episodic volunteers, some of whom only worked a few hours at a particular location. While the interviews were being conducted, the staff moved ahead with other tasks. It was efficient, effective, and frugal. Does this technique work? If you saw the 1988 Olympics on television, you already know the answer to that.

(f) The Recruiting Team

The use of a recruiting team could ease the burden of work on the volunteer director or program manager. The team can set numerical targets for recruiting, design the screening process, review job descriptions, and design and carry out advertising and recruiting strategies. The volunteer program manager has a workforce to implement the new program. Members of the planning team, supplemented by additional workers, can make up the volunteer recruiting team.

Those who recruit are members of the organization, or at least people who believe in the organization's work but may not currently be members; parents, partners, relatives, and friends of the clientele of the organization are ideal recruiters (Macduff, 1993, p. 117). Avoid recruiting currently active volunteers to serve on this team—they already have volunteer assignments. If you want to avoid burnout, concentrate instead on people who have recently retired from volunteer positions in your organization.

Recruiters need to develop specific campaign plans based on the goals and objectives established by the planning committee. These include guidelines (the job description for a committee) for the work of the recruiting team, which detail such things as the type and number of people serving on the recruiting team. If the planning committee has not developed this information, the recruiting team starts by laying out their tasks.

The recruiting team 1) sets goals for the number of people to be recruited; 2) establishes time lines to meet the goals; 3) divided duties or jobs between members; 4) assigns each member a "territory," much like a salesperson, in which to carry out recruiting.

The team also is instrumental in designing tools for recruiting—brochures, print ads, radio and television ads, and posters. By involving the recruiting team in the decision-making process they clearly understand their job, the "product" they are selling, and to whom. Recruiters are motivated and energized by ownership over the process and the procedure they must carry out.

The team needs a packet of information about the organization and all its activities. If the organization provides any service that is controversial or misunderstood by the public, the team needs special information to help people answer any questions they might encounter. The last thing a volunteer recruiter should do is inadvertently misrepresent a position of the organization to a potential volunteer. The recruiting team must manage its recruiting effort within the constraints of the resources available: It must have a budget.

Once the mechanics of the recruiting team effort are in place, the last step before it begins its work is training. The following list shows areas in which team members are likely to need training:

1. Brief history of organization and the place of episodic volunteers within it
2. The benefits to the prospective volunteer of volunteering
3. Details of the various types of episodic volunteer opportunities available, including copies of job descriptions
4. Discussion of how this organization and its various volunteer opportunities (continuous, episodic, intern, etc.) are different from those of similar organizations or agencies
5. Review of all recruiting campaign material (literature, deadline, publicity, goals, physical territory, etc.)
6. A system for reporting results
7. How progress will be measured and shared by the team—meetings, reports, phone calls, and so on
8. How to deal with "no" as an answer

What is required here is more than simply passing on information. The team member must learn how to use this information in the recruitment effort.

9.4 SUSTENANCE: PROVIDING SUPPORT FOR THE EPISODIC VOLUNTEER

The development of a short-term volunteer program does not end with bringing recruits through the door into an organization, agency, or program. An episodic volunteer program also includes strategies to sustain and support volunteers during their service.

Notice that the word used to describe support for the episodic volunteer is *sustain*. Sustenance is the process of "supplying with the necessaries of life, nourishment" (Ehrlich et al., 1980, p. 691). The process of supporting the long-term volunteer is best described as maintenance. This is "to continue to support or preserve" (Ehrlich et al., 1980, p. 400). The difference between sustenance and maintenance is a subtle but significant one for the short-term volunteer.

(a) Training

The best place to begin the process of sustaining the volunteer is with training. The episodic volunteer does not have time to attend lengthy training sessions. Fortunately, appropriate jobs for episodic volunteers rarely require a significant investment in training. One effective method to develop and design training is to invite both experienced volunteers and experts in adult education to serve on a volunteer training committee.

Training for episodic volunteers must be concentrated. This is the time to think about stand-alone types of training: a video, a self-study guide, training delivered via telephone. Episodic volunteers need the basics: "Do this!" "Do not do this!"—and they need the information quickly.

The orientation process for episodic volunteers should help dispel anxiety or confusion (Ilsley and Niemi, 1981, p. 67). It should help the volunteer feel comfortable and a part of the organization. It needs to send a clear message that *all* volunteers are welcome and *needed*, no matter their length of service. Sending that clear message helps volunteers generate stronger commitments to complete the assigned tasks, thus making them more effective at their jobs.

Deciding on the type of training needed begins with the planning committee. It establishes the learning criteria for each episodic volunteer before beginning service. The committee then decides on the most appropriate training delivery approach.

For example, a volunteer working a four-hour shift on an event might receive the following training:

1. When volunteers are accepted, they should be mailed a packet containing a brochure about the organization, a one-page history of the event that details the contributions of the episodic volunteers (how many there are, how much money they've raised, how many clients they serve, and so on), a copy of their job description, their supervisor's name and phone number.

2. New volunteers' supervisors—volunteer or staff—should call the volunteer to review their duties and any other relevant information that could make the job more comfortable, including tips on parking, clothing, costs, identification, and on-site training. This is also the time to find out what the volunteers already know about the job.

3. When the new volunteers arrive at the service location there should be an orientation to the actual job duties. This can often be conducted by another episodic volunteer who returns from one year to the next and is willing to work longer hours. The person responsible for the work area prepares a written list of responsibilities, ensuring that the training is consistent from one person to the next. Refinements can be made in the basic list, if needed.

4. Volunteers need to know how they will be evaluated. Share with them the standards of performance for the work they are doing. Explain how their performances will be reviewed and discussed with them.

(b) Supervision

Supervision of short-term volunteers can be done quite effectively by long-term volunteers. A large national volunteer organization is exploring the idea of designing programs to recruit a small number of long-term volunteers who agree to serve 15 to 20 hours per week for a minimum of three to five years. The agency will dramatically change the support and education provided to these continuous-service volunteers, who then become key players as supervisors and planners for the greatly expanded episodic volunteer corps. This makes the volunteer program director the "supervisor of volunteers who supervise other volunteers." This intriguing idea is best done in a field study situation but has extremely interesting possibilities for such organizations as Hospice, the Humane Society, orchestras, hospital volunteer programs, youth agencies, and many more.

Supervision in many volunteer programs is haphazard at best and damaging in the worst cases. Volunteer satisfaction is influenced by adequate supervision and assistance. Effective work is done by those who know their roles and responsibilities and receive support and monitoring to do the job more effectively. Yet few organizations provide formal training for paid staff or volunteers designed to enhance skills they need to supervise the continuous volunteers, let alone the episodic volunteers. As with any volunteer program, training to work with volunteers is essential. Volunteer managers and administrators need to lobby for in-service time with paid staff to teach the skills needed to effectively oversee the work of volunteers. Volunteer managers also prepare training programs for volunteers who supervise other volunteers.

Fisher and Coal (1993, p. 125) outline the skills that a supervisor of volunteers needs to be successful. They suggest that a *supportive environment* is made up of elements designed to enhance the worker's ability to perform and be satisfied with that performance. This includes such things as "training, a clear understanding of job assignments, information about standards, expected levels of performance, and instruction in how to do the job. Resources necessary to do the job are provided and conditions harmful to performance are corrected" (Gidron, 1983). With an episodic volunteer this communication must be immediate and helpful in order to bring about effective performance immediately. Some supervisors are better at building long-term relationships with volunteers over time. The episodic volunteer has no time for that; direct information is needed. Skill-building workshops can teach techniques to supervisors so the volunteers' manager can do this without offending the volunteer.

Creating an environment in which volunteers and staff work together on a team is desirable. Learning the skills to *build teams* includes knowing and communicating the reasons for working together, a personal commitment to the fact that team work is a most effective means to work, developing strategies to bring about accountability from members of the team, and understanding skills necessary to build work teams with a membership that is diverse in age, gender, cultural diversity, income, motivations, and pay (Fisher and Cole, 1993, p. 127). Episodic volunteers often work with people who have vastly greater experience and history with the organization. It is easy for that group to dismiss the skills of the short-tenure volunteer. The supervisor's job is to help the more experienced volunteers respect the ideas of newcomers and the newcomers not to act as if they have all the answers. Training sessions using a case study format can help supervisors develop specific strategies to deal with these types of problems.

The ability to *delegate responsibility* to volunteers is a skill supervisors must have. Delegation is assigning tasks and activities to volunteers and giving them real responsibility to carry out those tasks. It is not giving people jobs and then making them do it the way you would do it. Delegation also does not mean giving jobs to volunteers and letting them sink or swim alone. A supervisor must "choose the right task, choose the right person to do it, give clear instructions, turn the task over to the worker but stay in contact, give authority, and review results with the worker" (Fisher and Cole, 1993, p. 129).

Supervisors must constantly monitor and improve their *communication skills.* Verbal and written skills are essential for success in any type of management or administrative position. Supervisors must strive to achieve "accurate and mutually understood communication" (Fisher and Cole, 1993, p. 129).

Written communication is sometimes as important as verbal communication for episodic volunteers. If volunteers can read and learn about their jobs at home, their on-site training can take less time. However, the written material they are sent must be digestible. A five-page single-spaced memo may be thorough, but it is unlikely that anyone will read it. Claudia Dalton, the volunteer program manager for a senior service program, prepares written material using all the principles of good graphic design—lots of white space, bold type to highlight important information, cartoons to break up blocks of text, and humor. Her materials are so inviting that it is hard to resist reading them (Dalton, 1993).

Similarly, verbal communication is critical to bring the episodic volunteer up to performance standards as quickly as possible. Direct, clear communication can be learned in skill-building workshops. Active listening is essential in any relationship, but it is particularly important when working with someone with whom there is little time or opportunity to develop a long-term understanding. Two-way communication is particularly important between episodic volunteers and supervisors to ensure that volunteers understand the requirements of the job.

Feedback is an essential element of effective supervision. Feedback provides a continuous circuit of communication from the volunteer to the supervisor and back again. It is informal and is provided on a regular basis. Volunteers need to know about their work on a regular basis, not just when things are going wrong. Feedback can take a variety of forms, including verbal praise, suggestions for improving performance, written outlines of information to help performance, a postcard after the job is complete saying "thanks," or sharing the work done by episodic volunteers with others in the organization being sure the volunteers get the credit.

For episodic volunteer the type of evaluative behavior mentioned above is usually the only type received. They are rarely given annual performance evaluations. The person-to-person information about performance is immediate and designed to enhance performance. This is not the time for personal criticism; rather, it is specific to the job or service being performed—"It is descriptive rather than judgmental" (Fisher and Cole, 1993, p. 131); praise is essential. Models or samples of work can be used so that volunteers can measure their performance against them.

Self-assessment is a useful technique to use with episodic volunteers. It can be as simple as, "How do you think you are doing with this task?" Or the volunteer is asked to detail which tasks they are doing well and which tasks they would like to do better. In this way, the volunteer tells the supervisors where help is needed. Effective supervisors can guide volunteers in learning what they want to learn and guide them in areas where improvement is needed. "The guidance and support an organization provides to its volunteer staff are essential to their successful performance and to the achievement of organizational goals" (Fisher and Cole, 1993, p. 136).

(c) Recognition

Recognition *is* awareness. It is seeing something and acknowledging it. The most effective recognition for volunteers is personalized and directly related to the work the volunteer has done. Recognition initiatives are part of an ongoing, year-long process, not just an annual event that happens in the spring. Records are kept of awards presented. There are both formal and informal recognition activities (MacKenzie and Moore, 1993, p. 88).

Evaluation is one way to recognize volunteers. For example, auction volunteers might receive a short report on the results of the event and thus their work. You could include total receipts, attendance, net receipts, the money earned, and its relationship to client services. This short report and a thank-you letter is a powerful way to acknowledge the volunteer's job and reinforce the agency's mission.

The *sustenance* of episodic volunteers does not happen accidentally. Like the recruitment, selection, and screening of short-term volunteers, it is best done in a planned and organized manner.

9.5 LAUNCHING THE EPISODIC VOLUNTEER PROGRAM: FIELD TESTS

Too often in nonprofit and voluntary organizations administrators and leadership volunteers rush to implement new programs or services, only to have them fail. The notion of field testing is often ignored. *Field testing* includes organizing a program or service for a small group and then implementing it. The testing period involves close scrutiny of every aspect of the program. "Market testing [field testing] is the stage where the product and program are introduced into more authentic consumer settings to learn how consumers react to use . . . and how large the market is" (Kotler, 1983, pp. 293–294).

The directors of a large performing arts center decided to implement an episodic volunteer program. The episodic planning team completed all the steps listed in this chapter. At the advice of the volunteer program director it was decided to field test the program and evaluate the results. The performing arts center was located in a large city with many colleges and universities. The planning team decided to target selected colleges with performing arts or theater arts programs. For three months they coded advertising, targeting only the schools selected. They were seeking volunteers to accept assignments of one week or less, with a minimum of four hours per day. The episodic volunteers were to work in administrative offices throughout the building.

By starting small, using current volunteers, and gradually building the confidence and trust of the staff, this organization was able to launch a successful episodic volunteer program. It took less than six months from the first committee meeting to the launch of the field test. The volunteer administrator saw her role as supportive and advisory. The program was seen as a new volunteer opportunity owned by the continuous-service volunteers who had created it. Its chances of long-term success were improved by that ownership.

Within a month over 30 volunteers had been placed, and paid staff and continuous-service volunteers were clamoring for more help. The episodic volunteer planning committee knew which of its advertising and promotional techniques had been most effective. The field test allowed them to increase the scope of the program and reach out to a greater pool of episodic volunteers, and to avoid making large (or very public) mistakes. It also afforded the opportunity to refine various aspects of the volunteer opportunities—advertising and promotion, job descriptions, and the screening process (Shapiro, 1992).

Studies such as the one undertaken by J.C. Penney's/National VOLUNTEER Center, tell us that episodic volunteering is the wave of the future. The organizations and programs that learn to diversify the way in which people can serve will flourish, like their brothers and sisters in the for-profit sector, which are diversified. Episodic volunteering is only one way to offer the opportunity to serve. National community service programs, jobs to attract volunteers who are disabled, and youth volunteer initiatives are all effective means to diversify and reach out to new markets of volunteers. Like episodic volunteering, they require new management strategies for the volunteer administrator.

REFERENCES

Bryson, John M., and Robert C. Einsweiler. 1988. *Strategic Planning: Threats and Opportunities for Planners*. Chicago: Planners Press, American Planning Association.

Butler, Lorna Michael, and Robert E Howell. 1980. *Coping with Growth: Community Needs Assessment Techniques*. Corvallis, Oreg.: Western Rural Development Center.

Dalton, Claudia. 1993. *Foster Grandparents' Handbook*. Clark County, Washington.

Ehrlich, Eugene, Stuart Berg Flexner, Gorton Carruth, and Joyce M. Hawkins. 1980. *Oxford-American Dictionary*. New York, Oxford University Press.

Fisher, James C., and Kathleen M. Cole. 1993. *Leadership and Management of Volunteer Programs*. San Francisco: Jossey-Bass.

Gidron, Benjamin. 1983. "Sources of Job Satisfaction among Service Volunteers." *Journal of Voluntary Action Research* 12(1) (January–March): 20-35.

Ilsley, Paul J., and John A. Niemi. 1981. *Recruiting and Training Volunteers*. New York: McGraw-Hill.

Kotler, Phil. 1983. *Principles of Marketing*. Englewood Cliffs, N.J.: Prentice Hall.

Macduff, Nancy. 1991. *Episodic Volunteering*. Walla Walla, Wash.: MBA Publishing.

Macduff, Nancy. 1993. *Recruiting and Retention: A Marketing Approach*. Walla Walla, Wash.: MBA Publishing.

MacKenzie, Marilyn, and Gail Moore. 1993. *The Volunteer Development Toolbox*. Downers Grove, Ill.: Heritage Arts Publishing.

McCurley, Steve. 1988. *Volunteer Management Forms*. Downers Grove, Ill.: Heritage Arts Publishing.

National Volunteer Center. 1989. *National Volunteer Center and JC Penney Study on Volunteer Activity*. Arlington, Va.: National Volunteer Center.

Pearce, Jone. 1993. *Volunteers: The Organizational Behavior of Unpaid Workers*. New York: Routledge Press.

Shapiro, Heller An. 1992. *Kennedy Center for the Performing Arts*. Washington, D.C.

Vineyard, Sue. 1984. *Marketing Magic for Volunteer Programs*. Downers Grove, Ill.: Heritage Arts Publishing.

Wilson, Marlene. 1976. *The Effective Management of Volunteer Programs*. Boulder, Colo.: Volunteer Management Associates.

CHAPTER 10

VOLUNTEER AND STAFF RELATIONS

Nancy Macduff
Macduff/Bunt Associates

10.1   Introduction

10.2   Volunteers and Staff: A Team

10.3   Characteristics of the Effective Volunteer–Staff Team

10.4   Symptoms of Poor Volunteer–Staff Relationships

10.5   Causes of Poor Volunteer–Staff Relationships

10.6   Sequential Process to Build the Volunteer–Staff Team

10.7   Tips to Enhance Volunteer–Staff Relations

       References

10.1 INTRODUCTION

In *Volunteers: The Organizational Behavior of Unpaid Workers* (Pearce, 1993, p. 177), the author devoted a section to the research data on the relationship between volunteers and staff. She began that section by calling it "the dirty little secret of volunteerism." The author of this chapter, who read and commented on the draft manuscript, applauded her bravery in dramatically underscoring the seriousness of the issue. Regrettably, the editors of her book sanitized it to read, "The tension that can exist between volunteers and employee co-workers remains one of the unpleasant secrets of nonprofit organizations"(Pearce, 1993, p. 142).

It is unfortunate that her original statement did not survive the editor's pencil. The relationship between volunteers and staff needs the attention of both scholars and those who manage volunteer programs. As Pearce discovered, the research data on the state of relationships between volunteers and staff are not voluminous, despite the apparent severity of the problem. She reviewed studies on grassroots organizations that had few staff and were controlled by volunteers. Not as much data is available from those organizations where "volunteers work as adjuncts to employees in organizations controlled by employees" (Pearce, 1991, p. 142).

A brief review of handbooks for those who coordinate and manage volunteer programs found little information on volunteer–staff relations. There were, however, many admonitions to guard against poor volunteer–staff relations, with attendant advice to help everyone work happily together. There was little discussion describing the characteristics of an effective volunteer–staff partnership, the symptoms of poor relations, how to survey the relationship, or what to do to improve the situation if it is bad.

More than ever it is the relationship between volunteers and staff that can influence the success or failure of a program, fund-raising event, changes in leadership, and the ability to make positive organizational changes. When people work together as teams, at all levels of an organization, agency, or program, efficient and effective services are delivered to clients, patrons, or members. Harmony is achieved not by accident but by attention to the needs of both sides of this vital equation.

10.2 VOLUNTEERS AND STAFF: A TEAM

A set or group of people who work together for a common goal is a team. Another type of team are those players forming one side in certain games and sports. In this context the team is a thing—a group, an association, an entity. Change the grammatical usage, however, and team becomes people's willingness to act for the good of the group rather than their own self-interests.

In selecting members for a board of directors or advisory board one issue considered by nominating committees is a candidate's ability to rise above the single issue to look at the big picture and thus the welfare of the entire organization. Sometimes volunteers are asked to set aside ways in which they have operated for years and move into a new mode. Those who do have subordinated what is good for them personally and put the organization's needs first. The good of the team takes precedence.

At the time of her installation, a new president of a nonprofit organization asked all those serving on committees to leave their current assignments and join new committees. There was discussion about the need to bring fresh ideas and perspective to all areas of organizational operations. After a few months of grumbling most volunteers and some staff who had been moved began to enjoy their new associates and found they were looking at all areas with a new view. However, there was one person who had served on the same committee for 22 years. Now, 18 years after being asked to change committees, she still does not speak to the president of the organization who asked her to move.

Team also is used to describe transport or conveyance. The joint working relationship between volunteers and paid staff in the Boy Scouts allows children to build their citizenship skills; in orchestras it brings music to the community; in hospice it provides skilled and sensitive support to the dying and their families; in libraries it fights censorship; and in humane societies it supports the work of caring for a community's unwanted and unloved animals. Volunteers and staff have the capacity to transport and carry over the cares and concerns of other people into creative solutions.

"A team's performance includes both individual results and what we call collective work-products" (Katzenbach and Smith, 1993, p. 114). Those work products reflect the joint contributions of the members. The effective volunteer–staff team is greater than the participation of any one member.

10.3 CHARACTERISTICS OF THE EFFECTIVE VOLUNTEER–STAFF TEAM

Teams are a manageable size.   "Virtually all effective teams we have met, read or heard about, or been members of have ranged between 2–25 people. The majority of them have numbered less than 10" (Katzenbach and Smith, 1993, p. 112). In most voluntary organization this means that the large group of 100+ volunteers and 12 staff are in subgroups or teams. Those serving on the advisory board or board of directors are one team, the people who work every other Thursday in the organization's office are another team, the committee that plans the annual fun-run fund-raiser is yet another.

People are appropriately selected to serve on a team.   Putting together the right combination of volunteers and staff in terms of personality, skills, influence, communication styles, and ability to perform is important. The more time and care spent in selecting the right combinations for the team, the greater the chances of success.

Team leaders are trained.   Whether team leaders are unpaid volunteers or paid staff members, they deserve and should be required to receive training. Leaders who think they must do all the jobs or have little capacity to delegate make poor team leaders. Find a Tom Sawyer, someone who knows how to paint the fence but gets others to do it. This is someone who has the makings of a team leader, who must plan, delegate, and motivate.

Teams are trained to carry out their tasks. The board of directors or advisory board is a team. They need training on how to carry out their responsibilities and tasks. For example, they must understand the fundamental differences between governance and administration. Governance is the policy-making role of the board. Administration of the policy is carried out by the staff. Volunteers serving as school aides need to understand appropriate and inappropriate behavior in relationship to the children. The teacher (staff) and volunteer aide need to have an understanding of the same set of expected behaviors.

Teams are the foundation of the organization. Voluntary organizations, whether or not they are staffed by paid personnel, are founded on the notion of people working together for a common good. Such a foundation means everyone affiliated with the organization is in some way connected to everyone else. Working together effectively and efficiently is the foundation that builds and strengthens the organization or agency.

Volunteers and staff are supported by administration. Managers and administrators of organizations need to understand the importance of their commitment to the working team, both volunteers and staff. Any program is enhanced through a formal policy statement that outlines the role of volunteers and explains the nature of the volunteer-staff relationship.

Teams have goals and objectives. Effective volunteer–staff teams share a vision of their mission. Usually, they develop a plan with purposes, goals, objectives, and work plans to guide their efforts. "Effective teams develop strong commitment to a common approach, that is, to how they will work together to accomplish their purpose" (Fisher and Cole, 1993, p. 26). Trust cannot be ordained. It develops when people work together successfully. Having a plan helps to build the mutuality of experience that builds trust over time.

Volunteers and staff trust and support one another. People come to trust each other when they have shared positive experiences. In a voluntary organization this means that everyone knows the purpose of the organization and the tasks at hand. Goals are arrived at by members of the team who work together. Some orchestra boards of directors, for example, decide how much money is to be raised by a guild or association during their budget building process and do not consult with the volunteers whose responsibility it is to raise the money. This undermines trust and support among governance volunteers, fund-raising volunteers, and the staff who must work with both.

Communication between volunteers and staff is both vertical and horizontal. The common notion about communication deals with the sending and receiving of messages. Communication is really about sending "meanings" (Wilson, 1976, p. 163). It is less a language process and more a people process. It involves the active and continuous use of such things as active listening, providing feedback, telephone trees, and one-page memos; clarifying perceptions; reading body language; and noticing symbols that communicate meaning. It travels in all directions. Leadership volunteers communicate with direct-service volunteers. Staff communicate with volunteers all the time. Hierarchical blocks to communication are bridged when volunteers and staff work together effectively. It is also true that working together is best facilitated by good communication.

The organizational structure promotes communication between volunteers and staff.   Volunteers and staff need policies, procedures, and structures that permit and encourage them to communicate. A group of volunteers who raised a great deal of money for an organization and led educational programs had a small office read closet in the administrative offices of a large nonprofit group. In a management shuffle the new executive director saw no reason why these women (the group was largely female) couldn't work out of their homes so he could use the small office for storage. Volunteers who could once walk down the hall and talk with paid staff colleagues about their plans and activities were now forced to deal with the voice mail structure and making appointments to share information. This is an example of the organization creating roadblocks to effective communication.

The work of volunteers and staff has real responsibility.   Millions of volunteers stuff envelopes each year for organizations, agencies, and programs. Seems like an unimportant job except that it provides information, education, and news to constituents, clients, or members. Most volunteers know this and willingly fold and stuff for hours because it is a real job with real responsibility. All jobs need to be as clear to the people doing them, whether volunteer or staff.

Volunteers and staff have fun while accomplishing their tasks.   Harmonious relationships between volunteers and staff are readily apparent in the amount of fun exhibited during planning meetings, at activities, or during evaluation sessions. A group of volunteers and staff recruiting parents to serve as leaders of youth clubs heard many people say no before someone would agree to serve. Reporting meetings were sometimes quite grim. A volunteer came to a meeting and said, "I think I have heard the worst excuse yet for not volunteering. A woman told me yesterday she couldn't be a leader of her son's club because she ironed." This brought laughter all around and generated other "best excuse" stories. Someone produced a book and they were recorded. The recording of best excuses was institutionalized by the group. It went on for years. New members, volunteers and staff, were indoctrinated with readings from the book by returning members. The humor and affection exhibited by the group while finishing a task built a sense of fun and reinforced the concept of mutual responsibility.

There is recognition for the contributions of volunteers and staff.   Volunteers publicly recognize the work of staff. Staff publicly acknowledges the efforts of volunteers. There are both formal and informal expressions of appreciation for the work accomplished by groups. Management or administration encourages this and organizes ways to make it easy for the recognition to occur. This effort at recognition is consistent, public, and visible.

Volunteers and staff celebrate their successes.   Celebrations with food, frivolity, and friendship are a hallmark of effective volunteer and staff relationships. These activities are often spontaneous and inexpensive. They are encouraged by the leadership of the organization and might often be led by them. Budgets in nonprofit organizations are planned to pay for celebratory events to herald the effectiveness of the volunteers and staff who work together to achieve the mission of the organization.

The entire organization sees itself as promoting and encouraging the health of volunteer and staff teams.   Building effective volunteer and staff relationships works only when everyone in the organization sees him or herself as part of a volunteer–staff partnership and actively promotes such relationships.

(a) Types of Teams

There are three different types of teams, with many variations. The following descriptions give some idea of how they might be managed effectively.

(i) Volunteer–Staff Teams That Make or Do Things

These groups provide the most direct service—stuff envelopes, visit shut-ins, deliver library books, walk dogs, take blood pressure, lead Girl Scout or 4-H clubs, teach nutrition, weigh rice into one-pound sacks, and make soup for the homeless. The work these teams do has no end date because their activities are ongoing. Managers need to observe and assess these types of teams on a continuing basis. By measuring productivity and performance on a regular basis, alterations are made in how work groups are organized; the training they receive; and client, member, or patron responses. Feedback must be quick, clear, and concise.

(ii) Volunteer–Staff Teams That Run Things

The board of directors, an advisory committee, or a group overseeing some functional activity of the organization or agency is a team that is in effect governing. The key here is to help the team avoid being like the make or do things groups described above. If the volunteers and staff want to organize as a team, they must have goals and objectives separate from those encompassed in the mission of the organization. Boards of directors, for example often focus their planning on accomplishing the mission of the organization, to the exclusion of the development of their own skills as governance volunteers. The board needs separate and distinct goals and objectives, apart from the organizational goals and objectives. These might include such things as communication skill training, risk management presentations, or skills to manage conflict.

Governance groups, boards of directors, or advisory groups frequently have teams within the larger group. Standing or ad hoc committees make up smaller teams. They are in no way the only small team within the larger group.

As executive director of a nonprofit organization for almost 15 years, the author developed a team relationship with five succeeding presidents of the board, and in several cases the team was enlarged to include other officers. The volunteer and staff pairing allowed for creativity in problem solving, leadership development of others, program innovation, policy direction, and organizational change. These small teams did not operate to exclude others but to develop the plans and strategies to enable other volunteers and staff to perform as effectively as possible.

(iii) Teams That Recommend Things

Nonprofit and voluntary groups rely heavily on task force, advisory panel, and project groups. These are groups with a short time period to accomplish their tasks or solve a problem. A chapter in this book recommends the use of an episodic volunteer planning team. Initially, this is a task force type of group—a group that must get off to fast start and meet deadlines for recommendations or activities.

The key component of building teams that recommend is an early and clear role definition and the opportunity for volunteers and staff to create their own goals and objectives. The relationship between volunteers and staff can be enhanced if members are selected carefully. This is often the time to put together people who have a track record of working effectively. It is also critical to include among the volunteers and staff people whose responsibility is implementing the recommendations. That way, it is far more likely that it will happen.

Building effective volunteer–staff teams involves more than implementing training programs on communication. It includes knowing the types of teams that can be formed, what skills its members need, how to match tasks with skills and interpersonal style, and how to address the challenges faced by the teams.

A band that played an open-air concert at a county fair had several members who sang, played, and worked the front of the stage. Additional musicians behind them served in a more supportive role. The obvious harmony of this team came from their agreement about programming, their communication while on-stage, the fun they had with each other, and their willingness to listen to all members, those in front and those further back, in order to enhance the concert. This musical team was a delight to watch. "Usually when this occurs it is that the unique and separate talents of all those involved were somehow blended into a whole that was greater than all of its parts" (Wilson, 1976, p. 181). It is also the ideal to which all volunteer and staff teams should subscribe.

10.4 SYMPTOMS OF POOR VOLUNTEER–STAFF RELATIONSHIPS

In some organizations there is a lack of communication that influences the very survival of the institution. Volunteers and staff are locked in adversarial roles detrimental to the health of the entire organization. This usually begins gradually and at first is noticed by few staff or volunteers.

Symptoms include the increasing use of "us and them" language. Volunteer managers hear things like, "They always do things like this to us." "We would never do something like that to them." There is uncertainty among volunteers and staff about roles and responsibilities. Individuals are often uncooperative about working on joint projects. They do not communicate directly, but go around each other to get questions answered and problems solved.

Volunteers and staff often carve out territory and guard it tenaciously. For example, programs become the sole property of staff, volunteers stake out a fund-raising event and won't entertain suggestions from staff, or board members go into secret meetings to establish budgets and do not consult direct service volunteers or paid staff.

When volunteers and staff have poor relations there is little information sharing. In territorial environments information is seen as power. "Withhold information and you are in control" is the philosophy. A large city orchestra had to cancel its concert season due to a severe money shortage. Leaders asked season ticketholders to donate the purchased tickets and not to request refunds. Several months after this dramatic action the president of the volunteer association knew little about any plans to improve the financial situation, despite the fact that the association would be expected to raise several hundred thousands dollars to help balance the budget. Withholding of information is a way for the board and senior staff to demonstrate their ownership of the budget. It is also a flashing road sign warning that the relationship between volunteers and staff is not healthy.

How can management and voluntary leaders determine the current state of volunteer–staff relations and then develop strategies to improve the staff–volunteer work environment to increase productivity? The first step is to conduct an audit of current volunteer–staff relations, and the second is to implement appropriate steps or strategies to improve the relationship between the two groups.

(a) The Volunteer–Staff Climate Audit

The volunteer–staff climate audit (Exhibit 10–1) assesses the current state of volunteer–staff relations and provides a way to monitor changes in the working environment. It is distributed to randomly selected members of staff, volunteers, clients/patrons/members, and perhaps people outside the organizational family who regularly interact with staff and/or volunteers (if an outsiders' perspective is needed).

The process begins with the organization of an audit committee, which is led by a volunteer–staff team. Members include volunteers from all areas of the organizations and representatives of staff (including people who do staff support work). The person who coordinates or manages volunteers is a likely candidate to provide staff support to this committee. The audit committee needs the support of management and administration in the form of a budget and resources to carry out its work. The commitment of leaders in the organization to an assessment of volunteer–staff relations will be judged not just by words but by the actions taken to support the efforts designed by the audit committee.

The audit committee should follow all the recommendations for effective teams listed in Section 10.6 of this chapter. Their work begins with a purpose statement and a list of goals and objectives that are measurable, achievable, demanding, flexible, and observable.

A random sample of volunteers, staff, and clients should be surveyed, with each group receiving one-third of the questionnaires. For example, if you want to survey 30 people, each group is sent 10 questionnaires. If you add outsiders to the group, they receive half the number distributed to the three main groups. In the sample of 30, only five outsiders receive questionnaires. The number distributed depends on the size of the organization, how many volunteers it uses, how long it will take to compile the results, and the cooperation expected from those completing the form.

The audit distributed with a cover letter explaining the purpose of the activity, who is conducting the survey, how confidentiality is maintained, when the results are available, and how a respondent can see the results. If the survey is mailed, it should include a stamped return envelope.

◆ **EXHIBIT 10–1   The Volunteer–Staff Climate Audit**

Directions: Read each situation and decide how frequently it occurs. Check the appropriate box. Try to respond to each situation.

Situation	Usually	Sometimes	Rarely
1. "They never" or "we always" are words heard when staff members refer to volunteers.	1	2	3
2. Volunteers ask for credits or measures of their worth. Examples: paid parking, discounts, mileage allowance, etc.	1	2	3
3. Volunteers and staff both use such words as "together, we," "our project" (meaning staff and volunteers), etc.	3	2	1
4. Reports on volunteer activities during management meetings come from other staff, not just the person responsible for volunteer coordination.	3	2	1
5. Volunteers are visible on board of directors or advisory board committees.	3	2	1
6. Decisions affecting volunteers are made by staff without consulting the volunteers.	1	2	3
7. Decisions affecting staff are made by volunteers without consulting the staff.	1	2	3
8. Volunteers say "thank you" to staff publicly.	3	2	1
9. Staff treat volunteers who serve on the board of directors or advisory board with more respect than other volunteers.	1	2	3
10. Projects are planned collaboratively between staff and volunteers.	3	2	1
11. Volunteers focus on the past rather than on future possibilities.	1	2	3
12. Volunteers jump appropriate organizational structure lines to get answers to their questions from staff.	1	2	3
13. Staff are too busy to explain the rules of the game to volunteers.	1	2	3
14. The leaders of the organization (staff and/or volunteers) are visible at volunteer events.	3	2	1
15. Volunteers are asked to give input and assistance in most organizational projects, not just fund-raising.	3	2	1
16. Staff says "thank you" to volunteers publicly.	3	2	1
17. "They never" or "we always" are words heard when referring to staff.	1	2	3
Total			

Scoring: Add the numbers in all the boxes you checked. If there are situations for which you did not check any boxes, add 2 points for each situation. Then add the three numbers for your grand total. 38–51 means you have excellent volunteer–staff relations (but don't let up!); 28–37 means you are doing some things right but could use tuning up in some sections (the situations can help you identify those areas); 36–17 means that you have a serious problem and need to take action immediately.

Grand total _____

Are you? Volunteer _____ Staff _____ Other _____ Date _____

The audit committee tabulates the responses and prepares a statistical report for its deliberation. The first step in the deliberation is to have the person who was responsible for tabulation explain or clarify statistics without offering opinions. Then, the group discusses conclusions they can infer or draw from the statistics provided and come up with recommendations based on the conclusions of the group.

The final report is a copy of the statistics, the conclusions, and the recommendations. The co-chairpersons are responsible for delivering written copies of the report to those in leadership positions. They can also present an oral report to interested groups within the organization. The results of the audit are shared with the leadership of the organization, volunteer leaders, and the staff management team. People participating in the audit may want to see the results. A decision on the wider distribution of the results of the audit is made jointly by the members of the organizational leadership team.

The director of volunteer services at a large institution felt that the relationship between volunteers and staff was less than desirable. There had been reports by both volunteers and staff criticizing the other group's work, turnover seemed on the increase, and there was some "us and them" language used by volunteers and staff. A study was conducted to evaluate the attitudes of volunteers and paid staff toward each other as employer and unpaid worker (Macduff, 1991, p. 349). The result of the attitude survey questionnaire was that "paid staff and volunteers generally have positive attitudes toward one another's performance" (Macduff, 1991, p. 355).

The use of a quantifiable measure of attitudes of staff and volunteers provided information for a volunteer advisory committee and allowed the director of volunteers to enhance what was essentially a healthy situation. She discovered, for example, that the turnover was only a problem among volunteers assigned to work with an untrained (and sometimes unresponsive) supervisor. Supervisors were less sure than volunteers about the performance standards (Macduff, 1991, p. 356) for their jobs. There are easy remedies for this.

This experienced and capable volunteer manager misread cues on the state of volunteer and staff relationships. It is easy to do. The use of the volunteer–staff climate audit is a method to reduce overreaction, identify specific areas of concern, and develop a plan to improve the relationships throughout the organization.

10.5 CAUSES OF POOR VOLUNTEER–STAFF RELATIONSHIPS

Pearce suggests three causes for the negative tension that can exist between volunteers and staff: professional status, profiting from charity, and management systems (Pearce, 1993, pp. 143–147). Paid staff have a higher status than unpaid staff. The status is greater in proportion to the degree of specialized training for the occupation (Pearce, 1993, p. 143). The tension caused by the difference in status was reduced in several of the studies she reviewed when volunteers were seen as officeholders and there was "a careful deference on the part of paid [staff] members" (Pearce, 1993, p. 144).

The notion of profiting from charity is twofold. First is the idea that once there are employees in an organization you have the volunteers and staff working at cross purposes. The volunteers are raising money to fund worthwhile causes, while employees' goals are related to good wages and benefits. Second, volunteers are perceived by some employees as being a direct threat to their livelihood. For example, in the mid-1970s New York City had a budget crisis and 40,000 city jobs were lost. The mayor's solution was to enlarge the volunteer contingent. Despite the mayor's pledge that no department would replace employees with volunteers some departments did just that. "Incidents like these can do little to reassure public employees that volunteers pose no threat to their livelihood" (Brudney, 1990, p. 33). Pearce's review of the research backs up the notion that some hostility between volunteers and staff can be traced to job threat. She found that "those employees who were most hostile to volunteers were the ones most threatened by them" (Pearce, 1993, p. 145).

The third cause of tension between volunteers and staff falls in the lap of management systems. It appears that blurring the lines between volunteers and staff is a way to reduce the potential damage from hostility. This is especially true when paid staff leave their positions only to return to the organization or agency as volunteers. It is as if neither volunteer nor employee see the work as "just a job" but rather as a calling (Pearce, 1993, p. 146).

Susan Ellis, in the book *From the Top Down,* discusses the refusal of an employee to accept an assigned volunteer as a symptom of poor relations. "As long as salaried staff are given the choice or act as though they have the choice of accepting volunteers as co-workers, top administration is sending messages about volunteers" (Ellis, 1986, p. 63). This is a management problem. Sometimes the refusal to work with volunteers is based on inaccurate stereotypes. No one wants to work with a person who is incompetent, paid or unpaid. Ellis contends that a well-managed volunteer program recruiting the right people for the right jobs should be an expectation of management. Staff are encouraged to see volunteers as co-workers.

Pearce concludes a comments section on volunteer and staff relations by saying that there is a better chance of improved relations "when volunteers become more employee-like" (Pearce,1993, p. 178). This happens when the selection, orientation, training, and supervision of volunteers is done using standards similar to those used for staff. Pearce also suggests that volunteer and staff relationship is an area begging for more definitive research. Only a few studies have been done so far, and they have used small samples. Large institutional settings such as hospitals have been left out of the research (Pearce, 1993, p. 151). To truly understand the underlying causes of the tension between volunteers and staff, more volunteer managers and administrations must collect quantifiable data.

Despite the lack of abundant hard evidence on the causes of tension it seems clear that management strategies can help reduce tension. Building teams of volunteers and staff as co-workers seems like a successful strategy to enhancing communication and thus effectiveness.

10.6 A SEQUENTIAL PROCESS TO BUILD THE VOLUNTEER–STAFF TEAM

Volunteers and staff who work together to achieve the mission of the organization are a team. The committee that plans a fund-raising event, the executive committee of the board of directors, individuals who work with staff to deliver direct service to clients, members or patrons, and those who provide support services are all part of teams that make up the organization. All the teams working together make up the organizational team.

To build an effective and efficient volunteer team requires a sequential process. Attention to each of these steps can enhance the opportunity for volunteers and staff to work together more effectively.

1. Begin the process of building effective relationships by allowing members of work teams to develop their own goals and objectives. People who have a hand in defining the outcomes are generally more committed to seeing that they happen. A fund-raising team can establish a time line and target financial goals or benchmarks for measuring success. The goals belong to the team and are arrived at by volunteers and staff working together.

Once a work team of volunteers and staff has determined goals and objectives they are written and distributed to all members, thus becoming tools to evaluate progress. Each member of the volunteer–staff team makes a personal commitment to the goals by agreeing to take some responsibility for their completion.

2. Internal role expectations are those written and unwritten rules that describe the appropriate behavior of both volunteers and staff. For example, many boards and committees have an established internal expectation that members may have three excused absences from regularly called meetings. After the third absence their membership in the group is called into question. Some groups enforce this rule, others do not. By clarifying the role expectations, ambiguity is reduced and each half of the equation—volunteer and staff— knows what is expected.

It is also important to address the issue of multiple expectations and possible overload. For example, the secretary to an executive director was asked to represent support staff on a planning committee. Her job was to participate in committee deliberations, not to take notes and type up the minutes. That role had to be clarified for her. She did volunteer to do much of the note-taking for the group. The chair of the committee was careful to ask if it was too much or if she was feeling that the group expected her to do this. As time passed other members of the team picked up the message and both volunteers and staff agreed to share secretarial work. This is also an example of what could have become role conflict.

Another type of role conflict happens when board members are also direct-service volunteers. As board members they discuss governance issues, while as direct service volunteers they are concerned with issues that directly affect clients or members. "As association members, they are 'owners' of the organizations; as 'direct service volunteers' they are workers obligated to perform in accordance with directives and subject to performance surveillance" (Pearce, 1993, p. 178).

Role confusion can result if a volunteer or staff also receives the services of the organization or agency. Clarity and conscious attention to the roles for volunteers and staff keep lines of demarcation clear.

3. External role expectations are another area of concern for volunteer managers. Volunteers and staff need to know with whom it is appropriate to share their concerns, praise, suggestions, or turmoil. Are they only allowed to talk to an immediate supervisor? That is an unrealistic expectation. It is better to help both volunteers and staff understand the importance of knowing the limits and scope of their own influence and how using it will affect the team with which they work. A persistent problem for nonprofit organizations is when one spouse is a direct-service volunteer and the other serves on the board. The board spouse frequently brings administrative concerns to meetings dealing with governance issues. Similarly, the direct-service spouse may share information on new policy directions with friends when no firm decisions have yet been made. Helping people deal with their loyalties and appropriate avenues of communication is important to positive relationship between volunteers and staff.

4. Communication between volunteers and staff is critical. Are two newsletters produced to keep people informed about the organization—one for staff and one for volunteers? Could they be folded into one? The volunteer manager can map the flow and frequency of communication among volunteers and staff. This helps identify areas of weakness. It is also critical that all volunteers and staff be participants in the information flow, which should cross status and authority lines.

5. Decisions made by effective work teams are determined uniformly. The group needs to decide on a process for decision making. Leaders should not assume that everyone wishes to use a consensus model. Discuss alternatives and let the group make a conscious decision. The discussion includes those involved in the process of making decisions. Many people might be consulted, but only a few might make the final decision.

There are two other important issues to address before beginning work on a project—the problem-solving techniques to be used by the group, and the way conflict is managed. If volunteers and staff have been working together on a team for years, this information is reviewed annually whether or not there are new members.

6. Leaders of volunteers and staff must be skilled. This means appropriate training must be provided to staff who supervise volunteers *and* to volunteers who supervise other volunteers. It is not optional. Leaders need skills as facilitators, meeting managers, problem solvers, and conflict resolvers. Volunteers and staff work harmoniously when they are led by people with good skills.

7. All groups have norms, whether or not they acknowledge them. These are the unwritten rules that guide organizational and personal behavior. The best norms are those that encourage positive relationships between volunteers and staff. For example, the way volunteers and staff greet newcomers is often an indication of the state of volunteer–staff relationships. There are rarely policies about greetings, but they can immediately tell volunteers and staff if a team spirit exists in a group. For instance, volunteers arrive at a meeting and find that the attendees are all paid staff. No one greets them or helps them find seats. A paid staff person attends a meeting of all volunteers. The staff person is not included in the discussion or consulted about decisions that must be carried out by other staff members. Inclusion or exclusion is the basis of many organizational norms. If the organization runs on staff in-groups or volunteer in-groups, others can be excluded, and that does not build effective volunteer–staff teams.

10.7 TIPS TO ENHANCE VOLUNTEER–STAFF RELATIONS

The following are tips to enhance volunteer–staff relations:

- ◆ The position of the volunteer manager is challenging, time consuming, and vital. Coordinating volunteer programs is a complex professional job that requires a variety of skills and strategies. Most programs are in hot competition for qualified volunteers. Recruiting and retaining volunteers is a key factor in overall organizational success. It is also a major challenge. Building a strong volunteer–staff team means delegating tasks and responsibilities. An effective volunteer manager learns to delegate to others because it results in efficiency, productivity, and highly motivated people.

◆ Training on team building enhances volunteer–staff relations. Knowledge of team-building strategies helps both volunteers and staff manage more effectively. Sending volunteers and staff together to a team-building workshop sends a clear message about the goals of the organization.

◆ Volunteers find alternative lines of communication in an organization when they don't get their questions answered. Staff and volunteers in leadership roles need to monitor constantly the types, forms, and frequency of communication to members of the work team.

◆ Open, honest evaluation of tasks and positions within the organization, both volunteer and staff, is done on a regular schedule. Volunteers need to evaluate their own efforts and have opportunities to assess staff who work directly with them. This is a joint effort, not a session where staff outlines a list of transgressions. Volunteers can improve only if *they* identify and plan to correct weaker elements of their performance. Similarly, when a staff member works on an event or program, the evaluation process is done jointly.

◆ Volunteers and staff are evaluated on supervision and management competencies. The organization's performance appraisal form or process includes an area that assesses staff ability to work effectively with volunteers. If a staff member does not work with volunteers, that portion of the performance appraisal is marked "Not Applicable." If management does not take volunteer–staff team work seriously enough to evaluate staff on a regular basis, why should the staff? Similarly, volunteers in leadership roles are evaluated on how they might enhance their skills. The person conducting the assessment for the volunteer is the paid staff or volunteer to whom they report. For example, the president of the board of directors and the CEO of an agency meet annually to discuss their respective performances as it relates to the management of volunteers and staff, and both fill out a standardized management competencies form, which asks for self-evaluation. During the meeting they share the form and make adjustments based on the other's observations of their work. This is not part of CEO's formal evaluation.

◆ Clear communication means:
   straight talk from both volunteers and staff
   active listening by volunteers and staff
   emphasis on building a team-work environment
   volunteer work areas in close proximity to staff
   pay volunteers by means of a constant flow of information
   staff working continuously with volunteer leadership to understand the larger needs and goals of the organization
   "Thank yous" coming often to volunteers—publicly—even when volunteers contributed only part of the total job

◆ Monitor how often volunteers are included in planning for new projects. For example, a director of volunteers in a large urban setting uses as one measure of volunteer–staff relations how consistently the volunteers are invited to participate in discussions of service goals or projects. This means everything from determining how to stuff envelopes to meeting with the director of development at a problem-solving session on reaching a targeted group for contributions. This volunteer manager knows things are okay if requests increase for the special expertise that volunteers bring to the team.

◆ The volunteer coordinator is seen by both volunteers and staff as fulfilling a key linking role. One important responsibility is to communicate the views of volunteers to the paid staff and explain the roles and responsibilities of paid staff to the volunteers.

◆ Mutually define roles and responsibilities.

◆ Paid and nonpaid staff relations are often improved through training and orientation that is specifically about working in a nonprofit organization. The training session might focus on the concept of paid and unpaid staff to begin to reduce barriers that might exist between volunteers and staff.

◆ Volunteers can sometimes see themselves as operating to the side, away from the organization. A team approach to volunteer–staff relations means that everyone works *together* to further the mission. Decisions that affect the volunteers and the service they deliver or the money they raise are arrived at jointly with paid staff. Volunteers consult staff as they make decisions about how they will carry out an event or activity.

◆ Some staff members, representing the entire staff, may be on the volunteer-boards; some direct service volunteers, representing all direct service volunteers, may be on the board of directors or the advisory committee. Paid and unpaid staff also make good contributing members of management committees.

Every volunteer program or nonprofit organization faces unique problems and challenges in building an effective team, but efforts to build such a team have a practical, powerful payoff. Teams can deliver results efficiently and effectively when their members truly work together. The power of the team is in creating the kind of environment that enables individuals and organizations to perform at their peak.

Farmer Jones and Farmer Chin owned two dray horse they used to drag produce wagons to market. They decided to sell their horses. Farmer Alvarado decided to buy the two horses, hook them up to a larger wagon and carry more produce to market. The horses were raised differently; the food they ate, how they were disciplined, the shelter they had from the weather, the love and affection from their owners, and the weight of their wagons were all different. The farmer and the horses had to develop the means to work together. By pulling together they were able to accomplish the mission of getting more produce to market for Farmer Alvarado. (Macduff, 1965)

These horses represent the choices volunteers and staff face. They can pull the organizational wagon to market or pull it into kindling.

REFERENCES

Brudney, Jeffrey. 1990. *Fostering Volunteers Programs in the Public Sector.* San Francisco: Jossey-Bass.

Ellis, Susan. 1986. *From the Top Down: The Executive Role in Volunteer Program Success.* Philadelphia: Energize Associates.

Fisher, James C., and Kathleen M. Cole. 1993. *Leadership and Management of Volunteer Programs.* San Francisco: Jossey-Bass.

Katzenbach, Jon R., and Douglas K. Smith. 1993. "The Discipline of Teams." *Harvard Business Review* (March–April).

Macduff, Elizabeth. 1965. *Childhood Story.*

Macduff, Nancy. 1991. "Attitudes of Volunteers and Paid Staff on Job Performance," *Conference Proceeding: 1991 Association for Research on Nonprofit Organizations and Voluntary Action (ARNOVA),* "Collaboration: The Vital Link across Practice, Research and the Disciplines. Chicago.

Pearce, Jone. 1993. *Volunteers: The Organizational Behavior of Unpaid Workers.* London: Routledge.

Wilson, Marlene. 1976. *The Effective Management of Volunteer Programs.* Boulder, Colo.: Management Associates.

CHAPTER  11

REWARD AND RECOGNITION SYSTEMS FOR VOLUNTEERS

E. Brian Peach
Kenneth L. Murrell
Department of Management/MIS
The University of West Florida and Empowerment Leadership Systems

11.1   Behavior Theory Overview

11.2   Typical Reward and Recognition Systems

11.3   Opportunities Provided by New Organizational Forms

11.4   Managerial Guidance for System Design

11.5   Reward and Recognition System Redesign

11.6   Reward and Recognition Techniques That Work

11.7   Professionalization of the Volunteer Role

11.8   Leaders' or Managers' Role in Adjusting to Changing Conditions

11.9   Symphony Orchestra Case Study

         References

11.1 BEHAVIOR THEORY OVERVIEW

The design of reward and recognition systems within any organization (for-profit, nonprofit, volunteer, government, and so on) has as its goal influencing member behaviors to benefit both the individual and the organization. The fact that volunteers are not paid for their services should not be viewed as a critical deficiency in motivating performance. Firms in the profit-making sector have become increasingly aware that simply paying employees is not enough to ensure their continuing organizational loyalty, high levels of productivity, attention to quality and customer service, or any of the myriad other desired employee performances. One study found that job applicants rank salary as the ninth most important on a list of 18 rewards (Posner, 1981), and pay is not the single necessary factor in motivating performance that many people consider it to be.

Designing or redesigning reward systems starts with the premise that understanding what motivates people is helpful in designing systems to influence behavior. Researchers in a variety of disciplines have expended great effort over many years in an attempt to gain a deeper understanding of what motivates people to act. Organizations that rely on unpaid volunteers for provision of critical services can benefit from this increasing body of knowledge as well as contributing to the development of theory and improvement in management practice.

(a) Theories of Motivation

Motivation is the drive that energizes, sustains, and directs a person's behavior. Understanding why people do what they do—that is, what motivates their behavior—is the concern of researchers in many fields, including psychology, sociology, and organization science. Relevant theories of content and process motivation as a foundation for subsequent development of reward and recognition systems keyed to the special attributes of volunteers are reviewed briefly in this section.

(i) Content Theories of Motivation

Content theories of motivation focus on *what things* motivate people to act—or in other words, the *needs* individuals are attempting to satisfy through their actions. The earliest significant contributor to needs theory was Henry A. Murray, who developed a 20-item list of manifest needs (Murray, 1938). Murray believed that several needs could motivate a person simultaneously and so he did not arrange his list in order of importance. Environmental conditions, he believed, would determine which needs would manifest themselves. His needs each had two characteristics, direction and intensity.

Needs as a basis for motivation were later popularized by Maslow through his hierarchy of needs (Maslow, 1943, 1954). The five needs in ascending order are physiological, safety and security, belonging, esteem, and self-actualization. Maslow's contention was that lower-order needs must be satisfied before a person will try to satisfy higher-order needs. At any given time, one of the five needs would be prepotent (primary) and would drive behavior. Maslow felt that an organization's management should recognize the need level at which members were operating and adjust its response to suit those needs.

Maslow was followed by Herzberg, who proposed a two-factor theory (Herzberg, Mausner, and Snyderman, 1959). Sometimes referred to as satisfiers and dissatisfiers, Herzberg labeled them motivators and hygiene factors. *Motivators* are factors that encourage action; as motivators are increased, motivation is increased. *Hygiene factors* do not motivate, but inadequate levels of hygiene factors cause dissatisfaction and thus stifle motivation. Once enough of a hygiene factor is present to produce satisfaction, further amounts provide no additional benefit. Herzberg also promoted the concepts of intrinsic and extrinsic motivators. *Intrinsic motivators* originate within a person, while *extrinsic motivators* come from the outside. We will come back to motivators in our discussion of linking needs and rewards because of their critical importance in volunteer-based settings.

Mahoney (1975) extended Herzberg's two-factor theory by establishing optimality functions for hygiene factors (Exhibit 11–1). Mahoney contended that increased amounts of motivators (line A in Exhibit 11–1) will continue to increase satisfaction and influence performance positively. Some hygiene factors (line B) increase motivation with increased factor amounts until a certain point (satiation); after that, there is no benefit with increased factor amount. Others (line C) increase motivation to satiation, but after that increased factor amounts adversely affect motivation. The message here is that for rewards to have a maximum possible benefit (optimality points), providing additional rewards at best will not benefit the organization and may be counterproductive in influencing positive behavior.

A third important theory is McClelland's modes for success (McClelland, 1965). McClelland devoted most of his research to three needs—affiliation, achievement, and power—with a major focus on the achievement need. Such needs are often classified as secondary motives (Luthans, 1985) and are more learned than innate drives. McClelland treated power as the drive to have influence, either with others in a socialized form or in a more negative sense as control. His achievement motive is often incorrectly equated only with a desire for financial success. McClelland viewed achievers as people who want to perform to standards of excellence, to achieve success through their own efforts, and to take personal responsibility for any success or failure; people who desire timely feedback on their performance. Such characteristics are common to successful entrepreneurs, and from this derives the confusion over equating achievement needs with a purely monetary drive.

◆ **EXHIBIT 11–1   Optimality Functions**

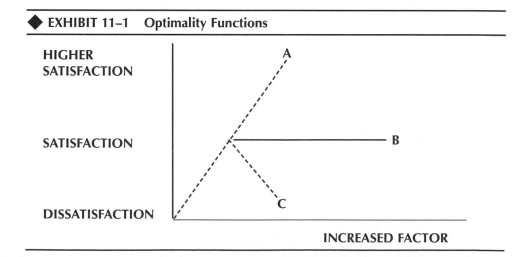

Achievers want to do things faster, more efficiently, and with less effort, and such a need can be satisfied in a variety of settings, not just with monetary inducements to work. Their risk-taking behavior is in the range where success is perceived as difficult but likely.

Need theories are important in understanding *what* motivates people, but they have limitations in practice. In many cases it is difficult to know which need is dominant in a person, especially since different people within groups may well be experiencing different needs. Need theory alone, therefore, does not adequately describe what motivates work performance.

(ii) Process Theories of Motivation

Process theories focus on *how* people are motivated. Two major process theories are Adam's equity theory (Adams, 1965) and Vroom's expectancy theory (Vroom, 1964).

Equity theory predicts that individual motivation is affected by perceptions of the ratio of personal outcomes divided by personal inputs compared to the same ratio for a relevant comparison person or group. In other words, under equity theory, people realize and are willing to accept that they work more or less hard than others and will therefore receive correspondingly more or less in the way of rewards or recognition, but they expect the ratios to be equal.

$$\frac{\text{My rewards (outcomes)}}{\text{My contribution (inputs)}} = \frac{\text{Your rewards (outcomes)}}{\text{Your contributions (inputs)}}$$

Two considerations derive from equity theory. The first is that both overrewarding, and underrewarding can cause feelings of inequity. The second is that feelings are based on an individual's perceptions, which may not match the perceptions of others. When people perceive an inequitable situation, they may take one or more of the following actions to restore equity. First, they may lower their contributions or attempt to increase their rewards. Second, they may compare themselves with a different person or group. Third, they may adjust their perceptions. Fourth, they may leave the situation. In making comparisons, people use five groups: themselves over time, a person in the same workplace in an equivalent job, a person in the same workplace in a nonequivalent job, a person in another work setting with an equivalent job, and a person in another work setting with a nonequivalent job.

Clearly, managers and leaders must not just rely on their own perceptions of equity, but must be careful to assess the worker's perceptions of equity as well. This is complicated because studies have shown that over 80 percent of the workforce believes that they are above average, and managers often falsely assume that their sense of reality is objectively right and therefore is shared by the workforce.

Expectancy theory predicts that the force (motivation) to engage in efforts to accomplish a task depends on three things: expectancy, instrumentality, and valence (Exhibit 11–2). Expectancy is a belief that a particular act will result in a particular outcome. Instrumentality is believing that achieving the outcome will result in receiving a reward. Valence is the sum of the rewards for accomplishing the task and should be of sufficient value to justify the effort. Thus, when presented with a choice of activities, we will perform the one most likely to lead to the most valued reward.

The message here is that three things must occur for motivation to be sufficient to stimulate activity. First, we must believe that we are capable of performing the

◆ **EXHIBIT 11-2   Expectancy Model**

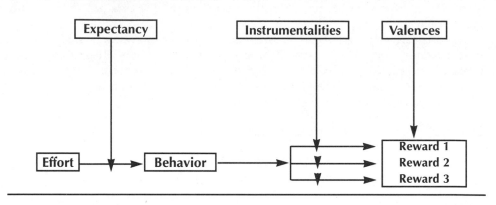

task. The more we doubt our ability to perform a task, the less likely we are to act, regardless of how much we value the reward. Second, we must believe that successful accomplishment of the activity is linked to the reward—that is, we must trust those who control the rewards. The greater our suspicion concerning the linkage, the less likely we are to act regardless of the ease of task accomplishment or the value we place on the reward. Third, we must value the rewards of this activity more than we value the rewards of alternative or competing activities or of doing nothing at all.

For example, a volunteer working in a fund-raising campaign with a specific campaign goal is faced with the choice of working on the fund drive or on one of a number of other activities. The volunteer has an *expectancy* that fund-raising effort will lead to additional contributions. The volunteer's *instrumentality* is a belief that those additional funds will result in achieving the organizational goal. The volunteer's *valence* for achieving the fund drive goal is the sum of all positive outcomes for the fund drive—the intrinsic reward of improved personal feelings, extrinsic rewards of recognition and praise from co-volunteers, social rewards of working with valued friends, increased status within organization and community, and so on. This valence competes with rewards for other possible activities—social rewards from partying with friends, status or power rewards from working extra on a project for work, spending time with family, and so on.

The first consideration is whether the volunteer believes that additional effort will actually result in additional contributions. If the volunteer believes that more effort will not raise additional funds, then to the extent that the volunteer's primary rewards are derived from *results*, not *effort*, the volunteer will not apply additional effort. Second, the volunteer has to believe that obtaining additional funds will result in achieving the campaign goal. For example, if the additional funds would result in only a minor change in the total, which would still fall short of the goal, there is little motivation to put forth the effort. Finally, the reward (valence) to the volunteer for achieving the campaign goal must be greater than competing rewards for other activities. Thus the volunteer must believe that additional effort will lead to raising additional funds (expectancy), which will lead to achieving the campaign goal (instrumentality), and all of this somehow provides a more positive and rewarding outcome (valence) than other available choices.

Porter, Lawler, and Hackman (1975) developed an extended expectancy model as depicted in Exhibit 11–3. They included equity effects as well as ability considerations. They believe that motivation does not lead directly to performance but is mediated by abilities and role perceptions. More important, their model illustrates that satisfaction is a result of successful performance rather than a primary motivator. The greater the ability to achieve the desired results and the more compatible the person feels with the role behavior needed, the greater the motivation. This is the key focus for managerial influence on motivation because given a trust relationship, training and self-esteem development can promote higher levels of volunteer motivation.

11.2 TYPICAL REWARD AND RECOGNITION SYSTEMS

(a) How Reward and Recognition Systems Work

The basic functions of any reward and recognition system are to recruit, retain, develop, and motivate to perform. At the simplest level, reward and recognition systems work by satisfying the needs of those already performing in the volunteer

◆ **EXHIBIT 11–3   Porter, Lawler, and Hackman Model**

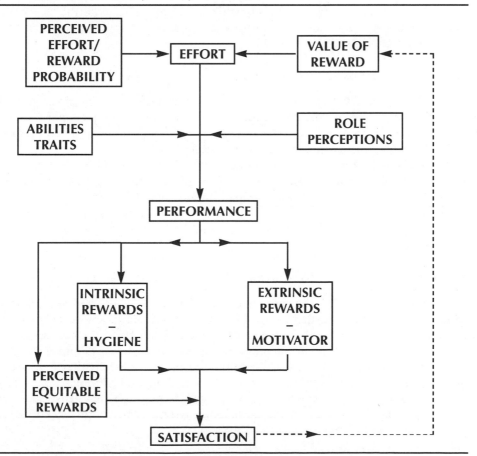

role, and convincing those considering a volunteer role that some of their needs will be satisfied through volunteering. For-profit organizations rely primarily, and many argue far too much, on money as a need satisfier and motivator. Although money, per se, is not considered a motivator, it often can be used to purchase satisfaction for a wide variety of needs. Thus it acts as a surrogate satisfier of needs. Volunteer organizations, however, must provide rewards that respond directly to individual needs, and this should be considered more and more as a competitive advantage. The use of direct rather than surrogate rewards is one reason why management theorists consider voluntary organizations an important area of study.

An effective reward and recognition system in a volunteer organization, therefore, will match the array of its available rewards to satisfy the specific needs of each volunteer. This may seem a daunting task, and in reality while it is simple in concept, it can be complex and challenging in execution. In a later section, we discuss specific approaches for the various types of needs identified. Most volunteers will have several needs at work at any given time and thus will seek multiple rewards to satisfy those needs.

(b) Vital Purposes and Contributions of Reward and Recognition Systems

Effective reward and recognition systems support the organization in many ways. In addition to motivating volunteer behavior by satisfying individual needs, reward systems should also be supportive of organizational goals. Behavior that is generally desired of all members should be rewarded and recognized for the good of the total organization and its stakeholders.

(i) Contributions to Productivity

Productivity typically is defined as an output–input ratio. Here we mean it as the effective channeling of volunteer effort toward the successful accomplishment of organizational goals. Volunteer time and effort is generally a precious commodity—it should not be squandered in irrelevant or useless tasks.

A critical step in increasing the productivity of volunteers is task selection and assignment, because it is crucial for volunteer organizations to match the desires and abilities of the volunteer with assigned tasks as carefully as possible. Much of the potential reward for volunteers derives from successful task accomplishment. Thus volunteers will be less motivated by (and less productive at) tasks they find irrelevant or inappropriate.

(ii) Contributions to Retention

Individuals volunteer with the expectation of satisfying some unfilled need. Because safety needs must be satisfied before social and self-actualization needs, volunteer organizations do not have the same control over individuals as the companies that issue their paychecks. Volunteers whose needs are unsatisfied will either withdraw from effective participation or leave for other organizations, where they perceive the potential rewards to be greater. By accurately identifying and addressing the specific needs of individuals and providing rewards and recognition that satisfy the need expectation, an effective reward and recognition system increases the likelihood that a volunteer will remain with the organization.

(iii) *Contributions to Morale and Esprit de Corps*

Key elements of an effective reward and recognition system are establishing clear performance goals and expectations, clearly linking individual tasks and performance to the overall organization mission, and satisfying individual needs to increase individual satisfaction. People dislike ambiguity, and providing volunteers with specific objectives focuses their efforts. To the extent that individuals feel that they are performing well at an important task, their morale will be enhanced. To the extent that individuals believe that they are working effectively with others for an important overarching organizational goal, their esprit de corps will be enhanced. As the leadership of an organization demonstrates concern for the volunteer through appropriate task assignment and performance recognition, the volunteer's sense of personal satisfaction and willingness to participate will increase.

(c) Weaknesses and Failures of Typical Reward Systems

Most often, organizations, both for-profit and volunteer, establish reward and recognition systems without recognizing the individuality of member needs. To some extent, for-profit organizations succeed because the monetary rewards they provide employee, can be used to acquire a variety of satisfiers for their actual needs. Many volunteer organizations succeed despite their reward systems rather than because of them. The reward system fails to encourage high performance because there is a lack of clear performance expectancy, lack of desired reward (desired by the worker, *not* preferred by the manager), or a lack of match between individual and task (Exhibit 11–4).

For example, the leadership of an organization motivated primarily by altruism and personal dedication to the organization's goal may consciously or unconsciously assume altruism to be a motivation for all of the organization's membership. They may assign tasks without regard to member preferences and expect volunteers just to pitch in and do the work; or they may fail to explain why the work is important and how it supports the organization's overall success (Exhibit 11–5).

Members motivated either by altruism or by achievement needs desire significant jobs they perceive as important to organizational success. In many cases, they

---

◆ **EXHIBIT 11–4   Reward Systems That Fail**

- ◆ Rewards that benefit <u>only</u> the individual or the organization without concern for the other, or for the integration of the individual's and the organization's needs
- ◆ Rewards that "buy" inputs without quality or commitment issues identified
- ◆ Rewards assumed to be good for everyone without regard for individuality
- ◆ Rewards based on what the leaders or managers value rather than what the volunteers value
- ◆ Rewards systems perceived as inequitable based on personal or comparison group performance (other volunteers treated better)
- ◆ Rewards inconsistently administered, resulting in a lack of trust
- ◆ Confusion about whether efforts will lead to expected rewards
- ◆ Rewards external to the volunteer—no connection to work or person

---

♦ **EXHIBIT 11–5**   **Recognition Systems That Fail**

- ♦ Recognition built on culturally based assumptions of leaders or managers and not connected to the lives or values of volunteers
- ♦ Recognition given whether performance merits it or not
- ♦ Assumption that only money and altruism motivate, with failure to develop alternatives
- ♦ Use of standardized symbolic or trivial systems that are easy to administer but are impersonal and treat everyone the same
- ♦ Recognition that is disconnected from accomplishments: too little, too late
- ♦ Assumption that the organization's mission is sufficient justification to volunteer—with no recognition, celebration, or appreciation
- ♦ Excessive recognition, celebration, and self-congratulation—managers must seek balance

---

desire some degree of control over the performance and want realistic goals and feedback. When volunteers are given tasks but are allowed little latitude in deciding how they are to be performed, or kept uninformed about how their contributions help the overall effort, the level of their need satisfaction will be diminished and their drive to perform dampened.

11.3 OPPORTUNITIES PROVIDED BY NEW ORGANIZATIONAL FORMS

In this last decade of the twentieth century, everything we do and know about organizations is in a state of change. So rapid are these changes that it approaches chaos. Managers and leaders of voluntary organizations may take some hope because many experts suggest that other organizations should look to them for new responses to organizing in these periods of turbulent change. Peter Drucker, one of the most respected management authorities, believes that managers of volunteers often deal first with the challenges that the rest of the management profession will be facing more and more (Drucker, 1990). The broader field of organizational studies takes seriously the potential for experimentation and innovation in organizing volunteers who dedicate their limited time for no direct economic gain. Volunteer organizations represent what many organizations of the future may look like— at least those organizations where skilled, world-class employees are in limited supply.

How to help organize and manage volunteers around the world who want to work together to provide services, solve problems, or make their voices heard is a significant question. Forming answers to that question is a major preoccupation for many management experts.

(a) Approaches and Strategies for Developing the Organization

Three general approaches or strategies exist for creating the systems through which we can effectively develop volunteer organizations. The first choice, and the one most often taken, is to attempt a replication of the historically dominant organizational models. Several reasons explain this duplication strategy, not the least of which is that it has sometimes worked. Today, though, when these traditional, predominantly hierarchial and bureaucratic models are being rejected, a volunteer manager or leader should be able to see beyond these habitual responses. He or she should be able to examine seriously the second choice for organizing, which is to look at the more successful contemporary forms and the innovative structures currently emerging. These new forms, many of which have been advocated for over 20 years, are often flatter organizations with much more emphasis on team-based structuring and intense and increased focus on both external and internal customers.

The preferred option is a third choice or strategy built on the understanding and even appreciation of the first two. It is a strategy dedicated to the development of contingent organizational forms. These models not only respond to the significant environmental changes that are occurring around them but also acknowledge and respond to the fact that volunteers are essentially different from employees who must work to survive financially.

Organizations built *for* volunteers—better still, organizations built *by* them—will reflect this third choice or strategy. A strategy to create systems grounded in the unique assumptions of volunteer employees is also a strategy that can be developed to take the potential of volunteer organizations even further into the next century.

This is one of the reasons why such management authorities as Peter Drucker look to nonprofit and volunteer organizations for lessons on how to organize effectively when the workforce—especially people with highly demanded skills and abilities—will be able to choose among many different organizations in a seller's market. These future employees, like volunteers, have many choices as to where, when, and how they want to work. It is likely that managing volunteers today foreshadows managing employees tomorrow in for-profit firms.

So the question, then, is how best to organize and use these workers or volunteers today. Many of the forms proposed have yet to be created, but there is much that can be learned by looking at new forms that are in place today. A first rule to hold in reviewing these new models is that the future may well have one of everything. No one single best, do it this way or else, is likely to emerge. Diversity is more than a slogan; it is an increasingly rich reality, and appreciation for differences will be an essential ingredient for new organizational forms. To manage diversity well or to tap into it for collective gain does assume that the organizational forms of the future will be more open environments, where relationships take on especially significant importance. The world of the volunteer is one in which individual contributors must be given a high level of basic respect and honor. In fact, this is one of those core reasons why volunteer organizations are looked at as future models. However, these values of respect should be deeply grounded in the organization; they should not be just written statements of board policy that are printed at the end of funding proposals or in glossy brochures.

(b) Embedding Organizational Values

To create organizational forms to reflect these values is possible only if the organizations leadership or management itself holds these values or is willing to learn them. If this situation does exist, then the next challenge is to see that it is supported in the structural or organizational forms that are developed to achieve the organization's goals. This is more difficult but still possible, because the new organizational models can reflect positive community values about how organizations should function. For example, if a core value is that all members are to share in the responsibility for deciding how the organization should operate, then the power relationships reflected in this value should support an empowerment principle of creating power and not a control assumption of distributing it. Volunteer organizations that have multilayered hierarchies where the levels of influence decrease limit volunteer workers' empowerment potential. This structure is even more controlling if lower-level employees are managed only as separate individuals with little or no linkage to the others with whom they accomplish larger tasks. Team-based models of volunteers working together can function if the organization is empowering. If the organizational structure is used primarily to lighten the administrative load while individual contributors' hours are needlessly wasted in nondirected discussions or endless committee meetings, then the organization might help leaders and managers feel good but will not establish an empowered volunteer workforce.

This new empowered volunteer organization model more closely resembles the small business unit or profit center, where a more self-directed team is aided by an organizational structure that provides it with real power, not just the hope of it or a discussion about it. Other structural components of a new volunteer organization are innovations that facilitate rapid and responsive actions as well as creativity, and are led from a contingency perspective that assumes that different volunteers may seek very different experiences from working together.

(c) The Future is One of Everything

Just as with the future, the organization may be a model with one of nearly everything. This does not make management easier; it just makes the organization more respectful of the uniqueness of its volunteers. If people feel that they can best offer five to seven hours of their individual efforts to raise funds, then a team might well be established to support them so that they can do what it is they do best. When volunteers want to work with a specific team, not only should those requests be considered but so should the provision of the necessary skill training and resources needed for those teams to be successful. The volunteer manager may be expected to manage a multitude of people and teams in forms that rely on shared responsibility, accountability, and empowerment. This is exactly what many large business corporations attempt as they spend millions of dollars on training for their managers and their workforce.

In this way the use of the second strategy—replicating current cutting-edge organizing models—will lead to the third strategy—evolving even more innovative organizational forms unique to the volunteer worker culture. This culture, or set of assumptions held by the volunteer of the future, should lead to the creation of effective structures, not vice versa, where the organizational forms used historically serve to limit and not promote change.

One of the most appealing structural forms, given an assumption of empowerment as a strong core value, is something loosely labeled a *liberating structure*. In this organizational form or design the principle becomes: In what unique and appropriate manner can the organization promote empowerment? Empowerment of individuals and teams is created by interactive application throughout the organization of responsibility, authority, resourcing, and accountability. When applied together these four core values help create the organizational environment needed to improve customer focus and satisfaction, to engage participants as professionals, to increase productivity, and to foster high morale and esprit de corps. The study of empowering or liberating structures is a developing area of interest, where field research is leading us to design beyond the self-directing and self-regulating team model toward organizational forms that build in coordination as well as in self-energizing functions. The concepts emerging from this area of interest look into cogenerative models such as those of Max Elden and Morton Levin (1981), as well as the creative power structures discussed by Bill Torbert (1991). These are organizational forms noteworthy more for their organic nature (that is, they are flexible and growing) than for any one particular form or fixed structure. As Elden discusses in his action research experiments, to be cogenerative is to share the organizational design task with the participants or volunteers so that the form is created by all the participants, who consider the unique needs and environments of their organization. Torbert proposes a similar process, so that people work together to create their own organizational forms, considering what they are capable of doing and what will work given the conditions they are facing.

Organizational form is created and re-created as needed, and that form should match the organization's function to help achieve its goals. If it has liberating structure, the organization helps create power rather than assuming a distributive function of power as a means of control. The organization's decision making and action taking occurs on the level at which it is needed, and so the organization does not rigidly follow principles of hierarchical control. Thus, the process of organizing is not cookie cutter simple; rather, it is open and responsive to volunteers as well as to the organization's mission and other stakeholders. Successful structures are then created and re-created instead of being inherited from past generations or imposed from top-down control-oriented leaders. In this way, the organization grows and changes, and in times of turbulent change this can be a distinct advantage over inflexible and bureaucratic organizational structures.

11.4 MANAGERIAL GUIDANCE FOR SYSTEM DESIGN

(a) Monetary Measures

In our discussion of motivation, a variety of models and processes has been mentioned. Traditionally, for-profit organizations have attempted to use money, in the form of wages, incentives, bonuses, and so on, as a proxy satisfier for the true needs of employees. Increasingly, successful motivation is limited by the value that employees place on money as an appropriate surrogate or channel for obtaining what they truly value. Volunteer organizations are restricted by not being able to offer a broad proxy incentive such as monetary rewards. They have, however, a significant advantage in being able to directly provide the rewards that people value. The key is first to identify what needs a person has, and then to provide the appropriate reward.

(b) Nonfinancial Measures

In general, the motives that people have for voluntary action can be placed in three categories: altruism, rationality, and affiliation (Puffer and Meindl, 1992). Altruism is the desire to help others without regard for personal self-interest or gain. Rational motives involve volunteering for reasons of self-interest. Affiliative motives derive from the desire to interact socially, to identify with a group, and to form affective bonds with others. Individuals volunteer for one or a combination of these three types of motives. The types of rewards provided by the organization should be targeted to these motives.

(i) Altruistic Volunteers

Altruistic volunteers seek intrinsic rewards—internal feelings of doing good, of helping, of making a positive difference. Their major objective or need is to obtain an intrinsic reward derived through performance on the job. All too many managers in volunteer organizations, who are personally consumed with the organization's overall mission, make the assumption that volunteers are driven only by altruism; the opportunity to undertake any task, however trivial, will be accepted gratefully; and the job will be carried out with zeal. However, volunteers motivated by altruism, driven by the need to feel truly good about helping others, desire a sense that their tasks are important and meaningful, and that they can contribute to their successful completion. This is especially important because over half of those interviewed in a Gallup poll reported that the desire to help others was their primary reason for volunteering (Hodgkinson and Weitzman, 1989).

Job enrichment was popularized by for-profit firms, which recognized that money alone was an insufficient motivator (Herzberg, 1968). Key elements of this approach can be extracted and used by volunteer organizations. To perceive their participation in a task as meaningful, volunteers must be given jobs that are clearly aimed at achieving organizational goals. They must also be given sufficient control over the task to clearly feel accountable for its success or failure. Today, empowerment is a recognized tool for placing decisions at the appropriate level, for both organizational effectiveness and worker motivation (Murrell and Vogt, 1991). For the altruistic volunteer empowerment is especially important.

The assignment of rote tasks or small pieces of a major project provide little opportunity for intrinsic feelings of accomplishment. If volunteers cannot see how their efforts mesh with the efforts of others to accomplish meaningful goals, their feeling of helping others is diminished. Also, tasks at which volunteers are unlikely to perform well, or where organizational limitations almost preordain failure, are unlikely to elicit the rewards that altruistic volunteers need. Challenging and complex tasks can be highly motivating, but fruitless ventures will result in frustration and lack of motivation.

Once the task has been properly structured, volunteers' intrinsic feelings can be augmented by external acknowledgments of the significance of their contributions. Verbal communications cannot be substituted for reality—the task must be perceived as important and job performance as good by the volunteer. However, public recognition by someone with credibility can enhance and reinforce volunteers intrinsic feelings and increase their positive feelings toward the task and the organization.

Thus, appropriate organizational rewards for altruistic volunteers, should be structured in two ways—they should be given challenging but accomplishable tasks and their efforts should be praised,both verbally and in other ways.

(ii) Rational Volunteers

Rational volunteers join organizations out of self-interest, but this should not be interpreted as a criticism or deficiency. Many talented people find themselves with a workplace position that does not satisfy their needs for power, achievement, or personal enhancement. Using Maslow's hierarchy of needs terminology, they are unable to fully satisfy their needs for self-actualization through their jobs. Using McClelland's needs terminology, they have unsatisfied needs for power or achievement. It is to the mutual benefit of both the individual and the volunteer organization to provide a mechanism for such people to satisfy their needs through activities that support both the volunteer's and the volunteer organization's goals.

Providing satisfaction to a need for power should not be misunderstood. Any organization needs leaders who are effective at providing direction and vision. Satisfying the need for power should not be equated with granting dictatorial rights but rather with the opportunity to act in an influential manner, and often to do this with others who are also positively power-oriented. The very nature of volunteer organizations, and the dependency on people who willingly participate, augers against the arbitrary or capricious use of authority. Rather, satisfying the power need lies in providing situations where a volunteer, through ability, dedication, unique skills, specialized knowledge, or other characteristics, may act in a leadership role. For people whose lives do not provide adequate opportunity to act in leadership roles, participating in voluntary activities may well provide needed opportunities.

A number of other rational self-interests may be gratified by volunteer organizations. In many cases, volunteer organizations provide opportunities for people to learn or polish new skills that they can use to improve their positions in the workplace. A computer systems analyst may be limited to certain software or hardware and welcome an opportunity to work with different hardware or to develop new software for use in a volunteer organization. Such opportunities provide win–win situations for both the individual and the organization.

In today's society, many for-profit companies either formally or informally endorse the notion of community action. Some for-profit organizations have socially conscious cultures or management policies that advocate active participation in voluntary community activities. Encouraging employees to volunteer for worthwhile causes is a part of their culture, and in some cases volunteering affects employees' performance evaluations. Despite the tacit requirement that these employees volunteer, the fact that they selected a specific organization indicates their interest in its functioning and success. These volunteers should be prized because they may be willing to take on tasks less likely to satisfy the needs of other volunteers, and also because they may be able to make the services and resources of their primary organization available to the voluntary organization.

The message here is that for a volunteer motivated primarily by rational needs, simple reliance on recognition and societally valued tasks is insufficient. Rational volunteers expect need satisfaction through tangible (extrinsic) rewards. These may include new or improved skills learned through the volunteer effort, or career enhancement through visibility, status, skills, and so on.

(iii) Affiliative Volunteers

Affiliative volunteers have social needs. They want to feel a part of an organization, to identify with others in a common effort and develop friendships. No matter how intrinsically rewarding, tasks they do by themselves will have little motivation for these volunteers. Lack of opportunity to meet and work with people will not lead to performance or retention. Volunteers motivated by affiliative needs should be given social activities to organize or participate in—for instance, they could be asked to organize formal reward ceremonies or other social activities necessary to the organization.

(c) Structure

Some techniques exist to hold the interest and ensure the cooperation of volunteers. One is the use of a voluntary service agreement (Meltzer, 1988). Such an agreement should spell out what is expected of the volunteer in terms of knowledge, experience, work times, attendance, and other items important to the organization. Volunteers want clearly defined activities (Geber, 1991). As volunteer workers shift from women not employed outside their homes to career people and retirees, clarification of organization requirements and expectations aligns the individual's activities with organizational requirements.

Gary Gerhard (1988) found that volunteers need to know that they are part of the organization, with both rights and responsibilities. He found that when they understood the organization's mission and goals and had a clear knowledge of their individual roles, volunteers became more productive.

It is useful to administer a questionnaire to determine what volunteers want (Curtis et al., 1988). Appropriate rewards must be based on what they value, not what the organization's leadership believes they value. This can be especially important if there are social or other differences between leadership and volunteers. Crittenden (1982) found that organizations dominated by younger workers had goals focused on satisfying member needs, whereas older members focused on external objectives.

Another possible difference is between long- and short-term volunteers. Often organizations run campaigns or other short-term projects that involve groups of volunteers who work for short periods. Short-term or episodic volunteers should receive less training and more frequent recognition (MacDuff, 1991).

11.5 REWARD AND RECOGNITION SYSTEM REDESIGN

The three Rs of volunteer management—reward, recognition, and redesign—might be expressed as the three Res plus three more. *Re*ward systems drive behavior in certain directions and serve as excellent analytic foci for understanding the organizational culture. The same can be said for the *re*cognition methods used, which, as discussed in an earlier section, are subject to *re*design on a continuing basis. The three additional Res of management in the 1990s are *re*newal, *re*invention, and *re*engineering. These are the three Res that are now being seriously considered by management.

These additional three Res depend highly on the reward and recognition systems in place. Even if your organization's history is only numbered in days, the reward and recognition (R&R) system is quickly established. If the organization has existed for many years, the R&R systems are firmly in place and can be rigid and difficult to change. In either case, the approach to redesign and change requires clear knowledge of what currently exists, and then an appreciation of how the evolving theories of renewal, reengineering, and reinvention can help the organization develop.

(a) Change Guidance

If change management is the issue, then (as is true for most change strategies) it will be necessary first to know what is in place now. To do this, a reward and recognition system audit or study is a first step in understanding the current culture. This process is not so much difficult as it is time consuming. R&R systems, particularly in a volunteer-based organization, are customized systems built around each unique voluntary organization. The issue is: What is it that people now perceive as the existing rewards and recognition factors—either working or promised? Managers first must assess how people are now rewarded. Next, is the redesign question "What kind of a R&R system do we want?" or specifically "What are the behaviors desired, and how can recognizing these effectively help us?" The general philosophy is to emphasize the positive side in hopes of driving out negative or nondesirable behaviors. This can work to some degree, but the whole process is limited in effectiveness if it is not opened up for input and participation at a very broad level. This is doubly important if the R&R redesign is to support developing a more empowering culture and help create more effective liberating structures of self-awareness and self-management.

To do this, it is legitimate to ask people not only what is currently rewarded and recognized but what new approaches should be considered. "What are the reasons you volunteer your time to work here?" and "How might we, working together, better design R&R systems." These issues are often kept below the table, hidden from view; if they were allowed to surface they could be addressed, and the issues they raise managed much more effectively.

Volunteer work settings offer lessons to for-profit companies. In using more actualized work contracts many of our more altruistic volunteers in progressive organizations are attempting to build intrinsic reward systems. For-profit organizations designed around renewal and reengineering programs also emphasize intrinsic rewards, high involvement, and active participation as essential for improving the organization. These more empowering work designs, which rely heavily on intrinsic reward structures, are attempting to stay competitive in a demanding global economy where doing more with less is absolutely necessary. Organizations, facing the increasing demands and shrinking resource bases, are forced to redesign using more radical change strategies.

New forms and structures of organization are emerging daily out of the private sector's experiments with the three Res of renewal, reinvention, and reengineering. In many of these new organizations, it is not necessary to recruit and maintain involvement exclusively through economic incentives. Much research argues that even in nonvolunteer work settings this economic incentive is only one of many reasons why people participate, and seldom the method used to release the human spirit in work. Why a person seeks to contribute time and effort is that this spirit of human growth is often associated with a desire to be a part of a growing and dynamic organization. These are not yet universally accepted ideas, but the management leadership literature that seeks to understand and harness these intangibles of spirit is expanding rapidly. After all, this spirit in work is what people are capable of and why we have many volunteer organizations in the first place.

11.6 REWARD AND RECOGNITION TECHNIQUES THAT WORK

Given that the design and management of reward and recognition systems provide both challenges and opportunities, there are a number of techniques that are helpful in achieving effective programs. Exhibits 11–6 and 11–7 summarize a number of such techniques.

11.7 PROFESSIONALIZATION OF THE VOLUNTEER ROLE

The demographics of volunteers are changing. Traditionally staffed by women who did not hold paying jobs outside their homes, volunteer organizations are looking more toward nontraditional volunteers (Sabo, 1994). Many organizations' volunteers are becoming more representative of the general population; increasing numbers of professional working people volunteer. With the disappearance of the single-income family, and with workweeks that often extend well beyond 40 hours, professionals who choose to volunteer have limited time to give.

Guessing the needs and motivations of professionals is problematic, as they represent a rather diverse array of backgrounds and interests. In many cases, asking volunteers what they value is the quickest and most accurate method of

---

◆ EXHIBIT 11–6   Reward Systems That Work

- ◆ Rewards that integrate the needs of the individual and the organization in a win–win understanding
- ◆ Rewards based on a deep appreciation of the individual volunteer as a unique person and that address individual needs and perceptions
- ◆ Rewards based on job content, not conditions—rewards intrinsic to the job or task work best
- ◆ Selection or assignment of tasks that can be performed effectively, leading to intrinsic need satisfaction
- ◆ Consistent reward policies that build a sense of trust that effort will receive the proper reward
- ◆ Rewards that can be shared by teams or the entire organization so that winning is a collective and collaborative experience

---

◆ **EXHIBIT 11–7   Recognition Techniques That Work**

- ◆ Carefully constructed systems that are built on the motives and needs of volunteers—individualized need recognition for each person
- ◆ Recognition integrated into task performance, where clear performance goals are established
- ◆ Growth and development goals also become opportunities for recognition
- ◆ Longevity and special contributions recognized frequently, not just every five to 10 years
- ◆ Creative and innovative approaches built on both individual and organizational uniqueness; recognition fits mission and helps lead to vision
- ◆ Recognition grounded deeply in the core values of the organization; what is recognized helps as a role model and sets high expectations and empowers

---

determining the most valued reward. In a study of professionals who were volunteer faculty at a clinical facility, the most valued reward was tuition credits allowing volunteers to take graduate courses. Awards, recreational facilities, and discounts were not as highly valued (Curtis et al., 1988).

Although care must be taken in matching organizational rewards to individual needs for any volunteer, developing rewards that match the needs of professionals can be more demanding. The effort is justified, however, as professionals represent an important source of volunteers; they are becoming more numerous and bring many needed talents and skills.

11.8 LEADERS' OR MANAGERS' ROLE IN ADJUSTING TO CHANGING CONDITIONS

Much has been written about the increasing pace of change in the word today. The volunteer leader or manager must be cognizant of the need to be responsive to change in two arenas—the external environment and the internal environment.

(a) Changes in the External Environment

As the needs of the environment change and evolve over time, successful volunteer organizations must adapt. They might have to revise their organizational missions and strategies to ensure that they can continue to provide necessary and beneficial services to their constituencies. Volunteer organizations depend heavily on congruency between environmental and organizational goals. As they make changes, volunteer organizations must ensure that such changes are explained to their volunteers, who may have joined in support of what they perceive to be substantively different objectives. Because volunteers want to feel that their contributions are important and useful to society, any changes in organizational goals must be communicated to the volunteers to maintain both membership and productivity.

(b) Changes in the Internal Environment

Volunteer organizations must anticipate and be responsive to forces of change arising from two internal sources—organizational initiatives and changing individual needs.

(i) Changing Organizational Initiatives

As all organizations grow and evolve, they modify structures, redefine jobs, change task assignments, and discontinue some services while adding others. Each of these changes poses different challenges to volunteer organizations than those posed to for-profit organizations. In many cases the volunteer's reward is derived from the specific task being accomplished or the social setting of the task. Any changes must be undertaken only after consideration of how it will affect the motivation of the volunteers involved.

(ii) Responding to Changes in Individual Needs

Individual needs and expectations about the organization will inevitably change over time (Fisher and Cole, 1993). Fisher and Cole cite conflicting research evidence about the changing needs of volunteers. Brudney (1990) cites a Gallup poll which indicates that volunteer motivations are generally consistent over time. However, findings by researchers such as McCurley and Lynch (1989), Ilsley (1989), and Pearce (1983) indicate that not only are the motivations different for different volunteers, but these needs change differently over time. Pearce and Ilsley warn that failure to identify and respond to these changes in needs over time will result in the departure of substantial numbers of these volunteers.

Matching organizational rewards to volunteer needs is thus a recurring requirement for the organization's leadership. The constant challenge is to provide a mix of rewards that best matches the current needs of volunteers in motivating performance that is supportive of organizational goals.

11.9 SYMPHONY ORCHESTRA CASE STUDY

The board chair of a regional symphony orchestra in the southeastern United States was concerned about the long-range future of her organization. The symphony had a long and successful history, providing cultural benefits to the surrounding communities. A volunteer board of directors played a major role in establishing and perpetuating the symphony's success.

The current president of the symphony asked two academically based consultants to help in directing the symphony's future. She believed that the symphony's previous success was due primarily to the leadership and participation of its board. She perceived the symphony as facing two challenges: an increasing variety of competitors and effective attainment of symphony goals.

As the consultants held discussions with the president and other board members, they began to see that one of the problems had to do with the way the role of board members had evolved over time. Historically all board members had been active participants in the organization, assuming personal responsibility for fund-raising and achieving concert attendance and symphony membership goals. The current board membership had a number of members who essentially had joined for the status it brought them in the community. They had been invited to join the board because they were well known in the community and it was thought they would bring in substantial contributions. The result was a significant number of members who did not attend meetings or even buy tickets to the concert series. This created a situation where board membership satisfied the need for status for a number of members, but those members did not contribute appreciably to the success of the organization.

The problem was identified as an R&R system that was rewarding membership but was not effectively rewarding member actions that were supportive of organizational goals. Part of this problem was addressed by adopting a new recruiting approach. Prospective board members were asked what they felt they could contribute to the symphony, and they were also provided with a list of specific expectations and tasks. Requirements such as regular board attendance, financial support, purchase of season tickets, and active participation on board subcommittees were spelled out in the informational packet. This process resulted in the recruiting, final selection, and acceptance of individuals who clearly understood the organizational mission and board membership requirements, and thus had personal needs and goals that were aligned with organizational goals and needs.

Prior to the board's first formal session, the president had one of the consultants facilitate a retreat for all incoming board members, both new and old. The retreat began with clarification and reinforcement of board member responsibilities. Key board members gave short presentations on the requirements of various committees and why they felt the duties were important and rewarding. Under facilitator leadership, board members discussed the role and structure of the existing committees and identified both new committee requirements and redundant and unnecessary committees. When a consensus was reached, changes were made. With this clear understanding of each committee and how it meshed in the overall organization structure, board members were then asked to volunteer for the committees of their choice, meet, and come up with specific goals for the coming year.

The new board now consists of a mixture of older members and younger professionals still active in the marketplace. The retreat process resulted in matching the rational, affiliative, and altruistic needs and interests of board members with the requirements and goals of the organization. The older members believe in bringing culture to their community and derive intrinsic rewards from task accomplishment. The younger members clearly have altruistic motives and needs but are filling rational needs as well. A junior member of a CPA firm heads the finance committee and is able to fill social, power, and skill-building needs. Similar actions apply to other members.

By bringing in volunteers whose needs are oriented with the organization's need and reward structure, and then allowing them to self-select tasks they found meaningful and rewarding, the symphony now has a more interested, motivated, and productive board.

REFERENCES

Adams, J. Stacy. 1965. "Inequity in Social Exchange." Pp. 267–299 in L. Berkowitz (Ed.), *Advances in Experimental Social Psychology,* Vol. 2. New York: Academic Press.

Brown, E.P., and J. Zahrly. 1989. "Nonmonetary Rewards for Skilled Voluntary Labor: A Look at Crisis Intervention Volunteers." *Nonprofit and Voluntary Sector Quarterly* 18(2) (Summer): 167–176.

Brudney, J.C. 1990. *Fostering Volunteer Programs In The Public Sector.* San Francisco: Jossey-Bass.

Crittenden, William F. 1982. "An Investigation of Strategic Planning in Voluntary, Nonprofit Organizations." Ph.D. dissertation, University of Arkansas.

Curtis, Elpida S., Kinda L. Klimowski, Thomas Burford, and Roger Fiedler. 1988. "A Study of Benefits Offered Volunteer Clinical Faculty." *Journal of Allied Health* 17(4) (November): 309–318.

Drucker, Peter F. 1990. *Managing the Nonprofit Organization.* New York: HarperBusiness.

Elden, Max, and Morton Levin. 1981. "Co-generative Learning: Bringing Participation to Action Research." In William F. Whyte (Ed.), *Participatory Action Research.* Newbury Park, Calif.: Sage Publications.

Fisher, James C., and Kathleen M. Cole. 1993. *Leadership and Management of Volunteer Programs: A Guide for Volunteer Administrators.* San Francisco: Jossey-Bass.

Geber, Beverly. 1991. "Managing Volunteers." *Training* 28(6) (June): 21–26.

Gerhard, Gary W. 1988. "MVP: A Volunteer Development and Recognition Model." *ERIC microfiche ED299451* (November).

Handy, Charles B. 1990. *The Age of Unreason.* Boston: Harvard Business School Press.

Herzberg, Frederick. 1968. "One More Time: How Do You Motivate Employees?" *Harvard Business Review* (January–February): 109–120.

Herzberg, Frederick, Bernard Mausner, and Barbara Snyderman. 1959. *The Motivation to Work.* New York: Wiley.

Hodgkinson, Virginia Ann, and Murray S. Weitzman. 1989. *Dimensions of the Independent Sector: A Statistical Profile,* 3rd ed. Washington, D.C.: Independent Sector.

Ilsley, Paul J. 1989. "The Voluntary Sector and Adult Education." In S. B. Merriam and P.M. Cunningham (Eds.), *Handbook of Adult and Continuing Education.* San Francisco: Jossey-Bass.

Luthans, Fred. 1985. *Organizational Behavior,* 4th ed. New York: McGraw-Hill.

MacDuff, Nancy. 1991. *Voluntary Action Leadership.* Washington, D.C.: National Center for Voluntary Action (Winter), pp. 22–24.

Mahoney, Thomas. 1975. "Another Look at Satisfaction and Performance." Pp. 322–334 in Thomas A. Mahoney (Ed.), *Compensation and Reward Perspectives.* Homewood, Ill: R.D. Irwin.

Maslow, Abraham H. 1943. "A Theory of Human Motivation." *Psychological Review 50:* 370–396.

Maslow, Abraham H. 1954. *Motivation and Personality.* New York: Harper & Row.

McClelland, David C. 1965. "Achievement Motivation Can Be Developed." *Harvard Business Review,* (November–December): 6–8, 10, 12, 14, 16, 20, 22, 24, 178.

McCurley, Steve, and Rick Lynch. 1989. *Essential Volunteer Management.* Downers Grove, Ill.: VMSystems and Heritage Arts Publishing.

Meltzer, Phyllis. 1988. "Volunteer Service Agreements: A New Strategy for Volunteer Management." Paper presented at the 34th annual meeting of the American Society on Aging, San Diego, Calif. (March).

Murray, Henry A. 1938. *Explorations in Personality.* New York: Oxford University Press.

Murrell, Kenneth L., and Judith F. Vogt. 1991. "The Manager as Leader in an Empowering Organization: Opportunities and Changes." In J. William Pfeiffer (Ed.), *1991 Annual: Developing Human Resources.* La Jolla, Calif.: University Associates.

Pearce, Joni L. 1983. "Participation in Voluntary Organizations: How Membership in a Formal Organization Changes the Rewards of Participation." In D.H. Smith and J. Van Til (Eds.), *International Perspectives on Voluntary Action Research*. Washington, D.C.: University Press of America.

Porter, Lyman, Edward E. Lawler, III, and Richard J. Hackman. 1975. *Behavior in Organizations*. New York: McGraw-Hill.

Posner, Barry. 1981. "Comparing Recruiter, Student, and Faculty Perceptions of Important Job Applicant Characteristics." *Personnel Psychology* 34: 329–337.

Puffer, Sheila M., and James R. Meindl. 1992. "The Congruence of Motives and Incentives in a Voluntary Organization." *Journal of Organizational Behavior* 13: 425–434.

Sabo, Sandra R. 1994. "Discovering the Volunteer." *Association Management* 46(3): 67–68.

Torbert, William R. 1991. *The Power of Balance: Transforming Self, Society and Scientific Inquiry*. Newbury Park, Calif.: Sage Publications.

Vroom, Victor H. 1964. *Work and Motivation*. New York: Wiley.

CHAPTER ◇ 12 ◇

THE ROLE OF VOLUNTEERS IN FUND-RAISING

Ellen G. Estes, LL.B.
Estes Associates

12.1 Introduction

12.2 Purpose of Fund-raising for Nonprofit Organizations

12.3 Background: Sources of Funds for Nonprofit Organizations

12.4 Types of Fund-raising Activities from Private (Nongovernmental) Sources

12.5 Categories of Volunteers Who Can Be Involved Effectively in Fund-raising Activities

12.6 Steps for Creating a Volunteer Fund-raising Corps

12.7 How to Obtain the Support of Board Members and Other Volunteers for Fund-raising

12.8 Training

12.9 Recognition and Cultivation

12.10 Marketing

12.11 What Volunteers Expect When They Become Involved in Fund-raising

12.12 Commonsense Pointers

References

12.1 INTRODUCTION

One of the key uses of volunteers by nonprofit organizations is in connection with fund-raising. Volunteers comprise a major source of potential donors, and more important, they are a very effective and efficient conduit to the larger community. Volunteers are also a solicitation corps that can augment the efforts of staff and professional fund-raisers. In this chapter the ways that volunteers can fit into the overall development program of a nonprofit organization are explored, as well as how to work with volunteers in the fund-raising program to maximize results and increase the bottom line.

12.2 PURPOSE OF FUND-RAISING FOR NONPROFIT ORGANIZATIONS

The major importance of fund-raising is to provide funds to support the organization's mission. Although many nonprofits may generate earned income (for example, through fees for such services as providing physical fitness programs, revenue from ticket sales and admission fees, membership fees and so on), the income that most organizations actually can earn usually will not be sufficient to sustain operations. Therefore, additional funding becomes necessary, and that is where fund-raising comes into play.*

12.3 BACKGROUND: SOURCES OF FUNDS FOR NONPROFIT ORGANIZATIONS

(a) The Public Sector: Federal, State, and Local Governments

Some organizations rely heavily on governmental funding for support. Governmental support can be in the form of a legislative grant to support the organization's general activities, or it can be in the form of fees for services (for example, fees for teaching handicapped students, a service that the government would have to provide if it did not pay the organization to do so). Although such funding can provide the bulk of the money needed to cover an organization's operations in the short run, relying too heavily on this source can often prove dangerous, since government priorities are likely to change over time, leaving a once well-funded agency without funds for its future.

(b) Foundations

Foundations can often provide funding for specific projects that will benefit the organization and its constituency. Obtaining foundation funding often involves discussions with foundation leaders about the kinds of activities they support, making sure that the organization's mission will be furthered by such activities, and then drafting and submitting a proposal for funding for that project.

---

*An in-depth analysis of fund-raising appears in *The Nonprofit Management Handbook* (Connors, 1993). Readers are referred to that publication for detailed information about establishing, managing, and marketing a successful fund-raising program. Here we will focus on the *involvement of volunteers* in the fund-raising process and what volunteers expect when they become involved in fund-raising for a nonprofit organization

(c) Corporations

Corporations often provide funding to nonprofit organizations whose mission and programs are perceived to benefit the corporation, its employees, and/or its customers. Corporations also often consider some forms of contributions (for example, sponsoring a golf tournament or subsidizing a theater event) to be helpful advertising for the corporation as well as a benefit for the nonprofit organization involved.

(d) Individuals

Probably the most effective way to build long-term support for a nonprofit organization is by cultivating individual prospects—people who will become involved, care about, and ultimately support the organization. Statistics show that nearly 90 percent of all gifts to nonprofit organizations from the private sector each year come from individuals (Kaplan, 1994). Corporations and foundations combined donate about 10 percent of all gifts to charity each year, so that relying too heavily on foundations and corporations for support can lead to problems, because these entities can often change their funding priorities. Since the lion's share of charitable donations comes from individuals, it seems clear that every well-run nonprofit organization should develop and implement a plan to raise funds from individuals in its constituency.

12.4 TYPES OF FUND-RAISING ACTIVITIES FROM PRIVATE (NONGOVERNMENTAL) SOURCES

(a) Special Events

Many nonprofit organizations start out in fund-raising by sponsoring special events such as dances, dinners, theater parties, golf tournaments, walk-a-thons, and the like. One attractive feature of these events is that they can bring volunteers together to work enthusiastically toward a shared, short-term goal: providing friends, fun, and funds for the organization. The event itself should also raise the visibility of the organization in the community and attract new supporters. Often the event does not prove to be a big moneymaker. Nevertheless, even though they are time consuming and labor intensive for both staff and volunteers, special events should not be overlooked, since they provide an excellent way to generate favorable publicity and attract new supporters. Just keep in mind that special events are usually "friend-raisers, not fund-raisers."

   Volunteers can be especially helpful in the area of special events—in deciding on what kind of event to undertake in the first place, planning the event, providing the brains and the muscle to organize and implement the project, getting family, friends, and others to attend and/or to give financial support, helping with the marketing of the event, selling tickets, publicity, and so on. If the event generates excitement among your volunteers, you should do all you can to encourage and provide the necessary staff support and supervision to allow them to be successful.

(b) Annual Gifts

Many organizations solicit funds from friends and supporters on an (at least) annual basis, usually by mail and/or telephone. This process usually includes mailing solicitation materials that make a case for supporting the organization, along with a cover letter signed by a person who is known and respected by the constituency, asking the prospect for a gift. An especially effective approach to the annual gift solicitation can be to have volunteers suggest the names of annual fund prospects, and write personal notes on solicitation letters to people they know. Also, having volunteers follow up by telephone with prospects several weeks after the solicitation mailing can also increase gifts dramatically.

(c) Major Gifts

It is hoped that an organization will have several prospects who have the financial capacity, interest, and involvement in the organization to make major gifts. What is considered a major gift will differ from organization to organization, but generally, it is a gift that is substantially (five to 10 times) larger than the donor's average annual gift. The solicitation of a major gift prospect should be viewed as a minicampaign, and major gift prospects should always be solicited personally. They should also receive special recognition for their gifts (unless they wish to remain anonymous) and be thanked in other ways. Tasteful public recognition and thanks will serve not only to make the donors feel special but also will show others that people really *do* make major gifts to *this* organization, and that such gifts are welcome and appreciated.

Volunteers can play a pivotal role in successful major gift cultivation, solicitation, and recognition. Volunteers cannot only identify major gift prospects and help to get them involved in the organization but can also help determine the prospect's interests and help strategize an appropriate solicitation approach. The effective volunteer can also make the actual solicitation or pave the way for another solicitor. With major gift solicitations, the peer-to-peer "ask" can often turn a token gift into a major commitment.

(d) Planned Gifts

Planned giving is an extension of the major gifts program. Once a donor has decided to support the organization with a major gift, the next step is to determine how that gift should be made (What kind of asset should be used? How should that asset be given?) to maximize the benefits for both the donor and the organization. Once an organization has a solid annual gifts program and a loyal core of donors, it should consider the next step, initiating planned giving, to build endowment and preserve and protect its financial security into the future. Volunteers can be most helpful in marketing a planned giving program, in talking with prospects and donors about gifts, and in serving as examples by making their own planned gifts.

(e) Capital Campaigns

Organizations often have needs that require funding beyond the annual support they receive from donors (for example, constructing a new building, purchasing additional equipment, building an endowment, or funding a special program). To achieve these expanded goals and help the organization fulfill its mission more effectively, a capital campaign may be considered. To be successful, a campaign must have a compelling case that is communicated effectively and convincingly to the constituency to engender enthusiasm and support.

Volunteers normally play a critical role in a capital campaign. They can help with the identification of special needs, have input into the planning of the campaign, and especially help with marketing the campaign and encouraging others to support it. The role of committed volunteers in soliciting gifts for a capital campaign can make the difference between the success or failure of the entire effort. Consequently, key volunteers should be involved in the planning and strategies of the campaign, receive training in the process of soliciting gifts, and receive ongoing thanks and public recognition for their part in making the campaign successful.

(f) Corporate Gifts

It has been said that corporations give to nonprofit organizations because of the corporation's enlightened self-interest. Also, corporations give to nonprofits in the communities where they and/or their employees are located to improve the quality of life in these communities. In any case, the nonprofit organization that hopes to generate corporate donations will have to make a compelling case for funding by showing that it provides goods or services that have demonstrable benefits for the corporation, its employees, and the community. The corporation must be concerned with its bottom line and the interests of its shareholders, so it will be critical to make a compelling case in order to win the corporation's support.

Corporate gifts often are made outright for general purposes, or they can be restricted for specific programs. Another way that corporations often give support is through sponsorships: for example, underwriting special projects, such as paying the costs of a theater production or subsidizing the costs of a major fund-raising event. Providing sponsorships can give wide visibility to both the corporation and the nonprofit organization, benefiting both.

Volunteers can play an important role in identifying friends in middle and upper management positions at corporations and by soliciting these people for funds or by opening the door so that others can solicit funds on behalf of the organization. Having the CEO or another executive of a major corporation on the nonprofit's board can often lead to gifts from that corporation. However, the organization must continue to show its importance and worth to the corporation and the community for the corporation's giving to continue into the future.

(g) Foundation Gifts

There are literally thousands of foundations in this country that provide funding for worthy causes. However, given the economic realities—limited funds and the enormous number of worthy nonprofits with financial needs—there is never enough foundation funding to go around. Consequently, the wise nonprofit will research a foundation thoroughly before applying for a grant: What types of organizations does *this* foundation support? What kinds of projects are most likely to receive funding? Will the project be of unique value to the community, or is it duplicating programs that already exist? Volunteers can be helpful in evaluating prospective foundation donors, and they can be especially helpful in opening doors and doing personal solicitations when they have personal contacts in the foundation.

12.5 CATEGORIES OF VOLUNTEERS WHO CAN BE INVOLVED EFFECTIVELY IN FUND-RAISING ACTIVITIES

(a) Board of Trustees

Virtually all nonprofit organizations have a board of trustees to oversee the operations of the organization, to provide guidance to the organization in fulfilling its mission, and to help preserve and protect the organization's future. Individuals are invited to serve on nonprofit boards for a variety of reasons, such as prominence in the community, personal wealth, access to wealth, professional expertise in a field related to the organization's mission, and personal commitment to the cause. One of the primary responsibilities of board membership is fiduciary: to assure that the organization has the needed financial resources—earned, contributed, and invested—to provide financial security for the future. To fulfill this responsibility, the board must become involved with and responsible for the fund-raising activities of the organization.

Board support is critical to the success of an organization's fund-raising efforts. Without strong commitment and involvement, fund-raising efforts may simply languish. With active board support, in terms of making personal gifts, identifying and soliciting prospects, and committing the necessary resources (staff, time, and money), the effort can be successful. Board members also set the standard—act as examples for others—for supporting the organization. The old adage, "Unless the family supports you, no one else will" is applicable here. If the closest people to the organization (board members and other committed volunteers) do not support the organization, no one else will. Board support can be effective in all of the organization's fund-raising activities—special events, the annual fund, major and planned gifts, and capital campaigns. Board members can also provide access to foundation and corporate gifts and sponsorships.

(b) Participants (Users of an Organization's Services and Their Families)

Individuals such as alumni, theater-goers, and museum members can become effective spokespeople for an organization in its fund-raising activities. These volunteers are usually well aware of the organization's mission and have actively participated in its success in some way. They can be involved effectively in special events, the annual fund, and in major and planned gifts. If they have the appropriate connections, they can also provide access to corporate and foundation grants.

(c) Volunteers Who Work on the Organization's Programs

Individuals who help the organization provide services such as delivering meals on wheels, running the organization's blood drives, planning and supporting special events, providing teaching assistance to clients, and working as aides in the hospital, can also become ambassadors for the organization in ways that can help its fund-raising efforts. These volunteers can be utilized in approaches to donors in ways that emphasize the value of the organization's services. Also, if they have an interest, they can often provide a valuable workforce for such fund-raising activities as helping with special events or with mailings for the annual appeal. In addition, just by spreading the word in the community about the value of the organization and its services, these volunteers can raise the visibility of the organization and help create a more positive environment for the organization's fund-raising activities.

(d) Community Volunteers

Individuals in the community who provide special assistance to nonprofit organizations, such as people who are recruited to canvass door to door for specific fund-raising drives, or service clubs (such as the Rotary, Lions, or Kiwanis) that sponsor specific events, can also provide assistance in an organization's overall fund-raising program.

Different organizations will have a different mix of volunteers available depending on the kind of organization involved. In assessing the availability of volunteers for fund-raising, it is important to keep in mind their wishes and desires, including the amount of time, energy, and effort they are prepared to expend and the types of activities they find personally rewarding. It may be that their current participation is based on an interest in the organization's mission as a whole or more geared toward the specific activities they have volunteered to do rather than in becoming involved in mailings, special events, or other fund-raising activities. It is important not to have a negative impact on the valuable services they now give in other areas. However, organizations that can identify the kinds of volunteers available to them who may be interested in fund raising, and can motivate them, help them focus on specific objectives, and support them in their fund-raising tasks can generate an extremely valuable corps to accomplish the organization's fund-raising goals.

12.6 STEPS FOR CREATING A VOLUNTEER FUND-RAISING CORPS

(a) Determine the Needs of the Organization and the Availability of Resources

What are the specific fund-raising needs of this particular organization that have to be addressed? Also, what kind of potential volunteers are available to the organization to help with fund-raising? Virtually all organizations will have a board of trustees. However, there may also be other types of volunteers available to provide additional fund-raising assistance. For example, colleges and schools have alumni groups, churches have parishioners and congregations, theaters have subscribers who attend performances, museums have members, and so on. These are all groups of people who, if properly cultivated and motivated, may be willing to become involved in fund-raising. Some social service organizations, such as soup kitchens or agencies for the homeless, may not have a built-in participant pool. However, these organizations may appeal to others in the community for whom community values are paramount, and these people may be willing to participate in fund-raising activities.

(b) Formulate a Strategic Plan for Fund-raising

Once the fund-raising needs are determined and the volunteer resources are identified, it will be important to develop a plan for utilizing the resources most effectively to meet those needs. The planning process should involve board, staff, and other key volunteers. The planning process should first assess the organization's present situation. (Where are we now? How did we get here?) Next, it should look at where the organization hopes to be in one year, three years, and five years. The planners should then set priorities, goals, and objectives and decide the best way to achieve these goals. The result of this process should be the creation of a fund-raising plan that will address such issues as:

1. What are the fund-raising goals this year? Over the next three to five years?
2. What are the most appropriate fund-raising methods to reach these goals? (Special events? Annual appeal? Major gifts? Planned giving? Several or all of them?)
3. How can volunteers be involved most effectively in each aspect of fund-raising?
4. How will volunteers be recruited, trained, supervised, evaluated, recognized, and rewarded?

12.7 HOW TO OBTAIN THE SUPPORT OF BOARD MEMBERS AND OTHER VOLUNTEERS FOR FUND-RAISING

(a) Clarify the Board Member's Role

Identify potential candidates for the board and recruit them with the explicit understanding that fund-raising is an important part of the board member's role. Start off on the right foot when recruiting new members. Do not say, "Please join our board. We just want to use your name. You won't have to *do* anything." Tell it like it is: "We hope that you will consider joining our board. You would be a wonderful addition and lend support to our most worthy cause . . ." Then discuss the job description, which specifically includes fund-raising responsibilities [see (c) below].

(b) Educate the Board

If possible, have a presentation made to the board, preferably by an outside consultant or an executive from a similar organization, about the importance of a carefully developed fund-raising program and each board member's role in making it work. Make sure that the presenter is an inspiring speaker who can engender enthusiasm for the project.

(c) Board Job Description

Prepare a job description (Exhibit 12–1) that outlines the board member's responsibilities, including fund-raising, and make sure to discuss the job description with each candidate before he or she comes on the board. (No surprises!) Also, the job description should be discussed individually with members already on the board, preferably by the chairman or other well-respected peer, in a way that will allow a

---

◆ **EXHIBIT 12–1   Sample Job Description: Board Members**

---

1. Select, support, and evaluate the CEO.
2. Review and approve the organization's mission.
3. Participate in the organization's strategic planning process.
4. Help ensure the financial solvency of the organization.
   a. Participate in the fund-raising process.
   b. Make your own gifts on a regular basis—both current gifts and by will.
   c. Oversee the fiscal management of the organization.
5. Become an ambassador for the organization. Spread the word about the organization and its mission throughout the community.
6. Communicate the perceptions of the community *to the organization*. Represent the community perspective to the organization to help it better serve the community.
7. Perform a periodic self-assessment and evaluation. How is the board doing?
8. Provide oversight and evaluation of the organization itself. Is the organization fulfilling its mission most effectively?

---

board member to resign gracefully if he or she is not willing to accept the stated responsibilities.

(d) Development Committee

Consider creating a development committee of the board to concentrate on fund-raising. The role of the development committee is to help set policy, approve program design and implementation, and help with the identification and solicitation of prospects (Exhibit 12–2). The development committee approach encourages specific board members to take responsibility for the fund-raising success of the organization and gives them a sense of ownership of the program that will help it succeed. The chairman will also be the development committee's liaison with the entire board, to keep the board informed about and involved in the organization's fund-raising efforts. (Please note that the members of the development committee are not the only ones responsible for fund-raising. All board members, as well as other volunteers, should be involved in the fund-raising effort, and that fact should be clearly enunciated on an ongoing basis to all concerned.)

(e) Board Participation

Promote the goal of 100 percent board participation in each and every aspect of the organization's fund-raising efforts: the annual appeal, special gifts, capital campaigns, special events, and so on. The amount of the gift is not as important as the fact that each board member has given support. You may need some "behind the scenes" peer pressure by the chair or other respected person to achieve that goal. Work with one or two committed board members to enlist their aid in soliciting others. Hopefully, you will achieve your 100 percent goal over time, but the process will require patience and gentle, continuing perseverance.

◆ **EXHIBIT 12–2   Sample Job Description: Development Committee**

---

1. Review the financial needs and objectives of the organization.
2. Decide what types of fund-raising will be most effective to accomplish goals.
3. Set policies regarding types of gifts to promote and parameters for accepting gifts.
4. Identify prospects for gifts.
5. Help to solicit prospects, as appropriate.
6. Help to organize and assist with special events and other fund-raising activities.
7. Help to determine appropriate recognition for donors.
8. Monitor the progress of fund-raising activities
9. Report to the board regularly on the status of the development program.
10. Become an ambassador for the organization—promote awareness and interest in the organization throughout the community.
11. Make your own gift to each fund-raising appeal.

(f) Involvement in Other Activities

Consider innovative ways to involve board and other volunteers in the activities of the organization on a regular basis. Find ways to provide meaningful interaction not just busy work. Try to make all volunteers feel wanted, needed, and important to the organization. Ongoing recognition, cultivation, and involvement are the keys to having happy volunteers who remain committed to the organization's cause.

(g) Planning

Include board members and key volunteers in strategy sessions, when appropriate, to help determine the design and structure of a fund-raising program. Volunteer input can be quite valuable to expand horizons and explore new opportunities. Also, volunteer involvement in the planning process can lead to their ownership and support of the fund-raising program, giving them a stronger commitment to make it succeed.

(h) Give before Asking

Keep in mind that the volunteer who has made his or her own gift will be a much better, more convincing solicitor in encouraging others to give. Make sure to communicate this fact to all volunteers.

(i) Application to All Volunteers

Keep in mind that the recruitment and cultivation techniques for board members are equally appropriate in encouraging other volunteers to become involved in the fund-raising program. Make sure to identify potential volunteers and to cultivate them and invite their participation. The goal is to generate interest and enthusiasm for supporting the cause.

(j) Don't Ask for Too Much

Finally, remember that board members and other volunteers should not be over-burdened with fund-raising activities. The same people cannot be expected to carry the fund-raising burden all of the time. It will be essential to find ways to maximize the fund-raising efforts of volunteers without making the demands so great that they just succumb to burnout.

12.8 TRAINING

(a) Overview

If an organization expects its volunteers to help with fund-raising, it will be important to provide the training necessary to prepare them for this task. The object of the training is to inform them about the organization (its mission, programs, and the services it provides to the entire community) as well as to provide the tools necessary to raise their comfort level in asking for gifts—to overcome the inevitable anxieties of asking. A fund-raising expert, either a consultant or a respected staff person, should conduct the training. The more information, case studies, and role-play the training session can provide, the more confident and secure the volunteers will become and the more likely that they will be enthusiastic solicitors for the cause. Keep in mind that volunteers will be willing to go out and ask for gifts *only if* they feel confident and competent to do so. Therefore, training that builds volunteer skills and confidence is critical to producing an effective fund-raising team (Exhibit 12–3).

12.9 RECOGNITION AND CULTIVATION

Recognition and cultivation are part of an ongoing process during which volunteers are thanked for their efforts and involved further in the organization's activities making their commitment to the organization grow even stronger. Effective cultivation and recognition are important for an organization's fund-raising effort in at least two ways. First, the volunteers themselves must be made to feel wanted, needed, and special. Second, all donors and prospects should be thanked publicly (and tastefully) in order to generate their continuing interest in and support for the cause.

Some of the elements of recognition and cultivation include:

1. Say thank you often, and in different ways, for gifts and services to the organization.
2. Recognize volunteers and donors in publications (get permission first).
3. Keep volunteers and donors informed. Send them a constant flow of information about what the organization is doing and why it is important to the community and to themselves.

◆ **EXHIBIT 12–3   Sample Outline of Training Session for Volunteers: What Should Be Included**

---

1. Background information about the organization. This should include a statement of its mission, a brief history of its accomplishments, and its goals for the future.

2. Information about this particular fund-raising effort. Why does the organization need the money it is asking for? What are the goals of this effort? What benefits will this fund-raising effort provide if it succeeds?

3. Information about the research being done on prospects for this fund-raising effort. Show the volunteers that they will be armed with background research and information about each prospect they are asked to solicit, to calm their fears about making these calls.

4. Information about objectives that might be raised by a prospect. Have there been recent problems that have concerned members of the constituency? The training should address these issues and prepare solicitors to answer difficult questions.

5. Information about the ways that donors can make gifts. It is strongly recommended that this be a *simple explanation* of the basic gift options and opportunities that solicitors can discuss with prospects.

6. Case studies and role-play. Work through sample solicitation scenarios to show volunteers how to conduct a solicitation. This is important to let volunteers know exactly what to expect during a solicitation visit—to calm their fears about the unknown. (For a detailed description of how to ask for a gift, see Estes, 1994.)

7. Written materials. Review the materials related to this fund-raising effort. Explain how and when to use pledge forms, when to leave brochures, and so on.

8. A discussion of follow-up procedures. These activities include reporting on the visit, following up with staff, sending information the prospect requested, preparing for the next visit, and others.

Note: Be sure to meet separately with each solicitor before he or she makes a solicitation call, to brief him or her on the particular prospect to be visited, and to review the entire solicitation process one more time.

4. Involve volunteers and donors in the organization's projects and programs.

5. Invite volunteers to events designed especially for them. Find ways to make them feel that they are part of the inner circle.

6. Invite volunteers to visit the organization to experience firsthand what their work is helping to accomplish.

7. Keep in touch. Send birthday cards, interesting magazine or newspaper articles, notes after events, and so on.

8. Do whatever you can to make volunteers and donors feel special. Show that you care about them not only about what they can do for your organization.

12.10 MARKETING

In the context of a nonprofit organization, marketing involves the continuing process of communicating the organization's clear, concise, compelling case about its mission and services to a broad constituency to influence them to support its efforts. Some of the methods of marketing for fund-raising purposes include:

(a) Written Materials

Newsletters, magazines, annual reports, brochures, and special information pieces all provide excellent ways to spread the word about the organization and its mission. Usually these materials are generated by staff and/or professional writers, but volunteer input regarding subject matter, format, appropriateness for a particular audience, and so on, can be extremely helpful.

(b) Direct Mail

Many organizations have begun to solicit funds by mail from a wide target audience. Direct mail provides a way to inform the public about the organization and its mission, to engender interest, and ultimately, to generate financial support for the cause. In this age of modern technology and automation, large direct mail projects are generally handled most cost-effectively by outside professionals, without much involvement by volunteers. However, for smaller annual appeals, special appeals, invitations to special events, and so on, volunteers can be quite effective in reviewing the materials, writing personal notes on letters, following up on mailings by telephone, and many similar activities.

(c) Phonathons

Many organizations establish programs to telephone donors and prospects in order to generate additional gifts. If done sensitively and in a low-key manner, phonathons can provide substantial gift income to the organization. Volunteer involvement in making the calls can be extremely effective, especially if the callers receive proper training before they call.

(d) Face-to-Face Solicitations

The most effective way to raise significant major gifts is through face-to-face solicitation. In a majority of cases, a volunteer asking a prospect who is a peer for a gift will be the most successful approach and produce the best results. For the solicitation to be successful, the organization should provide as much training and assistance as possible to support its volunteers in this critical effort.

(e) In General

As stated earlier, volunteers can become excellent ambassadors for the organization, sharing their interest and enthusiasm and raising the visibility of the organization in the community. The personal approach can be quite effective, especially when coordinated with the overall marketing plan of the organization to spread the word about the organization and its mission to a wide constituency.

12.11 WHAT VOLUNTEERS EXPECT WHEN THEY BECOME INVOLVED IN FUND-RAISING

The author conducted a small, informal survey of fund-raising volunteers to discover what *volunteers* consider important when they are asked to help with fund-raising. In general, volunteers said that they volunteered in the first place because they had an interest in the mission and programs of a particular organization, or they were asked to serve by a friend, or they wanted to sharpen their professional skills in a particular area, or they wanted to be affiliated with a particular organization, or for business reasons, or for a combination of these. When asked what *they* expected when they were asked to become involved with fund-raising, the responses were virtually unanimous.

(a) Personal Satisfaction

All the volunteers stated that they achieve great personal satisfaction from raising funds for an organization and seeing their efforts succeed (watching the organization grow stronger and become more effective, seeing its programs serve more people better, and so on). The feeling that they are doing something worthwhile is what motivates volunteers to continue to work on behalf of the organization. This means that the organization must continually inform volunteers about the results of their efforts—to show them why their involvement is so important and valuable.

(b) Communication

Volunteers need to be kept informed about what is going on at the organization on a regular basis. This means that the volunteers should know about current projects and programs as well as plans that management may have for the future. An informed solicitor will be the best solicitor, because he or she will feel close to the organization and can talk confidently about the organization and answer the prospect's questions.

(c) Preparation

Volunteers expect management and staff to think through the fund-raising issues and to plan and organize the fund-raising effort in advance. Volunteers have limited time to commit to an organization, and they especially want the nonprofit to "be organized" about fund-raising and "not waste my time." Volunteers need to be provided with basic information about the organization's mission and a simple, clear case statement to use in preparing for solicitations. They need to have a valid reason to go out and ask for money.

(d) Sharing Responsibility

Volunteers sometimes feel overwhelmed if they feel that they have to "do it all alone." Management and staff should make sure that the tasks are shared among volunteers and staff and that each person is given specific assignments, guidance, and a manageable time frame for each task.

(e) Staff Support

Volunteers need a dedicated staff, educated in the art of fund-raising, to prepare them for their fund-raising tasks and to provide materials, training, and follow-up, so that the volunteers can just go out and ask. Volunteers can provide effective peer outreach, but they must have guidance and strong logistical and administrative support if the effort is to be successful.

(f) Recognition and Appreciation

Volunteers expect the organization to listen to *their* ideas and suggestions about fund-raising (and other issues) and to give some weight to their recommendations. Also, they expect to be recognized for the work they do for the organization. Some prefer public recognition (to be given credit in published materials, to have their successes acknowledged at annual dinners and board meetings and so on); others prefer a more personal approach (a letter from the CEO or president, a certificate, small pin, or pewter mug, and so on). In all cases, volunteers like to feel that the organization appreciates the efforts they devote to fund-raising (and other activities) to feel that their efforts are not in vain.

12.12 COMMONSENSE POINTERS

1. Make sure to let your volunteers know what you will expect of them *before* you ask for their involvement.

2. Try to learn the interests and strengths of each volunteer and involve each person in those areas, to maximize the personal talents and expertise of each volunteer.

3. Remain open to suggestions from volunteers about different ways to approach organizational issues and problems.

4. Make it easy for volunteers to do their jobs. Be sensitive to their needs and aspirations. (For example, don't call a committee meeting on the first day of duck hunting season when a hunter is on the committee!)

REFERENCES

Connors, Tracy Daniel. 1993. *The Nonprofit Management Handbook: Operating Policies and Procedures.* New York: Wiley.

Estes, Ellen G. 1994. "How to Ask for a Major Gift." *Planned Giving Today.* (September Newsletter.) 1–2, 5–6. For additional information, call Roger Schoenhals at (800)KALLPGT.

Estes, Ellen G. 1994. *Planned Giving: Plain and Simple.* Manual Woodbridge, Conn.: Estes Associates. For additional information, call Ellen Estes at (203) 593-3159.

Kaplan, Ann E. (Ed.). 1994. *Giving USA.* New York: AAFRC Trust for Philanthropy, Inc.

MANAGING CORPORATE AND EMPLOYEE VOLUNTEER PROGRAMS

Keith Seel, M.A.
Volunteer Centre of Calgary

13.1 Introduction

13.2 Identifying the Stakeholders

13.3 Defining an Employee Volunteer Program

13.4 Defining the Impacts on Stakeholders

13.5 Defining the Levels of Company Support

13.6 Management Considerations Unique to Employee Volunteers

13.7 Preparing the Company and Employees

13.8 Developing Structure

13.9 Developing Corporate Policies

13.10 Liability and Risk Management

13.11 Receiving Benefits

13.12 Preparing the Agency

13.13 Four Steps to Approaching a Corporation

13.14 Evaluating the Employee Volunteer Program

13.15 Critical and Emerging Issues

13.16 Conclusions

References

13.1 INTRODUCTION

If you are a leader in a nonprofit organization, ask yourself how many of your organization's volunteers are employed. If you are an employer, how many of your staff are volunteering in charitable agencies? The simple fact is that nearly two-thirds of employees also contribute time as volunteers, in their communities (Ross and Shillington, 1989). Employees are a significant volunteer force throughout North America. As a group they are also a force with some unique needs and expectations. Traditional approaches to volunteer management may not be effective in cases where the employee's company adds its expectations to the mix facing managers of volunteers. To be effective, management of this incredibly diverse volunteer resource must include careful consideration of the needs of the employee, the company, and the community at large. Managerial skills that can address each of these stakeholders would yield incalculable benefits as the tremendous energy of this group of volunteers is mobilized and focused on the issues facing communities across North America. This chapter provides meaningful information for managers of volunteers in nonprofit organizations, managers and employees in a business environment, and those who are interested in the vast potential of an employee volunteer program.

13.2 IDENTIFYING THE STAKEHOLDERS

Employee volunteers represent a unique management issue since they are both employees *and* volunteers. This raises a complex set of management considerations. Managers associated with employee volunteer programs will need to recognize and factor into planning the differing priorities and objectives of three stakeholder groups: the company, the community, and the employees.

Exhibit 13-1 demonstrates the existing interdependence of these stakeholder groups. The fact that there is a very real, even synergistic and interdependent relationship between these stakeholder groups is frequently overlooked. These valuable links can be weakened or broken, however, if one stakeholder group takes sole ownership of the employee volunteer program and excludes the other stakeholders from formative activities. The following list outlines how stakeholder groups are necessarily interdependent:

- Employees live in the community, perhaps receive services from community agencies, and work for an employer such as the company.
- The company is made up of employees and is situated in a community that purchases services or products from the company.
- The community is made up of a rich blend of employers, employees, and citizens on whom it relies for tax dollars, volunteers, and a sense of social responsibility.

An ideal employee volunteer program would assess and carefully plan to meet the needs and expectations of each of these stakeholder groups. Because each of these stakeholder groups is comprised of constituent stakeholders, managers need to be well informed about the individual stakeholder in the particular mix

◆ EXHIBIT 13–1   Key Stakeholder Groups for Employee Volunteer Programs

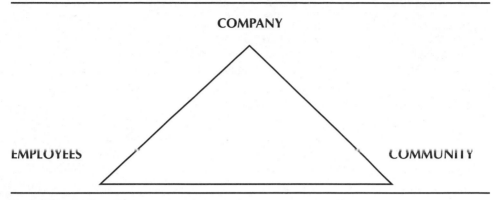

COMPANY

EMPLOYEES   COMMUNITY

represented by their employee volunteer program. Exhibit 13–2 gives examples of the constituents who could make up each of the three stakeholder groups. Each of these constituents will have different interests, needs, and expectations of the program.

Being able to assess the vested interests, needs, and expectations of a stakeholder group and its constituents is a key managerial skill. If an assessment is not done, it will be more difficult to meet the emerging needs of the participants. An assessment can provide focus and support the growth of an employee volunteer program. An employee volunteer program is "green" in that it is continually growing and changing; therefore, assessments need to be ongoing. This means that the manager or managers associated with the program will need to establish practicable assessment methodologies that continually monitor the attitudes and feelings of the constituents of the stakeholder groups directly effected by their program. A series of questions such as those in Exhibit 13–3 may help guide the managers in their

◆ EXHIBIT 13–2   Sample Constituents of Stakeholder Groups

Company Stakeholder Group	Employee Stakeholder Group	Community Stakeholder Group
Shareholders	Social clubs	Nonprofit agencies
CEO,COO	Employee groups	Social service agencies
Senior managers	Unions	Community associations
Department managers	Department staff	Neighborhood groups
Branch managers	Branch staff	Politicians
Plant managers	Plant staff	Government
Allied companies		Funders
		Citizens
		Religious groups
		Educational institutions
		Advocacy groups

◆ **EXHIBIT 13–3**   Sample Stakeholder Interests

Company	Employee	Community
◆ Can the employee find time to do his or her job and volunteer? ◆ Will the employee's volunteer work cost the company anything? ◆ Will the company get any benefits from the employees' involvement, such as publicity, skill enhancement, and community relations? ◆ Should the company support the employee through grants or flex time? ◆ Will the community be healthier or safer as a result? ◆ Will the company see a positive bottom-line return?	◆ Am I doing something meaningful for my community? ◆ Am I learning new skills that will help me in my work? ◆ Am I making new connections and expanding my network? ◆ Am I making a difference? ◆ Am I improving the skills that I have? ◆ Can I have fun? ◆ Can I do this with my family? ◆ Can I volunteer with some of my friends, as a group?	◆ Do we have the resources in place to meet the needs of our volunteers, consumers, and staff? ◆ Are we building strategic alliances between our agency, any companies, or other agencies in the community? ◆ Do we have the skills necessary in our human resource base to provide an effective and efficient service to those who need it? ◆ Will a partnership with a company mean that we have to change our mission statement and values?

---

monitoring and evaluating the employee volunteer program. Exhibit 13–3 is a short compilation of stakeholder interests that commonly arise during the course of developing and implementing an employee volunteer program.

Managers working with employee volunteer programs will face numerous challenges as well as opportunities. Some of the challenges evolve from the historical context of each of the stakeholders. For example, many corporations have a component dedicated to making donations to nonprofit organizations. Typically and historically, these donations have been monetary. However, with economic downturns, companies interested in maintaining a high level of community involvement look to alternative forms of support. One such alternative has been loaning the talents of employees to nonprofit organizations to provide technical assistance; that is, skill-based consultancies. Another approach has been to give employees flexible work hours to pursue volunteer service during office hours. Yet another option is channeling limited monetary donations through employees to the nonprofit organizations where the employees volunteer. In this kind of channeling, employees are responsible for directing some of the company's donations budget. Gift-in-kind donations of hardware or services often support all of these emerging initiatives. Clearly, the response to an economic change that affected traditional forms of corporate philanthropy has been varied. Every such challenge to the traditional way of doing things should be seen as an opportunity for innovation. Employee volunteer programs are a marvelous case in point.

A coordinated approach to linking corporations and the community exists through entities called *corporate volunteer councils, business volunteer councils* or *workplace volunteer councils.* These have been a relatively recent innovation by visionary members of the stakeholder groups. These councils work to leverage and coordinate the resources of several businesses and focus them on community issues in an effort to effect real social change. Frequently, the approach taken is project based. This means that a need is identified and a project designed to meet that need. Nearly all areas of the nonprofit sector have enjoyed this kind of employee volunteer and company project. While often short term in effect, such projects have galvanized communities and focused media attention on a social issue and on the efforts of the businesses and employees trying to improve the situation. A concern with this kind of project-based relationship is that too often only trendy, high-profile issues are addressed. Needs that may be just as critical but not as much in the public eye may be overlooked. Short-term projects that involve companies and employees should be seen as one useful tool in a broader approach to effecting real change in a community.

In other cases, the corporate council conducts a community focus group session to gather information on current and emerging critical needs. For example, members of the Calgary Corporate Volunteer Council (CCVC) agreed that they wanted to focus their efforts toward making a difference for youth who are at risk. A community focus group was held with several executive directors from youth-serving agencies who provided the CCVC with information on who "youth" are, what their current needs are, and what their needs will be in the near future. As a result, members of the CCVC can work at a broad range of projects directly affecting a very real community issue area while meeting their individual corporate and employee needs.

A trend is clearly evolving in which companies support their employees' efforts for the nonprofit sector by donating services or supplies, by loaning employee talents on company time, or by matching employee donations of time with a monetary grant. This will be discussed in greater detail throughout the chapter, and Exhibit 13–4 should provide the reader with a sense of how corporations are approaching matching grants.

To summarize, an employee volunteer program includes a variety of company-sponsored supports for employees and/or retirees who wish to volunteer their time and skills in service to the community. Such company support varies widely and can include:

- ◆ Providing information on volunteer opportunities to employees
- ◆ Providing a volunteer referral service for interested employees
- ◆ Providing recognition to employees who volunteer
- ◆ Encouraging and enabling employee volunteer projects
- ◆ Conducting training and related human resource development opportunities around volunteer work
- ◆ Making monetary grants available to employees who volunteer for the nonprofit agency of their choice

---

◆ EXHIBIT 13–4   Chevron Employees' Involvement Program

The Chevron Employees' Involvement Program is designed to promote and recognize volunteerism by Chevron employees in a wide variety of community organizations.

Through grants, Chevron enables employees to direct company financial resources towards helping their communities.

Chevron Employees' Involvement Program Funding Guidelines

The Employee Involvement Program supports a wide range of charitable and non-profit organizations, and volunteer activity.

Employee Eligibility

The program is accessible to all full-time and part-time employees of Chevron Canada Resources/CPTC who are actively volunteering and who have been employed by Chevron for a minimum of one year. As well, applicants must have completed three months of volunteer service with the organization prior to the application date.

Chevron annuitants living in any Chevron Canada Resources operating locale, including Calgary, are eligible to apply for funds.

Organization Eligibility

Organizations providing services in education, community affairs, health, social services, culture and sports are eligible for consideration under this program.

The application for funds, which may be approved for any amount between $100 and $1,000, must be submitted with a reasonable cost breakdown, and an acceptable explanation of what and how the grant will be used.

The organization must be a non-profit group open to all community members and provide a needed community service (political organizations or activities, fraternal organizations, and sacramental activities of churches and religious organizations are ineligible).

Grant Guidelines

Grants range up to $1,000 per application. The amount awarded will be proportional to the degree of volunteer participation as determined by the CEIP Committee.

Employees associated with a particular organization may only apply for one grant per organization per calendar year. Organizations may only receive two grants per calendar year.

If a Chevron employee is a volunteer for several organizations and wishes to submit a second application on behalf of another organization, the new request will be considered on its own merit in accordance with program guidelines.

In order to further promote the program and encourage Chevron employee participation, organizations are required to provide written acknowledgement and a photograph within 90 days.

Application Criteria and Procedure

Each application is evaluated by a committee of Chevron employees based on the following criteria:

◆ length of an employee's volunteer service,
◆ employee's volunteer time commitment to the volunteer service,
◆ nature of the employee's volunteer involvement,
◆ type of volunteer organization in which the employee is involved

Each request is evaluated on its own merit, with the final decision regarding eligibility and grant amount determined by the Employee Involvement Committee.

◆ Partnering with a volunteer center to maximize its knowledge of community needs and issues and to receive some of the services a volunteer center can provide, such as recruitment and referral to community volunteer opportunities

13.3 DEFINING AN EMPLOYEE VOLUNTEER PROGRAM

Two terms come to mind when one begins to explore the linkages between employees, the company, and the community: *corporate volunteerism* and *employee volunteerism*. Evolving as a positive force in community development, it is not surprising that volunteerism is understood differently by the company and its employees. Some corporate volunteer councils (Seel, 1994a) have differentiated these perspectives to communicate more effectively with stakeholder groups. A clear understanding of these two terms will help a manager develop a program that is finely tuned to the needs and expectations of those involved.

◆ *Corporate volunteerism:* tends to involve activities that are done under the name of the company, such as sponsorships, "dollars for doers," or employee granting programs. It may also refer to things that only the company can give, such as release time, gifts-in-kind, and loaned expertise.

◆ *Employee volunteerism:* tends to refer to the genesis of a volunteer movement by the employees in a company. It can include employee-initiated projects as well as the activities that individuals or groups of employees do on their own time.

Corporate volunteerism could be viewed as a top-down initiative, whereas employee volunteerism is more of a bottom-up initiative (Exhibit 13–5). If a volunteer program is defined as corporate volunteerism, the program could be seen to be moving from the company stakeholder group toward meeting the needs of the employees and community. On the other hand, if the volunteer program turns out to be a form of employee volunteerism, then the program is moving from the employee stakeholder group toward meeting the needs of the company and community stakeholders. Whether the program is a form of corporate volunteerism or employee volunteerism, we can see that there is a definite directionality to how the program will be rolled out. The mechanics of implementing programs defined to be corporate volunteerism will be significantly different from the process of implementing programs from the domain of employee volunteerism. Four questions can help orient the manager to the task:

1. Who is initiating the program, the employees or the company?
2. Why is this group initiating the program?
3. How and when will the purpose and goals of the program be communicated to the other two stakeholder groups?
4. What are the priority issues for each of the stakeholder groups?

13.4 DEFINING THE IMPACTS ON STAKEHOLDERS

The type of volunteer program—employee or corporate—will determine the impact on the key stakeholders. Effective managers recognize the type of initiative behind the employee volunteer program and the anticipated impacts those initiatives will

◆ **EXHIBIT 13–5 Differentiating Corporate and Employee Volunteerism**

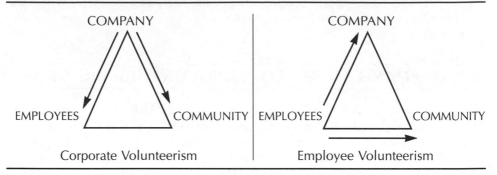

have on the stakeholders. Exhibit 13–6 outlines some of the stakeholder interests for each type of volunteer program, employee or corporate. Although similar in some ways, two distinct themes emerge. First, companies will feel greater owner-ship or have a greater stake, so to speak, in a program that could be classified as a corporate volunteer program. Second, that employees will have the greatest interest and ownership of programs that fall into the area know as employee volunteerism. Not every stakeholder will have all of the indicated vested interests all of the time. Employee volunteer programs are growing and changing continuously, so that the interests of stakeholders change over time. Exhibit 13–6 indicates broadly the types of vested interests that could emerge over a period of time.

13.5 DEFINING THE LEVELS OF COMPANY SUPPORT

Each company will approach volunteerism from a different perspective. The wide variety of approaches means that managers must be able to assess the level of employer support for volunteerism quickly. Lautenschlager (1993) conceptualizes five types of employer support:

Type I	Acknowledgment;
Type II	Promotion;
Type III	Encouragement;
Type IV	Endorsement; and
Type V	Sponsorship.

These types of support are not a continuum. The type of support, instead, depends on the company or the employer more generally speaking, and the community in which it is located (see Exhibit 13–7).

13.6 MANAGEMENT CONSIDERATIONS UNIQUE TO EMPLOYEE VOLUNTEERS

Employee volunteers come to nonprofit organizations with their own special man-agement requirements. No two people necessarily have the same expectation for

◆ **EXHIBIT 13–6   Sample Stakeholder Interests in Employee Volunteerism and Corporate Volunteerism**

Stakeholder	Sample Interests Associated with a Corporate Volunteer Program	Sample Interests Associated with an Employee Volunteer Program
Company	◆ Assumes employees' allegiance to company supersedes allegiance to volunteer activity. ◆ Resources to be allocated to short-term events only, not to long-term program development. ◆ Evaluation assesses changes in public awareness of the company as a result of the sponsorship. ◆ Events fit within donations policies. ◆ Expectation that community acknowledge and recognize corporate participation in the event. ◆ The public image of the company improved and new customers reached. ◆ Corporate liability. ◆ A cost-benefit analysis was conducted.	◆ The cost to the company resulting from employee involvement (i.e., time away from work) is an important factor. ◆ The cost of supports, if any, that are required, must be included. ◆ Program goals align with business goals and values. ◆ The program is open to all employees who want to participate.
Community	◆ The event was sponsored and/or utilized employee volunteers. ◆ The event was well attended by the target audience. ◆ A client group received better service. ◆ The company and the employees were appropriately recognized. ◆ An evaluation was conducted showing cost, benefit, and outcome.	◆ The event was sponsored and/or utilized employee volunteers. ◆ The event was well attended by the target audience. ◆ A client group received better service. ◆ The company and the employees were appropriately recognized. ◆ An evaluation was conducted showing cost,

◆ EXHIBIT 13–6 Sample Stakeholder Interests in Employee Volunteerism and Corporate Volunteerism (Cont.)

Employees	◆ Employees are consulted about the kinds of events the company supports. ◆ Release time from work is given by the company to volunteer at the sponsored event. ◆ The sponsorship meets a business objective and a community need. ◆ A good time was had by all. ◆ Employees were recognized by the company for their participation. ◆ The event and the company received positive coverage by local media. ◆ Job security was enhanced.	◆ Employees are guiding the development of the program through an advisory group. ◆ Community agencies are willing to help as a partner. ◆ A need in the community was met. ◆ New skills were developed. ◆ A good time was had by all. ◆ People feel better at work. ◆ Employees are recognized for their volunteer work. ◆ Upcoming events and event summaries can be included in the company newsletter. ◆ The program is being evaluated to improve and enhance its impact on employees, the community, and the workplace.

their volunteer experiences. Whether employees volunteer individually or as a group, at least seven dimensions of involvement need to be considered (Seel, 1994a):

1. *Frequency*—addresses how frequently the employee will be expected to volunteer in the community—for example, annually, monthly, weekly, or daily.
2. *Duration*—addresses how long the employee will be expected to commit to the volunteer role—for example, a one-day commitment for a special event or a two-year commitment as a board member.
3. *Time*—raises the question of when the employee's volunteer work will take place—for example, during the day at the office, evenings, or on the weekend.
4. *Human Resources*—includes assessing human resource needs required to complete the volunteer work—for example, a single employee volunteer, a small team of employee volunteers, or a large group of employee volunteers.
5. *Activity*—addresses the issue of what the employee will be doing as a volunteer—for example, being directly involved in service delivery with a client group, making policy as a board member, providing technical assistance, or volunteering as an administrative assistant.

◆ **EXHIBIT 13–7   Forms of Employer Support for Volunteerism**

A wide range of possibilities

The support and encouragement that an employer gives to its employee's volunteer activity can take many different forms. There is great flexibility here, depending on the needs of the company and the intensity of its commitment to employee volunteerism. A variety of approaches can be chosen specifically to reinforce or complement one another.

This range of activities can be organized into five basic categories, but elements from these different categories can be combined to create a unique blend that may be the most appropriate strategy for a given company. In some ways, these different forms of employer support could be viewed as steps along a continuum.

Type I: Acknowledgment

The first form of employer support involves *practices that acknowledge that employees are involved as volunteers and try to accommodate this reality* whenever possible.

This type of support is not necessarily formalized in a policy or a philosophy statement. The possibilities include:

- ◆ Counting relevant volunteer work as experience when considering a candidate for a position or promotion
- ◆ Allowing leaves of absence without pay for volunteer work
- ◆ Allowing employees to adjust their work schedules to make it possible to carry out their volunteer work activities (where the demands of the job allow for flex-time)
- ◆ Allowing employees access on their own time to facilities and equipment (such as computer, fax machines and meeting rooms) for their volunteer work activities

Type II: Promotion

With the second form, employer support is demonstrated in a more formal way. A key element is the *recognition of employees who are involved with voluntary organizations* and highlighting their activities and achievements. Examples are:

- ◆ Sending a letter or memo to all employees in which the CEO expresses his or her views on the value of volunteer participation
- ◆ Sending a thank-you note to employees during National Volunteer Week (or any time during the year)
- ◆ Writing commendations or letters to employees concerning their volunteer activities
- ◆ Publishing activities or a regular column in company newsletters or magazines profiling the volunteer work of employees
- ◆ Organizing special lunches or receptions hosted by senior managers to recognize employees for their volunteer work
- ◆ Giving awards or some form of special recognition to one or more employees who have been nominated as outstanding volunteers
- ◆ Conducting a survey to find out about the volunteer activities of employees

---

◆ EXHIBIT 13–7   Forms of Employer Support for Volunteerism (Cont.)

Type III: Encouragement

With the third form, support is offered through *policies which encourage employees to volunteer* in a more active way. Guidelines, procedures and criteria are required to ensure fairness in terms of the competing demands of the needs of the workplace and the volunteer needs of employees. Potential activities include:

- Encouraging volunteer work as a legitimate way to gain skills and experience for professional or career development
- Encouraging executives and other staff to serve to boards of directors of voluntary organizations that they choose
- Offering pre-retirement seminars promoting volunteer work
- Permitting the posting of information on local voluntary organizations and volunteer positions in the community
- Featuring appeals in internal newsletters from employees on behalf of organizations they support
- Holding a volunteer fair on company premises or participating in a larger event in the community (that is, a display and information booth organized by a volunteer centre or a group of local voluntary organizations to inform employees about volunteer opportunities and services in the community)
- Inviting speakers from voluntary organizations to address employees
- Allowing employees to use office communication channels for announcements to publicize events or volunteer opportunities in the association they work with (for example, through company newsletters, bulletin boards or information in pay packets)
- Referring employees on request to a local volunteer centre or agencies that refer or place volunteers
- Encouraging and supporting volunteer clubs and employee groups that are involved in the community
- Establishing formal volunteer programs for retired employees

Type IV: Endorsement

The fourth form involves *the company working actively with voluntary groups to encourage employees to do volunteer work.* Nevertheless, the choice of the voluntary organization and the volunteer activity would still rest exclusively with the individual employee. Examples are:

- Making information about volunteer opportunities in the community available to employees on a regular basis through in-house publications, notices on bulletin boards, et al
- Liaison with the local volunteer centre on a regular basis or maintaining a clearing house to make employees aware of volunteer jobs available in the community
- Allowing voluntary organizations to have direct access to employees and to recruit volunteers on the company's premises
- Developing a skills bank to record the skills and experience of employees who are interested in volunteer positions

◆ **EXHIBIT 13–7   Forms of Employer Support for Volunteerism (Cont.)**

- ◆ Allowing time off with pay to employees for volunteer activities of their choice during the regular working day (that is, a specific pre-determined amount of time available on request, such as longer lunch breaks or early leaving)
- ◆ Offering help in kind or free services to the organizations for which employees volunteer without requiring the organization to identify or publicize the source (for example, access to surplus furniture or equipment, access to specific services or technology)
- ◆ Offering cash support to organizations for which employees volunteer (a popular model is the community fund program whereby grants are given to organizations as a form of recognition of outstanding volunteer work by employees)
- ◆ Giving cash donations to match funds raised or time volunteered by an individual employee or team of employees for a given organization
- ◆ Supporting community projects that have been organized spontaneously by employees
- ◆ Publicizing the work of employee volunteers in a public way in the community

Type V: Sponsorship

The fifth form relates to very active forms of employee volunteerism whereby *volunteer work is done under the auspices of the company* which employs the individual. Here the company is the intermediary for the community involvement and provides direct support to a community organization, event or cause. By some definitions, this is true 'corporate volunteerism'.

Activities in this category are often viewed as being part of the public relations function of the sponsoring company. They may be directly linked to the mandate of the company. Support for volunteer activities of employees is an integral part of the business strategy and, as such, tends to be 'corporate-driven' rather than 'employee-driven'.

Typically, this type of support involves selected types of volunteer involvement and specific organizations and requires highly structured involvement by the employer (that is, staff time is dedicated to the coordination of the employee volunteer program).

Types of support include:

- ◆ *Appeals to employees to volunteer* for specific organizations
- ◆ Programs to *recruit and refer volunteers* into specific organizations in the community
- ◆ Invitations to employees to become involved in *projects that endorsed by the company*
- ◆ *Cash, goods or services* are given to voluntary organizations for which employees volunteer with the employer clearly identified with the donations
- ◆ *Professional assistance* to identified voluntary organizations either on an ad hoc or a regular basis (in the past, this has generally involved only managerial, technical and professional staff)
- ◆ *Nomination of employees to serve on the board* of a specific voluntary organization (in the past, this has often been limited to managerial and professional staff)

♦ EXHIBIT 13–7   Forms of Employer Support for Volunteerism (Cont.)

- ♦ *Employer-sanctioned "volunteer" time*; the best example would be the time that employees devote to a United Way campaign during working hours

- ♦ *Company projects* that take place in regular working hours; these are company–sanctioned projects or committee–chosen causes that have been endorsed by the company; they may be either one-shot or ongoing projects

- ♦ *Lending employees* to a company-sanctioned voluntary organization at the employer's expense; this is often in an area linked to the product or service provided by the company and is generally restricted to managers and professionals (for example, loaned executives programs); it is commonly used for developmental assignments for staff in the early to middle stages of their career and for longer-term assignments for those in the middle to advanced stages of their career; for the employees involved, this is a work commitment, since they are still accountable to their employer

Company–sanctioned projects

In the case of company-sanctioned projects, three different concepts are possible:

1. *Sponsorship*: examples include the United Way campaign (which ranks first in terms of sponsorship in Canada) and adopt-a-charity schemes;

2. *Joint partnership projects* done in collaboration with a voluntary organization: a good example is a Meals on Wheels program run by a company;

3. *In-house projects where* the company works totally on its own without the involvement of a voluntary organization, except perhaps as a beneficiary; this is a model for community development that is common in the United States; adopt-a-school projects and tutoring of youth on company premises are popular examples.

Adapted with permission from Janet Lautenschlager, *Volunteering in the Workplace: How to Promote Employee Volunteerism.*

6. *Skill*—requires determining the skills the employee will need to have, or need to learn, in order to perform the volunteer work—for example, social skills sets, professional skill sets, or technical skill sets.

7. *Location*—emphasizes that some consideration must be given to the location of volunteer activity—for example, at home, at work, or at an agency.

In assessing a program, it is advisable to reflect on the expectations the agency has of the volunteer. The seven dimensions provide a general guide to matching the stakeholder interests of the company and the community agency with those of the volunteer. A volunteer position description that identifies expectations across each dimension provides clear criteria to an employee volunteer.

Ideally, an employee survey is conducted within the workplace. The survey would ask questions from each of the seven dimensions to determine the parameters of employee involvement. With a completed workplace survey, the company and the manager could work together to meet each of their respective needs. The employee survey would serve the additional purpose of encouraging employee involvement by making employees aware that "something is happening" with regard to volunteerism in the workplace.

A final point to be made here is that in the early stages of designing an employee volunteer program, managers or representatives from each of the stakeholder groups should be involved in assessing the menu of volunteer opportunities to be offered to employees. Recognizing the diversity inherent in a workplace, a menu approach that reflects a rich mixture of volunteer opportunities will act as a powerful recruitment tool. The seven dimensions of involvement can help managers ensure that there is a full range of volunteer opportunities, appealing to a wide range of interests.

13.7 PREPARING THE COMPANY AND EMPLOYEES

Upon starting an employee volunteer program, both the company and the employees need to be involved in the planning process. In an excellent resource, the Points of Light Foundation (1993) has documented the kinds of management considerations that need review. Six areas are developed for consideration:

1. Setting goals
2. Developing structure
3. Working with volunteers
4. Developing corporate policies
5. Receiving benefits
6. Conducting evaluations

The steps suggested follow a commonsense order. Experience from corporate volunteer councils across Canada and the United States has shown, however, that this sequence of events usually occurs out of step. A common example: Each of the stakeholder groups may be working with employee volunteers before there is any structure to the program. While the sequence of steps may occur out of turn, at some point each step will need to be addressed if an employee volunteer program is to reach its full potential. To assist managers in understanding the basic elements of planning an employee volunteer program, these management considerations are explored in the remainder of this section.

(a) Setting Goals

As already discussed, the manager of an employee volunteer program needs to consider the stakeholders in the process, including:

◆ The company
◆ The community
◆ The employees

The Points of Light Foundation (1993, p. 6) suggests three areas for management consideration:

1. Managers should identify the benefits that the company would most like to receive from the employee volunteer program. Asking a senior leader or a senior management decision-making group such as a board of directors is one recommended strategy.
2. Managers should analyze the annual report of the company. The mission statement, values, current business priorities, and projected corporate initiatives should be reviewed. An employee volunteer program that links with each of these areas is more likely to be endorsed by the company.
3. Managers should generalize their contacts within a company to ensure that an employee volunteer program meets the needs of several departments or branches.

A review of the vested interests of the company will identify expected benefits to the company from any employee volunteer program (see section 13.4). Several benefits suggested the research can be used to promote an employee volunteer program to the three stakeholder groups.

(i) Benefits of Employee Volunteer Programs

Companies report 12 possible benefits of employee volunteer programs (The Conference Board, 1993, p.37). In order, from the most frequently reported benefit to the least, the top 12 ways in which companies that support employee volunteer programs benefit from the program are:

1. Helping to create "healthier communities"
2. Improving corporate public images
3. Enhancing impact of monetary donations
4. Improving relations with community and/or government
5. Building employees' teamwork skills
6. Improving employee morale
7. Attracting better employees
8. Enhancing employee training
9. Improving employee retention
10. Enhancing corporate strategic goals
11. Enhancing employee productivity
12. Enhancing company productivity

(ii) Creating an Employee Profile

Employees are a heterogeneous group, and assessing their interests may require that the manager:

◆ Conduct surveys
◆ Hold focus group sessions
◆ Review current employee interests in existing employee or corporate events associated with volunteerism

Involving a cross section of employees in these processes will help to ensure that the employee volunteer program will be of interest and accessible to the widest possible range of employees. To achieve such a cross section, managers could use existing communications vehicles in the company, such as electronic mail, bulletin boards, and newsletters.

One of the most common approaches used by managers to create an employee profile is a survey. A typical employee survey asks employees about:

- *Personal information:* name, department, demographic data
- *Current volunteer activities:* agency, hours volunteered, task done
- *Volunteer interests:* individual and group activities

If a survey is used, it is critical that employees be told what will be done with the information. A circulated follow-up showing the trends demonstrated by the survey is a good idea. People who are surveyed deserve a response from those who are conducting the survey. Experience has shown that a survey that is not appropriately implemented and followed up can create barriers to developing an inclusive employee volunteer program.

(iii) Community Needs

Community needs can be assessed in cooperation with a local volunteer center, United Way, or nonprofit agencies. Community needs will vary from place to place, so it is important that managers become familiar with the networks and coalitions that could be supportive. Finding a contact who can provide information on emerging and existing need areas in a community may take awhile, particularly if the employee volunteer program does not have a strong tie to the nonprofit sector. Once such a contact has been found, however, the program will have gained an important link to the community.

If your community has a volunteer center, it is a natural starting point in the process of designing and implementing a community needs assessment. Volunteer centers can be an important contact to a local corporate volunteer council, provide insights to the social issues facing a community, and facilitate linkages to the nonprofit agencies that deliver so many of the services required by people in need (Exhibit 13–8).

13.8 DEVELOPING STRUCTURE

The most frequently used organizing structures within a company to administer a corporate volunteer program are (Points of Light Foundation, 1993, p. 12):

1. A single staff person who is responsible for the employee volunteer program, usually administering and coordinating all program activities.
2. A staff person who coordinates a committee of employees who plan and manage the employee volunteer program's activities. This committee follows a predetermined company policy on employee involvement.
3. An outside consultant manages the program and coordinates the activities of the employee volunteer program.

◆ **EXHIBIT 13–8   Calgary Corporate Volunteer Council**

The Calgary Corporate Volunteer Council (CCVC) was looking for a focus for its corporate members. The CCVC had developed a strong relationship with the local volunteer centre during the negotiations that led to the formation of the council. The Volunteer Centre of Calgary became a founding member of the CCVC and helped to guide one of the community initiatives of the corporations participating on the council. When the CCVC wanted to focus its energies on an issue area, they requested that the Volunteer Centre of Calgary contact executive directors of local agencies. By matching the feedback from agencies and the needs of the companies, the issue area of "Youth At Risk" was selected. The Volunteer Centre of Calgary contacted several agencies working with youth and facilitated a series of focus group sessions to explore areas of possible involvement. The results of the focus group sessions were presented back to the CCVC members who used the information in planning new activities in the community.

Exhibit 13–9 is an example of a mission statement developed by AGT Limited for their corporate volunteer program—EXTENSION. Many companies will develop mission or vision statements for their programs, and thereby create a fit between the company and the volunteer program.

(a) The Single-Person Manager

An important consideration in the single-manager form of organization is the percentage of time the manager has available to dedicate to the employee volunteer program. The kinds of tasks and activities that can be undertaken will depend on the answer. The staff person who manages the employee volunteer program probably comes from the community relations, public affairs, corporate donations, or human resources staff, and spends only a small portion of time on the program—20 percent according to the Conference Board (1993, p. 12), and 16 percent according to Barnes (1993, p. 6). Managing an employee volunteer program is rarely a full-time position. This means that compared to the many other things a manager faces, an employee volunteer program is a relatively low priority. Given this situation, the task becomes finding a creative way to manage the program.

(i) The Management Team

To share the responsibility of managing the employee volunteer program, the single-person manager should consider establishing an advisory committee or team of employees. These employees may identify themselves during an employee survey or can be approached based on the manager's personal knowledge of their volunteer involvement. However, managers should be careful about using such personal contacts, because they should try to prevent the advisory committee from gaining the reputation of being somehow "specially connected," or "exclusive."

The single-person manager on the management team should consider four key management issues:

◆ **EXHIBIT 13–9   Sample Employee Volunteer Program Mission Statement from AGT**

EXTENSION, AGT's employee volunteer network, provides corporate support and endorsement for volunteer efforts of individual employees. The program matches skills and interests of current and retired employees with community needs in an organized way, thereby promoting a partnership between the corporation, its employees, and the community.

NAME RATIONALE
The name "EXTENSION" was selected to represent the volunteer program's mission. This program will "extend" employee talents and energy into the non-profit sector; give employees the opportunity to "extend" personal growth and self-worth; "extend" goodwill throughout the community.

Source: Reprinted with permission from AGT Limited.

1. It is important to try to get the CEO or senior management of the company to sanction the decision-making team and perhaps set parameters or assign areas of authority.

2. Select an advisory committee that reflects as much diversity as possible. Try to get a cross section of the employee population, including seniority, age, gender, racial, and cultural diversity. In many ways this concept echoes the idea behind the cross-function team approaches associated with the quality management movement.

3. Ensure that an orientation process is established for the advisory committee. This helps to create a common sense of purpose and aligns the team so that everyone knows what is to be done and why. An orientation also helps to make this team of decision makers aware of the mission and goals of the program.

4. Ensure that the advisory committee has some way of communicating its suggestions and activities to the employees of the company.

Working with Volunteers

After working out the context for the program and the role of the employee-driven advisory committee, the next step is to recruit volunteers into the program. In beginning to recruit, an eye should be kept on how to reward the voluntary efforts of the employees (Points of Light Foundation, 1993, p. 17).

(i) Types of Volunteer Activities

As an expert in the field of corporate volunteerism, Shirley Kennedy Keller advocates the use of a grab bag of activities to appeal to the diverse individual needs of employee volunteers (Keller, 1993). One way of considering this grab bag is to think of the various dimensions that effect potential volunteers when they review a volunteer opportunity. The terms describing the seven dimensions (discussed in detail earlier in Section 13.6) that need to be considered are *frequency, duration, time, human resources, activity, skill,* and *location.* Generally speaking, within each of these dimensions there are wide ranges of volunteer opportunities:

- A short-term group project (refurbishing a senior's house)
- Longer-term governance activities (serving on a board of directors)
- Direct service with a client (counseling individual clients)
- Administrative support (helping with mailings)
- Technical assistance (helping to conduct a technology audit)
- Management assistance (training a new treasurer or accountant)

(ii) Volunteer Recruitment

"To achieve variety in the ways you go about getting attention and persuading employees to volunteer, vary your recruitment strategies" (Points of Light Foundation, 1993, p. 18). This is sage advice when it comes to recruiting employee volunteers. Recruiting volunteers is an activity that calls for creativity. Volunteers respond to recruitment activities in much the same way that potential customers respond to advertising. The key is to decide on a clear message, perhaps involving a logo or a slogan, and then to go about promoting all employee volunteer opportunities using that logo or slogan. A constant image links the various promotional approaches that can be used, such as (Points of Light Foundation, 1993, p. 18):

- Placing tent cards on cafeteria tables
- Placing posters in elevators
- Including a brochure with employee paychecks
- Placing exciting recruitment messages on electronic and traditional bulletin boards
- Hosting a volunteer or agency fair
- Advertising in employee newsletters
- Advertising in corporate newsletters

When it comes to recruitment and recruitment ideas, volunteer centers can be a natural connection for corporate volunteer programs and managers of volunteers. Most volunteer centers act as brokers of both volunteers and volunteer opportunities. Volunteer centers are a source of both expertise and services that can enhance your program. Volunteer centers can:

- Help you start a volunteer program that is based on sound volunteer management practices, including conducting a needs survey, defining liability and other insurance requirements, and helping to determine what a budget for the program might look like (Seel et al., 1994, p. 8).
- Provide volunteer management expertise, including volunteer–staff relations, recruitment strategies, retention strategies, and recognition strategies; and ensuring that the program is targeted to a community need (Seel et al., 1994, p. 9).
- Suggest program management ideas, such as writing volunteer position descriptions, training needs, evaluation criteria, record-keeping systems, media relations, and marketing strategies (Seel et al., 1994, p. 9).
- Facilitate the links among the community, company, and employees.
- Promote the employee volunteer program and the work that it is doing in the community throughout the center's networks, including other nonprofit organizations and the media.

13.9 DEVELOPING CORPORATE POLICIES

Policies serve to bring employee volunteer programs closer to the core of business and nonprofit practice. The result is twofold (Points of Light Foundation, 1993, p. 26):

1. Policies sustain the corporate commitment to the volunteer program during times of change.
2. Policies indicate the degree of importance that volunteering holds for the corporation.

Policies can cover such things as:

♦ Parameters for corporate donations
♦ Flex time for employee volunteers
♦ Release time for employee volunteers
♦ Long-term leaves for employee volunteers
♦ Community investment donations attached to employee volunteer activities
♦ Partnership processes and limitations
♦ Liability coverage
♦ General insurance coverage

Depending on what the policy covers, different stakeholders will need to be involved. Managers should reflect on the roles and functions the stakeholder groups have in policy development. For example:

♦ Senior management
♦ Human resources departments
♦ Marketing departments
♦ Nonprofit boards of directors
♦ Community representatives
♦ Diverse groups, representing differences in culture, ability, gender, race, age, and so on

A more complete list appears in Exhibit 13–2.

The possibility exists that if one of these individual stakeholding groups was not properly involved in the development of policy affecting an employee volunteer program, it could emerge later as a "benign saboteur." Involvement for some stakeholders may simply mean that they are kept informed of developments. For others it will mean that they are part of the total policy development process. Managers should also be aware of initiatives such as quality management, benchmarking, continuous improvement, and similar programs when writing policy. Management initiatives such as these will have a direct impact on how the policy is written and implemented.

13.10 LIABILITY AND RISK MANAGEMENT

The final consideration in this section has to do with managing legal liability in an employee volunteer program. Volunteers deserve insurance protection. The question that is frequently asked is: should the company extend its insurance to its employee volunteers? Should the nonprofit agency insure volunteers coming to it to help with projects? The answer varies from case to case and can be negotiated as part of a partnership between the company and the nonprofit agency.

Tremper and Kahn (1992) compiled a thorough analysis of liability and risk management for corporate volunteer programs. In their work many issues that affect managers of volunteer programs are explored. A partial list of these issues includes:

♦ *Legal liability:* negligence, company liability for acts of its volunteers, company liability for injuries to its volunteer personal liability, and liability shields

♦ *Insurance and indemnification:* liability insurance to protect the company and insurance for volunteers

♦ *Strategies for controlling liability risks:* risk management, including written policies and procedures, positions describing training and supervision, and restriction on volunteer activity

As Tremper and Kahn observe:

As businesses expand their community service role from making contributions to involving their employees in volunteer programs, liability issue become more prominent. To reduce liability fears, volunteer program managers must recognize, understand and control the risks of their operations, just as product development directors and plant managers explicitly factor risk into every decision. (1992, p. 1)

Exhibit 13–10 is an excellent example of corporate guidelines detailing employee, agency, and corporate responsibilities pertaining to liability and indemnification.

13.11 RECEIVING BENEFITS

A study cosponsored by the Conference Board and the Points of Light Foundation found that 454 responses from 1,800 of the largest U.S. public companies produced a list of benefits attributed to corporate volunteer programs. These benefits can be grouped under three classifications (percentages of companies in agreement noted in parentheses).

1. Indirect community benefits including:
   ♦ Helps create healthier communities (94%)
   ♦ Improves corporate public image (94%)
   ♦ Enhances impact of monetary contributions (92%)
   ♦ Improves relations with community/government (85%)

2. Employee benefits including:
   ♦ Builds team work skills (93%)
   ♦ Improves morale (91%)
   ♦ Attracts better employees (90%)

◆ **EXHIBIT 13–10   Sample Policy Statements**

EXTENSION, AGT's employee volunteer network, provides corporate support and endorsement for volunteer efforts of individual employees. The initiative matches skills and interests of current and retired employees with community needs in an organized way, thereby promoting a partnership between the community, the corporation and its employees.

Guidelines

◆ For the purposes of EXTENSION, volunteer activities will be defined as those which AGT employees participate in outside normal working hours. Where such activities overlap or conflict with employee's regular scheduled tour of duty, flexibility will be given at the discretion of the employee's immediate supervisor. Priority, however, will be given to the productivity requirements of the job.

◆ **AGT Responsibility–EXTENSION Projects**

If a current or retired employee acting as a volunteer is involved in an incident where there is an injury to another person or damage to property of others and the employee is found personally liable, AGT will indemnify (pay any defense and settlement costs) for amounts which are not recoverable under the employee's personal insurance programs.

This indemnity is not available to family members or friends of an employee, or if the employee has acted in a dishonest, malicious, or grossly negligent manner. Also AGT will not be responsible for damage to employee's vehicles or personal property used while volunteering.

◆ **AGT Responsibility–Volunteering with an agency**

Since AGT is acting only as a referral body, and has no control over the activities of the outside agency or non-profit organization, AGT cannot assume responsibility for the actions of its employees while volunteering in this manner. Such responsibility should remain with the organization undertaking and directing the activities.

Reprinted with permission from AGT Limited.

◆ Enhances training (86%)
◆ Improves employee retention (77%)
3. Bottom-line benefits including:
 ◆ Enhances corporate strategic goals (77%)
 ◆ Increases employees productivity (74%)
 ◆ Enhances company productivity (63%)

In a comparative survey of 155 companies with and without employee volunteer programs, the Corporate Volunteerism Council of the Minneapolis/St. Paul Metro Area found different benefits. Although generally in agreement with the Conference Board's findings, new and interesting details emerged, such as: "Volunteer and community relations programs also are viewed as integral to team building, cultural diversity, environment and quality improvement goals" (Corporate Volunteerism

Council, 1993, p. 2). In the same study, when companies were asked to look into the future, those that were members of corporate councils saw school partnerships, organizations with cultural diversity, family-oriented volunteer activities, and agency partnerships as directions for employee volunteer programs. As the report notes (Corporate Volunteerism Council, 1993, p. 10): "Seeking out opportunities to explore cultural diversity will be a focus for both companies providing volunteers and agencies seeking those individuals. Fifty-three percent of nonprofit organizations listed an emphasis on cultural diversity as their primary strategy for attracting new business volunteers."

13.12 PREPARING THE AGENCY

Nonprofit agencies need to be prepared for partnerships with corporations. The few publications on nonprofit agency partnerships with corporations (e.g., Bosetti, Webber, and Johnson, 1993; Spiess and Robertson, 1993; Rostami and Audet, 1992; Audet and Rostami, 1993; Allen et al., 1987) can be of help to managers working with employee volunteer programs. The challenge is to overcome an inherent and historical imbalance in power between a corporation (seen to be powerful and wealthy) and a nonprofit agency (seen to be poor and powerless). Stereotypes exist within each of the stakeholder groups in an employee volunteer program, and overcoming them on the way to an equitable working partnership may take considerable time.

Audet and Rostami (1993, p. 20) suggest 11 elements that need consideration is a positive, equitable partnership is to develop: attitude, team composition, communication, commitment, trust, power, resources, stakeholders, management, stability, and creativity. Representatives from each stakeholder group could work through a values-based process to explore each of these issues. The result of such a process would be not only a solid understanding of the needs and expectations of each partner, but also an excellent framework for an employee volunteer program.

Unlike grantors, private foundations, or subsidy-granting government agencies, corporations would like to see evidence of a return on investment for the company, the employees, or both. As Spiess and Robertson observe:

> [nonprofits] are not *selling your soul* to the company. You are simply making a mutually beneficial arrangement where your organization receives funds, services, corporate volunteer support, or gifts-in-kind in exchange for some form of corporate recognition. This recognition may take the form of publicity of an event or on your promotional material, or if may simply be access to your market. This combination of non-profit needs and corporate marketing interests can be the basis for and successful partnership. (1993, p. 11)

An assessment can be an important step in the process of agency preparation. Assessments an agency understates, may cover (Spiess and Robertson, 1993, pp. 11-14):

> *Organizational assessments,* which review the mission statement, the goals, and even the values of the organization, as well as its commitment to client service

Environmental assessments, which review existing sociopolitical issues in the community, possible competitors, and potential supporters

Needs assessments, which assess a specific need within the agency, including resource, program, and strategic approaches to service delivery

Support assessment, which is an assessment of the philanthropic interests of the companies the agency may approach for support to enable the agency to align its resource needs with corporate interests and/or values

13.13 FOUR STEPS TO APPROACHING A CORPORATION

Spiess and Robertson suggest a logical series of steps toward a partnership with a corporation. These steps can be understood as a process of preparation and readiness on the part of the nonprofit agency (Spiess and Robertson, 1993, pp.17–18):

Step 1. *Research.* The nonprofit agency should make sure that it has the most current information available on the company. This may include the company contact's name and title, company policy on donations, and levels of employee involvement.

Step 2. *Review and align.* The nonprofit agency should make sure that there is a fit between corporate-giving guidelines or policy and the nonprofit agency's mission, values, goals, and needs.

Step 3. *Make the request.* The nonprofit agency needs to consider the request very carefully and in the context of other decisions being made.

Step 4. *Prepare and submit request.* The agency should be brief and very clear. Be aware of application deadline and preferred formats for the submission.

13.14 EVALUATING THE EMPLOYEE VOLUNTEER PROGRAM

To better determine program effectiveness and to make decisions regarding program development, managers will need to evaluate the employee volunteer program. Evaluation can take many forms, including frequently combined, such as:

◆ *Quantitative*—statistical measures: counts on number of volumes or numbers of projects or numbers of things done/clients served; cost/benefit analyses

◆ *Qualitative*—collecting anecdotes, testimonials, stories, holding focus group sessions, running perception checks

◆ *Formative*—needs assessments, front-end evaluations to determine scope and need, preliminary community focus groups

◆ *Summative*—postactivity evaluations, program impact statements, concluding assessments, program reviews

◆ *Critical*—assessing power relations between groups and individuals during a change process

These different methods of evaluation are often combined.

Regardless of the kind of evaluation being undertaken, serious attention needs to be given to the following areas, as suggested by Volunteer—The National Centre (1987, p. 13):

- ◆ Know the questions to which you need answers.
- ◆ Plan the information-gathering process to provide the answers you need.
- ◆ Make sure that constant and ongoing communication occurs between you (or other planners) and data handlers.
- ◆ Report the data in a usable fashion.
- ◆ Have someone who can interpret the data.
- ◆ Have a process in place to ensure that the data are as accurate, reliable, and valid as possible.
- ◆ See to it that you protect each person's privacy in your data handling.

Korngold and Voudouris (1994) suggest five phases in the evaluation of employee corporate volunteer programs:

Phase 1	Record keeping
Phase 2	Process evaluation
Phase 3	Impact on employees
Phase 4	Impact on company
Phase 5	Impact on community

The model presented by Korngold and Voudouris represents the kind of sophistication that is needed to assess the value and impact on the company, the employees, and the community. Managers should familiarize themselves with this and other evaluation models. Being aware that having a variety of evaluation approaches gives the manager associated with an employee volunteer program the tools needed to customize both the program and the evaluation to the needs and expectations of all stakeholders.

13.15 CRITICAL AND EMERGING ISSUES

Employee volunteerism is an evolving dynamic in community building. It has emerged as a positive alternative to the traditional conveyor belt approach to service delivery, which has money flowing from the private sector to service delivery points in the nonprofit sector. It has emerged because of an increasing awareness on the part of citizens in a community that everyone has a role to play in addressing the tremendous social problems facing his or her community. The role that private and corporate citizens alike are being asked to fulfill is no longer at arm's length, so to speak, but is personal and close. The potential of employee volunteerism is the tremendous *human* potential represented by each of the stakeholder groups.

As the movement grows, six critical issues (Seel, 1994a,b) are emerging. They require serious thought and debate by all stakeholders:

1. Acknowledging that volunteerism is frequently a foreign concept to business
2. Defining employee volunteerism as a program or as a process
3. Responding to the quality management movement
4. Enhancing foresight and adaptability
5. Differentiating employee volunteerism from corporate volunteerism
6. Exploring partnerships and levels of commitment

These issues are explored below.

(a) Issue 1—Volunteerism as a Foreign Concept

Managers involved with employee volunteer programs will have to face the question: What does volunteerism have to do with the workplace? History shows a clear split between the nonprofit and profit sectors. Clearly a great deal of change has occurred, and we are encouraged to see many companies and nonprofit organizations beginning to work together. A significant proportion of that collaboration is on very short term projects and frequently on the employee's own time. For many companies, however, the level of involvement is limited and typically rests on a donation program whereby money is contributed to nonprofit agencies working to deliver services to the community. There are many notable exceptions to this, but considering that the business backbone of North America is small business, not the large businesses of the Fortune 500, very little progress has been made.

Until the independent business person or the small business embraces employee volunteerism as part of its operations within a community, employee volunteerism can only be partially successful. Many of these independent small businesses do contribute small amounts of resources to a few nonprofit organizations, but a true working relationship is not evident. This may be due to a couple of factors. First, a small business has fewer employees concentrated in one workplace. In some cases the small business has only a handful of employees, so an expansive employee volunteer program makes little sense. Second, the small business needs to see a much greater connection to its bottom line. Whereas a large corporation may be able to wait to see long-term benefits from its program, a small company needs immediate benefits. Frequently, immediate bottom-line benefits are not forthcoming.

Further, nonprofit agencies cannot be of much help to the employee volunteerism movement until they begin to outgrow the image of helplessness and poverty. Businesses everywhere are entering into strategic or symbolic alliances with other business because there is a great potential for mutual benefit. Until nonprofit agencies can put aside the begging hand image and extend a partner's handshake to business, volunteerism will continue to be foreign to the strategic interests of many businesses. Nonprofit agencies need to, and over time will, become equal partners with their business counterparts.

(b) Issue 2—Employee Volunteerism as a Program or as a Process

This issue could be considered to be one of fit. How will the various stakeholders view the employee volunteer program? If employee volunteerism is seen to be a program, then it will be somewhat removed from the valued core of the business and probably from the nonprofit agency as well. Programs are typically viewed as peripheral to the real heart of the company and are therefore vulnerable to being cut whenever times are tight. Programs are susceptible to changing economic and business fortunes as well as changing personnel. Frequently, a program slowly vanishes after the leader who drove the program leaves.

Employee volunteer programs are frequently viewed as being outside the core business. If a company manufactures a product, it may support an employee volunteer program through good economic times as part of its community relations. However, if the economic situation takes a downturn, if values change, or if there is a merger, the program may be cut as the company's management focuses its energies back on manufacturing.

When employee volunteerism becomes a process, it has closer ties to the valued core of stakeholder organizations. As a process it works with other processes to serve the strategic interests of the company, the employees, and the nonprofit agency. For example, employee volunteerism in this sense would enhance performance management initiatives such as leadership training and customer service skills, and provide training in a diversity of areas, thereby showing bottom-line business benefits. As a process, employee volunteerism would work toward a bigger-picture strategic vision rather than a focus on short-term projects. A context for involvement would evolve that would be responsive and meaningful to all stakeholders—a context that management would resist losing.

(c) Issue 3—Quality Service Orientation

Even though up to 80 percent of total quality management initiatives fail or show no improvement, two-thirds of those organizations report that they will continue to persist with TQM (William M. Mercer Lmt., 1993). The reality is that quality management principles and practices will continue to be part of the business world for some time to come. The consequence is that employee volunteerism needs to be a quality service that supports quality management initiatives and improves the competitiveness of the businesses involved. Although the business sector may have been working with the idea of quality management for decades, the nonprofit sector has only recently begun to express interest.

Managers involved with employee volunteer programs will have to be aware of quality management principles and practice. An employee volunteer program that is professing and practicing quality management is more likely to be reviewed favorably by stakeholders in the company. Moreover, many companies may assess partnerships or projects with a nonprofit agency based on quality management practices. An agency that does not reflect a quality environment will be at a significant disadvantage to an agency that does.

(d) Issue 4—Foresight and Adaptability

There is a tremendous need to break out of traditional lock-step planning models. Employee volunteerism involves numerous stakeholders and is in a continual state of flux as new issues, agencies, and employees become involved. A rigid plan will take considerable time to prepare and will probably be out of step with reality by the time the first activities begin. This is not to say that planning can be overlooked. What needs to be considered is a strategic approach to setting parameters for flexible action within the employee volunteer program. These parameters can come from employee surveys, company policy, community needs, and so on. A kind of values assessment of each stakeholder may provide enough of a framework to proceed with an employee volunteer program. A values assessment is different in that it establishes the foundation of consensus values upon which all activities will be built. When stakeholders understand these consensus values, a more dynamic planning approach can be taken, one that responds to changes without losing contact with the stakeholders along the way. The advantage of a values-based, flexible, and strategic approach to planning is that the employee volunteer program can respond to unanticipated change without missing a beat. While a rigid plan may mean that really significant issue go unaddressed because they did not make it into the plan, a flexible approach can adapt to continuously changing world.

(e) Issue 5—Employee Volunteerism or Corporate Volunteerism

Although this subject was discussed earlier (see Section 13.3), it is worthwhile to note that the lack of differentiation between the two terms will create innumerable difficulties for managers associated with employee volunteer programs. Currently, employee volunteerism and corporate volunteerism are often seen as synonymous, and it is only when a difficulty is encountered that people become aware of the difference. For example, if a company suddenly surveys its employees to find out what the employees are doing as volunteers in the community, this could be misunderstood by the employee as an invasion of privacy. In this case, employees may feel that the company is trying to take credit somehow for something that they are doing outside working hours, on their own time. What has happened is that the vested interests of the employee stakeholder group have become confused with the vested interests of the corporate stakeholder group. Clearly, differentiating the stakeholders' interests and concerns and designing a program that addresses these stakeholders appropriately is a strategy for avoiding confusion and misunderstanding. As Exhibits 13–2, 13–3, and 13–4 show, it is important to understand which stakeholder is initiating an employee volunteer program and to recognize that there will be significant differences between a program initiated by employees and one initiated by a company.

An additional spin is put on this issue when the community begins to initiate employee volunteer programs. In several cases in Canada, for example, volunteer centers have initiated corporate volunteer councils and have been working with companies to develop employee volunteer programs. In cases such as these, who the community agency approaches, the company or the employees, will have tremendous impact on what will evolve. A blended approach that involves contacting both the company stakeholders and employee stakeholders may yield greater results than will focusing on just one or the other.

(f) Issue 6—Partnerships and Commitment

Regardless of who initiates an employee volunteer program (the community, the company, or the employees) the success of the program is totally dependent on involving the other two stakeholder groups. In other words, an employee volunteer program that does not go out into the community to volunteer has no purpose and no reason for existing. The process of contact between stakeholder groups involves various degrees of partnering and commitment. It seems that little reflection is given to the variety of factors that come into play when stakeholders commit to becoming partners in the betterment of the community.

An informal kind of partnership where commitment between the stakeholders is low would typically be a short-term project. Perhaps a company and a community agency agree to hold a special dinner event for street youth. Some negotiation may occur in order to have all components of the dinner covered—volunteers must be enlisted to buy food, serve dinner, and clean up. When the event ends, so does the partnership. In these situations, the commitment to a deeper kind of working relationship is largely absent.

In a more formal kind of partnership, a deeper commitment is made between the stakeholder groups. School–business partnerships, for example, often are long-term arrangements that involve many people doing many things in both the company and the school. Partnerships that exhibit high degrees of commitment may have joint interorganizational teams that oversee the partnership. Strong loyalties to the partnership evolve and are added to the loyalties that each stakeholder group had before the partnership. Resources are often pooled and applied in a strategic manner to yield the greatest long-term benefit to the client group being served.

A partnership that involves more commitment between stakeholder groups may mean that the managers associated with the employee volunteer program have the skills of talented negotiators and visionaries. Longer-term partnerships will involve significantly different kinds of efforts to be successful than do short-term events. Regardless of what kind of partnership is considered, managers associated with employee volunteer programs need to consider the resources (in time, people, and money) and skills needed to achieve successful results.

13.16 CONCLUSIONS

Employee volunteer programs offer a rewarding solution to many of the needs expressed by companies, employees, and the community. For companies, maintaining positive relations with its employees and with the community where it does business helps improve visibility, workforce skills, and the bottom line. For employees, new skills and networks can be developed in an exciting and meaningful way. For the community, focused support and talent from the business community can make a real difference to the multiple social problems that harm its citizens. But employee volunteer programs pose very real management issues, involving human resource management, financial management, project management, negotiations, and so on. Managers associated with employee volunteer programs must work constantly to upgrade their skills and anticipate trends. By enhancing management competencies, the potential of employee volunteer programs can be realized.

REFERENCES

Allen, Kenn, Shirley Keller, and Cynthia Vizza. 1987. *Building Partnerships with Business: A Guide for Nonprofits.* Arlington, VA: Volunteer–The National Center.

Audet, Beverly, and Janet Rostami. 1993. *Partnership Strategies for Community Investment.* Findings of national consultations conducted by the Institute of Donations and Public Affairs Research. Ottawa: The Conference Board of Canada.

Barnes, R. 1993. *1993 Profile of the Community Relations Profession.* Ottawa: Research report from the Center for Corporate Community Relations at Boston College. Boston: The Center for Corporate Community Relations.

Bosetti, L., C. Webber, and F. Johnson. 1993. "Partnerships in Education: Trends and Opportunities." Papers presented at a seminar at the University of Calgary, May 4, 1993, Faculty of Education, The University of Calgary, Calgary, Alberta, Canada.

The Conference Board. 1993. *Corporate Volunteer Programs: Benefits to Business.* Conference Board Report 1029. Ottawa: The Conference Board of Canada.

Corporate Volunteerism Council. 1993. *A Report to the Community: Twin Cities Businesses and Volunteerism.* Survey produced by the Corporate Volunteerism Council of Minneapolis/St. Paul Metro Area.

Keller, Shirley. 1993. *Employee Volunteerism: A Different Approach, a Greater Return.* Symposium on Corporate Volunteerism presented by the Calgary Corporate Volunteer Council, March 18–19, 1993, Calgary, Alberta, Canada.

Korngold, Alice and Elizabeth Voudouris. 1994. *Business Volunteerism: Designing Your Program for Impact.* Cleveland, Ohio: Business Volunteerism Council.

Lautenschlager, Janet. 1993. *Volunteering in the Workplace: How to Promote Employee Volunteerism.* Ottawa, Ontario, Canada: Voluntary Action Directorate, Canadian Heritage.

Points of Light Foundation. 1993. *Developing a Corporate Volunteer Program: Guidelines for Success.* Washington, D.C.: Points of Light Foundation.

Ross, D., and R. Shillington. 1989. *A Profile of the Canadian Volunteer.* Ottawa, Ontario, Canada: National Voluntary Organizations.

Rostami, Janet and Beverly Audet. 1992. *Partnership Strategies.* Background paper produced by the Institute of Donations and Public Affairs Research. Ontario, Canada: The Conference Board of Canada.

Seel, Keith. 1994a. *Employee Volunteerism: Building on the Potential.* Resource kit for a Summer Institute on Employee Volunteerism presented by M. Parker and K. Seel for the Calgary Corporate Volunteer Council, July 20, Calgary, Alberta, Canada.

Seel, Keith. 1994b. "Corporate volunteerism: a different approach, a greater return." *Journal of Volunteer Resources Management* 3(3) (Summer): 8–11.

Seel, Keith, Lisa Holden, Nadine Pickard, and Terri Bilodeau. 1994. *Campus Volunteerism: A Handbook and Case Studies.* Calgary, Alberta, Canada: The Volunteer Centre of Calgary.

Spiess, Karen, and Linda Robertson. 1993. *Partnerships: Non-profit Organizations and Corporations Working Together.* Grant MacEwan Community College, Edmonton, Alberta, Canada: Resource Centre for Voluntary Organizations.

Tremper, C. and J. Kahn. 1992. *Managing Legal Liability and Insurance for Corporate Volunteer Programs.* Washington, D.C.: National Center for Community Risk Management and Insurance.

Volunteer. 1987. *Evaluating Corporate Volunteer Programs.* Arlington, Va.: Volunteer—The National Center.

William M. Mercer Lmt. 1993. "The Organization of the Future." Presentation made at the 11th Annual Conference of the Calgary Personnel Association and the University of Calgary, November 8, Calgary, Alberta, Canada.

P A R T

Volunteers and the Law

CHAPTER 14
General Liability and Immunities

CHAPTER 15
Board Member Liability and Responsibility

CHAPTER 16
Risk Management Strategies

CHAPTER 17
Volunteers and Employment Law

CHAPTER 18
National Service: Twenty Questions and Some Answers

CHAPTER ⟨14⟩

GENERAL LIABILITY AND IMMUNITY

Carolyn Quattrocki

14.1 Legal Responsibilities of Volunteers and Agencies to Injured Parties

14.2 Volunteers' Immunities and Defenses from Suit and Liability

14.3 Volunteer as Plaintiff

Suggested Readings

14.1 LEGAL RESPONSIBILITIES OF VOLUNTEERS AND AGENCIES TO INJURED PARTIES

Like all human beings, volunteers may in the course of their activities make a mistake, take an action, or fail to take an action that causes harm to another. Whether any liability can result from an injury to another person depends on many different factors. For example, liability can sometimes turn upon whether the volunteer acted intentionally or simply made a mistake. Liability can also depend upon whether the volunteer who took some action resulting in injury had a duty to act at all. In addition, who may be held liable can vary. Depending on the circumstances, the volunteer, the organization for whom the volunteer works, the volunteer's sponsoring organization, or all three can be held liable to the injured person. The various situations that may give rise to liability on the part of volunteers and/or organizations utilizing volunteers, and the protections that may be available to them, are explored in this chapter.

(a) What Is a Tort?

Volunteer liability is derived almost entirely from the category of wrongs in the law known as *torts*. A tort, although difficult to define precisely, can be understood generally to be a person's act or omission that causes reasonably foreseeable harm to someone to whom the person owed a duty. A tort is not a breach of contract or a crime. Rather, it is a civil wrong with three essential elements: a duty between two people, a breach of that duty, and reasonably foreseeable injury caused by the breach. There are virtually infinite variations on this basic concept. The types of wrongful conduct giving rise to the tort, the nature of the breach of duty, and the types of potential injury are widely varied.

(i) Types of Conduct

Many different types of errors, acts, and omissions can give rise to a tort. Examples of tortious conduct can include rear-ending another person's automobile; trespassing on another's property; striking or otherwise assaulting another person; publishing a false, defamatory statement about someone; arresting the wrong person; or telling a lie. This list, by no means exhaustive, is also expanding as the law continues to recognize new types of conduct as tortious. Many states, for example, provide that wrongfully discharging someone from employment, intentionally interfering with another's contractual rights, and intentionally inflicting emotional distress on another now constitute torts.

(ii) Types of Injury

The types of injury that can give rise to tort liability are also varied. Again, examples include physical, mental, or emotional injury; harm to real or personal property; economic harm; and injury to reputation.

(iii) Nature of the Breach

Finally, the nature of the breach of duty can be different. As explained further below, the conduct constituting the breach can be accidental when the person committing the breach acts with simple negligence. The tort may also result from grossly negligent or intentional misconduct.

(b) Liability of Individual Volunteers

Individual volunteers may be held liable for wrongful conduct only when the conduct constitutes breach of a duty the volunteer owed to the person harmed, the volunteer's conduct itself caused the harm, and the harm was reasonably foreseeable.

(i) Volunteer's Duty

A volunteer's duty toward a particular person will be defined by the scope of the volunteer's responsibilities. For example, a volunteer charged with transporting kidney dialysis patients for treatment assumes a duty to use reasonable care in transporting the patient safely. The volunteer would not, however, have a duty to provide medical care to the patient were an emergency to arise during transport. The volunteer may have a duty to attempt to obtain appropriate medical care, but not to provide the care itself. Similarly, a parent volunteer taking a class of schoolchildren on a field trip may have a duty to exercise reasonable care in ensuring the safety of the children on the class trip but would not have a duty to another group of children who happened to be visiting the same locale.

Volunteers should be careful not to take action outside the scope of their proper sphere of responsibilities. Where a volunteer, absent a duty, nonetheless assumes responsibility to take a certain action, the volunteer at that point assumes a duty to act carefully and not to make a situation worse. The volunteer transporting the dialysis patient, for example, does not have a duty to provide medical care to the patient, but if the volunteer were to attempt to do so, he or she could be held liable for any additional harm that might be caused, however unintentionally. Similarly, the parent volunteer on the field trip has no duty to children not in his or her care but could be held liable for attempting to assist a child outside the group if the child were harmed by the attempt.

(ii) Reasonably Foreseeable Injury Caused by Wrongful Conduct

Even where a volunteer's wrongful conduct is in breach of a duty, the conduct may still not constitute a tort. The conduct must cause an injury, and the injury must be a reasonably foreseeable result of the conduct.

As an example to illustrate this point, a volunteer driver could negligently fail to stop at a traffic light, thereby hitting another's rear bumper. This action constitutes wrongful conduct in breach of the volunteer's duty to operate the vehicle safely. Whether the conduct constitutes a tort for which the volunteer can be held liable, however, will depend on whether there is foreseeable injury caused by the wrongful conduct.

Sometimes these issues of injury, foreseeability, and causation are clear-cut. If the collision causes direct damage to the other car or any persons in or around the car, the volunteer will be liable. If the collision causes no damage to the car or to any persons in or around the car, the volunteer's act does not constitute a tort. While the volunteer's conduct was wrongful, it did not cause injury.

However, these issues may not always be so clear. For example, a volunteer's rear-end collision could cause no immediate injury to the other car or driver but be identified years later as contributing to a passenger's pathological phobia about riding in moving vehicles. While the volunteer's conduct was wrongful and may be linked in some fashion to another's mental injury, the volunteer might escape tort liability by showing that the wrongful conduct did not actually cause this injury, or was too remote in time, with too many intervening contributing factors.

Similarly, the collision could cause no injury to the car, driver, or passengers, but so frighten a child witnessing the accident from a nearby porch that the child would fall down the porch stairs. The child would have fallen because of what he witnessed, but his injury may not be considered a reasonably foreseeable result of a rear-end collision.

(iii) Exceptions

As explored further below, volunteers have various protections from liability even where their wrongful conduct has breached a duty and caused foreseeable harm to another. Depending on the organization for which the volunteer works and the state in which he or she volunteers, a variety of statutory and/or common law protections may shield the volunteer from liability.

(c) Liability of Organizations for Acts of Volunteers

Organizations utilizing or sponsoring volunteers may potentially be held liable for the acts of those volunteers in two ways. First, the organization may be vicariously liable, which means that it is liable solely because of its relationship with the volunteer, not on account of its own misconduct. Second, the organization may be liable for its own negligence or wrongful conduct, which ultimately resulted in the negligence or misconduct of the volunteer.

(i) Vicarious Liability

Vicarious liability is derived from the notion that an organization should be held responsible for what its employees or agents do in the scope of discharging their responsibilities for the organization. Originally, the doctrine applied only to employers and their employees, but it has since been expanded to other principal–agent relationships. Under this doctrine, often called *responde at superior,* the organization's liability is based not on its own conduct but on the fact that it exercises control over, or has some kind of "master–servant" relationship with, the person committing the wrongful act.

This doctrine of vicarious liability can be applicable to organizations utilizing and/or sponsoring volunteers. Where applicable, it can result in a sponsoring organization's liability even though the organization may have had nothing to do with the volunteer's actual misconduct and may in fact have taken adequate steps to prevent it. The organization may have sufficiently trained the volunteers and instructed them to use utmost care in performing their responsibilities. These precautions notwithstanding, the organization may be liable nonetheless for the volunteer's tortious conduct.

For example, if a hospital volunteer charged with transporting patients in wheelchairs fails to operate a chair correctly and causes the patient to fall, the hospital will be vicariously liable. This liability will attach even if the hospital initially screened the volunteers and conducted training in the use of wheelchairs.

Where an organization is held vicariously liable, its liability is not necessarily a substitute for the individual volunteer's own liability. Both the volunteer and the organization can be held jointly and severally liable. This means that the tort victim may elect to sue and/or recover from either the organization only, the volunteer only, or both. For example, where the hospital volunteer negligently allows the patient to fall from the wheelchair, both the hospital and the volunteer can be held liable. The patient can sue one or the other, or both.

In certain situations, it may not be clear which of two possible organizations can be held vicariously liable for a volunteer's tortious conduct. Where a volunteer's sponsoring organization is different from the organization where the volunteer is actually performing work, the question may arise as to which organization is liable for the volunteer's misconduct. The answer may be both but will in any event turn upon which organization, or the extent to which each organization, determines and authorizes the scope of the volunteer's responsibilities and directs the volunteer's work.

An important limitation on this doctrine is that an employer is not vicariously liable for an employee's actions that are not taken within the employee's authorized scope of employment. With respect to volunteers, therefore, the organization would not be vicariously liable for its volunteer's misconduct where the volunteer acts outside the scope of the volunteer work and responsibilities.

For example, an organization using volunteers to transport patients would be vicariously liable for a volunteer's negligence in a car accident occurring to or from the places of transport. If, however, after dropping off a patient, a volunteer had an accident while going to the grocery store, the organization would not be liable because such a detour was not within the volunteer's scope of volunteer responsibilities.

This limitation on vicarious liability historically meant that an employer could not be held liable for the intentional misconduct of its employees. The theory was that an employer never "authorized" intentional misconduct; it could never be considered within the scope of the employee's authorized responsibilities. The law, however, has gradually moved away from this protection. The prevailing view now is that vicarious liability extends even to intentional misconduct if it is done while an employee is discharging responsibilities in furtherance of the employer's business. In some cases, however, the employer may remain protected notwithstanding the fact that the conduct occurred during the employee's discharge of work-related responsibilities, if the employee's conduct is motivated wholly or largely by personal considerations.

For example, if a volunteer is distributing information about vaccinations and misrepresents some potential risks involved, the volunteer organization may be vicariously liable for resulting harm even if the volunteer's misrepresentation was intentional. The organization certainly did not authorize intentional misrepresentations, but the volunteer's wrongful conduct involved his authorized activities in furtherance of the organization's work.

On the other hand, if the volunteer intentionally punched someone in the face while performing his or her duties, the sponsoring organization may not be liable, since that kind of misconduct cannot be said to be in furtherance of the goal of disseminating medical information. As is evident even from this one example, however, these issues are not clear-cut and will often depend upon very specific details about the scope of the volunteer's work and the precise nature and motivations for the volunteer's actions.

(ii) Direct Liability

In addition to or instead of vicarious liability for its volunteers' wrongful conduct, an organization may be liable for any direct negligence of its own that may be traced to the volunteer's conduct. Where a volunteer has committed a tort, the organization may be found to have been negligent in recruiting, selecting, training, supervising, instructing, or entrusting certain responsibilities to that volunteer. For example, in the case of the hospital volunteer accidentally allowing the patient to fall, the hospital may be vicariously liable for the volunteer's negligence but could also be liable directly for failing to instruct the volunteer adequately in the skills necessary to operate a wheelchair safely or in entrusting this task to a volunteer not physically suited to it. Similarly, where the volunteer intentionally pushes the patient, the hospital might not be vicariously liable for the malicious conduct of its volunteer but could be directly liable for its own negligence in failing to check the volunteer's background to ascertain a tendency toward violence.

In some situations, the organization may be held liable for a volunteer's wrongful act even if the volunteer escapes liability. Where a volunteer acts at the direct instruction of an employee of the organization and the act results in harm, the volunteer may be able to escape liability by showing that he did not know, and had no reason to know, that the act would cause harm. The organization's employee, on the other hand, may have known, or should have known, that harm would result, and thus the organization will be held liable.

(iii) Exceptions

As with individual volunteers, there are certain statutory or common law rules that may protect certain kinds of organizations from liability. For example, some states do not hold charitable organizations directly liable for negligence in conducting such activities as recruiting, screening, and training volunteers. In addition, subject to certain exceptions explained further below, the organization vicariously liable for the acts of its volunteers can assert the same defenses and protections as those available to the volunteer.

(d) Types of Legal Responsibilities and Liabilities

As mentioned above, one of the factors determining whether and to whom liability will attach is the type of conduct at issue. There are three categories of misconduct that would typically apply to the acts of volunteers.[1]

(i) Negligence

Tort liability for negligence arises when a person's breach of the duty owed another results from failing to use reasonable care. The person does not intend to cause harm but could have and should have been more careful in his or her actions or omissions. For example, a volunteer who gives a nursing home patient the wrong dose of medicine after having hastily misread the prescription might be liable in negligence for any harm caused. The volunteer did not administer the wrong dose purposefully, nor did he or she fail altogether to check the prescription. Some

[1]There is a fourth category, strict liability, where liability attaches to certain activities regardless of any degree of negligence or fault. However, there are relatively few, if any, situations in which this principle would apply to a volunteer.

care was taken but not enough to be deemed "reasonable" under the circumstances.

(ii) Gross Negligence

Gross negligence involves a higher degree of culpability than simple negligence, requiring something more than merely making a mistake. The concept typically is defined as conduct exhibiting reckless disregard of probable harmful consequences. A person acting with gross negligence engages in highly unreasonable and dangerous conduct. The conduct is more extreme than ordinary inattention or lack of care but falls short of an actual malicious intent to cause harm. The volunteer administering medicine might be grossly negligent, for example, if he or she knew that an inaccurate dose would probably be harmful, did not know the required dose, yet did not bother to check the prescription. The volunteer did not actually intend to cause the patient harm, but his or her actions recklessly endangered the patient.

(iii) Intentional Misconduct

Intentional misconduct constitutes conduct that the individual knows will cause harm and intends to cause harm. A person liable for intentional misconduct can be said to have acted with malice.

(iv) Ramifications of Different Types of Misconduct

Most torts can involve any of these three types of conduct. A volunteer, for example, can cause a patient to fall from a wheelchair by acting negligently, with gross negligence, or intentionally.[2] The demarcation between these three levels of culpability can be important for several reasons.

First, as explained above, an organization may not always be held vicariously liable for the grossly negligent or intentional misconduct of its volunteers. Unlike in the negligence context, liability will depend on the particular circumstances of each case. In addition, most insurance policies carried both by individuals and by organizations cover negligent conduct only. Many statutory protections available to volunteers also apply only to acts of simply negligence, not to gross negligence or intentional misconduct. In the same vein, the statutes that substitute governmental liability for that of individual volunteers typically cover negligence only.

Second, the type and amount of damages for which the volunteer or organization may be liable will vary depending on the type of wrongful conduct. Negligence and gross negligence usually give rise only to compensatory damages (the amount of money or other type of payment necessary to compensate a person for injuries).[3] These damages are not limited simply to easily calculable amounts such as medical bills or lost wages. They can also be awarded for indeterminate injuries such as pain and suffering or loss of reputation. All of these types of damages, though, are awarded with the goal of compensating the tort victim for actual harm suffered.

[2] There are a few torts that do by definition require intentional misconduct. For example, a necessary element of fraud or the intentional infliction of emotional distress is a showing of malicious intent.

[3] There are exceptions to this, of course, since the boundaries between negligence, gross negligence, and malice are not always clearly defined. There are certainly inconsistencies in the manner in which damages are awarded in the courts. The distinctions between these three levels of culpability, therefore, are statements, of general principles only.

Intentional or malicious misconduct, on the other hand, can result in the award of punitive damages. Rather than seeking to compensate the tort victim for the injury, punitive damages are geared toward punishing the wrongdoer and deterring others from committing the same tort. The amount of punitive damages can be quite high, sometimes bearing little or no relation to the amount of compensatory damages awarded, although some states have enacted statutory caps on the permissible amount of punitive damage awards. Again, neither insurance policies nor statutory protections typically cover punitive damages.

(e) Standards of Care for Negligence

Although issues involving gross negligence or malice may arise from time to time with volunteers, the question of what constitutes negligence is most often of the greatest importance. Ensuring that volunteers exercise that degree of care required to escape liability for negligence will protect against most tort litigation.

(i) General Standard

The concept of negligence assumes a departure from some uniform standard of behavior. It is based essentially on a notion of what a reasonable person would know and do under a given set of circumstances. The "reasonable person" standard is for the most part objective. Whether a person was negligent does not depend on what that particular person or some other particular person actually knew and actually did in a particular situation. Rather, the inquiry is what a hypothetical reasonable person of ordinary intelligence and common sense would know and do in the same situation.

For example, if a hospital volunteer fails to call for medical assistance when a patient begins gasping for breath, the volunteer will not necessarily escape liability simply because he or she really had no idea that the patient was in distress. Rather, the inquiry will be whether a reasonable person would have or should have realized the patient's distress and called for help.

By the same token, a volunteer will not be held to a higher standard of care based on specialized knowledge, skills, or training. The volunteer faced with the patient grasping for breath would not be held liable in negligence for failing to administer emergency medical assistance. The volunteer organization, however, should be careful not to place volunteers in situations where such specialized knowledge or skill is needed, because liability for negligent failure to train or supervise its volunteers adequately might result. In addition, volunteers should be careful not to take actions requiring such specialized knowledge; they could be liable for unreasonable conduct in attempting to act outside their legitimate sphere of knowledge and/or responsibility.

(ii) Children as Volunteers

There are some exceptions to the reasonable person standard of behavior. A child who commits a tort will not be held to the same objective standard applied to adults in assessing liability. The rationale against application of the reasonable person standard is that children do not have, and should not be expected to have, the same capacity to appreciate and understand risks and to know what to do in response to them. Thus, a child's misconduct is evaluated not against the conduct of a hypothetical reasonable adult but against a view of what that particular child, given his or her age, intelligence, and experience, should be expected to know and do. The standard is far more subjective, taking the particular traits of the individual child into account.

For example, in the case of a volunteer witnessing the hospital patient gasping for breath, if the volunteer has not reached the age of majority the liability inquiry would focus on what that particular child volunteer could be expected to know and do under those circumstances. This assessment would examine what could appropriately be expected of other children of similar age, experience, and intelligence. Could that child be expected to have appreciated the risk and known what to do about it?

Because the standard applied to children is more subjective and less stringent, child volunteers may escape liability under circumstances in which adult volunteers would be held liable. For example, had the hospital volunteer administering medicine not yet reached the age of majority, the volunteer might not be held liable by showing that he or she did not understand or appreciate the risks involved in taking the wrong amount of medication.

Organizations using child volunteers, however, should be extremely careful about entrusting them with responsibilities beyond their capabilities, or placing them in situations where they cannot be expected to understand and appreciate anticipated risks and appropriate responses. Where injury results from the negligent or otherwise wrongful conduct of a child volunteer, even though the child may not be liable, the organization may be held responsible for negligent entrustment, supervision, training, and so on.

(iii) Professionals as Volunteers

The objective reasonable person standard is also not applied to licensed professionals under certain circumstances. While children are held to a lesser standard of care than adults, professionals such as lawyers, doctors, nurses, accountants, engineers, and architects are held to a higher one in situations involving their areas of specialized knowledge, training, and skills. Rather than being expected to know and do what an ordinary person of ordinary intelligence would do, they are obligated to exercise the degree of skill and care imposed by the standards of their particular profession. The rationale is that if certain persons undertake to perform functions requiring specialized knowledge and skills, the law requires them to meet a minimum standard of such knowledge and skill levels.

Professional volunteers, however, will be held to this higher standard only for volunteer work involving their area of expertise. For example, a volunteer building contractor would be judged by the standards of his profession for injury caused by a faulty construction but would be subject only to the reasonable person standard in volunteering to tutor disabled children.

14.2 VOLUNTEERS' IMMUNITIES AND DEFENSES FROM SUIT AND LIABILITY

Volunteers and their sponsoring organizations are not wholly without protections from liability. States have enacted statutes that in some cases expressly establish certain immunities for volunteers specifically, and in other instances provide broader protections that can apply to volunteers. In addition, there are several defenses originally created by the common law that can shield a volunteer from liability.

Volunteers and organizations should bear in mind, however, that at best, these immunities and defenses prevent injured persons from obtaining judgments against them; they do not necessarily prevent injured persons from bringing suit. Volunteers and organizations will in many cases still have to bear the cost of defending against lawsuits. In evaluating insurance policies, therefore, volunteers and organizations should be careful to ascertain whether coverage includes defense costs as well as judgments.

(a) Statutory Protections for Volunteers

The precise statutory protections available to volunteers will necessarily vary from state to state. The range of possibilities that may be available are identified in this section, but volunteers should check the actual laws in effect in the state in which they volunteer.

(i) Volunteers in State Government

States historically have been protected from liability and lawsuits by the ancient common law doctrine of sovereign immunity. Originating from the old maxim in English law that "the king can do no wrong," this doctrine in its purest form essentially bars anyone from suing a state for any harm. The harshness of this rule, however, has resulted in its gradual erosion in most states.

One of the most significant and widespread statutory inroads into the states' sovereign immunity has been the enactment of tort claims acts. These statutes typically eliminate the state's sovereign immunity from liability for the tortious acts of its agents and employees, and confer a corresponding immunity from such liability on those agents and employees. In other words, the state substitutes its own liability for that of its agents and employees. Many, if not all, state tort claims acts include the tortious acts of state volunteers within the scope of their protection.

The waiver of the state's immunity, with its correlative immunity conferred on state agents, employees, and in many cases volunteers, is usually limited in several respects. The tort claims statutes typically provide that the state waive its immunity only for the negligent acts of its employees and only for those acts or omissions taken within the scope of their public duties. The statutes also usually establish a cap on damages, extending the waiver of immunity only up to $100,000 or some other fixed amount.

The state agents and employees, therefore, are correlatively immune from liability only for negligent wrongdoing committed within the scope of their employment or public responsibilities. They can be sued for any grossly negligent or intentional misconduct, or negligent acts committed outside the scope of their public duties. They will not be liable, however, for any damages above the statutory cap; the fact that the state waives its immunity only up to $200,000, for example, does not mean that the state employee committing the tort will have to make up the difference should a judgment be in excess of $200,000.

As applied to volunteers, therefore, individual state volunteers may be protected by statute for any negligent acts taken within the course of their volunteer work.

The volunteer will remain liable for grossly negligent and/or intentional misconduct, and for tortious acts committed outside the authorized sphere of his or her responsibilities. The state agency for whom the volunteer works typically also will provide legal representation for the volunteer as long as there is no serious question about whether the volunteer was more than negligent or was acting outside the scope of his or her duties.

By the same token, state agencies utilizing volunteers will be liable for those acts for which the individual volunteers enjoy immunity. The agencies will not be able to assert sovereign immunity as a defense to lawsuits arising out of the negligent acts of their volunteers. The agencies' liability will be capped, however, by the statutory limits.

If there is an organization sponsoring the state volunteer, separate from the state agency, the immunity of the volunteer might also protect the sponsoring organization from vicarious liability. Because vicarious liability is derived solely from the liability of the organization's agent, where the volunteer is immune the sponsoring organization should not be held vicariously liable. However, organization may still be vulnerable to being sued directly for its own negligence in recruiting, screening, or training the volunteer if it is located in a state that recognizes such liability on the part of charitable organizations. The organization may also not be provided legal representation by the state agency.

(ii) Volunteers in Local Government

Most states have also enacted statutes applicable to local governmental bodies that are similar to state tort claims acts and apply to local government volunteers. These statutes typically provide that the local governments will provide representation and indemnity for governmental agents and employees for negligent acts taken within the scope of their duties, and that the local government will step in and assume liability for those negligent acts. Like state tort claims acts, the statutes do not protect employees from grossly negligent or intentional misconduct, and the governmental entities' liability typically is capped.

An issue that can arise in the local government context is precisely which local governmental bodies are covered by the applicable statute. Volunteers working for local governments, therefore, should ensure that their particular entity is actually included with the applicable statute's protection.

(iii) Volunteers in Community or Charitable Organizations

Community and charitable organizations, as well as their agent volunteers, historically enjoyed absolute immunity from liability. The rationale for this sweeping protection was that individuals donating to charities did so for the good of the beneficiaries of the charity, not to compensate tort victims. However, the courts, and in some cases state legislatures, have gradually eroded this immunity in most states. Some states have retained partial immunities, applicable only in certain limited situations, but the traditional broad protections afforded charitable organizations in the past are largely gone.

However, states have enacted statutes protecting the individual volunteers of charitable and community organizations. Some states provide that a volunteer is not liable for negligent wrongdoing to the extent that the sponsoring organization has insurance. Other states provide that volunteers are not liable beyond the limits of any personal insurance that they may have. Virtually no state, if any, offers statutory protection for acts found to be more than negligent but rather grossly negligent or intentional. The precise circumstances and scope of these statutory protections will vary, and volunteers and organizations should check their particular state laws.

(iv) Volunteers in Specific Organizations

As with charitable organizations, some states have enacted certain immunities applicable to volunteers in other kinds of organizations. Volunteers of emergency, medical care, and fire companies are common examples of these specific statutory immunities. Licensed physicians are another common beneficiary of "good samaritan" laws. These laws, as in the context of state and local government statutory protections, typically do not protect the volunteer from liability for grossly negligent or intentional misconduct but do insulate him or her from liability for simple negligence. The immunities offered may also be affected by any applicable insurance. Again, however, volunteers and organizations must check the specific laws in their individual states.

(b) Nonstatutory Legal Defenses Available to Volunteers

In addition to statutory immunities, the common law also offers certain protections from liability for volunteers. There are basically four possible common law defenses, although not all are available in all states.

(i) Waiver

Volunteers may act affirmatively to provide themselves with some level of protection from liability under a principle known as *waiver*. As applied to volunteers, the concept is that the persons in receipt of the volunteer's services agree that the volunteer will not be held liable for any harm resulting from the volunteer's tortious conduct. The recipients of the services essentially waive their right to compensation from the volunteer for any harm that he or she may cause.

This is not a statutory protection, nor is it automatically conferred upon volunteers by the common law. Rather, it is a protection that can be conferred by contract only. Thus the parties involved—the volunteer and the recipients of the volunteer services—must affirmatively agree upon this waiver and should memorialize that agreement in a written contract. To be valid and effective, this contract should be executed prior to the rendering of services. The volunteer's sponsoring organization may also be a party to this waiver, thereby protecting the organization from vicarious liability.

The precise nature of the waiver may vary depending on the type of service being rendered and the scope of the protection agreed upon. The waiver should provide essentially that the parties know and understand that the volunteer is going to provide certain services and that the recipients of those services agree to hold the volunteer harmless for any possible negligence arising out of the provision of services. This principle of "holding harmless" typically means that the recipients agree not to sue or otherwise seek to hold the volunteer liable for any negligence and resulting harm. The protection can be broader, however, depending on the exact language of the waiver.

For example, the recipients of services can agree not only to forgo their own lawsuits against volunteers but also to pay any judgments against volunteers obtained by third parties who were somehow affected by their negligence. The broadest hold-harmless clauses may even agree to pay volunteers' legal costs in defending against other lawsuits. Thus, in the case of a volunteer organization placing volunteers in a hospital, for example, the waiver could take several different forms. The hospital may agree simply not to sue the volunteers or the organization. Alternatively, the hospital may agree that if the volunteer or organization is sued by a patient, it will pay any judgment resulting from the suit and/or the volunteer's defense costs arising out of the suit.

There are some limitations to bear in mind with respect to this legal defense. First, waivers do not typically cover gross negligence or malice and may not be considered valid if they attempt to do so. Second, the waiver protects the volunteer and sponsoring organization only to the extent that it clearly and expressly so provides. Disputes may arise as to exactly what volunteer conduct is covered by the waiver or whether legal fees expended in defending against a lawsuit should be paid. Volunteers and sponsoring organizations should be careful, therefore, to ensure that the language of the waiver is as clear as possible and that they have completely understood exactly what they are and are not protected against.

(ii) Assumption of Risk

Volunteers may also be protected from liability by the common-law doctrine of assumption of risk. In contrast to the waiver, this is not a protection for which a volunteer need obtain express agreement from the recipient of the volunteer services; rather, a plaintiff's assumption of risk is deemed by the law to be implied in certain situations. The doctrine can, however, be used to support the validity of a waiver to which the parties have expressly agreed.

Assumptions of risk is based on the idea that a person should not be liable for negligent harm to another if that other person knew and understood the risk of harm, but nonetheless went ahead with the activity that resulted in the harm. The victim's voluntary assumption of a known risk essentially relieves the wrongdoer of a duty to the victim he otherwise would have had.

The defense requires the presence of three elements: the person assuming the risk must know of the risk; he or she must understand and appreciate the nature of the risk; and he or she must choose to incur that risk freely and voluntarily. The standard is subjective, inquiring into whether the particular person harmed knew about, appreciated, and voluntarily incurred the risk. If, because of age, experience, intelligence, or other factors, the person harmed did not appreciate a risk that a hypothetical reasonable adult would have, the defense may not apply.

In certain situations, therefore, volunteers may escape liability for negligently causing harm by showing that the recipient of the volunteer services assumed the risk of harm in receiving the services. For example, a volunteer organization sponsoring a carnival may escape liability for injuries caused by a roller coaster by asserting assumption of risk. Persons riding on the roller coaster may be shown to have known about and understood the inherent risk of such an activity and to have incurred that risk voluntarily.

Issues may arise regarding whether and the extent to which people actually knew about, appreciated, and consented to a risk, and precisely which risks they thereby assumed. For example, the organization sponsoring the carnival, although not liable for injuries caused by the roller coaster itself, may be liable for injuries traceable to negligent operation of the roller coaster by a volunteer who was intoxicated. The people riding the roller coaster assumed the risk of the dangers inherent in roller coasters, but they may not have known of or consented to the operation of the roller coaster by an intoxicated volunteer. Similarly, if a volunteer organization were to take a group of developmentally disabled adults to a picnic where there was a fireworks display and someone was injured, the liability of the organization would depend upon such issues as whether their clients were capable of understanding and appreciating the inherent risk of fireworks and/or whether they were free to leave if they did not want to incur that risk.

The assumption of risk defense is not popular, and some states have carved away at it, leaving in some cases virtually no such defense at all. In most states it is still viable, at least to a limited extent. However, even where still viable it is a defense to negligence only, never to intentional misconduct.

(iii) Contributory Negligence

Contributory negligence is another absolute defense, barring any liability on the part of the wrongdoer. Many states have abandoned this doctrine in favor of comparative negligence, as discussed below. In contrast to assumption of the risk where the wrongdoer is relieved of his or her duty toward the tort victim, contributory negligence is applicable where the wrongdoer had a duty and negligently breached that duty toward the injured party but the injured party's own negligence contributed to the resulting harm. Where both parties were negligent, the injured party's negligence negates the liability of the primary wrongdoer.

For example, if a volunteer organization sponsors an event at a location, negligently fails to clear away snow and ice, and a person attending the event falls, the organization may escape liability for its negligence if the injured person was running on the ice. The organization was negligent, but the injured person's own negligence contributed to the injury and thus prevents recovery. Similarly, if a volunteer driver negligently drives too fast, he or she may nonetheless escape liability for hitting a pedestrian if the pedestrian darted suddenly into traffic against the traffic signal. Like assumption of the risk, this defense must be proven by the volunteer who is asserting it; the injured party does not have the burden of disproving it. The defense may be unsuccessful if the injured party can show that notwithstanding his or her own contributory negligence, the volunteer had the "last clear chance" to avoid the accident or injury. For example, where the volunteer driver hits the errant pedestrian, he or she may be liable despite the pedestrian's own negligence if the pedestrian can show that the driver had enough time to stop but negligently failed to try.

(iv) Comparative Negligence

Because contributory negligence can result in harsh, unfair results, many states have adopted comparative negligence in its stead. Rather than completely barring any recovery to an injured party who contributed only in part to the injury, or forcing the other wrongdoer to bear the entire cost of an accident for which he or she was only partly to blame, comparative negligence attempts to apportion fault and responsibility equitably and to award damages accordingly. Only about 10 states still have not adopted any form of comparative negligence. Many states have enacted the doctrine legislatively and others have done so by judicial fiat.

There are essentially two forms of comparative negligence: pure and modified. Pure comparative negligence simply awards damages in direct proportion to fault. Where there are several wrongdoers causing the same harm, each wrongdoer will be responsible for that portion of the harm that he or she actually caused. Where both plaintiff and defendant are injured, each will compensate the other for that portion of the other's injuries attributable to his or her own negligence. For example, if a volunteer driver's negligence contributes in part to an accident, he or she will be liable only for that portion of the other party's injuries traceable to the volunteer's negligence.

Although on balance far more equitable than contributory negligence, this doctrine of pure comparative negligence can result in certain distortions. For example, it can result in a situation where the person primarily at fault may receive greater compensation from the party only slightly responsible for the accident, when the person primarily at fault sustains more severe injuries.

Modified comparative negligence, on the other hand, awards the injured party damages only where his or her negligence was less than, or in some states no more than, equal to the other wrongdoer's negligence. If both parties are injured, therefore, probably only one will recover damages.

The effect of comparative negligence on the joint and several liability of multiple wrongdoers varies. In some states all wrongdoers will remain both jointly and severally liable to an injured party who did not contribute to the accident. For example, in these states, if a passenger in a volunteer driver's car is injured and did nothing to contribute to the accident, both the volunteer and any other negligent drivers involved in the accident may all remain liable in full to the passenger. The drivers will be responsible to one another only in proportion to their share of the blame, but they will all be liable for full compensation to the passenger. The passenger may elect to sue only one, some, or all of them. In other states, however, liability to non-negligent injured parties is individual only. This means that the volunteer driver would be liable to the passenger, as to the other drivers, for only that portion of the passenger's injuries attributable to the volunteer.

14.3 VOLUNTEER AS PLAINTIFF

(a) General Principles

Generally speaking, the avenues for recovery available to a volunteer injured in the course of volunteer work will be the same as those available to any other person. A volunteer injured by another volunteer, for example, would have the same ability to sue that volunteer as would any third party, subject to whatever immunities and/or defenses that particular volunteer possesses. Similarly, the volunteer may also be able to sue the sponsoring organization involved for direct or vicarious liability, again subject to whatever protections the organization would otherwise possess.

Volunteers seeking compensation through lawsuits should be careful to protect their rights in a timely fashion. Most states require that lawsuits be filed within three years of the date the injury occurred.

In addition to these general avenues of recovery available to any tort victim, there are a few other alternatives available to certain volunteers by virtue of their particular volunteer status.

(b) Insurance

Volunteers may have access to insurance coverage for injuries from various sources.

(i) Self-insurance

First, the volunteer always has the option of purchasing his or her own insurance. The exact terms and coverage of individual policies will vary, so volunteers electing this option should take care to obtain the type of coverage suited to the nature of their volunteer work.

(ii) Insurance of Organization

In addition, the organizations sponsoring or using volunteers may have applicable insurance coverage. In many states, for example, insurers who provide liability insurance to fire and rescue companies are required to offer coverage for the companies' volunteers. This does not mean that the fire and rescue companies are required to purchase it, but many do.

(c) Workers' Compensation

Most volunteers would not be covered by workers' compensation statutes, because they apply generally to individuals receiving compensation or renumeration for their work. There are some exceptions, however, so an injured volunteer should ascertain whether workers' compensation in the particular state does apply to his or her volunteer activities. Public school volunteer aides and volunteer fire and rescue workers are two examples of volunteers typically covered by worker's compensation statutes.

(d) Claims against State and Local Governments

A final alternative for state and local government volunteers may be a suit against the governmental entity for the wrongdoing of its agent or employee. Most tort claims statutes providing the right to sue the governmental entity, however, have strict time limitations for such a suit, often requiring the filing of an administrative claim within a six-month period. The volunteer contemplating such a lawsuit should therefore be careful to protect his or her rights within the applicable time frame.

SUGGESTED READINGS

Keeton, W. and W. Prosser. 1984. *Handbook of the Law of Torts,* 5th ed.

Volunteers and the Law in Maryland. 1989. Baltimore: Governor's Office on Volunteerism and the Bar Association of Baltimore City.

CHAPTER 15

BOARD MEMBER LIABILITY AND RESPONSIBILITY

Katharine S. Vargo
Risk Management Services Co.

15.1 Board Member Liability

15.2 Board Member Responsibility

References and Suggested Readings

15.1 BOARD MEMBER LIABILITY

Most liability claims filed against nonprofit organizations are the result of an accidental injury or property damage. However, sometimes claims are made against individuals—such as board members, officers, trustees, employees, and volunteers—who while acting on behalf of the organization, might have accidentally caused an injury or damaged another's property. Some claims against individuals allege negligence in managing the organization. Board members of a nonprofit organization may believe that the responsibilities associated with operating the organization do not hold the same weight as those of a for-profit organization. Those operating a nonprofit organization should be aware, however, that in some ways they will be held to a higher standard because of the trust they hold on behalf of those benefiting from the services offered (Bailey, 1989).

(a) Legal Duties

Board members of volunteer organizations must manage the organization with the same diligence and attention they would apply to a for-profit organization. Board members are bound by the legal duties of care, loyalty, and obedience to the organization. All duties must be performed in good faith and in the best interest of the organization.

(i) Duty of Care.

Directors and officers must act with the care that an ordinarily prudent person in a similar position under similar circumstances would exhibit. This duty extends to questioning and monitoring the activities of the organization, including financial matters, personnel issues, programs, use and maintenance of property, and planning for the future. Board members must actively resist matters they think are not proper.

(ii) Duty of Loyalty.

Directors and officers are required to place the interest of the organization above their own personal interests. They must avoid even the appearance of a conflict of interest and take no action that would be detrimental to the organization in order to benefit themselves or another party.

(iii) Duty of Obedience.

Directors and officers must perform their duties according to the organization's charter and mission and according to all applicable statutes and regulations governing charitable institutions. A board member may be held personally liable if found to have willfully or negligently permitted the organization to engage in activities beyond the organization's authority.

(b) Personal Liability

Board members can incur personal liability in several ways:

◆ For their acts, errors, or omissions for decisions made as a director of the organization

- By their status as a director; for example, being held responsible for the acts of an employee
- For legal fees and expenses necessary to defend themselves against claims

According to Tremper (1991), personal liability claims against board members and officers of nonprofit organizations arise primarily from employment-related activities. The most common claims are for wrongful discharge, discrimination, and other labor law violations. Employment-related claims are made by employees or former employees. However, other claims may be made by anyone inside or from outside the organization. Fortunately, the vast majority of these other types of claims are filed against the organization and only occasionally name the board members. Exhibit 15–1 provides examples of sources of exposure to a personal liability suit and examples of wrongful management claims that have been filed against nonprofit organizations.

(c) Board Member Indemnification

State laws allow organizations to limit the personal liability of its directors subject to general standards for directors' actions. This is done by including an indemnification clause in the organization's articles of incorporation bylaws. This clause will allow the organization to assume the cost of defense and judgment or settlement payments in the event that a claim is made against the director acting on behalf of the organization.

Most directors will insist on indemnification before they serve on the board. Directors should be aware that there are limits to the scope of indemnification. The organization may not have the funds available to pay defense and other costs, or there may be limits placed on the use of funds that prohibit paying legal fees associated with indemnification. The organization may be unable to indemnify certain acts, such as criminal acts or misappropriation of funds, if such acts are perceived as being against public policy. Personal liability for fines and punitive damages may not be indemnified because of the public interest in holding individuals responsible when they willfully violate established rules.

In most states an organization is not allowed to indemnify its directors and officers if it does not carry general liability insurance and directors' and officers' liability insurance. General liability policies cover some types of losses caused by directors, officers, employees, or volunteers. These policies typically pay if their action causes property damage or bodily injury to another party (Tremper and Babcock, 1990). A discussion of directors' and officers' liability insurance follows.

(d) Directors' and Officers' Liability Insurance

Directors' and officers' (D&O) liability insurance is often referred to as executive decision-making insurance. D&O insurance is management or governance errors and omissions coverage that provides help in the event that a director or officer is accused of mismanaging the organization. It is essential if the organization has large investments, extensive programs or property holdings, or many employees or volunteers. Indemnification provides only limited protection for board members, and even though legislation in many states provides immunity, this does not prevent a lawsuit from being filed against the organization and its board members. Directors' and officers' liability insurance can provide a source of funds to cover legal costs

---

◆ EXHIBIT 15–1   Potential Claimants and Wrongful Management Claims

---

Potential claimants

1. The organization itself. The administrators of the organization may feel that a board member has been negligent in performing duties.
2. Other directors. One director may sue another for violation of duty to the organization.
3. Members may sue to protect their special interests.
4. Beneficiaries may claim that the services promised were not delivered or were delivered in an unacceptable manner.
5. Donors may sue claiming misuse of the donor's gift.
6. Outsiders may feel they have some how been harmed by the organization's activities.
7. The attorney general of the state may claim that the organization has been mismanaged.
8. Other government officials may find a violation of regulations.

Potential wrongful management claims:

1. Failure to preserve qualifications for tax exemption.
2. Exceeding authority granted by charter or bylaws.
3. Using funds granted for one purpose in another way.
4. Failure to act upon an apparent conflict of interest involving a board member.
5. Breach of employment contract.
6. Discrimination in membership standards.
7. Failure to administer medical programs properly.
8. Failure to maintain adequate financial records.
9. Oversight or error in conducting a major building program.
10. Failure to maintain educational standards.
11. Failure to pursue an insurance claim.
12. Failure to take effective steps to remove unsatisfactory personnel.
13. Unauthorized or imprudent loans or investments.
14. Failure to properly protect and safeguard the assets of the organization.
15. Excessive compensation paid to officers and employees.

---

and judgment and settlement fees associated with certain types of lawsuits naming board members as individuals. Many organizations purchase D&O insurance primarily to cover the defense costs of unwarranted claims.

For nonprofit organizations, it is not uncommon for D&O coverage to apply also to employees, volunteers, committee members, and to the organization itself (entity coverage). The administrator should ask for these extensions of coverage. D&O policies are very technical and singular in terms, conditions, definitions, and exclusions. It is very important that the organization be represented by a knowledgeable broker when shopping for D&O coverage. The broker should not only be familiar with the idiosyncrasies of D&O coverage but also have a good understanding of the organization he or she is representing to the carriers. By the time coverage is in force, the organization should have a clear understanding of the coverage benefits and limitations.

(e) Incorporating

Incorporating a nonprofit insulates the board members from personal liability. This will provide a barrier between the organization and the members that will protect them if they are sued for harm caused by others acting on behalf of the organization. An organization that is not incorporated is severely limited in its ability to indemnify its directors and officers.

(f) Volunteer Protection Laws

Many years ago the doctrine of charitable immunity shielded charitable organizations, directors, employees, and volunteers from responsibility for damage or injury occurring in the course of the organization's work. Over the years this doctrine has eroded in the courts. Most states have now passed volunteer protection laws that protect volunteers' personal assets to a certain degree; however, the laws differ widely in terms of which volunteers they protect and how much protection is provided. Furthermore, such laws do not place limits on all types of claims. Suits alleging intentional misconduct or violations of federal laws on employment, civil rights, taxes, and a variety of other matters are unaffected, and civil courts still tend to find a way to compensate injured parties.

Lawsuits against volunteers are usually based on injuries resulting from negligence. In legal context, negligence means not acting with the care that a reasonable person would use in similar circumstances. Volunteer protection laws bar lawsuits based on negligence, and suits cannot be filed unless harm results from something more than negligence. These laws change the standard to gross negligence, recklessness, or willful or wanton misconduct. Exhibit 15–2 provides a schedule of state volunteer protection laws prepared by the Nonprofit Risk Management Center in Washington, D.C. This schedule shows the standards for each state with special volunteer protection laws. Aside from using different liability standards, volunteer protection laws also differ in the scope of their application and the conditions they impose. Most apply to volunteers of any nonprofit organization, but as the schedule shows some are limited to volunteers from charitable or social welfare organizations. Other laws require that the organization itself be insured, and some limit recovery to the amount of insurance the volunteer has available.

As shown in the schedule, many states have separate laws for various types of volunteers. Most states provide the greatest protection to directors and officers. Twenty states also provide special rules for sports volunteers. Volunteers working in emergency situations may be protected by good samaritan laws (Nonprofits' Risk Management and Insurance Institute, 1991). Despite these laws, the nonprofit manager would be wise to understand that state statutes contain undefined terms and significant loopholes that can be used to the plaintiff's advantage. As Tremper (1991) tells us, enactment of state volunteer protection laws has had little effect on protecting volunteer organizations and their board members for the following reasons:

- ◆ Protection applies only to volunteers' personal liability; the liability of the organization itself is not affected.

◆ EXHIBIT 15–2   State Volunteer Protection Laws

Volunteer Protection Laws

State	Directors and Officers Org.	Std	Conds	Volunteers Generally Org.	Std	Auto Ex.	Conds	Sports Y/N
Alabama	●	W		●	W			
Alaska	○	GN						
Arizona	●	GN						
Arkansas	●	GN		○	GN	i	i,X	Y
California	○	GN	I					
Colorado	●	W		●	W			Y
Connecticut	●	R						
Delaware	●	GN		●	GN	i		
D.C.	●	W	I-	●	W		I-	
Florida	●	R						
Georgia	●	W		●	W			Y
Hawaii	●	GN						
Idaho	●	W		●	W			
Illinois	●	W		○	W			Y
Indiana	●	GN						Y
Iowa	●	W		●	W			
Kansas	●	W	I	●	W		I,i	Y
Kentucky	●	W		●	W			
Louisiana	●	W		●	W			Y
Maine	●	GN		●	GN			
Maryland	●	GN	I	●	GN		I,i	Y
Massachusetts	○	W						Y
Michigan	●	org. can amend articles						
Minnesota	●	R		●	R			Y
Mississippi	●	GN		●	GN	Y	X	Y
Missouri	●	GN		●	GN		X	
Montana	●	W		●	W			
Nebraska	●	W						Y
Nevada	●	GN		●	W			Y
New Hampshire	○	W		●	GN	Y		Y
New Jersey	●	GN		●	GN	Y		Y
New Mexico	●	R						Y
New York	○	GN						
North Carolina	●	R		●	GN	Y	i	
North Dakota	●	GN		●	GN	Y		Y
Ohio	●	W		●	W			
Oklahoma	●	GN						
Oregon	●	GN						
Pennsylvania	○	GN		○	GN	Y		Y
Rhode Island	●	W		●	W	Y		Y
South Carolina	○	R		○	GN			
South Dakota	●	W		●	W	Y		
Tennessee	●	GN						Y
Texas	○	R		○	R	i	i	
Utah	●	W	X	●	W	y	I	
Vermont	●	R						
Virginia	●	W						
Washington	●	R						
West Virginia	●	R						
Wisconsin	●	W		●	W	Y		
Wyoming	●	GN		●	GN			

Org (Type of Organization)
● Most nonprofits
○ Certain nonprofits (at least charitable)

Std (Liability Standard)
W Willful/Wanton
R Recklessness
GN Gross Negligence

Conds (Conditions)
I Only if organization is insured
i Liability limited to insurance
X Significant limitations apply

Auto Excl.: Does not apply to motor vehicle accidents.
Sports: Y for "yes" only if there is a law specifically for sports volunteers.

March 1994

This table is based on **State Liability Laws for Charitable Organizations and Volunteers** by the Nonprofit Risk Management Center, 1001 Connecticut Avenue, NW, Suite 900, Washington, DC 20036, 202-785-3891. Copies may be purchased for $12.50 plus $3.00 shipping and handling. Substantial quantity discounts are available for copies to be distributed to association members, affiliates, or clients.

Source: Reprinted with permission from the Nonprofit Risk Management Center, Washington, D.C.

◆ The laws do not limit liability under federal statutes, including civil rights, labor, and tax provisions.

◆ Claims can still be filed, requiring a legal defense and imposing associated costs regardless of who wins.

◆ The new standards of gross negligence, recklessness, and willful or wanton misconduct may not reduce liability significantly in practice.

◆ The constitutionality of the laws has not been tested (although in most states the possibility of invalidation is slight).

◆ Lack of uniformity across states undermines statistical assessment of the laws' effects on claims.

Volunteer protection laws do not reduce the need for D&O insurance because they do not protect the organization, they do not stop lawsuits from being filed, and they do not bar the most common types of employment-related claims (Tremper, 1991).

Several nonprofit associations continue to call for initiatives to establish a uniform standard limiting volunteer and board member liability that can be adopted by all states. Tort reforms are still being tested in the courts. It is hoped that in the long run these reforms will help nonprofits attract talented and qualified people to provide service to volunteer organizations.

15.2 BOARD MEMBER RESPONSIBILITY

Relying on indemnification, immunity statutes, and insurance for protection against personal liability losses is secondary to the board member's responsibility to manage actively with the intent to prevent all types of losses. After carefully reviewing the organization, directors of nonprofits often find that they have more risks to manage than does a for-profit organization. Nonprofits have risks associated with financial matters, employee relations, outreach programs, volunteers, funding sources, and government regulations, just to name a few. The responsibility of the board extends far beyond program concerns, to the daily operations of the organization. Other responsibilities of the board include:

◆ Ensuring a safe environment for employees, volunteers, and beneficiaries

◆ Reducing the anxiety and fear of liability of employees and volunteers

◆ Conserving the assets of the organization so that it can pursue its mission

◆ Ensuring compliance with legal requirements

◆ Ensuring that individuals harmed by the organization's activities receive adequate compensation (Tremper and Babcock, 1990)

Charitable organizations should develop and follow loss prevention guidelines that will help protect the organization and limit the liability of board members, employees, and volunteers. Loss reduction efforts may be an important factor in defending a lawsuit which alleges that the organization was negligent in its management, employment, or volunteer practices. Loss control programs should be part of the system of internal controls of the organization.

Most insurance carriers can provide guidelines for property maintenance and accident prevention. However, loss prevention techniques apply to far more than preventing fires, slips, or falls. Board members find that they are responsible for controlling the actions of employees and volunteers and all the various facets of a nonprofit program. Guidelines for several risks particularly troublesome for volunteer organizations—board liability, volunteer and employee liability, and vehicle liability—are provided below.

(a) Loss Prevention Techniques: The Board

Because everything the board does is subject to scrutiny, and because the primary role of the board is to lead and direct the organization, the board should start its development of loss control programs by taking an objective look at its role in the organization.

- ◆ The board should be of manageable size to be able to perform its role. Keep it small.
- ◆ The board must hold regular meetings and members must regularly attend the meetings.
- ◆ Minutes of board meetings should be prepared to reflect the board's decisions, including the facts on which they are based.
- ◆ The board must maintain its independence from management.
- ◆ The board should insist on timely communications and regular reports from administration on the organization's finances, budgets, programs, membership, personnel policies and practices, fund raising, pending litigation, and claims.
- ◆ The board should obtain independent legal and financial assessments of the organization.
- ◆ The board should perform a periodic assessment of its activities to evaluate whether it is meeting the challenges it faces running a volunteer organization in today's business and legal environment.
- ◆ The board should inform new board members of their duties and the mission of the organization, and provide them with historic, financial, operational, and program information.

(b) Loss Prevention Techniques: Employment Practices

Since the majority of nonprofit D&O claims arise out of employment-related practices such as wrongful termination, harassment, and discrimination, employment practices are important issues for a nonprofit organization. Although employment practices obviously apply to employees, it is wise to apply the same practices to volunteers. The organization may be accused by both employees and volunteers of discrimination, harassment, or wrongful termination. Management should be well informed about current legal standards related to employment practices. The standards concerning harassment, discrimination, and termination have changed over recent years and other standards are likely to increase in importance over time. In-house training sessions, informational material, and detailed employment procedural manuals should be used to improve the sensitivity and knowledge of all management employees (Bailey, 1989).

To reduce employment-related claims, the organization should develop the following practices (here, the term *employee* also refers to volunteers):

◆ Do not wait until an employee has been on the job for several months before reviewing performance. Many performance deficiencies are apparent in the first few weeks of employment. Manage employee performance from the employee's first day on the job.

◆ Provide all employees with a written job description.

◆ All employees should have a copy of the personnel policy and guidelines.

◆ Grievance procedures should be easy to understand, independent, and confidential.

◆ Include employees in discussions related to the design and expectations of their jobs.

◆ Review performance on a regular basis.

◆ Provide training on a regular basis.

◆ Initiate corrective actions when performance begins to fall off.

◆ Document each performance slip and actions taken to correct.

Many organizations, for-profit and not-for-profit, often feel paralyzed when faced with a difficult personnel situation. Remember that fear of taking corrective actions may result in greater harm to the organization than would making a responsible decision to correct a problem.

(c) Loss Prevention Techniques: Employees and Volunteers

Organizations may be held liable for the wrongs committed by their employees and may also be liable for wrongs, damages, and injuries resulting from the actions of volunteers. One of the best ways to reduce liability in volunteer organizations is to select and manage volunteers with the same care as employees. The following guidelines are written for volunteers but also apply to employees.

◆ All volunteers should complete an application that contains work or volunteer experience, education, and references.

◆ Establish a set of minimum qualifications.

◆ All volunteer applicants should be interviewed.

◆ After selecting potential volunteers, contact references and document the date, time, and information provided by the person providing the reference.

◆ If the volunteer will be working with people who would be vulnerable to abuse (children, the elderly) the organization must conduct a criminal background check. Contact local authorities for procedures.

◆ Volunteers should have a job description and understand the requirements and limits of the job.

◆ Volunteer activities should be monitored and reviewed on a regular basis.

◆ All volunteers should receive job training. While many volunteer positions require low-level skills, many other positions require very specific procedures that could be harmful if not followed closely.

(d) Loss Prevention Techniques: Vehicles

The remainder of this chapter concentrates on loss control for vehicles used in the organization's business. The volunteer board and managers may wonder why so much emphasis is placed on the board's responsibility to control vehicle losses. The first reason is because the potential for loss is so great both in terms of serious injury to driver and passengers and in terms of the potential for enormous financial loss for the organization. Next, insurance companies often express their concern with nonprofit organizations that use volunteer drivers. They are concerned about the driving records of volunteers, driver training, the number and types of passengers, and the age of volunteer drivers. It is in the best interest of the organization to be able to show the insurance carrier that vehicle loss control is a top priority.

In many volunteer organizations, employees and volunteers drive on company business. They might drive vehicles owned by the organization or they might drive their own vehicles. Each situation presents a unique exposure for both the driver and the organization. Commercial auto insurance can cover volunteers who drive vehicles owned by the organization. However, commercial auto coverage does not automatically cover volunteers driving their own vehicles on company business. Nonowned auto coverage is available for programs that have volunteers driving their own vehicles either by adding such coverage to the organization's vehicle liability policy or by purchasing separate coverage (see Chapter 16). This is secondary or excess coverage for the volunteer, which means that coverage will apply only after any other insurance, such as the volunteer's own vehicle liability policy, has reached its limit. An organization nonowned policy covering volunteer-owned vehicles is more readily available and much less expensive than trying to provide full coverage for volunteer-owned vehicles under the organization's insurance policy.

The organization must make it very clear to employees and volunteers that safe driving is a top priority, that the organization has strict criteria that must be met before anyone is allowed to drive for the organization, and that failure to meet these criteria or to meet safe driving standards will immediately prohibit an employee or volunteer from driving for the organization.

(i) Guidelines for Selecting Potential Drivers

◆ Obtain a motor vehicle record (MVR). MVRs can be obtained from the insurance carrier, broker, or Department of Motor Vehicles or local police departments:

Check that the driver has a valid driver's license

Check the driver's past driving record

◆ Do not allow anyone who has had *any* driving while under the influence (DUI) or reckless driving charges brought against them in the last five years to drive on behalf of the organization.

◆ Prepare an analysis of MVR violations to determine the number and type of violations that will prohibit an employee or volunteer from driving (Exhibit 15–3).

◆ Check driving records every six months during the driver's service with the organization.

(ii) Guidelines for All Drivers of Any Vehicle

◆ Provide defensive driving and passenger assistance training.

◆ Drivers must drive with care and obey all traffic laws.

◆ **EXHIBIT 15–3   Driver Selection**

Nonprofit organizations that use drivers—especially volunteer drivers—are always looking for benchmarks to help decide whether or not to accept a potential driver. A clean driving record is easy, but what about the applicant who once ran a stop sign? Or the potential volunteer with two speeding tickets? In some states, Hertz Rental Cars applies the following criteria to weed out dangerous drivers and protect its fleet. Compare your own rules to this list.

Hertz Rejection List

1. Have a suspended, revoked, expired, or otherwise invalid driver's license.
2. Have been convicted of drunk driving in the past 72 months.
3. Were at fault in two or more accidents in the past 36 months.
4. Have acquired eight points on your driving record in the past 24 months.
5. Have three or more convictions for moving violations within the past 36 months.
6. Reckless disregard for life or property within the past 46 months.
7. DWI/DUI within the past 72 months.
8. Three or more moving violations within the past 36 months.
9. Two or more charges from tickets within the past 36 months.
10. One or more accidents resulting in fatality or bodily injury.
11. Failure to report or leaving the scene of an accident within the past 48 months.
12. Operating a vehicle without insurance or a valid license within the past 48 months.
13. Permitting others to use vehicles without a license or insurance within the past 48 months.
14. Possession of stolen vehicle or use of a vehicle to commit a crime within the past 48 months.
15. Suspension, cancellation, or denial of a license within the state within the past 36 months.
16. Two or more incidents of failure to respond to fines.
17. Two incidents of insurance cancellations.

Source: Reprinted from Community Risk Management & Insurance, January 1994, with permission from the Nonprofit Risk Management Center, Washington, D.C.

◆ The driver and all passengers must wear seat belts. Children must be in car seats appropriate for their age.
◆ No one is allowed to drive while under the influence or with an open bottle of liquor in the vehicle.
◆ Drivers must report all accidents to the organization as soon as possible. The organization should provide procedures for reporting accidents (Exhibit 15–4).

◆ **EXHIBIT 15–4**   Vehicle Accident Reporting Procedures

---

1. Remain at the scene. Do not move the vehicles unless they present a safety hazard to others. Notify the police immediately. If someone is hurt, call for emergency medical service (EMS) immediately.
2. Gather accident information. Write down names, addresses, telephone numbers, and insurance company of persons involved. Write down the names, addresses, and telephone numbers of witnesses to the accident. Do not admit liability or fault.
3. Notify your supervisor as soon as possible. The organization's business manager is responsible for gathering information to submit to the organization's insurance carrier.
4. Accidents involving property damage must be reported within 24 hours. Accidents involving injury must be reported immediately.

- Use of an organization's owned vehicles should be limited to the organization's business. Do not allow employees or volunteers to borrow the organization's vehicles.

(iii) Guidelines for Employees or Volunteers Driving Their Own Vehicles on the Organization's Business

- The driver must have insurance coverage in place. Limits must be at least to the minimum standard required by state law. The organization could wisely choose to establish a higher limit that would provide greater protection for driver and passengers. Ask for proof of insurance.
- The vehicle must be in good shape. All parts essential for safety must be in working order: horn, lights, brakes, signals, tires, steering, windshield wipers, and so on. Ride in the vehicle to be certain that it is well maintained.
- Make it clear to employees and volunteers that their insurance coverage applies if they have an accident while on the organization's business. The organization's insurance will apply only to claims in which the organization is claimed to be negligent and possibly in excess of the driver's own insurance (if such coverage has been purchased).

(iv) Guidelines for Organization-owned Vehicle Inspection

- Inspect vehicles daily to be certain that all functions necessary for safety are in working order. All parts essential for safety must be in working order: horn, lights, brakes, signals, tires, steering, windshield wipers, and so on.
- Vehicles should receive regular preventive maintenance and a professional safety inspection.
- Keep inspection reports and maintenance records on file.

REFERENCES AND SUGGESTED READINGS

Bailey, Dan A. 1989. *Directors and Officers Liability Loss Prevention for Non-profit Organizations.* Warren, N.J.: Chubb & Son, Inc.

"Benchmarks." 1994. *Community Risk Management and Insurance* 3(1).

Kurts, D.L. 1989. *Board Liability: Guide for Nonprofit Directors.* New York: Moyer Bell Ltd.

Lai, Mary L., Terry S. Chapman, and Elmer L. Steinbock. 1992. *Am I Covered for . . . ? A Guide to Insurance for Non-profits,* 2nd ed. San Jose, Calif.: Consortium for Human Services, Inc.

Nonprofits' Risk Management and Insurance Institute. 1990. *State Liability Laws for Charitable Organizations and Volunteers.* Washington, D.C.: The Institute.

Nonprofits' Risk Management and Insurance Institute. 1991. *Answers to Volunteers' Liability and Insurance Questions.* Washington, D.C.: The Institute.

Studebaker, Dennis. 1994. "Are Your Volunteers Covered?—Drivers." *Community Risk Management and Insurance* 3(1).

Tremper, Charles R. 1989. *Reconsidering Legal Liability and Insurance for Nonprofit Organizations.* Lincoln, Nebr.: Law College Education Services, Inc.

Tremper, Charles R. 1991. *D&O . . . Yes or No?* Washington, D.C.: Nonprofits' Risk Management and Insurance Institute.

Tremper, Charles R. and George Babcock. 1990. *The Nonprofit Board's Role in Risk Management: More Than Buying Insurance.* Washington, D.C.: NCNB Governance Series.

CHAPTER 16

RISK MANAGEMENT STRATEGIES

Katharine S. Vargo
Risk Management Services Co.

16.1   Introduction to Risk Management

16.2   The Risk Management Process

16.3   Risk Management Techniques

16.4   Volunteers and Risk Management

16.5   Insurance for Volunteer Groups

References and Suggested Readings

16.1 INTRODUCTION TO RISK MANAGEMENT

Risk management is a common business management technique used to protect, conserve, and increase the assets of an organization. Risk management goes beyond protecting the obvious physical assets of an organization, but recognizes that all the resources and assets—volunteers, employees, investments, property, loyal clientele, goodwill—work together to make an organization operate successfully. The fundamental elements of a risk management program for a volunteer organization are described in this chapter, and an overview of the types of insurance coverages available and necessary to protect the organization are provided. The specific insurance needs of the volunteer organization should be discussed with an insurance agent or broker who specializes in insurance programs for volunteers and nonprofits.

In *Risk Management and Insurance for Nonprofit Managers,* Byron Stone and Carol North list the benefits that an effective risk management program offers to nonprofits.

- *Risk management encourages safe actions.* Volunteer and employee education is an important part of the risk management program. The well-trained person does the job better and thereby reduces risks to the organization. Safe actions protect the life and health of everyone concerned.
- *Risk management protects assets.* Basic to all effective risk management programs are methods for reducing the risk of devastating property loss.
- *Risk management conserves assets.* A major goal of risk management is getting maximum, but safe, use of equipment.
- *Risk management increases employee loyalty and productivity.* Huge corporations have found that it is good business to practice risk management and provide safety and health programs for their employees. When volunteers and staff can perform their duties without stopping to worry about their personal safety, productivity is increased and morale is improved.
- *Risk management may reduce insurance costs.* Insurance rates are computed on industry or group experience, but *experience credits* may be applied to individual organizations when they have an effective risk management program (1988).

16.2 THE RISK MANAGEMENT PROCESS

Risk management is an orderly process that carefully identifies and evaluates the variety of ways in which a loss could occur in an organization, and selects and implements the best methods of dealing with those losses consistent with the goals and objectives of the organization. Risk management should not be confused with insurance management. Purchasing insurance is only one part of the risk management process.

(a) Identifying Potential Losses

Identifying potential losses is a painstaking process worth the valuable time of an organization's administrator. The administrator will list potential sources of injury, threats to people's well-being, or situations that could jeopardize the assets of the organization, result in penalties or damage to the organization, or lead to a lawsuit. The administrator has several sources of information that can be used to identify major and minor potential loss sources. The administrator can conduct a physical inspection of the operation, use questionnaires to ask the staff and volunteers about exposures and hazards particular to their activities, and analyze flowcharts showing the flow of goods and services to identify potential bottlenecks, hazards, and liabilities. Discussions with administrators from similar organizations may help to identify losses from other sources. Financial statements can be used to identify major assets that should be protected. Records of prior losses and claims data and knowledge of safety regulations and codes can be very helpful in identifying loss exposures.

The administrator will look for potential losses in the following areas:

1. Property losses—buildings, contents, vehicles
2. Liability losses—potential for bodily injury or property damage to other people or property
3. Losses resulting from job-or service-related injuries or disease
4. Losses from fraud, criminal acts, and employee dishonesty
5. Death or disability of key people
6. Employee or volunteer benefits loss exposures
7. Board liability exposures

(b) Evaluating Potential Losses

After potential losses have been identified, the administrator should continue the risk management process by evaluating and measuring the impact of losses on the organization. This is done by estimating the frequency and severity of potential losses and classifying each loss as a particular exposure type (Exhibit 16–1). Frequency is the likelihood that a loss will occur. Workers' compensation and auto losses are often referred to as high-frequency losses; property damage losses are usually considered low-frequency losses. Severity is the size of the loss usually expressed in financial terms but should also be considered for the loss's effect on people and the working environment, including the physical health and emotional well-being of staff and volunteers and the consequence of loss of goodwill in the community.

◆ **EXHIBIT 16–1   Exposure to Potential Losses**

Exposure Type	Frequency	Severity
1	Low	Low
2	High	Low
3	Low	High
4	High	High

Frequency and severity are also important to estimate to determine the most appropriate techniques for handling the loss exposure. Small losses, even if somewhat frequent, would probably be handled out of the organization's operating budget. Large or unpredictable losses would require a combination of other techniques to handle the exposure. Severity of the loss is usually considered more important than frequency. A single catastrophic loss can destroy the organization. Considering the impact on the organization, preparing for such losses must be given a high priority. Further discussion of the various techniques for handling loss exposures follows.

16.3 RISK MANAGEMENT TECHNIQUES

After the administrator has determined the types, frequency, and severity of losses, the next step in the risk management process is to select and implement the most appropriate technique or combination of techniques to manage each exposure. These techniques are widely practiced by most organizations and include:

♦ Avoidance

♦ Retention

♦ Noninsurance transfers

♦ Loss control

♦ Insurance

(a) Avoidance

As a risk management technique, avoidance means the possibility of a loss is prevented in its entirety by not engaging in activities that present the risk of the loss. For example, a volunteer organization considering a new outreach program involving children might choose not to participate in this program because of the potential for abuse.

(b) Retention

Another technique for handling loss exposures is for the organization to assume all or part of the loss that results from a particular exposure. The organization can make a deliberate decision to retain a loss, or the decision may be unintentional if the organization is not aware of the possibility of the loss.

Retention may be used when there is no other way to handle the exposure. It is not unusual for an organization to discover that insurance carriers will not cover certain exposures and the organization is therefore forced to retain the exposure. This is common for sexual abuse exposures. The organization may exist to provide services to children and recognizes that the possibility of abuse exists in situations involving children and that a claim could be made against the organization. In this case the organization would probably retain the exposure and use other risk management methods to reduce the probability of loss.

Retention is also used when the worst possible loss may be small in terms of severity. Organizations often chose not to purchase physical damage on vehicles, thus retaining the loss. Retention is also used when losses are very predictable, such as workers' compensation losses. The organization may choose to retain part of the loss through deductibles or by self insuring the exposure. Deductible levels and self-insurance are usually determined by the financial condition and mission of the organization. A well-financed nonprofit organization my find that its donors or board of directors prefer to retain a certain portion of its losses in order to keep insurance premiums to a minimum. Other organizations may find that its board has no taste for large deductibles or self-insurance, and administration is required to insure the majority of its exposures.

(c) Noninsurance Transfers

Noninsurance transfers pass the consequence for a loss onto another party, usually by contracts, leases, indemnity, or hold-harmless agreements. Noninsurance transfers are useful because they can shift the burden of liability to another party, who may be in a better position to exercise control over hazardous situations. For example, if a Scout troop is using the organization's property to hold an event, the troop is in a better position than the organization to control activities occurring at the event. The troop would agree to be responsible for any losses that might occur during the event, including property damage and bodily injury. If the organization is named in a claim for injury or damages, the troop would be obligated by a hold-harmless agreement to arrange for defense of the organization and to make settlement payments. Be aware that indemnity agreements are useless if the other party is not covered by insurance for such losses or is otherwise financially unable to pay for the claim. As an extra precaution, the scout troop would provide proof of insurance to the organization (Exhibit 16–2).

Most organizations require participants in a program to sign a waiver or release that is intended to excuse the organization from responsibility for accidental injury, death, or property damage that might occur during the program. Waivers, releases, indemnification, and hold-harmless agreements can be useful but have limitations. The agreement may not be as tight as assumed when signed and may be subject to judicial interpretation. The injured party may claim not to have been aware that the document affected their legal rights. Also, the party agreeing to indemnify may not be financially able to defend the organization or may not have insurance in place that will cover contractual agreements. Some fear that such agreements reduce the incentive for an organization to monitor loss control. The same vigilance toward preventing losses should be in place regardless of who is believed to be responsible

---

◆ EXHIBIT 16–2   Certificates of Insurance

A certificate of insurance is a document issued by the insurance carrier, broker, or agent that simply indicates that an organization carries the particular kind of insurance and limits that is indicated on the document. An insurance certificate is issued when an organization is asked for proof of insurance. Any time the volunteer organization allows another party to use its facilities or hires a contractor, the organization should ask for a certificate of insurance. Without proof that the other party is insured, the volunteer organization could be taking on the obligation of providing coverage for both itself and the other party if an injury occurs. Certificates are quick and easy to obtain and they are free of charge.

---

for it. Because these agreements can obligate each party to very specific responsibilities, they should be drafted by legal counsel and reviewed by the organization's insurance carrier. Exhibit 16–3 provides an example of situations that call for indemnity, hold-harmless agreements, or waivers.

(d) Loss Control

Loss control refers to steps taken by the organization to reduce the possibility that a loss will occur and/or to reduce the severity of those losses that do occur. Driver training programs tend to reduce the frequency of losses. Sprinkler systems are designed to reduce the severity of loss from a fire. The organization considering an outreach program involving children would implement several loss control methods to reduce the likelihood of an abuse loss, such as checking references, obtaining a criminal background check, and having more than one adult in attendance.

The organization's loss control efforts are of great importance to the insurance carrier. The carrier wants to know if the organization is actively managing its risk, thus reducing the probability that a disaster will occur. Any organization will have an easier time finding good insurance coverage if it can document its efforts at loss control.

(e) Insurance

Purchasing insurance is considered the last technique used in developing a risk management program. All other methods should be analyzed and considered before insurance is put into place. Ideally, insurance should be used for losses that have a low probability of frequency of loss but a high probability of severity of loss. Insurance benefits the organization is several ways. If the organization has a loss, insurance will provide assistance to settle the loss in two ways:

1. As a source of recovery for injured parties. Injured parties can be either the organization or individuals.
2. To provide money for defense and payment of settlements or judgments.

◆ **EXHIBIT 16–3   Occasions to Consider Noninsurance Transfers**

When offering any classes or programs for children

When offering any medical treatment or exams

When taking any field trips

Any time when transportation is provided

When the organization's facilities, vehicles, or property are being used by others

When using another organization's facilities, vehicles, or property

Whenever a contractor or subcontractor does work for the organization on or off site

Whenever someone is driving his or her own vehicle on organization business

---

If, as the result of an automobile accident involving a volunteer, the organization is sued, the organization will want the security of knowing that it can survive if a judgment is rendered against it. Insurance also provides payment for property losses so that the property can be restored quickly and the organization can get back to work quickly. Insurance can protect the assets of individuals if they were to get injured or sued while working on behalf of the organization. Insurance also satisfies external demands placed on the organization by creditors, leaseholders, contractors, or government obligations. In addition to settling losses, insurance provides peace of mind for the board and administration. Uncertainty is reduced, which allows the organization to plan for the future. Finally, the insurance company can provide valuable services to the organization, such as settling claims, analyzing loss exposures, and providing loss control services.

(f) Which Risk Management Techniques Should Be Used?

Now that the administrator has gathered information on loss exposures and made an estimation of frequency and severity, how can this information be applied to the risk management process? A study of the matrix used to determine frequency and severity of potential loss exposures can be helpful to understand the vast array of potential exposures. Equally important is an understanding of management's commitment to loss control, the organization's budget and funding mechanisms, its taste for retaining a certain portion of a loss, and the level of comfort demanded by the board of directors. All of these factors taken into consideration will determine what combination of avoidance, loss prevention, retention, risk transfer, and insurance techniques will best protect the organization.

To succeed, there must be a strong commitment to risk management by the board of directors. The board must have a clear understanding of the benefits of a risk management policy and promote the fundamentals of risk management throughout the organization by insisting that everyone in the organization, from the chief executive officer to the occasional volunteer, be involved in implementing the policy (Tremper and Babcock, 1990). The commitment to risk management should be formalized in the board's minutes by adopting a risk management policy statement. An example of such a statement is provided in Exhibit 16–4. Insurance brokers and carriers also have samples available.

(g) Monitoring the Risk Management Program over Time

Once the risk management program is in place it must be monitored to determine if any changes are necessary to improve its effectiveness. It may be necessary to alter the assumptions made about potential losses and their place in the frequency and severity matrix. Monitoring also helps to determine if the risk management program has in fact had an influence on controlling or eliminating loss exposures and if any modifications are needed.

(h) Administering the Risk Management Program

In most volunteer organizations one person will have responsibility for the daily administration of the risk management program: processing claims, answering questions from volunteers, personnel, and insurance brokers, paying premiums,

---

◆ **EXHIBIT 16–4   Risk Management Policy Statement**

The volunteer management organization holds the safety, welfare, and health of its employees and volunteers as a high priority in all its operations. It is the objective of the organization to establish and maintain a risk management program that will achieve the following:

1. Preserve and protect the health and safety of employees, volunteers, beneficiaries, and the general public
2. Maintain the continuity of the mission of the organization
3. Preserve and maintain the property of the organization

This risk management policy is an intrinsic part of the organization's management policy and will govern judgment on matters of operations, personnel relations, and programs. It is the responsibility of all employees and volunteers to uphold this policy.

Source: Janet Lautenschlager, *Volunteering in the Workplace: How to Promote Employee Volunteerism* (Ottawa: Canadian Heritage, 1993). This publication is available free from the Voluntary Action Program, Canadian Heritage, Government of Canada, Ottawa, Ontario K1A 0M5, (613) 994-2255. Crown copyright reserved. Reprinted with permission.

maintaining insurance files, and so on. This person usually reports to the executive director or chief administrator of the program. In a small organization the executive director will be responsible for risk management. In a large organization the risk management function may be given to another management position. Very large organizations often will have a full-time position slated for a risk manager. Depending on the size of the organization, the person handling the risk management function will report directly to the board or to a manager with access to the board.

Tremper and Babcock (1990) acknowledge that there are often deep frustrations associated with implementing a risk management program. Developing risk management awareness may open the door to undiscovered opportunities, but it may also bring frustration when the most prudent choices are not available or the rewards are not immediately apparent. The principal benefit of risk management— reduced losses—may seem illusory, especially to the organization that has never been sued. Who can get excited because a bad thing that might have happened did not happen or happened in a way that was not as bad as it could have been? Nevertheless, risk management is a critical part of board responsibility.

16.4 VOLUNTEERS AND RISK MANAGEMENT

Legal precedent has established that an organization is responsible for the actions of its employees and volunteers. The legal doctrine of *respondent superior* holds that the "master," or organization, is responsible for the actions of its "servants," or employees or volunteers. It is likely that if a volunteer causes damage or an injury, the organization will be asked to participate in repairing the damages or providing compensation for the injury.

(a) Safety First

For this reason, many nonprofit organizations make risk management a cornerstone of their volunteer programs. The benefits Stone and North listed as resulting from an effective risk management program were itemized earlier in the chapter. The first item is that risk management encourages safe actions. Volunteer managers often worry that their volunteers will cause accidents. An organization that practices good risk management techniques will begin by finding the right kind of volunteers through carefully screening, training the volunteer to perform a job in a safe and efficient manner, providing detailed job descriptions, and supervising the volunteer to be certain that the work is performed correctly. The organization will do everything it can to prevent an injury to the volunteer, the beneficiary, or property. Safety becomes an integral part of the volunteer's activity.

(b) Indemnification

The volunteer may also worry about causing an injury and the possibility of a claim for damages against his or her personal assets. In addition to purchasing insurance, an organization may choose to indemnify its volunteers by agreeing to assume the risk. Most states are very permissive in the extent of indemnification allowed. Through indemnification the organization agrees to pay virtually any cost the volunteer may incur. Indemnification is useful for protecting the personal assets of volunteers, especially those serving on the board of directors, against judgments and other costs. If the organization agrees to indemnify volunteers for such expenses, the risk of personal liability is all but eliminated provided that the organization has sufficient resources to pay the expenses (Tremper and Kahn, 1992).

16.5 INSURANCE FOR VOLUNTEER GROUPS

(a) Presenting the Volunteer Organization to the Insurance Market

How the administration packages the organization will make a big difference in how it is received by the insurance market. To design the insurance program properly and underwrite or rate coverages correctly, the insurance carrier and the broker or agent must have a very clear understanding of the total operations of the organization. By putting a great deal of effort into preparing a package of information for the insurance market, the organization has a better chance of getting the best coverage at the best price. Insurance carriers like to make their decisions with as much information as possible, and more than anything else dislike being surprised by an unknown exposure after the policy is in place. Be advised, however, that portraying the organization in a favorable light is also important. Applying for insurance coverage is not the same as applying for a grant. An insurance carrier would probably be scared away if overwhelmed with the statistics supplied in a grant. Provide complete information but not the brutish details.

So what should this package of information contain?

◆ Detailed schedules and description of owned or leased properties
◆ Replacement cost value of owned properties

- Schedule of equipment and supplies and their value
- Description of operations at each location
- List of employees and volunteers and their job functions
- Salary information and job classification code if seeking workers' compensation coverage
- Copies of annual reports and budgets for the last five years
- All brochures that describe the organization and its programs
- List of staff certifications and memberships in national trade associations and accreditation organizations
- Summary of loss reduction efforts, such as the organization's compliance with regulations, property maintenance, applicant screening, accounting procedures, volunteer and employee training, and program guidelines

When the package has been compiled it is time to find an insurance broker or agent who likes to work with volunteer groups and an insurance company that likes to insure volunteer groups. Both should have experience with volunteer groups and nonprofit agencies. The broker should be willing to spend a lot of time getting to know the organization because the broker is the conduit to the insurance carrier and can make a huge difference in how the organization is received by the carrier. The carrier should be familiar with the types of losses associated with nonprofits and be comfortable with the organizational structure of a nonprofit. Find out what other nonprofits and volunteer groups they insure and if they stick with nonprofit business or go in and out of the nonprofit market when market conditions change. During the marketing process, the administrator can expect to be asked for additional information and to complete applications.

Nonprofits have a tendency to insure with someone who is a member or friend of the board. This is fine as long as they meet the criteria set forth above. Many brokers and agents specialize in nonprofits and can be found by contacting other volunteer groups or nonprofits, through associations, or by contacting the state association of nonprofits. Some brokers and insurance carriers that specialize in nonprofits advertise in nonprofit journals.

(b) Evaluating Insurance Coverage

The best way to tell if an insurance policy is right for the organization is for the administrator to read the policy and discuss concerns with the broker or the agent. The policy is a contract between two parties and, like any other contract the organization may enter into, the organization has a right to know what benefits it can expect to receive and its contractual obligations. Understanding several elements that are basic to any insurance policy can help guide the administrator through the policy.

All policies have declaration pages that give the most basic details of the policy. If any of these items are not correct, bring that fact to the attention of the broker or agent. These details include:

- Who is insured (the named insured)
- Address of the insured
- Type of coverage

- Policy number
- Dates of coverage
- Policy limits
- Deductible and coinsurance
- Locations covered by the policy
- Premium

The majority of policy wording deals with coverage issues. Every insurance carrier has a standard policy for each type of coverage from which modifications are made to fit the policy for the insured organization.

- The *insuring agreement* summarizes the major promises of the insurer to pay losses and to defend the insured organization. It tells what kind of losses are covered and how defense costs will be handled.
- *Definitions* might be included as a separate section or as part of the insuring agreement. A very important definition tells who is insured by the policy—and if employees, volunteers, directors, and officers are considered insureds.
- Another section of the policy deals with *conditions* that must be met by the insured party in order to receive the benefits of the policy.
- *Exclusions* list the types of losses that are not covered, the types of property not covered, and the causes of loss or perils that are excluded. Perils include damage from wear and tear, insects, nuclear activity, or war.
- *Endorsements* further define the policy by adding, deleting, or modifying the provisions in the original contract. Endorsements have precedence over any conflicting terms in the original contract. Endorsements can be used to change the policy to suit the organization it covers. The administrator has the responsibility to protect the organization and has the right to make a request to the insurance company to modify the policy to better protect the organization.
- Every policy contains *cancellation provisions*. Insurance carriers should be required to give at least 60 days' notice before canceling or not renewing a policy.

(c) Insurance Coverage

(i) Property Damage Coverage

Property damage insurance covers buildings and the contents of buildings. Policies are usually offered in two forms: a "cause of loss" policy or "all risk" coverage. All-risk coverage provides much better protection and makes it incumbent upon the insurance carrier to prove that a certain type of loss is not covered. It is important that proper replacement cost be determined to maintain adequate insurance coverage.

What to look for:

- All-risk or blanket coverage
- Replacement cost, no coinsurance (or 100 percent coinsurance)
- Earthquake and flood coverage if exposed to those risks
- Business interruption and extra expense coverage

- Coverage for:
  - Data processing equipment and data
  - Money, securities, and accounts receivable
  - Valuable papers, cost of research
  - Personal property of others
  - Outdoor property
  - Newly constructed or acquired property
  - Signs and glass
  - Sprinkler leakage
  - Sewer and drain backup

(ii) Commercial General Liability

Commercial general liability insurance covers accidental bodily injury and personal injury (slander, libel, defamation, false arrest) or accidental property damage to another's property. The principal purpose of the general liability policy is to protect an organization from the financial devastation of a lawsuit. The cost of legal defense and investigation will usually be covered until fault is determined or the claim is settled. Most general liability claims against nonprofits are the result of some type of injury to a person while on the nonprofit's property.

All insurance policies carry exclusions common to all policies and organizations, such as losses from war or nuclear disasters. Depending on the type of organizations being insured, the insurance carrier will add other exclusions to modify the policy. Some general liability exclusions common to nonprofits are sexual misconduct, employment practices, and professional liability. Ask your broker if these are covered by your policy. If not, ask how you can get coverage.

What to look for:

- Coverage for all locations and programs, on and off premises
- Coverage for all products
- Contractual liability
- Medical payments
- Employee benefits liability coverage
- Inclusion of employees and volunteers

(iii) Vehicle Insurance

The organization will insure its owned vehicles for liability coverage (bodily injury or property damage to other property) and may consider purchasing physical damage coverage for its owned vehicles. Many organizations choose to self-insure (or retain) physical damage.

What to look for:

- *Medical payments* pay for medical costs for passengers injured in the owned vehicle regardless of who caused the accident.
- *Uninsured or underinsured motorists'* provides bodily injury coverage if an accident is caused by an uninsured or underinsured motorist. It does not cover physical damage to any vehicle.

♦ The organization will also carry *hired and nonowned* coverage. This provides protection for the organization whenever someone from the organization leases a vehicle or drives another vehicle on organization business.

(iv) Volunteer Driver Excess Auto Liability

This coverage may be purchased as a stand-alone policy or may be tagged onto the organization's primary auto policy. Coverage is secondary to any vehicle liability policy the volunteer has in place, which means that the volunteer's own policy covers the loss first and the excess policy picks up after the volunteer's policy limits are exhausted.

(v) Umbrella or Excess Liability Insurance

An umbrella policy affords high limits of extra coverage for many liability exposures. Umbrella policies provide an easy way to increase policy limits and possibly broaden coverage at a reduced premium.
What to look for:

♦ Umbrella carrier must be aware of all underlying policies.
♦ Close attention is needed to any exclusions and endorsements.

(vi) Workers' Compensation

Every state has workers' compensation laws requiring employers to assume responsibility for employee injuries and some illnesses that arise out of and in the course of employment. Workers' compensation provides first-dollar medical benefits with no deductible or copayment. It provides loss of income benefits, rehabilitation, and benefits for survivors.
What to look for:

♦ In some states volunteers may be covered under workers' compensation. Any organization must be very aware of the trade-off made if volunteers are added. The cost of coverage may seem reasonable up front, but if volunteers are injured and claims are paid, the cost of those claims will be reflected in higher premiums for many years to come.

(vii) Commercial Crime Insurance

Also known as employee dishonesty or fidelity bond, it covers theft of property or money, fraud, embezzlement, or forgery by employees. Coverage can be extended to volunteers.
What to look for:

♦ Coverage for employees and volunteers, including directors and trustees
♦ Coverage on and off premises and in transit
♦ Coverage of losses resulting from theft by computer
♦ Coverage for losses resulting from dishonest acts of an employee of the bookkeeping firm handling the organization's accounts

(viii) Directors' and Officers' Liability Insurance

This was introduced to protect the personal liability of directors, officers, and trustees. D&O is management or governance errors and omissions insurance that provides help if a director or officer is personally accused of a wrongful act. A wrongful act means any actual or alleged error or misleading statement or act or omission or breach of duty by the insured parties while acting in their capacity as a director or officer. Whether to spend precious mission dollars on D&O liability insurance coverage has been a point of discussion for many nonprofits. It is essential if the organization has large investments, extensive programs and properties, is heavily involved in fund-raising, or has many employees or volunteers. When underwriting D&O coverage the carrier will ask for a completed application, annual reports including audit information, detailed information on the organization's structure, programs, employees, directors, and officers, and claims history.

What to look for:

- Coverage extended to the organization.
- Coverage for employees and volunteers.

Other coverage considerations:

- This is *claims-made coverage*, coverage that is in place only during the current policy period. Once the policy expires, the organization has no coverage.
- Defense costs are included in the policy limits. Most liability policies do not include payment for defense costs in the policy limits.
- The limits of a D&O policy may be exhausted by legal expenses before a settlement is reached.
- Traditionally, D&O policies provide only for reimbursement of expenses. They do not make direct payments for legal expenses or settlements. To be reimbursed as expenses occur, look for policy language that reads "pay on behalf of," "pay as incurred," "pay on a current basis," or "expenses paid upon notice."

(ix) Fiduciary Liability Insurance

This coverage protects the insured party, usually an administrator, director, or officer, from claims of a wrongful act committed or attempted while acting as a fiduciary or trustee for a pension or benefit program or for funds entrusted to the organization for specific investment management by the organization. Fiduciaries are those persons who have the authority to control and manage the operation and administration of a benefit program. These programs range from simple insurance programs to complicated trustee plans, from plans involving small amounts of money to plans managing millions of dollars. The benefit plans of most for-profit organizations are covered by ERISA (Employee Retirement Income Security Act of 1974) but nonprofit plans are not usually subject to ERISA requirements. This does not relieve the nonprofit from using the same standards of care as those required of for-profits. Lawsuits can be filed against any organization that is perceived as failing to care properly for the benefits promised to beneficiaries. Most fiduciary liability policies are claims-made coverage and carry a mandatory deductible. The underwriter will ask for a completed application, copies of the benefits plans, investment information, annual reports including audit information, and detailed information on the organization's structure, programs, employees, directors, officers, and claims history.

(x) Professional Liability Insurance

Some volunteer organizations provide professional services such as medical treatment or legal counsel. The volunteer organization should rely on professionals to carry their own professional liability coverage, which will protect them if a claim is made against them. The organization may need coverage to protect itself in the event it is brought into a professional liability claim. Coverage may be available on the general liability policy or by purchasing a separate policy. Given the diverse nature of volunteer groups, it is best to consult with the insurance broker to determine the best way to cover this exposure.

(xi) Employment Practices Liability Coverage

The decisions an organization makes regarding hiring, firing, and supervising its employees are referred to as employment practices. Employment practices liability is that resulting from actual or alleged wrongful termination, sexual harassment, or discrimination against an employee. Most general liability policies now exclude employment practices claims, so a new insurance product has been developed that responds to such claims. Coverage is provided for the organization and its directors, officers, and employees. This is claims-made coverage and because it is a fairly new coverage there are significant policy wording and pricing differences. It is important to consult with a knowledgeable insurance broker when considering this coverage (Vargo, 1994).

(xii) Association Liability Insurance

Usually, an insurance policy is designed to cover only one type of loss. Property policies do not cover liability losses; liability policies do not cover director and officer wrongful act claims. Association liability policies intend to wrap a variety of liability coverages into one policy, including general, directors' and officers', and fiduciary liability. An association liability policy is ideal for a small to medium-sized organization that has a fairly limited operation. Be aware that some policies, called association professional liability policies, cover only director and officer wrongful act claims.

(xiii) Volunteer Liability Insurance

This policy provides coverage for bodily injury and property damage accidents that a volunteer might cause while working for an organization. It is similar to coverage provided by a general liability policy but provides lower limits and is somewhat more limited. It is usually secondary coverage; that is, it pays for losses left after any other policies that may be available, such as an auto liability or general liability policies, have already paid out. If the volunteer or organization has no other coverage in place, then the volunteer liability policy would pay first. It is very economical. The other advantage to purchasing a separate policy to cover volunteer's liability is that it keeps small losses that have an adverse affect on rates from appearing on the commercial general liability policy.

(xiv) Volunteer Accident and Injury Coverage

Accident insurance provides a low limit of coverage for accidental injury to volunteers if they are injured while working for the organization. Coverage is secondary to any other insurance coverage that is available, such as the volunteer's personal health insurance coverage or an auto policy. Volunteer accident policies usually have no deductible and can be purchases at a very low rate per volunteer covered. Coverage may also include accidental death or dismemberment benefits.

(xv) Accidental Death and Dismemberment Insurance

This insurance may be purchased as a separate coverage providing death benefits and benefits for loss of limbs or eyes and some accidental injury medical payment coverage. This coverage can usually be purchased at a reasonable premium.

(d) Package Policies and Other Programs

Most small to medium-sized organizations find that purchasing property insurance and commercial general liability coverages together as a package is much less expensive than purchasing each coverage separately. The administrator should ask to review this and any other money-saving ideas that the broker or agent may have available. The broker may know of other types of insurance programs that may have coverage or financial benefits to the organization, such as group purchasing programs, risk retention groups, or insurance pools. Many of these programs are specifically designed to address the unique insurance needs of nonprofits and should be considered carefully.

REFERENCES AND SUGGESTED READINGS

Lai, Mary L., Terry S. Chapman, and Elmer L. Steinbock. 1992. *Am I Covered For . . . ? A Guide to Insurance for Non-profits,* (2nd ed.) San Jose, Calif.: Consortium for Human Services, Inc.

Rejda, George E. 1992. *Principles of Risk Management and Insurance,* (4th ed.), New York: HarperCollins.

Stone, Byron, and Carol North. 1988. *Risk Management and Insurance for Nonprofit Managers.* Chicago: First Nonprofit Risk Pooling Trust.

Tremper, Charles R. 1989. *Reconsidering Legal Liability and Insurance for Nonprofit Organizations.* Lincoln, Nebr.: Law College Services, Inc.

Tremper, Charles R. 1991. *D & O . . . Yes or No?* Washington, D.C.: Nonprofits' Risk Management and Insurance Institute.

Tremper, Charles R., and George Babcock. 1990. *The Nonprofit Board's Role in Risk Management: More Than Buying Insurance.* Washington, D.C.: NCNB Governance Series.

Tremper, Charles R., and Jeffrey D. Kahn. 1992. *Managing Legal Liability and Insurance for Corporate Volunteer Programs,* Washington, D.C.: National Center for Community Risk Management and Insurance, and the United Way of America.

Tremper, Charles R., Fiona Lally, and Dennis Studebaker. 1994. *Insurance Assurance for Volunteers.* Washington, D.C.: Nonprofit Risk Management Center.

Vargo, Katherine S. 1994. "Insurance for Employment Practices Liability." *Community Risk Management and Insurance* 3(2) (May).

Warren, David. 1985. *Risk Management Manual Guide.* New York: Risk Management Society Publishing.

CHAPTER  17

VOLUNTEERS AND EMPLOYMENT LAW

Peter J. Eide
Manager, Human Resources Law and Policy, U.S. Chamber of Commerce

17.1 Introduction

17.2 Nonprofit Organizations—Employers or Not?

17.3 Volunteers—Employees or Not?

17.4 Statutory and Regulatory Standards

17.5 Discrimination

17.6 Harassment

17.7 Common Law

17.8 Intentional Torts

17.9 Negligence

17.10 Contract

17.11 Conclusions

Suggested Readings

17.1 INTRODUCTION

Employment law is a short phrase for dozens of laws, and for volumes of regulations issued by government agencies, both federal and state, enforcing those laws, along with the court-made common law of every state, all of which establish the legal framework of the employment relationship. At stake are some of the fundamental rights of individuals and many of the basic tenets of society.

Most people in the United States are employees or employers at some point in their lives. Most are in one or both of those categories for most of their lives. It is their rights and responsibilities in the employment relationship that are created, affirmed, explained, restricted, or in some cases removed, through the statutes, regulations, and court cases that make up employment law.

The Constitution is the basis of all laws in this country, whether statutes or court-made common law. It empowers the government to adopt and enforce statutes and regulations. The Constitution authorizes the courts to enforce the common law, the body of court decisions that provides remedies and relief and governs everyday personal and business relationships in society. Most important, the Constitution also limits the power and authority of government and restricts government exercise of that power. The common law in the colonies and original states started with the courts in each state accepting the common law of England at the time as binding precedent in that jurisdiction.

The ancient English common law described the employment relationship as that of master and servant. In fact, a few frequently used law books still classify common law rulings in the employment area under the general heading of "Master–Servant." During the first 100 years of this country, employment was considered a relationship between a master and servant, with the latter having only the right to cease the relationship at will.

Not until the early twentieth century was it even contemplated that servants, or employees, had rights in the relationship with their employers. The growth of unions around the turn of the century, coupled with the unbridled exploitation of labor by some capitalists, exacerbated by the Depression, led to federal government action in the 1930s. Examples of early statutes include the Davis-Bacon Act of 1931 (requiring that contractors performing government construction work pay "prevailing"—union scale—wages), the Wagner Act of 1935 (giving employees the right to bargain collectively with employers through unions), and the Fair Labor Standards Act of 1938 (establishing minimum wages and maximum hours).

The early employment laws were the result of a perceived need to restrict employers from taking advantage of their dominant financial position relative to employees. Because it was primarily blue-collar workers who were seen as potential victims, these laws addressed primarily the private sector employment relationship based on a per hour or piece-rate wage.

For the most part, the rights of volunteer workers remain unchanged from what they were in the 1930s and before. That is, the relationship between the volunteer and his or her "employer" is entirely consensual. Neither party has greater financial power because, in theory, the relationship is not based on financial rewards for the volunteer worker and either party can terminate the relationship at any time and for any reason. The employer cannot take undue advantage of the volunteer worker because presumably if the volunteer feels oppressed or taken advantage of, he or she will terminate the relationship without financial consequence. Theoretically, the volunteer is not financially compensated—not paid wages—and cannot be coerced by the employer with possible denial of that compensation. The relationship must remain fair and mutually acceptable or one of the parties will terminate it.

In these circumstances, it cannot be assumed that volunteer workers have, or need, the rights granted to paid workers in profit-making organizations. Thus, with few exceptions, workers who truly volunteer their services do not enjoy the protections and rights granted in statutes covering the employment relationship.

That is not to say that volunteers have no rights under federal or state employment laws. The Fair Labor Standards Act (FLSA) and Department of Labor regulations issued under that law address volunteer workers specifically. As explained below, volunteers clearly have distinct rights, in certain limited circumstances, under the Civil Rights Acts of 1964 and 1991 (Title VII). Strong arguments can be made that the Civil Rights Act of 1866 applies directly to volunteer workers. Arguably, volunteer workers enjoy the protection of the Occupational Safety and Health Act. They do without question if they work alongside paid employees, all of whom are covered. The Americans with Disabilities Act (ADA) likewise provides protections, whether directly or indirectly, to disabled volunteers.

Just because they are providing services to a nonprofit organization, volunteers do not remove themselves from the protections of the common law. Although there was a time when the courts were reluctant to hold nonprofit or charitable organizations liable for damages, that is no longer the case in most jurisdictions. Now those entities can be liable under common law just like a major profit-making corporation.

17.2 NONPROFIT ORGANIZATIONS—EMPLOYERS OR NOT?

Most nonprofit or charitable organizations have some paid staff and leadership. In many cases the paid staff is augmented by volunteers who may work occasionally or on an unscheduled basis, or may devote their efforts on a frequent, scheduled basis. Without question, federal and state employment laws apply to these organizations and their paid staff. One of the few exceptions is the Title VII provision allowing religious organizations to hire based on the applicant's religion. Secular organizations are prohibited from discriminating against employees and applicants on the basis of religion.

Although most employment statutes do not expressly address true volunteer workers, volunteers in certain positions of authority can be considered agents of an organization and in that capacity violate a paid employee's rights under an employment law.

Virtually every employment law statute considers even a low-level supervisor or manager to be a spokesperson or agent acting on behalf of his or her employer. Thus, the acts of these individuals are considered the acts of the employer. For example, if the supervisor of a group of 10 office workers consistently assigns the most difficult and unpleasant tasks to a worker of a different race because of that worker's race, the employer may be found liable for unlawful discrimination against the worker even though higher-level managers in the organization were completely unaware of the situation.

Similarly, if a volunteer holds a supervisory or managerial position, or one that appears to the paid workers or others as having influence or control over the work or pay of paid staff, the volunteer could be found under the law to be a spokesperson or agent of the organization. As an agent, the volunteer could commit various acts that violate the rights of workers, resulting in substantial liability for the organization and, in some cases, the agent.

The law of agency also applies to the common law. A volunteer who is, or can be, viewed as an agent or spokesperson of the organization could commit a variety of employment torts or establish binding employment contracts, all of which could result in substantial costs to the organization.

Factors that suggest that a person is a supervisor or manager, and therefore an agent of the organization, include but are not limited to:

◆ A leadership, managerial, or supervisory title

◆ A leadership, managerial, or supervisory role

◆ Trappings of leadership (private office, parking space, perks and privileges, higher pay, eligibility for management bonuses)

◆ The ability or apparent ability to hire, fire, and/or discipline employees or effectively to recommend such

◆ The ability or apparent ability to direct the daily activities of one or more employees or effectively recommend such

◆ The ability or apparent ability to evaluate employee performance and set or recommend wages, bonuses, time off, and so on

◆ The ability or apparent ability to act on behalf of, or serve as a spokesperson for, the employer

Supervisors and managers frequently are named as defendants together with the plaintiff's employer in lawsuits alleging a violation of an employment law. Seldom, however, do courts find the individual to be liable for a violation even if the employer is held liable. Just being named as a defendant can be a costly, and often traumatic, experience for a manager or supervisor. If a volunteer is perceived to be a supervisor, manager, or otherwise an agent of the employer, the volunteer could find himself or herself named as a defendant.

Under Section 1981 of the 1866 Civil Rights Act, a person is more easily found liable, in addition to or instead of, the employer. Because this law provides unlimited compensatory and punitive damages and does not involve required mediation or conciliation as does Title VII of the 1964 Civil Rights Act, the individual defendant faces a much more dangerous situation.

Under state common law claims, which include wrongful discharge, wrongful hiring or retention, assault and battery, and intentional infliction of emotional distress, the individual who actually engaged in the alleged wrongful conduct is routinely named as a defendant along with the employing organization. In these cases the employment status of the alleged supervisor is of even less consequence than in actions taken under employment statutes. The danger to the volunteer who is held to be an agent is immense, as the individual defendant can be left to defend the suit alone if the employing organization establishes that the person's conduct was clearly outside the range of conduct for which the employer could reasonably be responsible.

17.3　VOLUNTEERS—EMPLOYEES OR NOT?

The employment statutes are clear—when paid employees are assigned by their employers to offer their services or time to an organization as "volunteers," they remain employees of the assigning employers. If they are paid on an hourly basis by their assigning employers, then there arises an obligation to pay them for all time spent carrying out the assignment to volunteer.

However, just because volunteers are paid by the assigning employers for their efforts, it does not mean that the organizations for which the volunteer work is performed cannot be liable for volunteers' misconduct under employment law. The law has developed the theory of *joint employer* for such circumstances. Under this theory, either the nonprofit organizations, the volunteers' regular employers, or both could be held responsible for violations of employment statutes or wrongful actions under the common law.

Department of Labor regulations issued under the Fair Labor Standards Act (29 C.F.R. Sec. 553.100, *et seq.*) provide that:

Sec. 553.101(b)—Congress did not intend to discourage or impede volunteer activities undertaken for civic, charitable, or humanitarian purposes, but expressed its wish to prevent any manipulation or abuse of minimum wage or overtime requirements through coercion or undue pressure upon individuals to "volunteer" their services.

(c)—Individuals shall be considered volunteers only where their services are offered freely and without pressure or coercion, direct or implied, from an employer.

Sec. 553.104(a)—Individuals who are not employed in any capacity by state or local government agencies often donate hours of service to a public agency for civic or humanitarian reasons. Such individuals are considered volunteers and not employees of such public agencies if their hours of service are provided with no promise, expectation, or receipt of compensation for the services rendered, except for reimbursement for expenses, reasonable benefits, and nominal fees, or a combination thereof, as discussed in Sec. 553.106. There are no limitations or restriction imposed by the FLSA on the types of services which private individuals may volunteer to perform for public agencies.

(b)—Examples of services which might be performed on a volunteer basis when so motivated include helping out in a sheltered workshop or providing personal services to the sick or elderly in hospitals or nursing homes; assisting in a school library or cafeteria; or driving a school bus to carry a football team or band on a trip. Similarly, individuals may volunteer as firefighters or auxiliary police, or volunteer to perform such tasks as working with retarded or handicapped children or disadvantaged youth, helping in youth programs as camp counselors, soliciting contributions or participating in civic or charitable benefits programs and volunteering other services needed to carry out charitable or educational programs.

Sec. 553.106(a)—*Volunteers may be paid expenses, reasonable benefits, a nominal fee, or any combination thereof, for their service without losing their status as volunteers.* [Emphasis added] (b)—An individual who performs hours of service as a volunteer for a public agency may receive payment for expenses without being deemed an employee for purposes of the FLSA. A school guard does not become an employee because he or she receives a uniform allowance, or reimbursement for reasonable cleaning expenses for wear and tear on personal clothing worn while performing hours of volunteer service. Such individuals would not lose their volunteer status because they are reimbursed for the approximate out-of-pocket expenses incurred incidental to providing volunteer services, for example, payment for the cost of meals and transportation expenses.

(c)—Individuals do not lose their status as volunteers because they are reimbursed for tuition, transportation and meal costs involved in their attending classes intended to teach them to perform efficiently the services they provide or will provide as volunteers. Likewise, the volunteer status of such individuals is not lost if they are provided books, supplies, or other materials essential to their volunteer training or reimbursement for the cost thereof.

(d)—*Individuals do not lose their volunteer status if they are provided reasonable benefits by a public agency for whom they perform volunteer service. Benefits would be considered reasonable, for example, when they involve inclusion of individual volunteers in group insurance plans (such as liability, health, life, disability, workers' compensation) or pension plans or "length of service" awards, commonly or traditionally provided to volunteers of State and local government agencies, which met the additional test in paragraph (f) of the section.* [Emphasis added]

(e)—*Individuals do not lose their volunteer status if they receive a nominal fee from a public agency. A nominal fee is not a substitute for compensation and must not be tied to productivity. However, this does not preclude the payment of a nominal amount on a "per call" or similar basis to volunteer firefighters. The following factors will be among those examined in determining whether a given amount is nominal: The distance traveled and the time and effort expended by the volunteer; whether the volunteer has agreed to be available around-the-clock or only during certain specified time periods; and whether the volunteer provides services as needed or throughout the year. An individual who volunteers to provided periodic services on a year-round basis may receive a nominal monthly or annual stipend or fee without losing volunteer status.* [Emphasis added]

(f)—Whether the furnishing of expenses, benefits, or fees would result in individuals' losing their status as volunteers under the FLSA can only be determined by examining the total amount of payments made (expenses, benefits, fees) in the context of the economic realities of the particular situation.

The Department of Labor also issued guidelines on when a paid employee of a nonprofit organization may volunteer his or her services on an unpaid basis. In the following circumstances, paid employees of a nonprofit organization may volunteer their time to their employer when:

1. The services are entirely voluntary, with no coercion by the employer, no promise of advancement, and no penalty for not volunteering.
2. The activities are predominantly for the employee's own benefit.
3. The volunteer employee does not replace another employee or impair the employment opportunities of others by performing work that would otherwise be performed by regular employees.

4. The employee serves without expectation of pay.

5. The activity does not take place during the employee's regular working hours or scheduled overtime hours.

6. The volunteer time is insubstantial in relation to the employee's regular hours.

17.4 STATUTORY AND REGULATORY STANDARDS

This section contains a brief description of the principal federal laws governing the employment relationship. For the most part, the following statutes were intended primarily to set standards for the workplace. Although they prohibit discrimination against employees who report noncompliance with those standards, the principal purpose of these laws is to assure that all employers will maintain certain minimum standards.

(a) Fair Labor Standards Act

The Fair Labor Standards Act (FLSA), passed in 1938, is administered by the U.S. Department of Labor (DOL). Its complex provisions cover both private- and public-sector (federal, state, and local government) employers. This law sets the federal minimum wage (currently $4.25 per hour) and the maximum number of hours (40 per week) an employee must work before receiving overtime pay (time-and-a-half). Either the DOL or an aggrieved employee may bring suit under this law in federal court. The government can bring a criminal action against the employer for "willful" violations. Included are restrictions on the use of child labor (an employee must be at least 14 or 16 years of age, depending on the type of employer and the work involved; he or she must be at least 18 for hazardous occupations).

The regulations cited above concerning the volunteer status of workers were issued by the DOL under the FLSA. A worker is not considered a volunteer merely because he or she considers the work to be volunteered or because his or her title or classification includes the term "volunteer." Rather, factors such as those listed above (for example, whether and how much the person is paid, whether the remuneration can be withheld for disciplinary reasons, the character of the person's work, and whether the work is performed alongside paid employees).

If a person is considered to be a volunteer and accordingly not paid wages under the requirements of the FLSA, and it is later determined by the DOL or a court that he or she should have been a paid employee, the employer could be liable for at least minimum wages for all hours worked (including overtime at overtime rates) and, depending on the circumstances, liquidated damages equal to the wages that should have been paid.

One especially dangerous wrinkle in such a situation is that there are probably no records of the hours that someone who was considered to be a volunteer would have worked; because it is required under the FLSA, there would be such records for someone who was considered an employee and had been paid for those hours. In the absence of these records, the DOL and the courts usually rely on the person's recollection about the number of hours worked. Since the statute of limitations under the FLSA can be up to three years, the total amount of unpaid wages for the previous three years along with the punitive liquidated damages could be huge.

(b) Occupational Safety and Health Act

This 1970 law, also known as the OSH Act, is based on the constitutional power of Congress to regulate and police interstate commerce. Most private-sector employers are covered, although a few-such as mine owners—are exempt because they are covered by other laws. The intent of this law is "to assure so far as possible every working man and woman in the Nation safe and healthful working conditions and to preserve our human resources."

The law establishes the Occupational Safety and Health Administration (OSHA), which is empowered to reduce the number of workplace hazards by issuing regulations (also called standards), that provide training programs for occupational safety and health specialists, establish an effective enforcement program, and require employers to keep records of accidents, injuries, and illnesses.

Employers are required to comply with OSHA's many standards. Failure to comply may result in civil penalties up to several thousand dollars for *each* violation. Employees are protected from discrimination because they exercise their rights under the OSH Act or report employer violations of OSHA standards. Under the act, an employee possessing a reasonable apprehension of danger may in good faith refuse to perform an assignment that exposes him or her to hazardous conditions.

Unlike the regulations issued under the FLSA, volunteers are not mentioned specifically. However, as the not-for-profit or nonprofit sector (sometimes called the third sector) continues its rapid growth and role in the economy,[1] its significant effect on interstate commerce grows as well. Nonprofit organizations are clearly covered under the OSH Act and as employers (of paid staff) they are subject to OSHA's standards and inspections for compliance.

The OSH Act specifically provides that OSHA inspectors may question "agents" of an employer. As discussed above, volunteers who have or exercise management or supervisory authority can be considered agents of a nonprofit employer. It would follow, then, that such agents could be held accountable in federal court for discrimination against an employee who has filed a complaint or testified in an OSHA proceeding.

(c) Family and Medical Leave Act (FMLA)

This 1993 statute requires employers with 50 or more employees to provide up to 12 weeks unpaid leave in any 12-month period (1) to care for a newborn or to provide child care upon the placement of an adopted or foster child; (2) to care for a child, parent, or spouse who has a serious medical condition; or (3) if the employee is unable to work because of the employee's own serious health condition.

The complex eligibility requirements essentially provide coverage of the act to all full-time and some part-time regular employees who have worked for the past 12 months. Leave may be taken on an intermittent basis when medically necessary.

Employees may be required to exhaust accrued sick and personal leave as well as vacation time before utilizing the leave provided under the act. Employees using

[1]Peter Drucker, a well-known writer on the science and art of management, says that the nonchurch part of the nonprofit sector of the economy is the growth sector in the United States. There are about a million organizations registered as nonprofit or charitable. Almost half of the adult population contributes at least three hours per week as a volunteer to nonprofit organizations. (Drucker, 1994, pp. 75-76).

leave provided under the act must be afforded health benefits under the same terms and conditions that would be in effect if they were working.

Remedies for violations of the FMLA include back pay and benefits as well as reinstatement and promotion. An employee is entitled to compensation for actual losses if the violation is classified as willful. Attorney's fees are also available.

It is not inconceivable that the FMLA could be found to cover a volunteer receiving allowable compensation and health benefits under the 29 C.F.R. Sec. 553.106 (discussed above). The FMLA is so new that a body of case law addressing the status of volunteers under the statute has not yet developed.

(d) Immigration Reform and Control Act (IRCA)

This 1986 law requires all employers, including state and local governments, to verify that new employees are either U.S. citizens or authorized to work in the United States. In addition, employers are required to complete an Immigration and Naturalization Service (INS) Form I-9 for each new employee. That form lists which documents an applicant may produce to document to an employer his or her citizenship or work authorization.

Employers must retain completed I-9 forms for three years after the date of hire or one for one year following the date of termination, whichever is later. The law also prohibits employer discrimination based on citizenship, national origin, or intention to obtain citizenship.

Civil and/or criminal penalties of several thousand dollars may be levied for hiring an illegal alien or for violations of the I-9 requirements. A finding of discrimination under this law can result in stiff penalties for the employer and an order to provide back pay to the victims.

(e) National Labor Relations Act (NLRA)

This 1935 law provides employees the right to form and join unions to represent them in collective bargaining. It also gives employees the right to engage in "concerted" activities affecting their employment. Thus, two or more employees may act in concert concerning their wages, hours, or working conditions. Employers are prohibited from discriminating against an employee who exercises a right protected under this act or testifies in a National Labor Relations Board (NLRB) proceeding.

Clearly, this law does not apply to volunteers. However, a volunteer easily could be found to be an agent of an employer covered by the NLRA. Accordingly, volunteers in supervisory or management positions, or who may appear to hold positions of authority, could engage in conduct for which an employer of employees covered by the NLRA is responsible.

Damages are limited to make-whole relief (back pay and reinstatement) for individuals discriminated against in violation of the NLRA. Unusual remedies the NLRB has ordered include returning the situation to the status quo (e.g., for unlawful plant closures) and reinstatement of wages or benefits that had been altered by an employer who had not bargained with a union that had been certified by the NLRB to represent its employees.

(f) Employee Polygraph Protection Act

This 1988 law prohibits the use of lie detector tests on employees or prospective employees. There are exceptions for the subjects of ongoing investigations, and national security, drug security, or drug diversion investigations.

The Secretary of Labor may levy civil fines of up to $10,000 for each violation. The aggrieved employee may sue in court, receive a jury trial, and obtain "appropriate" legal or equitable relief.

For the reasons discussed below in the section about coverage of volunteers under the Civil Rights Act of 1964 and 1991, to the extent that a nonprofit organization routinely refers its volunteer workers for employment in traditional paid jobs, such volunteers may be considered prospective employees, who are expressly covered under this law.

17.5 DISCRIMINATION

The primary purpose of the following federal statutes is to prohibit employment discrimination against individuals in certain protected classes. Increasingly, these laws are being applied to guarantee minimum standards of employer conduct.

(a) Age Discrimination in Employment Act (ADEA)

This 1967 law, administered by the Equal Employment Opportunity Commission (EEOC), applies to employers with 20 or more employees and prohibits discrimination against employees and applicants 40 years old and older. The ADEA allows jury trials and provides remedies such as back pay, liquidated damages (double the back-pay amount), injunctions, and reinstatement.

(b) Civil Rights Acts of 1964 and 1991

Commonly referred to as Title VII, these laws, enforced by the EEOC and covering employers with 15 or more employees, prohibit discrimination (including harassment—see the discussion below) against employees and applicants on the basis of race, color, national origin, religion, or gender. Available remedies include reinstatement, back pay, and in cases of intentional discrimination, compensatory and punitive damages. The parties to a suit alleging intentional discrimination are entitled to a jury trial.

These laws apply only to employment. Thus, one would not immediately look to them for a remedy affecting a truly volunteer relationship. However, courts have held that in certain circumstances a true volunteer may pursue a Title VII claim against the organization for which the volunteer service is provided.

In a New York case,[2] the plaintiff provided unpaid or volunteer medical services through the defendant hospital. The hospital subsequently denied her admitting privileges for discriminatory reasons. Thus, by not allowing her to render her services on a volunteer basis, the hospital prevented her from later practicing medicine on a gainful basis. The hospital was found to have prevented her from securing employment based on its unlawful discrimination and was held liable under Title VII.

In situations where an organization's conduct has an adverse effect on the ability of one of its volunteers to obtain subsequent employment, it may be found in violation of Title VII. This situation could easily arise when an agent of the organization provides a negative reference in response to a routine reference check conducted by an employer to which a former (or current) volunteer is applying for employment.

[2]*Beverly v. Douglas*, 591 F. Supp. 132 (S.D.N.Y. 1984).

Example

A national nonprofit professional association with a large staff of both paid experts and unpaid members who serve in policymaking volunteer roles routinely sends one paid staffer and one volunteer to an annual conference of a smaller association composed of professionals in a related field. Both organizations have historically been male-dominated and have had mostly male members. Conference participants are given a certificate and continuing education credits. Attendance at the conference often leads to lucrative job offers for attendees. The national association refuses to send any of its female volunteers to the conference. A Title VII claim based on gender discrimination by one of the few female volunteers is successful because the association denied her the opportunity to obtain a lucrative position when it refused to send her to the conference.

As unpaid volunteer work becomes an increasingly important part of everyday life in the United States for a large segment of the population, (Drucker, 1994, p. 76) it is conceivable that in the near future Title VII could be viewed by some courts as applicable to many unpaid or volunteer "employees."

(c) Civil Rights Act of 1866

Section 1981 of this post-Civil War statute provides that all citizens, regardless of their race, have the same right to make and enforce contracts as do white citizens. The Supreme Court has held that this section prohibits intentional employment discrimination based on race. In the Civil Rights Act of 1991, Congress expressly provided that this law applies to employment. Recently, the Court held that the term race under this law is defined as it was in the mid-nineteenth-century when the law was passed. As a result, many people now usually classified as "white"are also protected by this law, although by mid-nineteenth-century standards that classification was strictly limited to those of western-central European descent. Scandinavians, for example, were not considered to be white.

There are no administrative steps in the enforcement procedure and a person may sue directly in federal court. The court (or perhaps the jury) may award all equitable remedies, back pay, reinstatement, and full punitive and compensatory damages.

Because this law is not expressly limited to employment discrimination, it clearly presents special problems to organizations using volunteer (or unpaid) workers. If a person's right to provide volunteer services—to make a contract—is hampered because of race (as broadly defined), the organization and/or the person responsible for the interference could be found to have violated Section 1981 and be liable for the remedies listed above.

(d) Americans with Disabilities Act (ADA)

This 1990 law, covering employers with 15 or more employees, is administered and enforced by the EEOC. It prohibits employment discrimination against a person because of an actual or perceived disability. The ADA and its regulations require employers to make certain physical changes to the workplace to facilitate the movement and accommodation of physically disabled employees and applicants.

The law also prohibits discrimination against the disabled by providers of services and public accommodations. Thus, covered entities must remove architectural barriers and provide other forms of assistance and services to the disabled.

Available remedies include back pay and injunctions. If intentional discrimination is alleged, compensatory and punitive damages as well as a jury trial are available.

(e) Equal Pay Act

This law prohibits discrimination in the form of payment of lower wages to a person on the basis of gender. Remedies, which may be awarded by a jury, are back pay and liquidated damages (double back pay).

(f) Executive Order 11246

First issued in 1965, covering only employers holding government contracts of $10,000 or more, this order prohibits employment discrimination on the basis of race, color, national origin, religion, and gender. Large contractors (50 or more employees and contracts in excess of $50,000) are required to have a written affirmative action plan for minority and female employees. The order is enforced by the Department of Labor, which may terminate or suspend the federal contracts of violators and bar them from bidding on future contracts.

17.6 HARASSMENT

(a) Sexual Harassment

Increasingly, courts are finding violations of Title VII when an employee is subjected to a sexually adverse or unpleasant situation, whether it is someone's conduct or the environment in the workplace. Classic examples demonstrate these two basic types of gender-based harassment. An employer may be held liable for sexual harassment if a supervisor whose proposal of a romantic or social relationship with a subordinate employee was rejected by that employee, retaliates in some manner—for example, by denying a promotion or a raise, assigning more onerous work, or writing an unfavorable and unjustified evaluation. This type of harassment is referred to as *quid-pro-quo sexual harassment*—do what I want and I won't exercise my authority as your supervisor to hurt you.

An example of hostile environment sexual harassment is when a supervisor openly engages in offensive conduct, such as using off-color and degrading phrases to describe female workers or customers. Another example is when female employees are forced to walk through a large department of exclusively male employees to reach the isolated door to the women's restroom.

(b) Other Harassment

The basic principles supporting theories of sexual harassment are applicable to situations where the objectionable conduct or environment is based on race, color, national origin, age, disability, or religion. For example, if an employer permitted members of a predominantly white workforce to openly display various Ku Klux Klan symbols on their clothing or such personal property as briefcases or toolboxes, the employer could be the target of a racial harassment charge or lawsuit brought by employees belonging to a ethnic or religious minority.

17.7 COMMON LAW

The preceding sections dealt with the statutory framework of federal employment law. Most state and many municipal jurisdictions have similar if not identical statutes and ordinances applicable to the employment relationship. All states have a body of court-made common law broadly applicable to the employment relationship. Most of these principles do not rely exclusively on the master–servant or employment relationship but are equally applicable to a broad range of commercial and personal relationships. Accordingly, most are applicable to a relationship in which one party volunteers services to another in exchange for intrinsic rewards and satisfaction resulting therefrom.

Some of the more frequent common law claims raised in the employment context are described below. They are mentioned because a volunteer easily could be an agent of an organization and through his or her misconduct create substantial common law liability for an employing organization. Organizations using volunteers should take note because most of the principles discussed below could also be raised in a dispute between a volunteer and the organization to which he or she provides a service.

(a) Employment at Will

The common law of most states is based on the common law of England, which held that the employment (master–servant) relationship could be terminated by the employee or employer at any time for any reason or no reason at all. Thus, the master–servant relationship was characterized as "employment at will."

In most jurisdictions the basis of most employment is still the at-will relationship. Most employers take great care to advise applicants that employment with that organization will be based on the at-will principle. This basic principle can easily be changed, sometimes inadvertently, by the employer when it notifies or somehow promises employees that certain conditions will apply before, during, or after the employment relationship is terminated by the employer.

For example, if the employer through its handbook or by the assurances of an agent (supervisor, manager, officer, or spokesperson) informs an employee that the employment relationship will be terminated only for cause or only after a hearing, the employer may have eroded its at-will right to discharge the employee for any reason or no reason. Depending on the assurance given to the employee(s), the employer may have to demonstrate in court that the discharge took place for cause, if that was promised, or may have to show that a full and fair hearing was conducted prior to the adverse action.

Although the relationship between an organization and an individual voluntarily providing a service to that organization is not employment, in many respects it is similar to a master–servant relationship in that one party receives the benefit of the other party's services and that party presumably receives some degree of compensation if only in the form of psychological satisfaction or intrinsic reward. In theory, the relationship can be terminated by either party at any time for any reason or no reason at all. However, if the volunteer was promised or led to believe that severance of the relationship would occur only for cause or after certain conditions were met—for example, a hearing—then the organization may be found to have obligated itself to meet those conditions before terminating the relationship.

Under the common law, the wrongful conduct or speech of a person or organization can be classified as either a tort (intentional or negligent conduct that harms or damages another) and/or a breach of contract (the promise to do something in exchange for something else).

17.8 INTENTIONAL TORTS

(a) Misrepresentation

In the employment area, most claims of fraud or misrepresentation arise when an employer makes false promises or misleading statements about a position to entice someone to accept employment in that position. Similarly, an employer could engage in misrepresentation to discourage an employee from leaving a position for employment elsewhere. Misstatements about the status or condition of the hiring organization also could result in a misrepresentation or fraud claim.

To prove intentional misrepresentation or fraud, the plaintiff must prove that:

◆ The defendant, or its agent, made a false representation of fact, intention, opinion, or law.
◆ The defendant, or its agent, had knowledge or belief that the information was false.
◆ The defendant, or its agent, intended the plaintiff to rely on the misrepresentation and act or refrain from acting.
◆ The plaintiff in fact acted or refrained from acting in reliance on the misrepresentation.
◆ The plaintiff suffered loss, damage, or injury as a result of reliance on the misrepresentation.

Volunteers who may be considered agents of an organization should be extremely careful when recruiting or seeking to retain both paid employees of the organization and the services of other volunteers.

(b) Defamation

There are two types of defamation:

1. *Libel*—written or printed defamation
2. *Slander*—spoken defamation

A written or spoken communication may be defamatory if it tends to harm the reputation of another person or deters others from associating or dealing with the person who was the object of the communication.

In most states employers enjoy a qualified privilege to make what would other-wise be defamatory statements about employees, but only if that statement:

- ◆ was made in the good-faith belief that it was true.
- ◆ was made on a proper occasion (for example, future employer's reference check).
- ◆ was communicated only to the proper parties (for example, the future employer).
- ◆ served a legitimate business interest or purpose.
- ◆ was limited to the legitimate business interest or purpose.

Here, too, the volunteer who has what could be determined to be a supervisory or management role in the organization—the agent—must be careful not to defame individuals (either paid employees and other volunteers) associated or formerly associated with the organization. Many people do not realize that seemingly innocuous office gossip or the not unusual anger expressed by someone merely blowing off steam could easily contain highly defamatory statements.

Fortunately, truth is an absolute defense to defamation!

(c) Infliction of Emotional Distress

The claim of infliction of emotional distress may arise when an employer (or its agent) intentionally engages in actions that are so shocking and outrageous and so extreme in degree that they exceed all bounds of decency and are regarded as atro-cious and utterly intolerable in a civilized society.

As an essential element of this claim, the plaintiff must prove that he or she suf-fered severe emotional distress. However, in many situations the defendant's con-duct is so extreme or outrageous that the emotional distress is inferred by the court.

This tort arises in the employment context most often when supervisors engage in physical, sexual, or verbal harassment of subordinates and when a termination or other form of discipline is carried out in an especially embarrassing or demeaning manner.

It is not difficult to foresee a situation where a volunteer worker is subjected to emotionally damaging physical or sexual harassment either by an agent of the orga-nization or (with the actual or presumed knowledge of management) by a customer of the organization. A volunteer raising such a claim will be an especially appealing plaintiff likely to be viewed favorably by a jury.

(d) Invasion of Privacy

Privacy is often called the "right to be let alone." It is far more than the Fourth Amendment to the U.S. Constitution (which is applicable only to government action and therefore useful only to public-sector employers/employees). Privacy has long been protected by the common law and increasingly is the subject of state and federal statutes designed to restrict the unnecessary release of personal informa-tion. In addition, some state constitutions provide a separate right of privacy to cit-izens, irrespective of a government role.

Under common law the tort of invasion of privacy can be broken down into three distinct types:

(i) False Light Publicity

This situation arises when the defendant publicly attributes certain false character-istics, opinions, or conduct to the plaintiff so that he or she is placed in a false light. In one recent case an employer stated that a certain employee had filed baseless claims of sexual harassment. The harassment charges were settled before trial, so there was no determination as to their merit. The employee then successfully claimed that the public comments held her up in a false light.

(ii) Public Disclosure of Private Facts

This tort arises when the employer publicly discloses information about an employee when the information is of no legitimate concern to the public. For example, if an employer or its agent reveals to the public (or even to the employee's co-workers) highly personal medical information about the employee—for exam-ple, about a mastectomy, or psychiatric problems—the employer may be found to have committed the tort of invasion of privacy.

(iii) Intrusion upon Seclusion of Privacy

This action may arise if to a reasonable person the intrusion is highly offensive or the inquiry is patently unreasonable. Often, the issue in these cases is whether the complainant had a reasonable expectation of privacy in the circumstances.

For example, an employer, without warning or notice, might disable the lock on an employee's personal locker and conduct a search without good cause—for example, without a reasonable suspicion that the locker contained contraband, such as illegal drugs or weapons. Another problem situation might occur when an employer or its agent questions an employee about his or her sexual affairs. Usually, such information could not possibly be relevant to the organization or its functions.

(e) Interference with Contractual Relations

This tort is the intentional and unjustified inducement of another not to enter a contractual relationship or to end (or breach) a contractual relationship with a third party if that third party is harmed as a result. Sometimes called interference with prospective economic advantage, it clearly applies to employment that technically may not be based on an actual or implied contract.

The key elements of this tort are: (1) whether the inducement or interference was committed with the knowledge of contractual or prospective relationship, and (2) whether it was intentional. Absent such knowledge, the alleged interference cannot be that the act was intentional—a necessary element of the tort. The inter-ference also must be unjustified. As with defamation, relating a truthful fact to another, even if it may cause that party to refrain from entering a relationship with another party, is almost always held to be justified. On the other hand, knowingly communicating a false or misleading statement that results in interference may be the basis of a suit for damages under this legal theory.

Because the essence of this claim involves the improper conduct of a person—a supervisor, a manager, or an agent—often that person, rather than the organization on whose behalf he or she acts, must defend this claim in court.

Example I

A long-time volunteer worker in a day-care facility that was operated in conjunction with a parochial secondary school administered and managed by volunteers is considered by the facility's new director to be uncooperative and unwilling to adhere to new work schedules. The worker discontinues her volunteer work and applies for a full-time paid position at a nearby private elementary school. That would-be employer contacts the director of the day care facility in a routine preemployment reference check. The director depicts the applicant as both insolent and inflexible. As a result, the worker is denied employment at the school. She sues the director for unjustifiably and intentionally interfering with her prospective economic relationship.

Example II

A dedicated and much-praised volunteer maintenance worker at a homeless shelter is forced to leave the organization when the entire unpaid staff is discharged because several other volunteers are arrested for selling drugs in or near the shelter. Years later, the maintenance worker, who now owns his own home maintenance and repair company, enters a below-cost comprehensive maintenance contract with the preschool affiliated with his church. The preschool subsequently learns of the drug incident at the shelter and contacts the new manager of the shelter, who states that the entire volunteer staff was replaced because of their drug-related activities, thus clearly but falsely implicating the maintenance worker. Based on the new information, the school immediately terminates the contract. The resulting court case involves the maintenance worker's claims against the shelter manager for, among other things, defamation and interference with contractual relations.

(f) Assault and Battery

Assault and battery are actually two distinct torts. Assault may occur when through his or her acts a person intentionally causes another reasonably to fear that he or she will be physically harmed. Thus, actual contact is not necessary. Battery is the intentional and unpermitted physical contact with another regardless of whether that contact caused any physical or psychological harm. In most cases, but not all, a battery is accompanied by an assault.

Assault and/or battery is not common in the workplace or most other situations involving human interaction. Increasingly, however, allegations of sexual harassment in the workplace are accompanied by claims of assault and battery. Certainly, it is not difficult to understand how unwelcome physical contact by a co-worker or supervisor, especially if it appears intended to arouse or indicate sexual desire, meets the basic requirements of assault and/or battery—fear or apprehension, intentional conduct, and physical contact.

Example I

A teacher of an adult Sunday school class accompanied his students on a weekend retreat. On the beach, while the other participants were in or near the lake, the teacher came up behind a female student whom he had dated while they were both in high school 15 years earlier and wrapped his arms around her. She asked him to leave her alone and rebuked him for touching her without permission or warning. She later sought psychological treatment when the incident caused her to relive the severe and debilitating emotional pain she had experienced when their romantic relationship ended. Alleging battery, she sought compensatory and punitive damages from the teacher.

Example II

Having experienced several incidents involving violent and intoxicated fairgoers, the president of a 4-H club placed a small handgun under the cash register near the door to the exhibit hall at the county fair. When he was closing the hall one night, an obviously inebriated but otherwise well-behaved man asked him for change for the telephone. The president removed the gun, pointed it briefly at the drunk, cocked it, and then held it down at his side as he ordered the shaken man to leave the hall. Two years and 11 months later, just before the three-year statute of limitations expired, after having been in counseling, the man filed an assault claim against both the 4-H club and its president.

17.9 NEGLIGENCE

(a) Misrepresentation

This tort arises when a plaintiff relies on the defendant's seemingly innocuous statement—as it turns out, a statement that the defendant knew or should have known to be false. The essential elements of this action are present when:

- The defendant made a false representation of fact, intention, opinion, or law;
- The defendant knew or should have known that the information was false;
- The defendant intended the plaintiff to rely on the misrepresentation;
- The plaintiff in fact acted or refrained from acting in reliance on the misrepresentation, and;
- The plaintiff suffered loss, damage, or injury as a result of reliance on the misrepresentation.

Example

The unpaid chairman and vice-chairman of the board of directors of a well-known not-for-profit trade group convinced the president of a rival group to resign and take a similar position with their organization. Their biggest selling point was the financial strength of their organization, which was due to the long-time membership of two large multinational corporations. Both of those corporations had recently told the retiring president of their intent to drop their memberships and join the rival trade group. Within a few hours of announcing his resignation and taking the offered position, the new president learned that his employer's annual revenue would soon drop 50 percent because of the reduced membership. The new president sued both members of the recruiting duo for negligent misrepresentation.

(b) Hiring/Retention

This tort places liability on an employer who knew or should have known that an employee was unfit to hold the position, or perform the job, to which he or she was assigned. A plaintiff alleging this violation of common law must establish that:

- ◆ The employee was unfit for the job or should have been more closely supervised when performing the job;
- ◆ The plaintiff's harm or injury was the direct result of the employee's unfit status or the lack of supervision, and;
- ◆ The employer knew or should have known of the employee's unfit status or the need for close supervision.

Example

The unpaid president of a local office workers' union hires a member's out-of-work husband to clean the office two nights a week. The cleaner was unemployed because he was fired from his last job as a janitor upon his conviction for stealing various items from the office areas he cleaned. Soon after he started work at the union hall he stole several calculators, two dozen computer disks, and a keychain from the union's secretary's desk. Using the secretary's house key, he entered her home, stole her jewelry, and severely injured her husband. The union president's unsuccessful defense in the negligent hiring case was that she was not aware of the janitor's conviction. A routine preemployment reference check probably would have turned it up.

17.10 CONTRACT

(a) Handbooks

Many organizations provide employees with a handbook that describes many personnel policies, together with the organization's rules and regulations and expectations for employee conduct. Sometimes handbooks include useful information such as details about various services available to employees.

Handbooks often have been relied upon as contracts between employer and employee. Thus, if a handbook states that the organization's policy is to allow disciplined employees to appeal a suspension administered by a supervisor to upper management, and the employee is denied the opportunity to appeal such a suspension, the employee could seek a court's assistance, or even damages, for breach of contract.

Numerous lawsuits have been filed claiming that a little-noticed phrase in a handbook constitutes a contract. Plaintiffs in such lawsuits often claim, either directly or by implication, that they may not have continued the employment relationship but for that phrase. Accordingly, most employers include in such handbooks clear language stating that no portion of the handbook is intended to be, nor may it be relied upon, or construed as, a contract by employees, applicants, or anyone else.

(b) Implied Covenant of Good Faith

The courts in a few states hold that an element of the employment relationship is an implied promise by the parties to the relationship to act in good faith and with fair dealing. Dismissed employees bringing suit successfully under this theory argue that an employer's actions were contrary to its stated policies or were carried out in an arbitrary manner or in bad faith, thus breaching the implied agreement to act fairly and in good faith.

The courts in those states that do permit suit for breach of implied covenant have relied on numerous theories and rationales for justification. Because of the variety of legal theories serving as foundations for these actions, it is not practical to list a few essential elements of a plaintiff's case from a case brought on this claim.

Example

A large charity in a major metropolitan area hires a public relations spokesman to improve awareness of the organization's used-clothing drives in the suburbs. Shortly after he was hired the new spokesman was injured in a hunting accident, causing him to develop a long-term but not permanent speech impediment that prevented him from making public statements or speeches. He was summarily discharged for being unable to perform his new job fully. The court agreed with the discharged spokesman that the organization had violated the covenant of good faith and fair dealing implicit in its employment policies and lengthy employee handbook.

(c) Reliance

This contract-based action that may arise when a person relies to his or her detriment on the misrepresentations, whether negligent or intentional, of an employer. The key elements are whether the reliance was reasonable and whether the detriment was sufficient. Statements by agents for a recruiting employer often are deemed "puffery," not unlike statements a consumer might expect to hear on some used-car lots.

Some courts hold sufficient detriment to be relocating to a distant city to take an offered position, or foregoing another employment offer. Other courts require a combination of these and other elements to warrant damages.

Example

When he retires from elective office, a highly respected and well–known state politician is recruited by two influential state-wide professional societies. Both offer the politician an executive position with a huge salary, a long list of perquisites, and a lavish entertainment budget. The polititian accepts the offer of the larger of the two organizations. Within a year the long-running internal feud between the older members and their younger counterparts is settled by splitting the larger organization into two separate associations. The retired politician sues both new organizations, claiming detrimental reliance because neither will continue to employ him in any capacity.

17.11 CONCLUSIONS

The purpose of this chapter is not to lay out all federal and state statutes and regulations under those statutes that govern the employment relationship. Rather, the laws listed above represent the most commonly used federal statutes with which all employers must be somewhat familiar. The bibliography immediately following this chapter lists several excellent and far more comprehensive sources, which should be made available to the management of any employing organization.

Depending on the nature of the organization using volunteers in leadership or decision-making positions, under almost all federal employment statutes as well as their state counterparts their volunteers can through their actions and decisions commit violations for which their organizations can be held liable. Some insurance companies offer policies protecting against substantial losses resulting from such violations. However, it is questionable whether an insurance company will issue a policy covering the violative conduct of a person who is not a paid agent or official of the insured.

With few exceptions, most federal employment laws do not protect volunteers. It is clear, however, that volunteers are protected by those statutes to the extent that the organization to which they provide a service can affect the volunteers' future employment.

In light of the rapid growth of the nonprofit sector and its important role in every community and in the national economy, it is likely that courts and agencies gradually will extend coverage of employment laws and regulations to volunteers. To the extent that a volunteer relationship resembles that of an employment relationship, it is likely that the spirit and intent, if not the letter, of employment laws will be found applicable.

SUGGESTED READINGS

Adler, R. L., and F. Coleman, (1993). *Employment-Labor Law Audit.* Potomac, MD.: Laurdan Associates, Inc.

Bokat, S. A., and M. C. Zeiberg, (1994). *Labor and Employment Law; Corporate Law Department Forms and Policies.* Washington: ACCA Press.

Coulson, R. (1981). *The Termination Handbook.* New York: The Free Press.

Drucker, Peter F. (1990). *Managing the Non-profit Organization.* New York: Harper Business.

Drucker, P. F. (1994). "The Age of Social Transformation." *The Atlantic Monthly*, November.

Green, R. M. and R. J. Reibstein, (1992). *Employer's Guide to Workplace Torts*. Washington: BNA Books.

Ivancevich, J.M. (1995). *Human Resource Management*. Chicago: Irwin.

Kahn, S. C., *et al.* (1990). *Personnel Director's Legal Guide*, 2nd ed. Boston: Warren Gorham Lamont.

Kahn, S. C., *et al.* (1993). *Personnel Director's Legal Guide*, 2nd ed., 1993 Cum. Supp. Boston: Warren Gorham Lamont

Panaro, G. P. (1993). *Employment Law Manual*, 2nd ed. Boston: Warren Gorham Lamont.

Panaro, G. P. (1994). *Employment Law Manual*, 2nd ed., 1994 Supp. Boston: Warren Gorham Lamont.

Personnel Policy Manual. (1995). Louisville, KY. Personnel Policy Service, Inc.

Schlei, B. L. and P. Grossman, (1983). *Employment Discrimination Law*, 2nd ed. Chicago: American Bar Association.

Thorne, J. D. (1990). *A Concise Guide to Successful Employment Practices*. Chicago: Commerce Clearing House.

CHAPTER ◇ 18

NATIONAL SERVICE: TWENTY QUESTIONS AND SOME ANSWERS

Jon Van Til, Ph.D.
Professor of Urban Studies, Rutgers University at Camden

Frances Ledwig
Volunteer Development Associates, Colorado Springs

18.1 Introduction

18.2 Underlying Values

18.3 Operational Considerations

18.4 Practical Policies for Managers of National and Community Service Volunteers

References and Suggested Readings

18.1 INTRODUCTION

This chapter raises a number of questions about an important contemporary movement in the field of volunteer management—the provision of national service. National service gives rise to a number of questions, questions that will need to be addressed by those who work with volunteers in the years ahead, particularly as they begin to be confronted by cohorts of young people who want to serve in their agencies and communities.

Let us begin with an informal definition: National service involves governmental support of the performance of structured voluntary action by citizens, usually youths, toward the end of strengthening both values of citizenship and behaviors evincing caring and concern for others. As a policy initiative, national service has been supported in principle by nearly every incoming American president in the twentieth century. Few of these initiatives, however, have survived the press of other governmental priorities, and in recent memory, only the initiatives of Presidents Kennedy and Clinton have yielded legislation and programs. Kennedy's call to service gave rise to the Peace Corps and a variety of smaller domestic programs. Clinton's national service legislation has resulted in a national commission now known as Americorps.

In his inaugural address, President Clinton sought to define a vision of the kind of nation he wished to lead, a vision in which national service played a central role. Here is what he said:

> It is time to break the bad habit of expecting something for nothing from our Government or from each other. Let us all take more responsibility not only for ourselves and our families but also for our communities and our country. . . .
>
> I challenge a new generation of young Americans to a season of service; to act on your idealism by helping troubled children, keeping company with those in need, reconnecting our torn communities. There is so much to be done. Enough, indeed, for millions of others who are still young in spirit to give of themselves in service, too.
>
> In serving, we recognize a simple but powerful truth: We need each other and we must care for each other.

Just how it is that a governmental policy can bring about these lofty goals is a central issue to be explored in this chapter, which identifies 20 questions regarding national service, questions that volunteer managers will need to understand clearly as they confront the new realities of volunteer service, particularly by youth, in the years ahead. The questions are organized around two major categories, those dealing with underlying values and those involving operational considerations. The questions are:

(a) Underlying Values

1. What will emerge as the guiding vision for national service?
2. What are the core values of national service?
3. How will diversity be provided for in the face of societal tendencies toward increasing segregation and homogeneity?

4. Will participants in national service be residents or commuters?
5. Will the program be designed for the particular benefit of any socioeconomic class?
6. Will the program be universal or needs-based in its rewards?
7. How will the provision of employment training be balanced with that of general education?
8. Will national service be governed in a democratic or a paternalistic mode?
9. Will the focus be placed primarily on the provision of service or on the advocacy of change?
10. Will the program enhance the quality of American democracy? If yes, in which specific ways?

(b) Operational Considerations

11. How will agencies be selected for participation in the program?
12. What results will be expected from the service?
13. Will the program effectively counter prevailing cultural ethics of individualism and self-absorption?
14. Where and how will the interests and voices of client be heard?
15. Will the program seek to serve both civilian and military goals?
16. Will participants in the program be stipended, and if so, to what extent?
17. Will the program rely on a professional or a splendidly amateur management?
18. Will the program be mandatory for all youth or voluntary in its selection?
19. Will the program operate on both the domestic and international levels?
20. Will national service be able to garner enough public support to become an established part of American social policy?

The second part of the chapter traces the implications of these twenty questions for the practice of volunteer management. Criteria are presented for the identification and construction of successful programs as seen from the perspectives of the volunteer, the school, the nonprofit agency within which the service is performed, and the client.

18.2 UNDERLYING VALUES

1. What will emerge as the guiding vision for national service?

Here the question is not only of which vision might emerge and prevail, but whether any single vision will predominate. After all, it is possible that service will come to be institutionalized in our organization society as simply one more thing to be done, administered by a new class of "service-crats."

Initial participants in the development of national service did tend to speak of a movement, articulating a variety of visions in keynote speeches and grant proposals (some 450 of which were submitted for the first round Summer of Service awards in1993, from which 10 programs were selected for support). We see four visions contending:

1. Some see their work as the 1990s' extension of the civil rights movement, in which young people of every race and class will work together to develop new institutions of justice and opportunity. Some see the movement already betrayed by bureaucracy and power (cf. Horwitz, 1993, p. 43).

2. Others seek to rally the forces behind the flag of experiential education, in which students demonstrate that they learn best by doing.

3. Yet others, behind a flag first raised by John Dewey, find sustenance in the educational vision of the community school, in which universities and school systems join forces in opening schools to their surrounding communities, providing job training, continuing education, recreation, and a range of other collaborative social services.

4. A fourth vision focuses itself on voluntary action, framed in the context of democratic institutions and civic participation.

It is too soon to see which of these visions will predominate, and a likely outcome is that all four, and others as well, will from time to time inspire and inform the variety of programs that we may expect to see emerge in the years ahead. It is important to note, though, that "in the mid-1980s, however, long before Clinton proposed his national service plan, a renewed movement for community service took hold on college and high-school campuses. A generation of young people had been roundly accused of being a 'lost generation,' apathetic and having no social conscience. With the federal government retreating from social responsibility on all fronts under Ronald Reagan, young people eager to make a difference said let's *do something*. By the end of the decade, only the environmental movement could match it on college campuses for sheer size, vitality, and longevity" (Kallick, 1993, p. 2).

Countryman and Sullivan (1993) contrast the Bush–Reagan model of voluntarism with the Clinton model of *service entrepreneurship*. The voluntarism model focuses on the service of the volunteer and tends to neglect consideration of the impact of the service. Service entrepreneurship, on the other hand, "has come to mean the creation of funding and institutional mechanisms that give young people with good ideas the opportunity to test those ideas by establishing service projects in communities of need" (p. 31).

2. What are the core values of national service?

Underlying the various visions of national service are a number of core values that figure in most discussions. National service is said to provide an antidote to individualism in society, to encourage responsible activism, to fortify the moral currency of citizens, and to encourage the development of effective partnerships between governmental and voluntary organizations in society.

Kallick (1993) identifies the following core values of national service: reciprocity (assuring that both the service provider and the recipient of service gain), accountability to the community (assuring that the community benefits), youth leadership (providing a rite of passage to full participation in society), a multigenerational approach (providing role models for younger kids, allowing them to learn about careers from older folks), crossing the color line (developing sensitivity to others), and open-mindedness (welcoming all to come as they are).

Writing from a neo-conservative perspective, Cunningham (1993) notes the failure of national service programs to consider the use of private money, and the excessive trust in government shown by participants (p. 2). "'Grassroots' to these students means government doling out money at a local level. They find the idea of bureaucracy somehow offensive in the abstract and often refer to it." They "have no clue" about the cost of programs (p. 3).

From the values perspective, then, we may see that national service is highly valued by those who see as appropriate a partnership between government, citizen, and voluntary organizations in enhancing individual commitment to service and participation. For those suspicious of the role of government, however, national service takes on a more menacing appearance. From this perspective it is seen as an arm of an intrusive and overarching state, seeking to extend governmental power in realms properly left to governmental action. As such, then, national service tends to be viewed as an appropriate policy by liberals and with a certain amount of suspicion by conservatives.

3. How will diversity be provided for in the face of societal tendencies toward increasing segregation and homogeneity?

As Robert Reich has perceptively observed, American society has become "zip-coded." The quality of the schools our children attend, the tax burden we endure, the insurance rates we are charged, and the fund-raising solicitations we receive are all conditioned by our place of residence. As a result, our society is more rigidly stratified than ever before on grounds of social class, race and ethnicity, and age.

For national service, the zip-coding of America raises the question of the degree to which it is possible or desirable to establish programs in which the service providers themselves are culturally and socioeconomically diverse. Critics of national service have frequently worried that it would become a two-tier program, with a richer set of rewards and experiences provided to middle-class participants.

Since social class and race are rather strongly related in American society, the question of the degree to which minority and majority students will be represented among the service participants, both n absolute numbers and in the mix of individual programs, also arises.

A third diversity issue involves the extensive focus in current discussions on young people as participants in national service. Other forms of voluntary action in society have increasingly come to focus on adult members of the workforce and retirees. The role of the nonyoung typically is ignored in discussions of national service.

4. Will participants in national service be residents or commuters?

The importance of this issue may seem less grand in the United States than it has been in Trinidad, for example, where parents from the island's two major ethnic groups quashed a residential program out of fear that it might inspire intermarriage among their children. But as we have already seen, Americans have segregated themselves dramatically on the bases of class, race, and age. A major program that national service programs will face involve bringing service providers into physical proximity to those they will be serving. The problem is both theoretical and practical. The Jamaica example indicates the resistance that may be felt in society to mixing service participants by class and race, especially in residential settings.

On the level of logistics, many willing service participants are simply located too far away from the people who need the service to make for a workable program. Thus, in Los Angeles, a major problem exists in transporting high school volunteers to low-income recipients of service. Students in the Palos Verde schools, for instance, face a commute of over an hour to their service locations. Similarly, many colleges and universities find themselves situated in bucolic small towns too distant from low-income urban areas to make it feasible to ongoing service programs.

Clearly, urban universities are advantaged in the provision of residential service programs, as their location permits easy access to a wide range of low-income communities, and their student bodies themselves are typically more diverse than those of their nonurban counterparts. Urban areas, with their networks of public transportation, are also more readily suited to the establishment of "service commuting."

Although this problem has received little consideration in the literature on national service, it has not been ignored by prospective service providers. Surveys by the George H. Gallup International Institute indicate a strong preference on the part of young people to providing service in their own local community (56 percent) rather than in another community in the state (6 percent), elsewhere in the United States (16 percent), or in a developing foreign country (20 percent).

5. Will the program be designed for the particular benefit of any socioeconomic class?

Countryman and Sullivan (1993, p. 29) have noted that the "service movement needs to grapple with two weaknesses that have plagued it through the past decade: (1) the under-representation of young people of color and young people from working-class and poor backgrounds in the leadership of most of the nationally recognized service organizations; and (2) the failure to develop strategies that seek to solve the problems caused by persistent poverty, rather than just meeting the immediate needs of poor people." Horwitz (1993, p. 42) adds: "All too often, service neatly separates the haves from the have-notes, those with skills from those with needs."

It is easy to imagine that national service will become a fashionable activity of the middle class, part of a contemporary Sir and Lady Bountiful movement. It is also possible that it will become another mandatory hurdle for poor and minority youth to surmount on the difficult path toward eventual employment and economic security. In either of these cases, both youth and the nation are unlikely to gain.

The answer, once again, lies in the path of diversity, integration, and sensitive planning. National service will work only if it is supported and participated in by Americans of all backgrounds. It will be more effective if it brings people of different backgrounds together in well-constructed teams. And it cannot succeed if it does not address the systematic inequalities and discrimination that has come to characterize late-twentieth-century American society. Countryman and Sullivan (1993, p. 34) strike a judicious note with their observation that "Service opportunities should not be limited to poor youth, but the central mission of national service should be to strengthen the capacity of poor communities to solve their own problems. . . . The first step is to encourage poor youth to develop explanations for the realities they perceive in the community."

6. Will the program be universal or needs-based in its rewards?

The issue here deals with the monetary reward of national service, whose participants are not volunteers in the pure sense. Some, to be sure, will see them as stipended volunteers in the tradition of Peace Corps volunteers, people who receive a below-market wage payment at the completion of their term of service. Others, and with equally strong rationale, will call them low-wage public employees on deferred payment.

Volunteer managers are familiar with these debates and have become increasingly accustomed to dealing with stipended volunteers, whether they are enrolled in governmental programs, assigned as welfare recipients, committed by courts for the provision of community service, or enrolled in college and receiving course credit for performing the service as part of a civic education course. The prevalence of low-wage workers is so strong in the field that one leading scholar has urged defining as a volunteer anyone working for less than a market wage in a position of significance to societal need (Smith, 1994).

Gartner and Reissman (1993, p. 36) weigh this issue in a discussion of elitist and democratic themes in national service. They offer a number of items of advice for participants, primarily along the lines of making certain that a contribution is being made. They also reflect on an initial preference to make participation entirely voluntary but then recognize that this raises the dilemma of "creaming"—attracting only participants of such ability and background that they could afford to take a year off for the performance of service.

Gartner and Reissman urge that thought be given to involving large numbers of people in national service—"making the program a regular part of the curriculum in schools, for example. In thinking about national service, it is worth keeping in mind that democratizing help giving—making it available to the widest possible audience—can help transform the helping process itself. And that would go along way toward removing the pitfalls and problems associated with receiving help and giving help in our society."

7. How will the provision of employment training be balanced with that of general education?

This is an issue that really generates heat when national service supporters get together (Eberly, 1992). Those who see service as a way to get the dispossessed close to the mainstream argue that job training and preparedness must be central, as in a Job Corps or Youth Corps program. Liberal arts types tend to prefer their service pure, although they often note that it cannot hurt to have participation in such a program on one's resume.

Resolution of this issue would best seem to take the form of "both–and" rather than "either–or." It is surely the case that many young people, including among them college graduates, desperately need job training and employment experience as well as the discipline to focus on a single task for eight hours at a time. In addition, almost all young people will benefit from participation in a socially significant task, particularly if it is performed in a supervised group setting.

8. Will national service be governed in a democratic or a paternalistic mode?

National service typically is justified in the language of a full and participatory democracy. Claims are made that service will expand the horizons of individuals and extend the development of a caring and active society (cf. Barber and Battistoni, 1993). A question arises about the nature of the management of such an effort: Will it itself be participatory and democratic?

The initial Clinton national service foray, Summer of Service, got things off to a rocky start in 1993. As Countryman and Sullivan (1993, p. 33) put it: "There is no better example of what happens when youth of color encounter community service models rooted in voluntarism and service entrepreneurship than the training week for the Summer of Service program (SOS) that took place this June. Many of the week's problems were the result of the radical disjuncture between the training's emphasis on physical exercise and team-building, and the experiential understanding that the SOS participants who came from poor communities brought with them of what their communities need. What these young people craved was the space to have structured discussions about the causes of social problems in their communities, and an opportunity to develop specific ideas for how they might solve them."

Summer of Service planners and trainers were overwhelming white, male, adult, and middle class. Participants were overwhelmingly black, young, and of marginal economic background. It is not surprising that the training sessions were often chaotic and the program delivery uncertain at best. As national service matures, its leaders will need to consider the development and implementation of models of management consistent with the democratic vision that underlies the program (see question 1 above).

9. *Will the focus be placed primarily on the provision of service or on the advocacy of change?*

The issue here is one of the oldest dilemmas in the field of volunteer management. Is the aim of volunteerism solely to bandage the wounds of those injured by fate or structure in society? Or should volunteers aim as well at the identification of the societal sources that cause these wounds and seek to right these injustices? Liberals tend to support both forms of voluntary action; conservatives tend to be wary of any effort of youth to rectify society on the basis of social justice. When the Reagan administration came into office, for example, a decided effort was made to restrict voluntarism to the provision of service alone.

This may be another of those "both–and" questions. There is no question, as the longtime leader of the National Council of Negro Women, Dorothy Height, has argued, that when people need Band-Aids they need Band-Aids, not a cure for cancer. On the other hand, the voluntary tradition boasts a long and distinguished history of social movements, ranging from the antislavery crusade through the suffrage movement to more contemporary movements in the area of civil rights, gender equality, and the redress of poverty.

Countryman and Sullivan (1993, p. 30) identify the dilemma from the point of view of the young service providers assigned to work in an impoverished community: "Either you focus solely on the individual children who have that special something it takes to make it out of their community (talent, determination, a committed parent); or you begin to mobilize the local community to work for changes in government policies and programs that will improve the life chances of every child." Or, perhaps, you find a way to advance both goals within the confines of program, agency, and community.

10. *Will the program enhance the quality of American democracy? If yes, in which specific ways?*

Volunteer managers who venture into the national service arena will quickly become aware that volunteer and volunteerism are often used disparagingly to describe well-intentioned but ineffectual actions of middle-class individuals to relate to some societal issue or other. Long-time community organizer and writer Harry Boyte, among others (cf. Barber and Battistoni, 1993), has questioned the degree to which a focus on voluntarism will achieve goals of citizenship (in Peters, 1993, p. 47). Peters observes that "the language of the service movement is primarily a language of caring and concern, of private feelings and personal development, rather than a political language tied to the skills and concepts of public life" (1993, p. 47). He concludes: "Citizenship is not easy, but without it, there can be no democracy" (p. 50).

Volunteer managers who work with national service participants will find a real challenge in blending the strengths of community service with a management style that embodies democratic principles. They have the chance to implement participatory management and to assure that the young people with whom they work learn both how to serve and how to affect a range of issues of power, governance, and control that are vital to effective citizenship.

18.3 OPERATIONAL CONSIDERATIONS

11. How will agencies be selected for participation in the program?

Choosing which agencies will become suitable receptors for national service participants will be an important decision. In the public–voluntary partnership that national service is likely to involve, this choice will probably be made in a joint fashion between the state governing body and interested agencies. Federal legislation is likely to constrain the fields of placement, initially to education, recreation, law enforcement, and elder care.

Over time, advocacy organizations, whether left- or right-wing, whether they are engaged in voter registration, environmental policy, abortion provision or control, or the redress of social and economic grievances, will surely claim their share of national service participants. These claims are likely to be opposed by policymakers who fear the political backlash that association with a controversial cause is likely to engender. At the same time, these claimants will find patrons in those policymakers friendly to the causes and approaches undertaken.

National service may end up placing its participants only in programs whose purposes are so bland and generally acceptable that they arouse little political opposition. Considering the power that veto groups exercise in American democracy, it would seem difficult and unlikely that service participants will ever have the chance to work for such agencies as Greenpeace, Focus on the Family, or the National Abortion Rights League.

12. What results will be expected from the service?

If national service is structured so that placements are typically provided in agencies that have won a position by means of a competitive grants process, programs are likely to be evaluated in terms of the ability to provide a service in an innovative and original fashion. Such *service entrepreneurship* is a primary aspect of David Osborne's thinking on reinventing government and is widely valued within the Clinton administration.

In a sophisticated critique, Countryman and Sullivan (1993) note that this Clinton-Osborne service entrepreneurship approach may serve to "encourage the creating of funding and evaluation criteria that push young people toward the provision of services for poor people and away from efforts to empower poor people to find solutions to problems caused by poverty. The danger of service entrepreneurship is that it risks rewarding clever ideas and programs that may come and go, while diverting resources from established service and advocacy programs already operation within poor communities" (p. 32). A more suitable standard for the evaluation of such programs might well involve the acceptability of a wider range of outcomes than mere service innovation.

13. Will the program effectively counter prevailing cultural ethics of individualism and self-absorption?

We should not assume that voluntary action necessarily engenders an identification with the fortunes and misfortunes of those who the volunteer attempts to serve. Countryman and Sullivan (1993, p. 32) note that "the concept of entrepreneurship also brings with it the marketplace's fixation on the bottom line." The national service entrepreneur may well be in it for her or his own advancement.

A critical firsthand report by Cunningham (1993) finds that the "focus of Summer of Service corps members seems to be incredibly, unswervingly, on themselves. Many of their objections begin with boilerplate therapy lingo: 'I feel uncomfortable when you say. . . ' " (Cunningham, 1993, p. 7). Her article concludes with a bitter satire of bored and rowdy youth delighting when their clients did not show, leaving behind a messy picnic ground as they leave in their vans. "All that remained of the day—feathers, rocks, leaves, beer bottles and those enormous, ugly mushrooms— witnessed that America Had Been Served."

Programs ought to be evaluated, Countryman and Sullivan remind us, in terms of their impact on the community. As social scientists Mark Rosentraub, Louis Wechsler, andRobert Warren have suggested, such community social service budgets need to be developed to allow for the fullest assessment of how programs do and do not meet the needs of communities and their members.

14. *Where and how will the interests and voices of client be heard?*

It is very easy to overlook the felt needs, expressed or not, of those identified as the "served" in programs of national service. Those who planned the training module of Summer of Service, for example, noted only when they completed their deliberations that representatives of the communities to be served had not been invited to participate in their process. Volunteer managers will play a crucial role in assuring appropriate community input to programs of national service. If they and other community leaders do not speak for a full role for the served, programs of national service are highly likely to dish up prepackaged programs whose delivery will appear as the latest visit of Lady and Sir Bountiful.

Wolf (1993, p. 15) notes that the major recommendation for national service that emerged from her study of community leaders was the "need to involve community agencies and those they serve in the process early on. If individuals in the grassroots community are wanted as partners in this effort, ways must be found to reach out to them and offer them a real opportunity for involvement." Wolf identifies the following as crucial in evaluating the quality of community participation:

- Use of respectful language and vocabulary
- Appropriate placing and timing of public meetings
- Awareness of "diversity outreach"
- Involvement in search for funding
- Involvement in grant writing and planning
- Awareness of the context for action
- Flexible development of management plans
- Provision of appropriate training for participants

Wolf (1993, p. 14) quotes an agency director who has worked with youth volunteers: "When community service is top-down and bureaucratic, it never gets past the surface of the problem. It deals with cosmetic repair and nurse-maiding rather than structural renovations and social surgery."

15. *Will the program seek to serve both civilian and military goals?*

Viewed comparatively across national experiences, national service programs often involve military service as their major component (Sherraden and Eberly, 1982). In many countries of the world, a military leader directs the national service program.Changing valuations of the need and prestige of military service may restore military service to the equation in the United States, but for the present, only civilian forms of service are being discussed and developed.

16. *Will participants in the program be stipended, and if so, to what extent?*

This issue may be worth an intellectual or philosophical debate, but it has quite clearly been resolved as a policy issue. As was the case with previous federally funded forms of service, such as VISTA and the Peace Corps, those who serve will be paid about the minimum wage. Summer of Service participants, 5,000 of whom were recruited in 1993 for service at 10 sites, were provided $1,000 in college funding at the finish of their eight weeks of service. Participants in other programs (Boston's City Year, Georgia's Peach Corps) typically receive $5,000 for college expenses upon completion of the process. Thus the focus of these programs is on service, not on pure voluntarism.

17. *Will the program rely on a professional or a splendidly amateur management?*

Volunteer managers are likely to face resistance from national service participants if they introduce management tools perceived as excessively formal or bureaucratic into the placement process. Cunningham noted the fierce opposition of participants to any hint of bureaucracy in the Summer of Service program. (She also notes a startling similarity between that service program and the old Russian joke: "I'll pretend to work, you pretend to pay me.")

Volunteer managers will need to be prepared to explain to service participants why rules and regulations are necessary, why work needs to be supervised and done well, and why some participants will need to be separated from the program for insensitive or inadequate performance of duties. The bottom line must be maintained: The overarching aim of the service program is to help people and build communities.

18. *Will the program be mandatory for all youth or voluntary in its selection?*

The question of whether service should be universal or voluntary has been joined on campus in recent years with the development of university programs of civic and service education. At Rutgers University, for example, political scientist Benjamin Barber has articulated the view that requiring service is an appropriate decision for educators to make, just as it is appropriate to have a math or English requirement. Everyone needs to learn to be an effective citizen, Barber argues, and a university has the perfect right to assert this program as a required aspect of its curriculum. A similar position is taken on the secondary school level by legislation in the state of Maryland, where all high school students are required to meet a community service requirement.

Three main arguments are commonly held in opposition to the mandatory position:

1. Mandatory service is an oxymoron: If it is ordered by the state, it cannot be seen as voluntary.
2. Mandatory service is organizationally infeasible: It is impossible to find that many service placements.
3. Mandatory programs of service comprise an ill-conceived intervention by the state into realms of action appropriately left to individuals and communities (Cunningham, 1993, p. 4).

The reader is invited to assess this debate. For the time being, however, there is no evidence that a mandatory program of national service is being given any serious consideration in American society.

19. Will the program operate on both domestic and international levels?

This is another question that has not advanced to the current agenda. For the time being, national service is being viewed as entirely a domestic enterprise.

20. Will national service be able to garner enough public support to become an established part of American social policy?

By mid-1995, national service found itself in the uncomfortable position of having become an issue of considerable political controversy. On the one hand, President Clinton clung tenaciously to its support, calling it one of the most important pieces of legislation passed during the first two years of his administration. In opposition to this view, the newly elected Speaker of the House, Congressman Newt Gingrich of Georgia, identified national service as a prime example of the kind of wasteful government spending the new Republican majority had been brought to power to eliminate.

The outcome of this debate will be settled by appropriations and legislations adopted after the present volume has gone to press. However, the issues raised by the President and the Speaker will continue to face American society whatever the fate of the current national service initiative: Does the federal government have a role to play in supporting service? Or should service emerge only if initiated and entirely supported by voluntary organizations? Should the federal government play a direct role in helping equip youth to serve others? Or should such service be left to state and local governments to provide in a redesigned welfare state that sees a greatly lessened role for the federal government?

The half-life of issues is short in our society, and many a policy fades from public sight some scant months after initial proposal. It seems clear, however, that a significant part of the fate of the current national service initiative has come to rest in the hands of political leaders jockeying for electoral advantage and momentary publicity. If these leaders do come to an agreement to sustain the national service initiative, they will require the cooperation of professional volunteer managers, whose assessments of the initial programs will play an important role in the eventual success of whatever national service programs are launched and maintained in American society.

The second section of this chapter addresses the kind of practical challenges the Clinton initiative presents to volunteer managers, whatever the ultimate political fate of that initiative. If current programs are indeed zeroed out by Congress, these challenges will remain to face those new national service initiatives that will surely be proposed at some future point in the American experience.

18.4 PRACTICAL POLICIES FOR MANAGERS OF NATIONAL AND COMMUNITY SERVICE VOLUNTEERS

If we are serious about creating a society of citizens who value the common good, and who are willing, on occasion, to put the needs of others ahead of their own, then we must assure that the opportunities for service we offer (or mandate) through service learning or educational award programs are managed well from the perspective of the volunteers, the schools, and the agencies whose missions are served, as well as the clients.

The National and Community Service Trust Act of 1993 was signed into law by President Clinton on September 21 (cf. Waldner, 1995). The impact on volunteerism in the United States is likely to be monumental, especially on student volunteers, their teachers, and their sponsors (organizations or agencies that utilize their services). Since a major portion of the legislation addresses youth and student volunteering, a primary goal is to build a foundation for service among the nation's youth, inspiring them to serve and instilling in them the values and attitude to serve effectively after graduation (Lohmann, 1992, p. 225). Without careful attention to sound volunteer management principles, the effort could indeed become counterproductive. State commissions, schools, and nonprofit agencies will need to collaborate to create optimum experiences for students who will be involved in service learning and community-based programs that utilize their services.

(a) Overview of the Legislation

While our intent in this chapter is to focus on those programs that involve and affect youth volunteers, it is helpful to be familiar with the broader scope of the Trust Act. The legislation is complex. The comprehensive national service program will be administered by the Corporation for National Service, created by combining two existing federal agencies, the Commission on National and Community Service and ACTION.

The centerpiece program of the new national legislation, AmeriCorps, the National Service Initiative, is designed to solve problems by mobilizing young people in service to our communities and country. This new program offers educational awards to Americans who make a substantial commitment to service. Mandates for the National Service Initiative (AmeriCorps) that are of interest to organizations planning to develop a program or alter an existing program to meet the guidelines are:

◆ National service must address unmet educational, environmental, human, or public safety needs.
◆ The corporation and state commissions must establish priorities among these needs that programs must address.
◆ National service must improve the life of the participants through citizenship education and training.
◆ Participants may not displace or duplicate the functions of existing workers.

The legislation also addresses:

◆ Extension and improvement of programs in the National and Community Service Act of 1990 that enhance elementary and secondary education through school-related community service, support after-school and summer programs (Serve America), and fund service programs on college campuses (Higher Education Innovative Projects for Community Service)

◆ Support for the Civilian Community Corps, which provides service opportunities in areas adversely affected by defense cutbacks

◆ Support for the Points of Light Foundation, which supports volunteerism

◆ Extension and improvement of the VISTA and the Older American Programs, authorized by the Domestic Volunteer Service Act

◆ Acceleration of implementation of the Stafford Loan Forgiveness Program

The corporation has determined goals, standards, and guidelines for state commissions that must be established to receive and distribute the federal grant monies that will help fund the local programs. Specifics have been outlined for the structure of the corporation itself, for structuring state commissions, for allocation of funds, for program development, and for training and technical assistance. Federal funds must supplement, not supplant, state and local dollars.

(b) Where to Get More Information

Much of the preceding information was gleaned from the official White House summary of the new legislation. More information and timelines will be available from the new Corporation for National Service, 529 14th Street NW, Suite 452, Washington, DC 20045, 202/724-0600. Further information will also be available from state governments, particularly regarding specific state structures. Since a portion of funding allocated on a competitive basis, it is important for nonprofit organization leaders to be informed. The summary also states that in cases of comparable quality programs, there will be a general priority for nonprofit organizations.

What follows will apply more specifically to those formal programs of the National Service Initiative, Serve America, and Higher Education innovative Projects for Community Service, as well as informal volunteer programs and projects involving youth and student volunteers.

(c) Common Characteristics

As the organizational discipline of volunteer management continues to evolve, some benchmarks for accomplishing the desired results of a national service venture become more predictable. Successful formal programs associated with Americorps and Learn and Serve America, as well as successful informal volunteer projects involving youth and student volunteers, will probably exhibit many of the following characteristics:

From the Perspective of Students

1. The teacher or other leader has presented an historical perspective of voluntary service in the United States and has promoted community service as a valuable life experience, connected to other aspects of learning (Van Til, 1988, p. 26).

2. Students understand that there is an exchange of value in volunteering time and effort without being paid including:

   ◆ Giving back to their community some of the benefits they have received
   ◆ Encountering people and places different from their world
   ◆ Making a difference in others' lives by using their own skills and talents
   ◆ Learning about themselves—their interests, strengths, weaknesses, and beliefs
   ◆ Learning to be a responsible citizen in society
   ◆ Gaining experience and skills that can make them more employable
   ◆ Acting on their own priorities for developing a better world (Barnett and Losso, 1992, p. 1)

3. Students have been interviewed and placed in an appropriate position based on personal interests and motivations.

4. Students have received a concise description of what they agreed to do, how it relates to the mission of the organization, time and place to work, to whom they will report, where to get help, what orientation and training they will receive, and how they will be evaluated (Van Til, 1988, p. 26).

5. Students feel appreciated and recognized in a way that is meaningful to them, both as individuals and as members of the team of volunteers and staff.

6. Students have the opportunity to reflect on the volunteer experience with other volunteers at the work site and with fellow students involved in other types of community service (Van Til and Dunn, 1991, p. 1).

From the Perspective of the School

1. Educational objectives are clearly stated. Service learning relates to what is happening in the classroom. Students are given the option to choose a community service assignment that relates to the subject of their choice.

2. The program is carefully introduced and creatively promoted.

3. Agencies requesting student volunteers have been properly screened.

4. Appropriate positions have been secured for all students who want or need to be involved in community service. The community demonstrates its belief in the value of youth service by asking students to become involved in meaningful work for the good of the community (Van Til, 1988, p. 28).

5. Students have the flexibility and freedom to create their own planned experiences as long as they meet the school's service learning criteria (informal volunteering). Innovative projects with a long-range focus on solving problems are encouraged and recognized.

6. Prepared students are accepted by the organization as individuals with skills and talents worth sharing. Assignments challenge students and provide opportunities for them to make decisions (Hall, 1992, p. 263).

7. Administrators and teachers are enlightened in the principles of how to work effectively with volunteers.

8. Parents are informed about the value of service learning and encouraged to support their children—and to become involved themselves.

9. The service learning program is enhanced by the community's evaluation of students and service, as well as students' evaluations of their own experiences and the school's role in preparing them and providing group reflection.

10. The school is the primary advocate for the students. Risks are kept to a minimum. Accurate records are kept.

From the Perspective of the Nonprofit Agency, Organization or Other Site of Service:

1. The agency management team has made the decision to involve student volunteers and communicated that decision to everyone whose work will be affected by the decision.

2. Supervisors have designed age appropriate jobs for students, based on the needs and goals of the organization.

3. A primary concern is implementing the agency's mission, meeting client's needs. Students are there to help as part of the team.

4. Supervisors and other staff have been trained in how to work effectively with all volunteers (including students) and in supervisory skills, if needed.

5. The agency is able to accommodate flexible scheduling to meet the needs of students and families.

6. The agency budgets for and provides orientation, training, and recognition for all volunteers. Accurate records are kept.

7. The agency invites evaluation and planning input from student volunteers and their schools.

From the Perspective of the Client:

1. Students who are considered at risk, or who are or have been receivers of client services, are given an opportunity to make a difference in their own neighborhoods or schools through structured volunteer service.

2. Representative clients are asked to serve on the planning committee designing student volunteer jobs.

3. Clients are invited to evaluate the quality of service they are receiving from student volunteers and to offer suggestions for program improvement.

4. Clients show appreciation to students for valuable service.

Ultimately, schools and nonprofit agencies will be held accountable by the community for the kinds of experiences students have with National Service programs, whether good or bad. Collaboration and integration must occur among all the entities for success to be realized by any of them. Representatives of agencies, school administrations, and students must come together on a regular basis for planning, evaluation, and problem solving. Individual success will result from team effort and should be celebrated by the entire team. The process is demanding but has the potential to become an energizer for everyone involved.

Implementation of the National and Community Service Trust Act is certain to change the face of student volunteerism in the United States, in that it will set standards for the future. Nonprofits and other organizations wanting to take advantage of this promising source of volunteers must place themselves in a state of readiness to maximize opportunities for their programs. Agencies, schools, and students themselves can develop these characteristics of success, whether their community volunteer service is associated with a national program or is a private endeavor.

The goal is to create models for a responsive, caring citizenry by giving students positive experiences as community service volunteers (Van Til, 1988, p. 189). If success is realized, a lifelong pattern of volunteering is likely to develop. On the other hand, if students have bad experiences they are likely to be turned off by formal volunteering for life (Lohmann, 1992, p. 226). Administrators, agency directors, volunteer managers, teachers, parents, and students have the opportunity and an obligation to make community service a good experience. It will be worth the effort.

REFERENCES AND SUGGESTED READINGS

Barber, Benjamin R., and Richard M. Battistoni. 1993. *Education for Democracy: Citizenship, Community, Service.* Dubuque, Iowa: Kendall-Hunt.

Barnett, Bryan, and Grace Losso. 1992. *Getting the Most from Community Service.* New Brunswick, N.J.: Rutgers, The State University of New Jersey.

Buckley, William F. 1990. *Gratitude: Reflections on What We Owe to Our Country.* New York: Random House.

Countryman, Matthew, and Lisa Sullivan. 1993. "National Service: 'Don't Do For, Do With.'" *Social Policy* (Fall): 29–34.

Cunningham, Jill K. 1993. "Adrift in Utopia: Summer of Service Takes on Baltimore." *Philanthropy, Culture and Society* (November): 1 ff.

Eberly, Donald J. 1991. *National Youth Service: A Democratic Institution for the 21st Century.* Washington, D.C.: National Service Secretariat.

Eberly, Donald J. (Ed.). 1992. *National Youth Service: A Global Perspective.* Washington, D.C.: National Service Secretariat.

George H. Gallup International Institute. 1993. *America's Youth in the 1990s.* Princeton, N.J.: Gallup Institute.

George H. Gallup International Institute. 1993. *Perspectives on National Service.* Princeton, N.J.: Gallup Institute, 2 vols.

Gartner, Audrey, and Frank Riessman. 1993. "Making Sure Helping Helps." *Social Policy* (Fall): 35–36.

Hall, Peter Dobkin. 1992. *Inventing the Nonprofit Sector.* Baltimore: Johns Hopkins University Press.

Horwitz, Claudia. 1993. "What Is Wrong with National Service." *Social Policy* (Fall): 37–44.

Kallick, David. 1993. "National Service: How to Make it Work." *Social Policy* (Fall): 2–7.

Kendall, Jane C., and Associates. 1990. *Combining Service and Learning: A Resource Book for Community and Public Service.* Raleigh, N.C.: National Society for Internships and Experiential Education, 2 vols.

Lohmann, Roger. 1992. *The Commons.* San Francisco: Jossey-Bass.

Moskos, Charles C. 1988. *A Call to Civic Service: National Service for Country and Community.* New York: Free Press.

Peters, Scott J. 1993. "A New Citizenship in the Making?" *Social Policy* (Fall): 45–50.

Sherraden, Michael, and Donald Eberly. 1982. *National Service: Social, Economic,and Military Impacts.* New York, Pergamon Press.

Smith, David Horton. 1994. Comments at Inaugural Conference of International Society for Third Sector Research, Pecs, Hungary (July).

Van Til, Jon. 1988. *Mapping the Third Sector: Voluntarism in a Changing Social Economy.* New York: Foundation Center.

Van Til, Jon. 1993. "Here Comes National Service." Pp. 184–186 in Benjamin R. Barber and Richard M. Battistoni, *Education for Democracy: Citizenship, Community, Service.* Dubuque, Iowa: Kendall-Hunt.

Van Til, Jon, and James A. Dunn. 1991. *Report on the Rutgers/Camden Program in Civic Education and Community Service.* Camden, N.J.: Rutgers University Departments of Urban Studies and Political Science.

Waldman, Steven. 1995. *The Bill: How The Adventures of Clinton's National Service Bill Reveal What Is Corrupt, Comic, Cynical—and Noble—About Washington.* New York: Viking.

Wolf, Maura. 1993. "Involving the Community in National Service." *Social Policy* (Fall): 14–20.

A P P E N D I X

Sample Forms and Documents from State Volunteer Programs

Needs Assessment Questionnaire	Georgia Department of Community Affairs
Writing Job Descriptions	Georgia Department of Community Affairs
Volunteer Job Description	
Sample Volunteer Job Description	
Volunteer Interview Checklist	Georgia Department of Community Affairs
Nondirective Interviewing Suggestions	Georgia Department of Community Affairs
Application for Service as a Volunteer	Tennessee Department of Youth Developement
Criminal History Request	State of Oregon, Children's Services Division
Criminal Record Authorization	State of Oregon, Senior and Disabled Services, Department of Human Resources
Record Keeping	Georgia Department of Community Affairs
Volunteer Hours-Master Record	
Supervisory Record	

NEEDS ASSESSMENT QUESTIONNAIRE

1. What are the most pressing jobs/tasks that need doing right now?
   _____
   _____
   _____

2. Can any of these jobs be done by new volunteers? Indicate which ones.

3. Who should be responsible for these volunteers? _____

4. Should a management plan be developed to monitor and supervise the work of these volunteers? _____

5. Would there be any additional expense to the organization if these volunteer jobs are created? _____ How much? _____

6. How could we supplement the budget to accommodate them? _____
   _____

7. Do you think the organization is clear on what the job responsibilities actually are and how much time a volunteer should commit? _____
   _____

8. Would we need to provide training in any particular areas which the present Board and membership cannot provide? _____ If so, what and where could we get the trainers? _____
   _____

9. How much would the training cost? _____

10. Is there any free training that you know of available anywhere? _____
    _____ If so, where? _____

11. If we need to prepare job descriptions, who should write them? _____
    _____

12. Do you think it is a good idea to periodically evaluate the use of volunteers in this organization? _____ If so, who should conduct the evaluation and how should it be accomplished? _____
    _____

13. Should we build in a way to get rid of non-productive volunteers? _____
    How could this be done? _____

14. Do you think the elected officers and Board members of this organization understand the process for managing volunteers? _____

15. If not, how do you think they could be brought around? _____
    _____

16. Would you be willing to assist in developing a volunteer utilization plan based on proven volunteer management techniques? _____

17. If so, what could you contribute in terms of skills, time or finances? _____
    _____

WRITING JOB DESCRIPTIONS

Job descriptions for the volunteer staff are just as important as ones for the paid staff.

You can use the volunteer job description as a basis for:

> Recruitment
> Training Programs
> Supervision
> Assignments
> Evaluation of your volunteers.

If you don't have a volunteer job description (or have one that needs revision), here is a simple format for constructing one. Change it according to your specific needs.

A. JOB TITLE

Make a statementthat is straightforward and accurate. Don't "dress it up" (a janitor is some-times called a "maintenance engineer"). Do make it as attractive as possible ("receptionist" is more appealing than "switchboard operator").

B. STAFF COORDINATOR

Your position title, not your name, since you may be promoted.

C. VOLUNTEER JOB SUMMARY

After you have completed the following specific duties, summarize them in one or two concise sentences.

D. ACTIVITIES AND RESPONSIBILITIES

Make short, easy-to-understand action statements:
"Attends and participates in monthly board meetings."
"Operates independently a one-position switchboard (PBX, cord board)."
"Maintains order and discipline in a cabin with up to seven preteen boys."

Avoid Statements that cannot be measured-"loyal", "dependable", "works with. . . "

Include all of the specific duties. The stop.

E. NEEDED CHARACTERISTICS, EXPERIENCE AND TRAINING

If you list those factors that are absolute requirements (Examples: "Needs to be able to pass a beginning swimmers test"), the recruitment selection process is easier for you and the volunteer when both know and understand the specific expectations.

Avoid fuzzy words in this segment. Instead give specifics such as: "Must be able to deal in a firm but friendly way with minority group teenagers."

This tells the volunteer applicant specific expectations and allows the uncertain ones an easy opportunity to offer their services in another area.
"Should be available at least one Friday night a month." is much better than "Must be reliable in attendance."

F.   TIME COMMITMENT

This tells the volunteer applicant that a commitment is expected and allows you to find out how much time that volunteer is willing to give your program.

It should be clearly stated if the time commitment is flexible or is a specific job to be completed within a certain time period.

G.   SIGNATURE

If the volunteer wishes to accept the position, get a signature, and you sign it also. This has the psychological effect of a "contract" and formalizes the commitment.

Or you may wish to use a formal "contract" agreement.

Many job descriptions also include optional information such as:

Training
What will be provided for the volunteer in the area of orientation and/or training in preparation for the job and how much time it might involve.

Assessment Procedure
How and when the volunteer will be assessed.

Clarity, conciseness and understandability are three key concepts when writing job descriptions.

Does it say what the job is really about?

Does it state clearly what the volunteer will be required to do?

Did you make it sound like a job you would enjoy doing (but just don't have the time)?

(See blank Volunteer Job Description)

VOLUNTEER JOB DESCRIPTION

JOB TITLE: _____

STAFF COORDINATOR: _____

VOLUNTEER JOB SUMMARY: _____

_____

ACTIVITIES AND RESPONSIBILITIES:

1. _____

2. _____

3. _____

4. _____

NEEDED CHARACTERISTICS, EXPERIENCE AND TRAINING:

1. _____

2. _____

3. _____

4. _____

TIME COMMITMENT:

DAYS AVAILABLE	TIMES AVAILABLE
MON TUE WED THU FRI SAT SUN	_____
— — — — — — —	_____

_____   _____
VOLUNTEER   DATE

_____   _____
STAFF COORDINATOR   DATE

*SAMPLE VOLUNTEER JOB DESCRIPTION

TITLE: Cultural and Recreational Guide for the Blind

MAJOR OBJECTIVES: To offer blind persons self-confidence and a positive self image.

MAJOR RESPONSIBILITIES:

1. Plan and arrange outings with the client and serve as an escort/friend to the client.

2. Help client improve motor skills and develop self-confidence according to treatment plan.

3. Provide client the opportunity to attend cultural and recreational activities in order to stimulate clients's interest in community and hobbies.

4. Work with staff on the progress of the client and make the staff aware of any potential problems.

5. Help client development positive self image by reinforcing appropriate behaviors and attitudes.

QUALIFICATIONS: Mature individual, at least 18 years old. Ability to relate to people. Patient and non-judgmental in relation to client's interests and attitudes. Able to give guidance and support in a firm manner. Experience with working with the blind is helpful, but not necessary. Must have access to transportation.

TRAINING AND/OR PREPARATION: Orientation to DHR with emphasis on Vocational Rehabilitation and volunteer services. Volunteers will be given special courses designed for instructors for the blind, emphasizing attitudes often expressed by both the sighted and blind individuals towards blindness and development of communication, listening, and assertiveness skills. Classes will be conducted by Vocational Rehabilitation staff and appropriate resource persons. These sessions will last approximately one day. Follow-up training sessions will conducted periodically.

TIME AND PLACE: Volunteer will meet with the client in the Vocational Rehabilitation facility once a week. At the mutual agreement between client and volunteer, meetings may be conducted elsewhere as will outings.

COMMITMENT: Minimum six months. One year maximum

ON-THE-JOB SUPERVISION: The designated Vocational Rehabilitation staff person will meet with the volunteer on a regular bi-weekly basis.

*   Manual for Volunteer Services; Georgia Department of Human Resources; Office of Volunteer Services.

VOLUNTEER INTERVIEW CHECKLIST

PURPOSE

Give a brief overview of the volunteer opportunity and tell how it fits in with the program or service as well as the organization's philosophy. Tell the interesting and rewarding aspects of the job. Tell also the difficult and demanding parts. Be candid. Be fair. Be enthusiastic. Be honest.

JOB DESCRIPTION

Here is a chance to use that volunteer job description as a framework for your interview with the applicant. Use the specific items to make certain the volunteer understands the position and that you feel he/she is suitable for it.

SPECIAL INFORMATION

If you are going to coordinate the volunteer's work, explain how and when you will be available and the kinds of support and assistance to expect. Make sure the volunteer clearly identifies the recipients of his/her time commitment (who and how many) as well as the specific days and hours of that pledge. If other volunteers are involved in the same program, tell something about them. Before any volunteer starts on a job, BE CERTAIN he/she understands fire and disaster procedures, accident and first aid procedures and whom to contact in an emergency.

INTRODUCTIONS

When a volunteer has agreed to be a volunteer, introduce him to those friendly folk with whom he will be working - staff, clients, and other volunteers. Above all, don't say "be here Tuesday night at seven and someone will show you around."!!!

ASSESSMENT

Explain that, just as for a paid staff member, the volunteer will have an opportunity to discuss with the responsible staff coordinator (you or a colleague) his effectiveness in the volunteer assignment, the reaction of clients, other staff and volunteer co-workers. Set a date and time for this evaluation NOT MORE THAN TWO WEEKS after the volunteer starts. Give the applicant a volunteer handbook and go through it with him briefly. Assign a locker, or desk space if applicable; be certain to explain that if this trial effort doesn't work out, there are other volunteer opportunities that should be explored.

COMMITMENT

Explain that at the time of evaluation, or shortly thereafter, volunteers who are accepted for the program are expected to pledge a minimum number of hours and days over an extended program (usually six months, however it depends on the needs of your specific program). If you use a contract or pledge form, ask the volunteer to sign, after explaining that it is a moral and NOT a legal commitment.

NONDIRECTIVE INTERVIEWING SUGGESTIONS

Sample List of Open-Ended Questions

ATTITUDES:

    -What have you enjoyed most in previous volunteer assignments?
    -What have you enjoyed least?

INTERPERSONAL RELATIONS:

    -What kind of people do you work with best as a co-worker?
    -What kind of people are you most interested in as clients and why?
    -Are there types of people you feel you would be unable to work with?

MOTIVATION AND VALUES:

    -What would you consider to be the ideal volunteer job for you?

MOTIVATION:

    -Why are you interested in doing volunteer work?
    -What are your long-range objectives?

VALUES:

    -What do you like to do in your leisure time?

WORK HABITS:

    -What is your "energy" or "activity level" and how would you describe your
    work habits?

DECISION MAKING:

    -Thinking back, what are the most significant decisions you have made in your
    life and how do you feel about them?

EMOTIONAL STABILITY:

    -What makes you really angry - on the job or at home - and how do you deal
    with this anger?
    -Tell me about your family?
    -What has been the biggest disappointment in your life?
    -Describe your temperament.
    -If you could, what would you improve? What do you like best about yourself?

Department of Youth Development
Volunteer Services Section

APPLICATION FOR SERVICE AS A VOLUNTEER

Name:_____ Social Security No:_____

Present Address: _____City/State/Zip _____

Permanent Address:_____City/State/Zip_____

Previous Address(es) (Past 10 years): _____
_____
_____

County of Residence:_____ Driver's License #:_____ Expires:_____

Telephone No. (Home) _____ (Work)_____

Date of Birth:_____ Marital Status:_____ Level of Education:_____

Sex: ____ Race: ____ Do You Speak Other Languages?____ Specify_____

Location Desired for Volunteer Service:_____

For Students: Educational Institution Attending: _____

Major:_____ Career Interest: _____

Hobbies, Interest, Special Skills:_____

Community, Civic, Church Affiliation (Note offices or leadership positions held):_____
_____
_____

Type of Program Activity Desired:

____Arts and Recreation   ____Religious Services
____Community Service   ____Substance Abuse Prevention
____Education and Counseling   ____Other (please specify): _____
____One to One/Mentoring   _____

Number of Hours Requested Per Week:

____0–2 ____2–4 ____4–10 ____10–15 ____15–20 ____20–40

Can you use your car in connection with your volunteer service? _____

If so, do you have current automobile liability insurance? _____

REFERENCES:

Name:_____ Telephone No. (Home) _____
                                             (Work) _____
Address: _____City/State/Zip _____
No. of Years Known:_____

Name:_____ Telephone No. (Home) _____
                                             (Work) _____
Address: _____City/State/Zip _____
No. of Years Known:_____

YD–0319   Page 1 of 2

<u>**REFERENCES (Cont'd)**</u>

Name:_____ Telephone No. (Home) _____

(Work) _____

Address: _____ City/State/Zip _____

No. of Years Known:_____

PLEASE FILL OUT THIS SECTION COMPLETELY.

Official Job Title   Company Name   Type of Business

Title of Immediate Supervisor   Dept. Where Assigned

Employed: From: _____ To: _____   Weekly Work Hours: (Full–time) _____(Part–time) _____

Number and Titles of Employees You Supervise: _____

Your Job Duties: _____

Previous/Present Volunteer Services

Name of Organization: _____ Contact Person: _____

Business Address: _____ Business Telephone:_____

Job Duties: _____

Answers to the following questions will be considered for volunteer services purposes if relevant to the assignment for which you are applying. Have you ever been CONVICTED of an offense against criminal or military law, or are there criminal charges currently pending against you? (Exclude minor traffic violations) _____No _____Yes If "Yes", please give a detailed explanation about the nature of conviction and time since release from custody or probation.

CERTIFICATION

I certify that the statements made by me on this application are true and complete to the best of my knowledge and are made in good faith. I understand that any misstatement of fact may result in termination. All statements made on this application, including employment information, are subject to verification as a condition of volunteer services. I hereby give my permission for you to verify any information included in this application. I further understand that as a volunteer I may be exposed to some degree of danger in working with this population of clients.

Signature: _____ Date:_____

FOR OFFICE USE

	Comments	Signature	Date
References			
Employment			
Criminal Record			
Personal Interview			

YD–0319   Page 2 of 2

CRIMINAL HISTORY REQUEST
REQUEST WILL NOT BE PROCESSED UNLESS ALL INFORMATION IS COMPLETED.

☐ DHR VOLUNTEER(S) *   ☐ ADOPTION*   ☐ DAY CARE   ☐ PRIVATE AGENCY*
Documentation will be attached if record is found. $3.00 Per Person

The persons listed below are currently employed by us, are applying for employment, or are applying to adopt. We request criminal record identification checks pursuant to ORS 181.537, as printed on the reverse side of this form.

By the signature which follows their name, the below listed persons give consent to the Department of Human Resources to check their name through the Oregon Law Enforcement Data System (LEDS).

Juvenile employees or volunteers (any person under 18) must provide the names of their counties of residence for the past five years in the State of Oregon. Their names will not be in LEDS so county juvenile departments must be contacted.

It is understood that positive identification cannot be established without fingerprint comparison.

Central Office Use Only Record — No / Yes

NAME--Include last, first, middle, aliases, maiden name, previous married names.		No	Yes
Name (Please Print) Last, First, MI ☐ Male ☐ Female Date of Birth SS# (Optional)			
Other Names Used Signature: Date Mo - Dy - Yr			
Juveniles-List Counties of Residence for past 5 years:			
Name (Please Print) Last, First, MI ☐ Male ☐ Female Date of Birth SS# (Optional)			
Other Names Used Signature: Date Mo - Dy - Yr			
Juveniles-List Counties of Residence for past 5 years:			
Name (Please Print) Last, First, MI ☐ Male ☐ Female Date of Birth SS# (Optional)			
Other Names Used Signature: Date Mo - Dy - Yr			
Juveniles-List Counties of Residence for past 5 years:			
Name (Please Print) Last, First, MI ☐ Male ☐ Female Date of Birth SS# (Optional)			
Other Names Used Signature: Date Mo - Dy - Yr			
Juveniles-List Counties of Residence for past 5 years:			

Day Care Center/Group Home/Agency-Name _____

Address: _____   City: _____   State: _____   Zip Code: _____

Director/Agency Signature _____   Date: _____

CSD Central Office Use Only

LEDS Clerk Signature _____   Date _____

ease see reverse side for additional space and explanation of uses and authority.
ils form is not to be altered in any way! This form may be copied or additional supply is available upon request.

Mail To: Family Services Section/LEDS Clerk
Children's Services Division
198 Commercial Street S.E.
Salem, Oregon 97310

CSD 999 Rev. 1/90

State of Oregon
Department of Human Resources
Senior and Disabled Services Division

Criminal Record Authorization

Facility Name:

I authorize Senior and Disabled Services Division to obtain information about me from the Oregon State Police and other law enforcement agencies and courts:

Signature: _____ Date: _____

Signature: _____ Date: _____

Signature: _____ Date: _____

A criminal record check is now required on all persons providing care to Senior and Disabled Sevices Division clients. For Adult Foster Home applicants/providers, please provide the following information for all persons age 16 or over residing in your home (except residents receiving care). See instructions on back of this form for client-employed providers and volunteers.

Provider/Volunteer

Full Legal Name	
Maiden Name	Other Name(s) Used
Address	
Date of Birth	Social Security Number

Spouse (AFH Only)

Full Legal Name	
Maiden Name	Other Name(s) Used
Address	
Date of Birth	Social Security Number

Others (AFH Only)

Full Legal Name	
Maiden Name	Other Name(s) Used
Address	
Date of Birth	Social Security Number

Full Legal Name	
Maiden Name	Other Name(s) Used
Address	
Date of Birth	Social Security Number

SDS 303 (Rev.5/93)

RECORD KEEPING

While paperwork can be the bane of many a manager's existence, it is nevertheless important to consider whether or not records are important to the organization and the extent to which they should be used as management tools as well as documenting the work which is done. This chapter provides sample forms which many volunteer utilization agencies and organizations use to track and record the use of volunteers. They are provided for direction only in developing your own forms which record the things you need within your organization.

Reasons for keeping records:

1. to track individual hours of service by individuals, groups, teams on particular projects or tasks - useful in developing budget requests for paid jobs as well as setting up subsequent work schedules and calendars for volunteer projects..

2. to provide documentation on community involvement and/or commitment to an organization, community need, or agency need - useful in preparing grant proposals to foundations and other funding groups (including local government).

3. to provide a method by which the organization develops its recognition program for individual or group service to the cause.

4. to provide documentation on either "promoting" or "firing" a volunteer.

5. to give both the organization as well as the volunteer a method for evaluating programs or projects.

6. to give a formalized way to reinforce the importance to the agency of the volunteer and to convey the message that the organization is run like a business.

WHO KEEPS THE RECORDS?

At the time the volunteer program is developed, the person or persons responsible for record keeping should be determined. There is no need to adopt a record-keeping policy and then not maintain it. Usually the volunteer coordinator keeps the records or is responsible for seeing that they are kept by supervisors and some which are kept by volunteers themselves. All forms should be kept in the volunteer's individual file and put there only with his/her knowledge.

Volunteer Hours

Master Record

This is a monthly summary of individual volunteer time contributions and is the official record for volunteer time reports.

In the monthly blocks after each name show the total numer of hours (to the nearest half) contributed by that volunteer and the code indicating the using service.

Check One: _____
_____
_____

Year _____

Name	Jan.	Feb.	March	April	May	June	July	Aug.	Sept.	Oct.	Nov.	Dec.	Total

Supervisory Record

for the Month of _____

Volunteer	Weekly Contact	Weekly Contact	Weekly Contact	Weekly Contact	Monthly Suprv. Mtg.	Workshop	Group	Client	Contact

INDEX

A

Aboriginal community, 31
Absences, reporting, 180
Accidental death and dismemberment insurance, 337
Accident and injury insurance, 337
Accounts payable process, 108–116
Achievement, in learned needs theory, 26–27, 32, *33*, 67, 80, 224–225
Action science, 101
Adams, J., 225
Ad hoc volunteer efforts, 49
Administration. *See* Director of volunteer services; Management; Risk management; *specific tasks*
Advocacy, 78, 159, 183–184, 368
Affiliation, in learned needs theory, 28–29, 32, *33*, 67, 79, 236
Affirmative action policy, 135
Age Discrimination in Employment Act, 348
Agencies. *See* Volunteer organizations
Age of volunteers, 30, 63, 165
AGT limited, *277, 281*
AIDS, 157
Altruism, 13–15, 229–230, 234–235
"Altruism Is Not Dead" (Flashman and Quick), 15
American Red Cross, 135
Americans, volunteer participation, 37, 63, 83, 157
American Society for Quality Control, 120
Americans with Disabilities Act, 349–350
AmeriCorps, 373–374
Antidiscrimination policy, 135
Application and placement
  defined, 159
  director of volunteer services in, 163–167, 174–176
  for episodic volunteers, 191, *192, 198*
  policy, 143–144
  process, 57
  rejecting, 172
  serving on team, 208
  training and, 87–88
Application forms
  in determining volunteer satisfiers, 24
  elements, 69
  example, *70, 166*
Argentina, 31
Argyris, C., 101
Assault and battery, 355–356

Assessment. *See* Evaluation
Assignable causes of variability, 107
Association for Volunteer Administration (AVA), 52, 158–159, 184, *185*
Association liability insurance, 336
Assumption of risk, 305–306
Audet, B., 282
Audiotapes, for TQM training, *120*
Audit of volunteer-staff climate, 213–215
Avoidance in risk management, 325
Avoidance motives, 32

B

Barber, B., 371
Bauer, Rudolph, 5
Behavior modification, 17–19
Behavior theory. *See* Motivation theories
Beliefs. *See* Values and beliefs
Belonging in Maslow's theory, *20*
Benefits, for volunteers, 78
Berns, G. T., 22–23
Blanchard, K., 101
Block, P., 101
Board members
  for employee volunteer programs, 277
  in fund-raising, 249, 251–254
  goals and objectives, 211
  legal issues
    directors' and officers' liability insurance, 311–313, 335
    duties, 310
    incorporating, 313
    indemnification, 311
    liability, 315
    loss prevention techniques, 315–320
    negligence, 356–357
    personal liability, 310–311
    potential claimants and wrongful management claims, 312
    volunteer protection laws, 313–315
  motivation for volunteering, 14
  policies
    application to board members, 139–140
    development, 140
    in gaining access to, 131–132
  self-evaluation, 219
  team, 209
  training and continuing education, 99–100

view of voluntary organization, 5–6
volunteers on, 220
Bradner, J. H., 61
Brainstorming, 93
Bridges, W., 101
Brudney, J. L., 36, 41
Bryson, J. M., 193
Building a Customer-Driven Organization: The Manager's Role (CareerTrack Publications), 120
Burlington Parks and Recreation Department, 136
Business. *See* Corporations
Business Process Improvement (Harrington), 119
Buzz group, 93
By Definition: Policies for Volunteer Programs (Graff), 144

C

Cahn, E., 63
Calgary Corporate Volunteer Council, 263, 276
Calgary Winter Olympics, 199
California, 40
Capital campaigns, 247–248
Career ladders for volunteers, 53
Career motivational concerns, *17*
Car metaphor for society, 4
Carnivals, 305–306
Cars. *See* Vehicles
Carver, J., 129
Case studies, in training, 93
Cause-and-effect diagrams, 108, 112–113, *116*
Celebrations, in volunteer-staff relations, 210–211
Centralized approach, 51
CEO of agency, self-evaluation, 219
Chamber of Commerce, 121
Champoux, J. E., 103
Chance causes of variability, 107
Checksheets, 108, *109*
Chevron employees' involvement progam, *264*
Child care for volunteers, 66
Children, as volunteers, 300–301
Chile, 31
Chinese, 31
Citizenship, 368
Civil Rights Act of 1866, 342, 349
Civil Rights Acts of 1964 and 1991, 342, 348–349
Clary, E., 16
Clients. *See* Community
Clinton, W., 6–7, 362, 372

Cole, K. M., 52, 87, 96, 98, 99, 202
College students. *See* National service
Commercial crime insurance, 334
Commercial general liability, 333
Commitment of volunteers, 65–66
Committees, in leadership development, 98
Common law, 351–352
Communication
  about policies, 152, 171–172
  in fund-raising, 257
  supervisor skills in, 202–203
  in TQM, 105
  between volunteers and staff, 209–210, 212–213, 218, 219
Communitarian theory, 6–8
Community
  in employee volunteer programs, 260–263, *266, 267–268,* 275
  link with voluntary sector, 5
  in national service programs, 370–371, 376
  in society, 5
  view of voluntary organization, 5–6
  volunteer programs in relations with, 40, *42,* 43
Computers, for record-keeping, 57–58
Confidentiality, 25, 69
Conflict of interest policy, 138, 142–143
Conrad, W., 130, 132
Continuous improvement in TQM, 106
Contracts
  elements, 74
  example, *75*
  legal issues, 354–355, 357–359
  in policy compliance, 152
Control charts, 108, 109, *111*
Corporate volunteer councils, 263
Corporate Volunteerism Council of Minneapolis/St. Paul Metro Area, 281–282
Corporate volunteer programs. *See* Employee volunteer programs
Corporation for National and Community Service, 63
Corporation for National Service, 374
Corporations
  donations, 9, 246, 248, 262–263, 271
  link with voluntary sector, 5
  in society, 4
  sponsorship, 271
  volunteerism as foreign concept, 285
Cost-effectiveness, of volunteer programs, 39, *42*
Cost savings, vs. cost-effectiveness, 39
Countryman, M., 366, 368, 369, 370
Crime insurance, 334
Criminal records check, 72–73

Cryderman, P., 128
Cultural diversity, 30–31, 65, 365
Cultural ethics, 369–370
Cunningham, J. K., 364
Curriculum development, 92–94

D

Dalton, C., 203
Debates in training, 94
Decentralized approach, 50–51
Decision making, by volunteer-staff teams, 218
Defamation, 352–353
Democracy, 368
Demonstrations in training, 94
Department of Labor, 344–346
Designs for Fund-Raising (Seymour), 64
Development committee in fund-raising, 252
Direct mail, 256
Director of volunteer services, 157–186;
See also Management
  adjusting to changing conditions, 239–240
  in advocacy and education, 183–184
  in application process, 163–167
  benefits of position, 51
  business and service aspects, 5–6
  in decentralized approach, 50
  in episodic volunteer programs, 190
  in evaluation, 176–178, 183
  in exit interview, *181*
  in interview and screening, 163–164, 167–172
  in job description process, *175*
  in organizational hierarchy, 52
  in orientation and training, 172–174
  in placement, 174–176
  in policy development, 132, 134–135, 140–141
  in policy implementation, 160–162
  professional development, 184, *185*
  in recognition, 178–179
  in record keeping, 182
  in recruitment, 162–163
  in retention, 179–182
  role, 52–53, 157–160, *159*
  staffing method, 51–52
  in supervision, 176–178
  support for, 53
  support of volunteers and staff, 209, 218–219
  in volunteer-staff relations, 219–220
Directors' and officers' liability insurance, 311–313, 335
Directors of Volunteers in Agencies (DOVIA), 184

Direct service, volunteer-staff teams in, 211
Disabled volunteers, 66, 349–350
Disaster imaging, 134–135
Discrimination laws, 135, 348–350
Discussion groups, 93
Dissatisfiers in two-factor theory, 22–25, *26*
Diversity, 30–31, 65, 365
Double-looped learning, 101
Driving. *See* Vehicles
Driving under the influence (DUI), 318
Drucker, P., 84, 105, 230, 346
Duncombe, S., 41

E

Economic issues. *See* Financial issues
Educational background of volunteers, 88
Education, defined, 83, 159; *See also* Training
Ehrlich, E., 200
Eide, P. J., 339
Einsweiler, R. C., 193
Elden, M., 233
Elephant metaphor for voluntary sector, 5–6
Ellis, S., 44, 55, 129–130, 153, 216
Emotions, 165–166, 353
Employee dishonesty insurance, 334
Employee Polygraph Protection Act, 347–348
Employees. *See* Staff
Employee volunteer programs, 260–288
  adaptability of, 286–287
  agency role in, 282–283
  benefits of, 274, 280–282
  company support, 262–263, 266, *269–272*
  vs. corporate programs, 265, *266*, 287
  evaluating, 283–284
  as foreign concept to companies, 285
  identifying stakeholders, 260–265
  impacts on stakeholders, 265–266, *267–268*
  liability and risk management, 279–280
  management considerations, 266, 268, 272–273
  mission statement, *277*
  partnerships with company and communities, 287–288
  policy development, 279, *281*
  preparing company and employees, 273–275
  as program or process, 285–286
  quality service orientation, 286
  recruitment, 78
  structure development, 275–278

types of activities
Employment at will, 351–352
Employment law, 339–359
  application to volunteer organizations,
  341–342
  application to volunteers, 343–345
  basis of, 340–341
  common law, 351–352
  contract, 357–359
  discrimination, 348–350
  harassment, 350–351
  intentional torts, 352–356
  loss prevention techniques, 316–317
  negligence, 356–357
  statutory and regulatory standards,
  345–348
Employment practices liability coverage,
336
Employment, shortening workweek and
redistributing income, 8–11
Employment status of volunteers, 88
Empowerment, 48, 232–233
Environment of agency, 239–240
Episodic volunteers, 188–205
  barriers to, 189–191
  defined, 188–189
  field tests, 204–205
  job development and job descriptions,
  193–196
  needs assessment, 191, *192*
  planning for, 193
  recognition, 203–204
  recruitment, 196–197, 199–200
  screening, 198–199
  supervision, 201–203
  training, 200–201
Equal Pay Act, 350
Equity theory, 225
Esteem, *17, 20*
Estes, E. G., 244
Etzioni, Amitai, 6–8
Evaluation
  of board members, 139
  director of volunteer services in,
  176–178, 183
  of employee volunteer programs,
  261–262, 282–284
  mechanisms, 58
  of programs, *81*, 159
  in retention, 76–77
  in supervision and management, 219
  of training programs, 91, 94–95
  types of, 283
  in volunteer-staff relations, 219
Evangelical church-related organizations,
10–11
Executive Order 11246, 350
Exercises in training, 93

Exit interview, 24–25, 179–182, *181*
Expectancy theory, 15–17, 225–227
  connection with other theories, 31–32, *33*
Expense reimbursement, for volunteers, 78
EXTENSION, *277, 281*
External environment, 239

F

Fair Labor Standards Act, 343–346
False light publicity, 354
Family and Medical Leave Act, 346–347
Family members as volunteers, policy, 138
Feedback, in supervision, 203
Fiduciary liability insurance, 335–336
Field tests, of episodic volunteer program,
204–205
Filipinos, 31
Financial issues. *See also* Fund-raising;
Insurance
  cost-effectiveness of volunteer programs,
  39, *42*
  dollar value for volunteer contribution,
  63
  in employee volunteer programs,
  262–263, 281
  Equal Pay Act, 350
  Fair Labor Standards Act, 345
  funding of volunteer programs, 38, *41*,
  42–43
  as motivation for volunteer programs, 45
  in national service programs, 366–367,
  371
  paid community service, 9–11
Fishbone diagram, 112
Fisher, J. C., 52, 87, 96, 98, 99, 202
Flowcharts, 108, 110, 112, *113–115*
Foundations as source of funds, 245, 248
Fraud, 352
From the Top Down (Ellis), 216
Fund-raising, 245–258. *See also* Financial
issues
  marketing, 256
  purpose, 245
  sources of funds, 245–246
  types of activites, 246–248
  volunteers in, 249–258
Fun, in volunteer-staff relations, 210

G

Gartner, A., 367
Georgia, 41–43
Gerhard, G., 236
Gingrich, N., 372
"Give Five" campaign, 157
Glenn, W., 130, 132
Goals for volunteer programs, 44–46

Goals for volunteer training program, 86
Governing Boards (Houle), 99
Government. *See also* Legislation; Liability
  link with voluntary sector, 5
  in society, 4
  as source of funds, 9, 245
  volunteers in, legal issues, 302–303, 308
Graff, L., 125, 144
Greetings, 218
Grievance procedures, 78
Guided discussions, 93

H

Hackman, R. J., 227
Hamner, E. P., 17
Hamner, W. C., 17
Handbooks, 96–97, 357–358
Harassment laws, 350–351
Hayes, Jeffrey, 7–8
Health test, 73
Hertz rejection list, *319*
Herzberg's two-factor theory
  assignments based on, 25, *26*
  concept, 22, 224
  connection with other theories, 31–32, *33*
  dissatisfiers, 24–25
  in motivating volunteers, 22–23
  satisfiers, 23–24
Hiring, legal issues, 357
Hospitals, legal issues, 296, 298–301, 348
Hotlines, training for, 173–174
Houle, C., 99, 100
Hours worked, 8–11, 345
Hygiene factors, 224

I

Illegal aliens, 347
Image of agency, 14
Immigration and Naturalization Service,
347
Immigration Reform and Control Act, 347
Implementing Total Quality Management
(CareerTrack Publications), 121
*Implementing Total Quality Management:
How to Make TQM Work in Your
Organization* (CareerTrack Publications),
120
Implied covenant of good faith, 358
Income redistribution, 8–11
Incorporating, 313
Indemnification, 311, 326, 330
Independent sector, 37, 157
India, 31
Individual contributions, 9, 246–247
Individualism, 8, 369–370
Infliction of emotional distress, 353

Informal sector, 4
Instructional strategy, 92–94
Instructional television, 122
Instrumentality theory, 15–17, 30
  connection with other theories, 31–32, *33*
Insurance
  directors' and officers' liability, 311–313,
  335
  evaluating, 331–332
  presenting volunteer organization to
  insurance market, 330–331
  risk management and, 323, 327–328
  types of coverage, 332–337
  vehicle, 318, 333–334
  for volunteers, 308
Insurance certificates, *326*
Intentional misconduct, 299–300
Interference with contractual relations,
354–355
Internal environment, 240
International City/County Management
Association, 56
Interviews, 69–74
  application form, 69, *70*
  of board members, 139
  defined, 159
  director of volunteer services in,
  163–164, 167–172
  for episodic volunteers, 198
  exit interview, 179–182, *181*
  interviewer's report form, *72*
  open-ended questions, 69, 71
  questions to avoid, 171
  risk of program and, 71
  screening during, 71
  second interview, 73
  special needs of volunteers and, 71
  of staff, in volunteer job description,
  54–55
  training and, 88
Interview sheet, *170*
Intrusion upon seclusion of privacy, 354
Invasion of privacy, 353
Ismaili community, 31

J

Job descriptions, 175
  for board members, 251–252, *253*
  elements, 62
  for episodic volunteers, 193–196, 198
  example, *75*
  training and, 88–89
  for volunteers, 53–56
Job design, 54–55, 193–196
Job threat, 216
Joint employer theory, 343

K

Kahn, J., 280
Kallick, D., 364
Kanter, R. M., 101
Keller, S. K., 277
Knowles, M. S., 20
Korngold, A., 284

L

Labor relations. *See* Volunteer-staff relations
Labor unions, 10–11
Ladak, D., 14, 16, 18
Landy, F. J., 15
Latin Americans, 31
Lautenschlager, J., 266
Lawler, E. E., III, 227
Leadership programs, 98–99
Learn and Serve America programs, 63
Learned needs theory. *See* McClelland's learned needs theory
Learning, in training, 100–101
Learning modalities, 174
Leaves of absence, 77
Lecture-discussions, 93
Lectures, 93
Ledwig, F., 361
Legal issues. *See* Employment law; Liability; Risk management
Legal responsibilities. *See* Liability
Legislation
  for national service programs, 373–374
  protections for volunteers, 302–304, 313–315
Liability. *See also* Risk management
  board members
    directors' and officers' liability insurance, 311–313
    incorporating, 313
    indemnification, 311
    legal duties, 310
    loss prevention techniques, 315–320
    personal liability, 310–311
    potential claimants and wrongful management claims, *312*
    volunteer protection laws, 313–315
  in employee volunteer programs, 279–280
  episodic volunteers, 190
  immunities and defenses from
    assumptions of risk, 305–306
    comparative negligence, 306–307
    contributory negligence, 306
    statutory protections, 301–304
    waivers, 304–305
  of individual volunteers, 295–296

  of organizations for acts of volunteers, 296–298
  standards of care for negligence, 300–301
  tort, 294–295
  types of, 298–300
  volunteer concerns about, 66
  volunteers as plaintiff, 307–308
Liability insurance, 311–313, 333–337
Libel, 352–353
Liberating structure, 232–233
Libraries, 174
Life insurance application process, *107*
Lipset, S. M., 7–8
Literacy programs, 40
Loss prevention techniques, 315–320, 327. *See also* Risk management
Love in Maslow's theory, *20*
Ludeman, K., 91
Lulewicz, S. J., 82
Lynch, R., 48, 56

M

McClelland's learned needs theory
  achievement, 26–27, 67
  affiliation, 28–29, 67
  connection with other theories, 31–32, *33*
  power, 27–28, 67
  in practice, 29
McCurley, S., 29, 48, 53, 56, 135, 152
Macduff, E., 220
Macduff, N., 187, 206
Mahoney, T., 224
Management. *See also* Risk management; specific tasks
  of application and placement systems, 57
  of education and training systems, 57
  of employee volunteer programs
    agencies in, 278
    assessing stakeholder group, 261–262
    dimensions, 266, 268, 272–273
    emerging issues, 285–286
  evaluation of, 219
  importance of, 56
  of national and community service programs, 367–368, 371, 373–377
  personnel vs. program approach, 52–53
  of recognition systems, 58, 233–236
  of record-keeping systems, 57–58
  total quality management, 104–122
    continuous improvement in, 106
    nonprofit organizations and, 105
    process focus of, 106–116
    summary of, 104–105
    training in, 114–122
  of volunteer-staff relations, 216
  volunteer-staff teams in, 211

Managers. *See* Director of volunteer services

Managing Quality: The Strategic and Competitive Edge (Garvin), 119

Managing Today's Nonprofit Organization (CareerTrack Publications), 120

Manuals, 96–97, 357–358

Mapping Work Processes (Galloway), 119

Marketing, 256

Marketing Services: Competing Through Quality (Berry and Parasuraman), 119

Maslow's need hierarchy, 19–22, 223
  connection with other theories, 31–32, *33*

Media in marketing and recruitment, 197, 199, 256

Media resources, for TQM training, 119–122

Medical payments, in vehicle insurance, 333

Meetings, joint planning, 47–48

Meneghetti, Milena M., 12

Mentoring, 97

Metaphors, for voluntary sector, 3–6

Military, 371

Minneapolis/St. Paul Metro Area Corporate Volunteerism Council, 281–282

Misconduct, 299–300 Misrepresentation, 352, 356–357

Mission statements, *277*

Morale, recognition in, 229

Motivation
  application questions about, 165
  diversity and offering range of jobs, 56
  evaluation and recognition and, 58
  for fund-raising, 257
  types of, 66–67

Motivation and Personality (Maslow), 32

Motivation inventory or profile, 23–24

Motivation theories, 12–33
  altruism as, 13–15
  connecting motivation theories, 31–32, *33*
  contemporary issues in, 29–31
  content, 223–225
  equity theory, 225
  expectancy theory, 225–227
  Herzberg's two-factor theory, 22–25, *26*, 224
  instrumentality theory, 15–16, *17*
  McClelland's learned needs theory, 26–29, 67, 79–80, 224–225
  Mahoney's theory, 224
  Maslow's need hierarchy, 19–22, 223
  Murray's, 223
  process, 225–227
  process-based vs. content-based, 13
  reinforcement theory, 17–19

Motivators, 224

Motor vehicle record, 318

Multicultural perspectives in volunteering, 30–31, 65, 365

Multilogue, 8

Murray, H. A., 223

Murrell, K. L., 222

N

Nadler, L., 83

National and Community Service Act of 1990, 158

National and Community Service Trust Act of 1993, 184–185, 373–377

National Labor Relations Act, 347

National service, 63, 362–377
  defined, 362
  operational considerations, 363, 369–372
  policies for managers, 373–377
  sources of information, 374
  underlying values, 362–369

National VOLUNTEER Center, 188

Naylor, H. H., 56

Need hierarchy, 19–22

Needs analysis, 62, 89–91, 191, *192*

Needs theories. *See* Motivation theories

Negligence, 298–301, 306–307, 356–357

Networking, 97–98

New Republicans, 10–11

New York City, 216

Noninsurance transfers, 326–327

Nonprofit organizations. See Volunteer organizations

Nonprofit Organizations Policies and Procedures Handbook (Champoux and Goldman), 119

Norms, of volunteer-staff teams, 218

North, C., 323

O

Occupational Safety and Health Act (OSHA), 346

O'Connell, B., 130

Organizational affiliation policy, 138

Organizational structure, 230–233
  in communication promotion, 210
  of employee volunteer programs, 275–277

Orientation
  agenda, 74, *76*
  contracts, 74, *75*
  director of volunteer services in, 172–174
  questions, 74
  topics, 57, 96

Osborne, D., 369

OSHA (Occupational Safety and Health Act), 346

Outreach calls, 180
Owen, H., 100

P

Paid community service, coalition for
advocating, 9–11; *See also* National service
Paid staff. *See* Staff
Panels in training, 94
Pareto charts, 108, 109, *110*
Partnerships
  in employee volunteer programs, 282,
  287–288
  in national service, 370
Peach, E. B., 222
Pearce, J., 207, 215, 216, 217
Personal development
  benefits, 99
  defined, 83
Personnel file, for volunteers, 78
Personnel management, vs. program
approach, 52–53
Person-to-person recruitment, 196
Peters, S. J., 368
Philippines, 31
Phonathons, 256
Physiological needs in Maslow's theory, *20*
Picket lines, policy, 138
Placement. *See* Application and placement
Plaintiffs, volunteers as, 307–308
Points of Light Foundation, 273
Policies, 126–154
  for board members, 139–140
  compliance, 149–153
  defined, 126–127
  development process, 140–141
  director of volunteer services in
  development, 160–162
  for employee volunteer programs, *270*,
  279, *281*
  for episodic volunteers, 198
  functions
    gaining access to board, 131–132
    levels of policy, 129–130
    as program improvement tools,
    138–139
    risk management, 130–131, 133–135
    as rules, 137–138
    trends in voluntary sector, 128
    as values and belief statements,
    135–137
  loss prevention techniques
    board's role, 316
    for employee and volunteer acts, 317
    for employment practices, 316–317
    for vehicles, 317–320
  for national and community service
  programs, 373–377

priority scale, *147*
resistance to development, 153–154
risk management, 328, *329*
for volunteer-staff teams, 209
writing
  editing, 149
  principles of, 142–144
  prioritizing, 144–149
  tracking drafts and input, 149, *150*
Policy checklist, *145*
Policy volunteers vs. service volunteers, 37
Polish immigrants, 31
Polygraphs, 347–348
Porter and Lawler model, 227
Positive reinforcers, 17–19
Post-turnover survey, 24–25
Power, in learned needs theory, 27–28, *33*,
67, 80
Presentations, by volunteers, 77–78
Privacy issues, 353, 354
Procedures. *See* Policies
Process in TQM
  analysis tools and techniques, 108–116
  variability, 106–107
Process vs. program, 285–286
Productivity, recognition in, 228
Professional development
  benefits, 99
  for directors of volunteer services, 184,
  185
  employee volunteer programs in, 272
  for volunteers, 79
Professional liability insurance, 336
Professionals as volunteers, 29–30,
238–239, 301
Program description, for youth shelter, *168*
Program vs. process, 285–286
Progressive advocacy organizations, 10–11
Promotions of volunteers, 77
Property damage insurance, 332–333
Protective motivational concerns, *17*
Psychological issues, 165–166, 353
Publications, for TQM training, 119–122
Public disclosure of private facts, 354
Puffer, S. M., 30

Q

Quality. *See* Service quality; Total quality
management (TQM)
*Quality and Productivity Improvement
Through Statistical Methods* (Society of
Manufacturing Engineers), 121
*Quality Service: A Commitment to Customer
Satisfaction* (American Society for Quality
Control), 121
Question-and-answer periods in training,
93

R

Rational volunteers, 235
Reagan, R., 364
Recognition
  adjusting to changing conditions, 239–240
  characteristics of successful, 238, *239*
  choosing best volunteer, debate about, 80
  defined, 159
  in employee volunteer programs, *269*
  of episodic volunteers, 203–204
  for fund-raising, 254–255, 258
  managerial guidance for, 178–179, 233–236
  motivation and, 17–19, 79–80, 223–227
  opportunities in new organizational forms, 230–223
  professionalization of volunteer role, 238–239
  redesign, 236–238
  symphony orchestra case study, 240–241
  typical systems, 58, 227–230
  for volunteers, in retention, 79
  in volunteer-staff relations, 210
Recommendations, volunteer-staff teams in, 212
Record keeping, 57–58, 159, 182
Recruitment, 62–68
  balancing program and volunteer needs, 62
  defined, 159
  developing strong and diverse volunteer support, 64–66
  for employee volunteer programs, 278
  of episodic volunteers, 196–197, 199–200
  finding volunteers, 63–64
  generic vs. targeted, 162–163
  offering opportunity, 68–69
  offering range of jobs, 56
  other organizations in, 50
  person-to-person, 162–163
  preparation for, 62
  quality programs and measurable out comes, 62–63
  techniques, 67–68
  types of service and motivation, 66–67
Recruitment Is the Third Step (Ellis), 44
Redesign, 236–238
Reengineering, 236–238
Reference checks, 72, 139, 167, 355, 357
Reference form, *73, 169*
Referrals, of volunteers to other agencies, 172
Reimbursement, in motivating volunteers, 66
Reinforcement theory, 17–19
  connection with other theories, 31–32, *33*

Reinvention, 236–238
Reissman, F., 367
Rejecting applicants, 73–74, 143, 172
Reliance, 358–359
Renewal, 236–238
Republicans, 10–11
Research tools, 89–90, 108–116
Resources for TQM training, 119–122
Respect for volunteers, 78
Responsible voluntarism, 8
Responsive Communitarian Platform: Rights and Responsibilities, 7
The Responsive Community (Hayes and Lipset), 7*f*8
Resumes, 24
Retention
  defined, 159
  director of volunteer services in, 179*f*182
  factors in, 76*f*79
  legal issues, 357
  recognition in, 228
Retention in risk management, 325–326
Retirement Reconsidered (Cahn), 63
Rewards. *See* Recognition
Ridge, R., 16
Rifkin, J., 8–11
Risk management, 322–337; *See also* Liability
  administering, 328–329
  benefits, 323
  in employee volunteer programs, 279–280
  identifying and evaluating potential losses, 323–325
  monitoring program, 328
  policy in, 131–135, 146–148
  techniques
    avoidance, 325
    choosing, 328
    insurance, 327–328
    loss control, 327
    noninsurance transfers, 326–327
    retention, 325–326
  volunteers and
    function, 329–330
    insurance, 330–337
Risk Management and Insurance for Nonprofit Managers (Stone and North), 323
Robertson, L., 282, 283
Rogers, B., 97
Role expectations, in volunteer-staff relations, 217–218
Role-playing, 93
Roller coasters, 306
Root Cause Analysis (Wilson, Dell, and Anderson), 119
Rostami, J., 282
Rules, 137–138, 148

S

Safety in Maslow's theory, *20*
Sampling techniques, 90
Satisfiers in two-factor theory, 22–25, *26*
Scheier, I., 132
SCORE (Service Corps of Retired Executives), 49
Screening
    of board members, 139
    defined, 159
    director of volunteer services in, 163–164, 167–172
    episodic volunteers, 198–199
    during interview, 71
    policies, 148–149
    reference check, 72
    rejecting applicants, 73–74
    in risk management, 146
    second interview, 73
    special requirements, 72–73
    training during, 173–174
Seel, K., 259
Self-absorption, 369–370
Self-actualization in Maslow's theory, *20*
Self-evaluation, 203, 219
Seniors as volunteers, 30
Service Corps of Retired Executives (SCORE), 49
Service entrepreneurship, 369
Service quality. *See also* Total quality management (TQM)
    policies as improvement tools, 138–139, 148–149
    recruitment in, 62–63
    volunteer programs in enhancement, 40, *42*, 43
Service volunteers vs. policy volunteers, 37
Sexual harassment laws, 350–351
Seymour, H., 64
Shadowing, 97
Shaw, R., 127
Sikhs, 31
Silver, N., 129, 131, 132, 153
Slander, 352–353
Small Business Administration, 49
Smith, Nan H., 22–23
Snyder, M., 16
Social exchange theory, 14
Social motivational concerns, *17*
Social responsibility norm, 13
Society, car metaphor of, 4
Society of Manufacturing Engineers, 120
Socioeconomic class, 366
Software, for record-keeping, 57–58
Solicitation, 256
Sources of volunteers, 63–64
Special events for fund-raising, 246

Spiess, K., 282, 283
The Spirit of Community (Etzioni), 6
Sponsorship, corporate, 271
Staff. *See also* Director of volunteer services
    in fund-raising, 258
    involvement with volunteers, 39, *41*
        empowerment of volunteers, 48
        episodic volunteers, 189, 193
        in job description creation, 54–55
        policies, 46–48, 161–162
        recognition in, 229
        relations, 207–220
        as teams, 207–212, 216–218
        on volunteer-boards, 220
    leadership positions, 53
    legal issues, 316–320, 341–342
    planning for episodic volunteers, 193
    in policy development, 140
    total quality management, 104–105, 114–122
    training, 84–86
    view of voluntary organization, 5–6
    as volunteers, policy, 138
Staff meetings, 77
Status motives, 30
Status, of staff vs. volunteers, 215
Statutes. *See* Employment law; Legislation; Liability
Stepputat, A., 156
Stone, B., 323
Structure. *See* Organizational structure
Students. *See* National service
Succession planning, 98–99
Sullivan, L., 366, 368, 369, 370
Summer of Service programs, 367–368, 370, 371
Supervision, 176–178, 201–203, 219
Surveys, 54–55, 272–273
Symphony orchestra case study, 240–241

T

Tasks, for volunteers, 55, 78
Tax credit for volunteering, 9–11
Taylor, C., 8
Teams, volunteer-staff, 202, 208–212
Telephone calls
    to absent volunteers, 180
    phonathons, 256
    in recruitment, 197
Television, instructional, 122
Termination of volunteers, 136, 176–177
Thanks as motivator, guidelines for, 18–19
Theft, 357
Time sheets, 139
Torbert, B., 233
Toronto, 127, 135

Torts, 294–295, 352–356
Total Quality Management—Creating a Culture of Continuous Improvement (Society of Manufacturing Engineers), 121
Total Quality Management—The First Steps (Society of Manufacturing Engineers), 121
Total quality management (TQM)
  concept, 104–105
  continuous improvement in, 106
  in employee volunteer programs, 285
  nonprofit organizations and, 105
  process focus of
    analysis tools and techniques, 108–116
    training plan, 114–122
    variability, 106–107
Trainers, volunteers as, 79
Training, 83–102
  building effective program, steps in, 86–87
  curriculum development
    conduct training, 94
    instructional strategy, 92–94
  defining learning objectives, 91–92
  emerging trends, 100–101
  for episodic volunteers, 200–201
  evaluation of, 94–95
  in fund-raising, 254, *255*
  management, 87–91, 172–174, 183–184
  in national service programs, 367
  orientation, 57
  for recruitment teams, 200
  in retention, 77
  in risk management programs, 323
  for specific positions, 57
  vs. staff training, 84–86
  terminology, 83–84
  in total quality management, 114–122
  types of programs
    continuing education of boards, 100
    for members of the board, 99–100
    mentoring, 97
    networking, 97–98
    organizational handbooks, 96–97
    orientation, 96
    personal and professional development, 99
    shadowing, 97
    succession planning/leadership programs, 98–99
  of volunteer-staff teams, 208, 209, 218, 219, 220
Training and Development, 100
Transitions (Bridges), 101
Transportation. *See* Vehicles
Tremper, C., 280, 313
Trial periods, 176
Trumbo, D. A., 15
Turnover, 215

Two-factor theory. *See* Herzberg's two-factor theory

U

Umbrella liability insurance, 334
Understanding motivational concerns, *17*
Unions, 10–11
United States, volunteer participation, 37, 63, 83, 157
University students. *See* National service

V

Vacations, 77
Valence, instrumentality, and expectancy theories, 15–17, 31–32, *33*, 225–226
Values and beliefs
  belief in agency's cause, 13–14
  communicating during screening, 171–172
  embedding in organization, 231–232
  motivational concerns, *17*
  of national service programs, 363–369
  policies, 135–137, 148
  statements, 135–137
Van Til, J., 3, 361, 374, 375
Vargo, K. S., 309, 322
Variability in TQM, 106–107
Vehicle inspection, 320
Vehicle insurance, 333–334, 334
Vehicles
  legal issues, 295–296, 306, 307
  policy for volunteers, 133–134
  transportation reimbursement, 66
Videotapes, for TQM training, *121*
Vineyard, S., 20, 29, 141, 196
Vision for voluntary sector, 6–11
Vision for volunteer program, 79, 363–364
Voluntary action centers (VACs), 162
Voluntary functions inventory, 16
Voluntary sector, metaphors and visions, 3–11
Volunteer advisory council, 78
Volunteer Centre of Calgary and Calgary Parks and Recreation, 30
Volunteer Centre of Metropolitan Toronto, 127, 135
Volunteer driver excess auto liability, 334
Volunteer liability insurance, 336–337
Volunteer organizations. *See also specific aspects*
  backup for volunteers on duty, 133
  in employee volunteer programs, 265, 278, 282–283
  environment, adjusting to changes in, 239–240
  episodic volunteers, 193
  evaluation of, 159, 183

image, altruism and, 14
innovations, 10–11
legal issues, 296–297, 301–307, 341–342
measuring effectiveness, *81*
in national service programs, 369, 371
organizational capability expansion,
   39–40, *42*
policies, 125–154
   aspects covered by, 47–48
   for board members, 139–140
   defined, 126–127
   development process, 140–141
   empowerment of volunteers, 48
   functions, 133–139
   goals in, 45–46
   guidelines, 149–153
   reason for, 128–132
   resistance to development, 153–154
   for staff and volunteers, 48
   writing guidelines, 142–149
preparing for volunteers, 36–59
   advantages vs. disadvantages, 38–44
   climate of readiness, 62
   integrating participation, 49–51
   job descriptions, 53–56, 62
   leadership position for, 51–53
   needs assessment, 62
   paid staff in, 46–48
   rationale and goals for, 44–46
   strategies, 37
   systems and supports for participation
      and management, 56–58
risk management
   benefits, 323
   identifying and evaluating potential
      losses, 323–325
   insurance, 330–337
   techniques, 325–329
service quality, 40
structure, 230–233
   ad hoc, 49
   centralized approach, 51
   in communication promotion, 210
   decentralized approach, 50–51
   reliance on other organizations, 50
total quality management and, 105
Volunteer Protection Act, 183–184
Volunteer protection laws, 302–304,
313–315
Volunteers. *See also specific issues*
   agency preparation for, 36–59
      advantages vs. disadvantages, 38–44
      integrating participation, 49–51
      job descriptions for positions, 53–56
      leadership position for, 51–53
      paid staff in, 46–48
      rationale and goals for, 44–46

strategies, 37
systems and supports for participation
   and management, 56–58
on board of directors, 220
career ladders, 53
episodic volunteers, 189
   barriers to, 189–191
   defined, 188–189
   field tests, 204–205
   recruiting, 191–200
   supports for, 200–204
in fund-raising, 245–258
   categories of volunteers involved in,
      249–250
   creating volunteer-fund-raising corps,
      250–251
   expectations, 257–258
   obtaining board support for, 251–254
   recognition and cultivation, 254–255
   training, 254
interviewing and screening, 69–74
legal issues
   employment law, 339–359
   immunities and defenses, 301–307
   liability to injured parties, 294–301
   loss prevention techniques for actions,
      317
   loss prevention techniques for vehicles,
      317–320
   plaintiffs, volunteers as, 307–308
motivation theories, 12–33
   altruism as, 13–15
   connecting motivation theories, 31–32,
      33
   contemporary issues in, 29–31
   Herzberg's two-factor theory, 22–25, 26
   instrumentality theory, 15–16, *17*
   McClelland's learned needs theory,
      26–29
   Maslow's need hierarchy, 19–22
   reinforcement theory, 17–19
orientation, 74–76
policies, basis of, 161–162
recognition, 79–80
recruitment, 62–69
retention, 76–79
risk management and
   function, 329–330
   insurance, 330–337
tasks appropriate for, 55
training, 83–102
   building effective program, 86–95
   commonly used programs, 95–100
   emerging trends, 100–101
   as learning, 83–84
   vs. staff training, 84–86
   in total quality management, 114–122

view of voluntary organization, 5–6
as workers, perceived disadvantages,
38–39, *41*, 43
Volunteer-staff climate audit, 213–215
Volunteer-staff relations, 207–220, 347
causes of poor, 215–216
enhancing, 218–220
recognition in, 229
symptoms of poor, 212–215
as teams, 207–212, 216–218
in volunteer programs, 39, *41*, 43
*Volunteers: The Organizational Behavior of
Unpaid Workers* (Pearce), 207
Volunteer-The National Centre, 284
Voudouris, E., 284
Vroom, V. H., 225

W

Wages for national service program,
366–367, 371
Waivers, 133, 304–305, 326
Wheatley, M., 101

Wilson, M., 194
Wolf, M., 370
Workers' compensation, 308, 334
Workplace volunteer councils, 263
Workweek, 8–11

Y

Yourstone, S. A., 103
Youth shelter
application for, *166*
program description, *168*

Z

Zip-coding of America, 365